Human Evolution, Biological and Cultural Domains

The Evolution of Man
Ernst Haeckel (Author) Translated by Joseph McCabe
2021. ISBN: 978-1-53619-029-8 (Hardcover)
2021. ISBN: 978-1-53619-146-2 (eBook)

The *Homo* within the *Sapiens*
Jorge A. Colombo, MD, PhD (Author)
2021. ISBN: 978-1-53618-938-4 (Softcover)
2021. ISBN: 978-1-53618-373-3 (eBook)

From Molecules to Organisms
Alexander Poletaev, MD, PhD, Carmelo Rizzo
and Mohammad Ebrahimi, PhD (Authors)
2020. ISBN: 978-1-53617-551-6 (Hardcover)
2020. ISBN: 978-1-53617-552-3 (eBook)

What Makes Us Humans
Francisco J. Ayala, PhD, Michel Tibayrenc, MD, PhD (Authors)
2020. ISBN: 978-1-53616-853-2 (Softcover)
2019. ISBN: 978-1-53616-854-9 (eBook)

Our Animal Condition and Social Construction
Jorge A. Colombo, MD, PhD (Author)
2019. ISBN: 978-1-53615-357-6 (Softcover)
2019. ISBN: 978-1-53615-358-3 (eBook)

More information about this series can be found at
https://novapublishers.com/product-category/series/human-evolution-biological-and-cultural-domains/

Michael Charles Tobias
and Jane Gray Morrison

Terminal Philosophy Syndrome

Ecology and the Imponderable

nova
science publishers
www.novapublishers.com

DOI: https://doi.org/10.52305/CZHM8078

Library of Congress Cataloging-in-Publication Data

Names: Tobias, Michael, author. | Morrison, Jane, 1954- author.
Title: Terminal philosophy syndrome : ecology and the imponderable / Michael Charles Tobias and Jane Gray Morrison.
Description: New York : Nova Science Publishers, [2023] | Series: Human evolution, biological and cultural domains | Includes bibliographical references and index. |
Identifiers: LCCN 2022058595 (print) | LCCN 2022058596 (ebook) | ISBN 9798886974157 (hardcover) | ISBN 9798886974782 (adobe pdf)
Subjects: LCSH: Ecology--Philosophy. | Biology--Philosophy.
Classification: LCC QH540.5 .T628 2023 (print) | LCC QH540.5 (ebook) | DDC 577.01--dc23/eng/20221208
LC record available at https://lccn.loc.gov/2022058595
LC ebook record available at https://lccn.loc.gov/2022058596

Published by NOVA Science Publishers, Inc. † New York

Contents

Foreword

Michael Charles Tobias and Jane Gray Morrison have written a myriad of works that challenge conventional paradigms in science. Their many goals in doing so concern a clear summons that a universal biological clock is being stressed to the point of nearly unimaginable consequence(s). The Anthropocene is accelerating and the Earth, and humanity do not have the luxury of time for some if not many traditional methodologies of experimentation. Hence, their philosophical overview of the very consciousness in *Homo sapiens* that, for so many apparent reasons, is clearly grappling with fast-waning options to re-imagine solutions, and major paradigm shifts.

In reading this powerful and provocative book, their latest, *Terminal Philosophy Syndrome: Ecology and the Imponderable*, I was reminded of a fascinating time when, as a graduate student, I was required to read John R. Platt's "Strong Inference" essay published in the journal Science in 1964. Platt's sub-title, "Certain systematic methods of scientific thinking may produce much more rapid progress than others" has been validated in any number of historical and contemporary instances. (Platt, J.R., 1964. Strong Inference: Certain systematic methods of scientific thinking may produce much more rapid progress than others. Science, 146(3642), pp.347-353.)

And this requires deep deliberation. As echoed throughout Morrison and Tobias, there are significant flaws and vulnerabilities to the idea that endless experimentation is the answer. Leo Szilard, Einstein's close colleague and the man who actually obtained the patent for the notion of nuclear fission, described a rather revelatory insight regarding redundant experimentation at a biophysics conference in 1958. He talked about enzyme induction, protein synthesis, and the formation of antibiodies but reminded everyone present with the fact that "…there are only about 5 different ways [experiments], not 50!... to distinguish these." Many were uncomfortable with this razor-sharp insight and one electron microscopist retorted, "Gentlemen, this is off the track. This is philosophy of science."

Fast forward to 1961 when Melvin Calvin was the sole awardee of the Nobel Prize in Chemistry "for his research on the carbon dioxide assimilation in plants". Without a doubt, this is the most significant set of biochemical reactions, the ones that permit life on Earth to be possible. Here is a most relevant story about the underlying – not simplicity, but elegance – of Calvin's thinking. It speaks volumes to the questions and realizations raised within *Terminal Philosophy Syndrome*. I was a teaching assistant at The Ohio State University for William August "Bill" Jensen, who spent 27 years at the University of California-Berkeley and I was mesmerized by his account of how Calvin finally gained the insight that all of those reactants, and products with enzymes fit exquisitely into a tangible, absolutely critical cycle.

Calvin was the son of Russian immigrant parents who owned a grocery store in St. Paul, Minnesota. It was in a grocery store parking lot, waiting for his wife to return with her purchase, when Calvin pondered why he could not take all the various chemical compounds associated with fixing carbon and neatly make them fit in a linear pathway. The nagging question persists: Why would he want to do that? There is an answer, an unexpected one. As he watched customers pick up their grocery carts outside the store, bringing them inside one by one, filling them with items, only to exit the store with their purchases, before placing them in their cars, then routinely returning their carts where they had found them, a most un-routine truth was discovered. Calvin did countless experiments, practiced his scientific approaches to perfection, but the general fundamental question of "how" was missing. It was a philosophical spark, spawned by supermarket customers, that enabled him to express that "how". How, in the grand scheme of things, molecules hang together and cycle endlessly on our green planet. Every carbon atom in our bodies was at one time, sucked into the Calvin Cycle.

Over the span of my career in a field integrating botany, climate science, ecology, evolution and geology, I recognized that the "off the track" approach was essential and that every discipline I integrated into my work was hooked to philosophy, moved forward by creativity, and forged by gut reactions and emotions. Indeed, given the earlier referenced urgency spelled out implacably and relentlessly in Morrison and Tobias' latest work, philosophy is more relevant to science today than ever.

On one end of the spectrum, we have the philosophical considerations connected with climate change. Is it ethical for countries, like the United States, which built their economies on fossil fuels, including coal, to call out nations currently using coal as part of their energy equation to build competitive economies? Is it not morally irresponsible for a Bahamian (many young ecologists there being close colleagues of mine) to have to endure more risk of impact from sea level rise and increasing storm intensity resulting from climate change caused predominately by larger nations indisputably to blame for releasing gigatons of carbon? These kinds of philosophical considerations are massive, collective ethical concerns, and as we all know, have been tangled by politics and corporate power grabs. So how does one manage to navigate such an ambiguous world where emotions, ideas, and ideals interface with science? Can scientists themselves recognize that the practice of fine science is but one of several ways that humans can gain critical knowledge of the world around them? Engineers, common sense technicians committed to sustainability, indigenous wisdom passed down for millennia, powerful poets, and human inspiration in general, as derived from the vastly under-acknowledged genius of all biodiversity, must necessarily add to the equations of our scientific revolution, so called. At least, if it is to be relevant to a world that is currently hemorrhaging.

All of Jane Morrison's and Michael Tobias's collaborations unravel the interactions among emotions, a vast literature of ecological data and contemplations, and great science. In *Terminal Philosophy Syndrome*, the Authors have the reader follow them along a pathway, equipped with faith in the untapped potential of our imagination and consciousness, that enables us to address the immense environmental monstrosities threatening not just our own survival, but those of Others, whom they are not shy about itemizing. Nor do they hesitate to catalogue and analyze human inflictions on those trillions of Others.

How we think, how we use capacities we do not fully understand locked in our consciousness, and our ability to let our imaginations inspire our actions, will play major roles in our future as a species.

As a scientist, can I say science provides the silver bullets needed to slay all our species' threatening banes? In some cases, yes (to a degree); but more often than not, it is the synergy formed by melding our intellect, imagination and untapped consciousness to find a way that just might move us ahead. This is why I strongly urge scientists – indeed, everyone – to take the time and explore the roadmap that Morrison and Tobias propose for our species in their pivotal *Terminal Philosophy Syndrome: Ecology and the Imponderable.*

Melanie L. DeVore
Professor
Georgia College & State University
Milledgeville, Georgia, USA

Melanie L. DeVore is a Georgia College & State University Professor, Department of Biology & Environmental Sciences; Arizona State University, Adjunct Faculty Member, Center for Biology & Society and School of Life Sciences; University of Washington, Research Associate in Paleobotany, Burke Museum; New Jersey City University, Earth and Environmental Sciences, Adjunct Professor; University of Rwanda, Honorary Research Fellow in the Center of Excellence in Biodiversity & Natural Resource Management (CoEB-UR, CST).

Prologue

"The Golden Mountain May Yet Exist"

The duo of Michael Charles Tobias and Jane Gray Morrison is unlike any team of activists and researchers you have ever come across. It is nearly impossible to keep track of all they have achieved together: Sixty or more books, 170 films, cooperatively created over thirty years of marriage. This is what their day working together might be like:

> We went into our studio, which is a modest library facing a garden; a library with books all asking questions and pointing to human-alleged facts about nature. And there, on a carpet staring at us was a long, gorgeous, curled snake, the *Thamnophis proximus*, or western ribbon snake (bush snake, like a garter, as from the original Latin). All of the books – by the likes of Buffon, Dostoevsky, Darwin, Nietzsche, Ovid, Kierkegaard, Virgil, and so forth – were facing out from their shelves towards this remarkable Other, each book dumb and mute, confined the way most books are – all that learning, trapped between covers. He had clearly gotten in the way insects and spiders and the occasional rodent do. A crack in the universe of our house. A house that is not strictly *our* domicile, to be sure. We live here at the good graces of weather gods and social phenomena. The snake glided with its most elegant circuitousness to a corner, and then with our gentle directional urging headed right outside the door, into *its* home, the green sward, the forest, the riverbanks, the free air universe.

No reason they need any introductory words from me, since interconnected ideas, the firmament of ecology, just flow out of these two, on all and every topic under the sun and moon.

From my part I'll say I first became aware of Michael's work when I was a teenager, reading his compendium on altitudinal philosophy entitled *The Mountain Spirit*, where I first learned of the work of climber/philosopher Arne Naess, who became an important mentor and teacher for many years. I first met Jane when I worked with the two of them on the PBS series *Parliament of Minds*, where we interviewed a series of the world's most interesting philosophers, from Joe Margolis to Martha Nussbaum. I saw firsthand how seamlessly these two could create new work in a matter of days and weeks.

I'm not exactly sure how they divide the work between them, but I'm sure each needs the other to flourish and to dance through the ideas, leading to maximum effectiveness. Together they run the Dancing Star Foundation, which focuses on biodiversity protection, environmental education, and the promotion of animal sanctuaries all over the globe. There are no other thinkers and conservationists working as widely and intensively as Tobias and Morrison — they set the bar high for all the rest of us to ponder.

It is impossible to number *Terminal Philosophy Syndrome* among the pantheon of their books, since there are so many that have come before it. But I assure you this is one of their most profound and wide-ranging works. What they aim for here is to demonstrate that ecological thinking is primarily philosophical, while philosophy itself is fundamentally ecological. The structure of knowledge and reasoning is thickly entwined with the workings of nature and the Earth. Ecology is philosophy far more than it is biology:

> Thus far, neuroanatomy is nowhere close to explaining explanations, of itself; or accounting for reasoning. The morphology are so many mute stones.… The fact that 178 million years of mammalian cortical presence does not as yet reveal a window on that dimension says much. It empowers our belief systems, no matter what they are, to hang upon the cusp of dimensionless faith in the service of ideals that also remain uncommitted to matter, scientifically pre-contextualized. We simply have no idea from whence our ideas originate; or how to comprehend the power they exude, the measurements they eschew, the connections with other ideas that may be their shelf-life long after neurons have moved on. We know nothing.

Saying we know nothing doesn't mean there is nothing to be said. It simply shows science is not the primary parlay for the justification of our thoughts, and how these thoughts have led us to invent such a destructive way of living on this planet. We do not listen to the snake, or feel the full power of the wind!

More than any of their previous collaborations *Terminal Philosophy Syndrome* is a kind of live documentation of Morrison's and Tobias's collective dance-drama between science, emotion, and idea. We all know the terrible data streamed at us daily on the futility of continued human habitation on Earth, and this book aims to chart a way for us to navigate a path out of our malaise, moving from the horror of endless information to an intellectual faith in a better way. I continue to find so many pithy comments in this booming, buzzing adventure through ideas that I wish to share with you:

> In the meantime, our hope is vested in our schizophrenia, a word we use advisedly given that there are at least some people who are not perpetually craven, crass and tyrannical. These are people who truly endeavor to save lives, every life; to impound all that which kills, if we can, and seek transformative modes of being that are not hostile, or inane, but co-symbiotic.... We have seen incumbent indigenous deifications of the earth, rituals inciting every version of tree hugging. Such efforts, while laudable, have not re-invented antidotes to the absolute disasters of modern strangleholds, the real bastions of implacable power and reach. How we are likely to come by the stability of Dunbar's number in a fragmented amalgam of nearly eight billion strong is neither an arm's length distillation of disinterested theory, nor an enmeshed self-sacrifice to the ideal of ethical ecology. Somehow, from the contested and entangled inner trappings of humanity there is a quiet answer awaiting all of us, not in due course, but either sooner or never.

That quiet answer, some pristine response—how are we to locate it? Arne Naess would say everyone needs to find the right answer for themselves, but with such global challenges as we have now, collective agreement and understanding is essential. We're all in this together, though some are more guilty than others. And there is no solving planetary problems without the cooperation of all species into the discussion, a melee or Babel that lies far beyond language:

> The communal properties of an information system deriving from human companionship with Others is a far more ancient sociology than that simply concerning human-to-human relations.... We accept the notion that there are currently one trillion or more species on earth; and that each of those species

> remains a mystery.... It is a distributive conundrum in terms of today's other-than-human survivors. There may be billions of red billed sub-Saharan weavers (*Quelea quelea quelea*) and hundreds-of-millions of starlings; over 30 billion chickens, untold trillions of ants. But the most likely human contact species 350,000 years ago, given the largely African common denominator geographically, can only be vaguely surmised from the few tens-of-thousands of known examples of rock paintings, the majority of which date to less than 40,000 years ago. The mystery of interspecies communications involving human participants remains the same, unflinching enigma.

As someone who routinely plays music together with water scorpions, nightingales, and beluga whales I know that each species has its aesthetics, its vision for beauty, its way to want to survive in their imperiled habitats. We simply cannot think of our own kind alone if we are to forge a route beyond the end of the line that we hear so much about in these tragic times. We all need to read, to learn, to experience, to interact, and Tobias and Morrison are ideal guides and examples for such a task. There is a way to connect far beyond language:

> We will continue to identify the endless minutiae of our kind, but thousands of years of this incessant philosophical bent has not ethically rebalanced a statistically ascertainable number of individuals within the greater community. We can generalize upon such standards of behavior, as if there might be actual courtesies in an ideal biological world, from the brute force that is the continued penchant, and escalating tools, for consequential human violence. Conceptually, we have not altered the course of bloodshed. We might escape temporarily, as individuals, "the cloud imposed by symbols," as C.D. Scott referred to it, or convince ourselves (again and again) that we are apex linguists with corresponding behavioral wisdom, given the "multiple-network view" that has been advanced in attempting to understand all that which is happening "beyond the information...that enter primary sensory cortices."

All this language, all these ideas—still we humans remain trapped in the cloud of symbols, confused away from the deep need to do all we can to ensure our survival.

We all know that our survival is not guaranteed; after all, we're just one more strange species with an increasingly unsustainable way of living. Perhaps our time has come and gone. Yet what can we do? We simply have to hope our ideas can save us, that there remains much more we can offer this planet to remedy our centuries of mistakes. Did David Hume actually say "we can form the idea of a golden mountain, and from thence conclude that such a mountain may actually exist," thereby presaging René Daumal's quest for a Mount Analogue that offers his seekers the ultimate climb? Indeed, he did, but it took Tobias and Morrison to remind us, in this erudite and far-reaching work, that the power of human imagination and consciousness may have no limits. To survive beyond the twenty-first century, we thus need to think, explore, and act.

David Rothenberg
Distinguished Professor of Philosophy
New Jersey Institute of Technology
Newark, New Jersey, USA

Dr. David Rothenberg is distinguished professor of philosophy and music at the New Jersey Institute of Technology. He is a noted writer on themes connecting humanity, nature, and technology and music. He is the author of *Why Birds Sing* (Basic Books and Penguin UK, 2005), also published in Italy, Spain, Taiwan, China, Korea, and Germany, and turned into a feature-length documentary *Why Birds Sing* by Endemol UK for BBC4 in June, 2007. Rothenberg is also the author of *Hand's End: Technology and the Limits of Nature* (University of California Press, 1993), *Thousand Mile Song* (Basic Books, New York, 2008), *Survival of the Beautiful* (Bloomsbury, New York, 2011), *Bug Music* (St Martins, New York, 2013) and *Nightingales in Berlin* (University of Chicago Press, 2019 and Rowohlt Publishers, Hamburg, 2020) www.davidrothenberg.net.

"St. Francis Consoled By The Musical Angel," 1600, Engraving On Paper, 9 15/16 x 7 11/16 in. (25.3 x 19.5 cm). By Raphael Sadeler 1 (1560-61-1628 or 1632) After Francesco Vanni (1563-1610). Photo by © M. C. Tobias, Private Collection.

Preface

This treatise is focused upon biology and the imponderable; ecosystems lost and found. The problem of human consciousness in the Anthropocene, which is a very different crisis for the planet than ever posed before by our thinking, and the reactive thoughts and feelings of all Others (a word we use to guide one's image and interior sense of every individual of every other taxonomic rank on earth).

We cannot offer something otherwise, that would connote a validation of philosophical speculation. To do so is to live in a falsity, where the authentic, integral and protracted Consciousness that aspires to a facet of biology (and for some, physics) imports every buttress that can attempt to stave off, or at least delay reality, involving itself in everybody's business, believing fiercely that its very *Being* matters. When – though who can say – by all evidence it does so only in negative numbers and exponents. In square roots whose expressions are largely disastrous, save for the moments of kindness, the unstinting gestures, first responders, museums, those who have sworn to a Hippocratic Oath in whatever honest and virtuous form, all those cherished byproducts of this unlikely species. Recognition that our species' capacity to venerate nature in all her quirks and ellipses, stochastic incalculables and steadfast patterns, her graces and unimagined diversity, is our only chance of at least partial survival into an unknown future. Not that it matters in the least, whether we survive as a species, that is. Although, given the currents of our collective behavior – not to be entirely foregone in our conclusions – the one fact that appears to stand out in biological history is that the quicker we are gone, the better it will be. That is not a mean-spirited approach to a text, but a necessarily sobering one.

It must be admitted that the majority of human behavior – historical and contemporary – that can be discerned as the most obvious outward manifestation of such Being is conditioned by pillars of life that clearly want nothing of it, if we are to assemble the forensics and start speaking truth to ourselves. We could empty all the shelves, but there would be more to it than that, this much is clear. As in sleep, when chance permits it, we drift in and out of ideation, subsequent to a scattering of light-infused after images. Often not. In those intermezzo times of free improvisation there is a blank, where human metabolism is slowed down, our footprint light and airy. Until we wake up and start the cycle of destruction by so many means all over again. Many years ago, we termed this obvious syndrome World War III, the war our species has been waging against the earth.

As an evolutionary fact, we don't as a species care in the least about our own biology. In fact, we do everything possible to avoid it, save for externalities that reward the outering Self. To see the face of beauty, smell the aromatics, discern the curvaceous and wonder at the carefree. To dream of other lives, better ones.

Whereas, to glimpse upon the human autopsy is quintessentially anathematic to our senses of dignity, hygiene, order. The chaos of internal organs, its bodily wastes, odors and such are precursors – and we know it – to the same loathsome condition of a dead body that has not been disposed of for days, weeks, months. The scent of a deceased rodent is an emphatic, atavistic repellent. Almost at once time brings upon the corpse another set of life forms mobbing such entrails, fully disregarding any notion of disease. The many species of heterotrophic bacteria, a cornucopia of fly larvae (maggots) and flesh-eating flies, at least three taxa of beetle, thousands of mites, and then the moths that devour hair, and much more. This is our long-term fixity.[1]

A saga quite different from its sanitized literary version, the somewhat (by contrast) soothing Ecclesiastes 3:20, Genesis 3:19 and 18:27, or Job 30:19, "from dust and each returns to dust" or, still, the *Book of Common Prayer* (final 1662 version) invoking ashes. In dust and in ash our words and civilizations can rest unmolested, in a sense; unconcerned by galaxy cannibalism or that dead rat lurking in our ancestral memory.[2]

During this precious time of our lives we wield something beyond mere emotion or tragedy to bind the living upon the living, as "friends": "grapple them to thy soul," declares Polonius to his children Ophelia and Laertes[3] in the year of 1602, just months after Queen Elizabeth delivered to the 141 Members of the House of Commons her "Golden Speech," – her final speech to Parliament. "…we verily believe, that all you will (in your best judgement) discharge us from such guilts. Thus we commend us to your constant faith, and your selves to your best fortunes."[4] England passed an Act for the Relief of the Poor, at least; and that same year a Jesuit missionary from Italy, Matteo Ricci, created a map while living in Beijing with China (not Italy) at its center;

a massive cartographical work of the imagination that first named the Americas with its "wild horses," a place named Ka-na-ta, and told of a strange and wondrous Florida "the Land of Flowers."[5] Our lives are fraught in these ways, between times and what, in mathematics, are the components of any probability distribution.

Such be the odd phalanxes of disquisitions in untold number, on every variety of the curious semblances that give to life its fanciful and fearful. May we find justice in it? Or come to common parlance? Even so, we have no recourse to what would absolve the Queen's said "discharge" of "such guilts" for this is the very ecological clock that appears to keep track of all wastrels across the planet. Those who offer up only their corpse and nothing else. What should we have done, our species in its instant of perceived presence?[6] Instead of habituating ourselves to what we do and think, might we have thought and done differently? There is no other question for philosophy. To argue that the wager is obsolete is to assert that once, sometime far back or away, it was relevant. If once of importance, then why not again so? The answer lies without obscurity in the immediacy of the Anthropocene,[7] which measures in her own inscrutable fashion and metrics, everything that is done to her, the earth. By which we can only mean one thing, not two, or three, thus obviating the temptation to grab at solace among cosmic ambiguities. A mercy rule, not in cricket, but in rescuing one. The mercy that is truth in a human heart, without definition, which would cause ruin at the moment of self-recognition, at least in our species, as it has, though probably in no others.

Herein lies the root of our proposed points of discussion. That we only use our tools as fair tidings in their day, then let go of them. Seizing none of our goals, nor undermining – by their gimmick – the remaining prospects for whatever remediation and tenderness to Others might yet be manifest in a destiny otherwise quite solidly projected to have no other cause or context to go on living, but by this one last chance of loving. Because it cannot be collectivized, and scarcely exists outside the one upon the one. Such that no politic or science will remedy the trouble we are in, engineers and clergy; the young and the old; thought and lack of it. Together, there are not the means to carry forth any plan. We have lost that opportunity, perhaps fifty, or one-hundred thousand years ago – meaningless sketchbooks of our odyssey here. It was not one moment or another. Nor can we rightly visualize when the cumulative pressures overcame all else, what ecologists clumsily know to be some version or other of carrying capacity. The morals behind such capacity are murky; the information spheres obese with self-exonerations.

As remarked earlier, the closer we come to points of detail, the more hazardous our journey becomes recognizable. Injuries that have meaning only to the injured, as we sum up a planet in turmoil because of what we have done. These are true ecological sins, if such can be incited and tallied. However untidy a word, an ethic awkwardly Biblical, to posit our undoing in the midst of what we have done to fellow biologicals must quash the philosophy of hope, even whilst we continue to write of it.

The state of affairs is for real, as much as we can say so, or imagine it. We have seen it, with these and other eyes. Recognized the many destructions, projected in all probability theory, the hypotheses of self-annihilation. But what is more important today, and likely tomorrow, is whether philosophy, as she desperately searches for something to cling to, can reconcile her losses with a single gain. Can logic and every form of analysis settle for nothing more, nothing less than restraint in the actionable canons of everyday machination. Live between absolute hells for whatever seconds of freedom, during which eons, as it were, to help another in pain. To give comfort and think of nothing else.

An out-reigning, where once were the self-aggrandizing if vindictive rubrics and constraints of superegos; the hidden agendas of trade, communication, and sovereignties. Rather, to front a generosity of ideals propagated in the fidelity of unconditional love. Of loyalty to that which has brought us all to this cusp of hoped-for, if simplistic clarity, wherein we either allow our best to pour forth, or cling, as we have done all our lives, to the deathsail and its mythographical evocations; a way through the dust and the ash that we, for an instant in our dying embers, make believed could be a solid pathway. But there was/is not. For only in true conscience is there a tenable subject of consideration. A mirror image of what biodiversity proclaims with her every want and breath.

Endnotes

[1] "Corpse fauna," March 29, 2019, Australian Museum, https://australian.museum/learn/science/decomposition-corpse-fauna/

[2] See "Galaxy Cannibalism: The Milky Way's terrible table manners," by Daniel Zucker, *Science Illustrated*, August 13, 2010, https://scienceillustrated.com.au/blog/science/galaxy-cannibalism/

[3] "Hamlet," by William Shakespeare, Act 1, Scene 3, line 63, London, 1602.

[4] "The Golden Speech," by Queen Elizabeth I, 30 November 1601 (SP 12/282 ff.137r-141v), The National Archives, https://www.nationalarchives.gov.uk/education/resources/elizabeth-monarchy/the-golden-speech/

[5] "China at center of world in 1602 map," n.a., Globe Newspaper Company, Associated Press, January 13, 2010.

[6] For one uncannily interesting commentary on this, see Poetry Ireland Review of George Steiner's *Real Presences*, Issue 28, Edited by Michael O'Siadhail, https://www.poetryireland.ie/publications/poetry-ireland-review/online-archive/view/george-steiner-real-presences

[7] See for example, "National responsibility for ecological breakdown: a fair-shares assessment of resource use, 1970–2017," by Prof. Jason Hickel, Daniel W. O'Neill, Andrew L. Fanning, Huzaifa Zoomkawala, Open Access Published: April, 2022 doi: https://doi.org/10.1016/S2542-5196(22)00044-4, https://www.thelancet.com/journals/lanplh/article/PIIS2542-5196(22)00044-4/fulltext#; See also, Best, Steven (2021). "Failed Species: The Rise and Fall of the Human Empire". *Romanian Journal of Artistic Creativity*. 9 (2); and, Bradshaw, Corey J. A.; Ehrlich, Paul R.; Beattie, Andrew; Ceballos, Gerardo; Crist, Eileen; Diamond, Joan; Dirzo, Rodolfo; Ehrlich, Anne H.; Harte, John; Harte, Mary Ellen; Pyke, Graham; Raven, Peter H.; Ripple, William J.; Saltré, Frédérik; Turnbull, Christine; Wackernagel, Mathis; Blumstein, Daniel T. (2021). "Underestimating the Challenges of Avoiding a Ghastly Future". *Frontiers in Conservation Science*. 1. doi:10.3389/fcosc.2020.615419; and, Rott, Nathan (10 September 2020). "The World Lost Two-Thirds Of Its Wildlife In 50 Years. We Are to Blame". *NPR*. And, Kress, W. John; Krupnick, Gary A. (2022). "Lords of the biosphere: Plant winners and losers in the Anthropocene". *Plants, People, Planet*. doi:10.1002/ppp3.10252. S2CID 247388985. See also, *Anthrozoology: Embracing Co-Existence in the Anthropocene*, by M. C. Tobias and J. G. Morrison, Springer Publishers, New York, NY, 2017.

"Notornis Alba -Extinct," from *Extinct Birds*, by The Hon. Walter Rothschild, Hutchinson & Co., London, UK, 1907, Plate 33, p. 145, Photo © By M. C. Tobias, from Private Collection.

Chapter 1

Introductory Misgivings

Gandhi's Misreading

In his two, much discussed letters to Hitler in 1939/1940, and in assorted writings after WWII, when the full revelations of the Holocaust were made transparent to the world, it is profoundly clear that M.K. Gandhi (1869-1948) was both distracted, slightly biased, sadly naive and utterly incapable of reconciling his own professed non-violence and pacificism, with what, in his own words, was "the greatest crime of our time." Nonetheless, said he, "...the Jews should have offered themselves to the butcher's knife. They should have thrown themselves into the sea from cliffs...It would have aroused the world and the people of Germany...As it is they succumbed anyway in their millions."[1] In India, on the 150th anniversary of his birth, some critics focused only on the fact that Gandhi, who addressed Hitler as "Friend" triumphed philosophically over Hitler in the very true sense that Gandhi's "message" remains as ever, "relevant in the face of challenges posed by terrorism..."[2] Professor of Jewish philosophy at Bar-Ilan University in Israel, Ephraim Meir, suggests "Gandhi's understanding of Judaism was limited..." That the Mahatma failed to decipher its "peoplehood dimension."[3] Writing for The Jerusalem Post, Shmuley Boteach discusses the "make love not war" philosophies, "how many people have had these beliefs truly put to the test".[4]

It is an understatement to reiterate that *good and evil* preoccupy the annals of philosophy, comparative religions, key themes in ethnography, sociology, and ultimately, the natural sciences, although the latter umbrella of deliberations eschew human ascriptions to behavior, except in the sense of raw analogies. While ideas of teleology have predominantly favored those who harbor grandiose orientations to, and debate purpose, the sciences are preoccupied with a notion of pure objectivity, albeit a clairvoyant one that cannot escape its anthropic biases. No matter the experiment, none has ever achieved neutrality. By definition, everything our species investigates and espouses comes from our species. While this is self-evident, it also remains the most fundamental challenge in terms of ever achieving neutral objectivity; a struggle between human knowledge and knowledge in general (if the *kind* of knowledge we define as such even exists) that is exacerbated at both micro- and macro-observational levels. No matter what our deep history, big picture, or seemingly pure theories suggest, no cartography or topology will ever get it right, because *right* means that which has been ordained by a human. At even the most extreme hybridized or artificially intelligent non-human expression, every communication pathway is tainted by and incarnate within our own definition of whatever it is and has come to be articulated or displayed. Self-evident? One would think so. But there is great variance within the alleged evidentiary.

Our species finds it rather easy and preferential to criticize itself, a penchant that has nothing more to say than the ends achieved, at best, by self-reflection. We don't criticize other species in the same way. Indeed, those that may proffer risks, other carnivores, disease agents, natural disasters and the like we accept in the order of things. As will be discussed, evolutionary pivots in our own thinking and, to a much less extent, our behavior, do occur. Science records rapid changes of political policy, and the entire shifts in species, from mosquitoes to elephants; from salmon, to lizards and birds. Are such morphic re-locations (temporally, spatially, cognitively) Darwinian in the sense of survival, or is their predication for reasons strictly moral, intellectual, aesthetic? The latter query devolves to a different class of entelechy entirely. It remits to conjecture as if embryologically re-assigned the subject to both premises and predicates that may have nothing to do with the transitive targets of human knowledge, intuition or abstracted impressions. If one species is able to swiftly change course, does that suggest that all species are capable of it? If we disengage from the taxonomy of a species category, is morality the predominate driver of evolution? Or beauty? Or joy? Or is it pain and suffering? These unanswerables arise in the salient intersection of human self-observance where no face of God can ever be confirmed. Nonetheless, one civilization and culture after another invents a proliferation of faces, motives, surrogate explanations that require nothing more than faith, or the oppression by power for purposes of subordination.

The back-story of such extrapolations to Others is the hierarchical structure that fuels the animism, buttresses theodicy with the conditionality to considerations that for every perceived evil, we have the aid of moral reasoning to abet our belief in the underlying goodness of humankind. Do such contemplations possibly lead anywhere, or are all philosophical meanderings simply that, an ounce of mellow air troubling itself over other ounces of air which we have winnowed down descriptively to nothing more complicated than the very good and evil underscoring whatever notions of evolution we hold at any given time?

We think we are being wise, progressive, ethically generous and accurate by suggesting all species have intelligence. But, of course they do, perhaps far, far more so than *H. sapiens*, if so called intelligence is worth the letters that build up its exhibitions and vacuous popularity. We would argue nothing less. Yet, taxonomically, we think about sapientipotency as a strictly human quality, if not actually godlike, as contradistinguished from all other species, genera, orders, families, kingdoms and the like. Only the Sapiutan in Malay (wild ox) and sapindaceous genus of certain firs and pines have anything linguistically in common with us, for purely non-synonymous reasons. Etymologically, *Homo* dates to Carl Linnaeus's 10th edition of his *Systema Natura* in 1758. *Sapiens*, from the Latin present active infinitive, sapere, to "be wise" remains exclusively reserved for ourselves. It is the finest hour of egotism and separatism. It undercuts all self-criticism which, ultimately, is trapped on the possible cusp of positive or negative change. Changes which in today's technologically charged climate means gene editing.

Prima facie experience and the implications for some version of natural law that transcends the human blind alleys of historical, rational discussion: this is the labor camp of the idle. Ethicists quibble from their addictive ranks, parsing through the lexicons of words and phrases, like "pure land Buddhist paintings' with their obsessive depicture of the Amitabha Buddha descending into the land where all his faithful are waiting. Descriptive, prescriptive; ethical behavior, duty, moral theory, virtue ethics, consequen-tiality, deontology (the study and nature of obligations), pragmatism, utilitarianism, justice, distributive justice, inviolable laws, God's will, human nature. All the big questions are made far murkier in the molecular cauldrons of bioethical and proprietary zeal.

In each instance, in every documented cultural representation of an ethical purview, the relationships between goodness and unethical behavior are reversible, both in theory and more importantly in practice. What is good for an individual may not be good for a community, and vice versa. While the variola virus (Smallpox) was eradicated in the wild in 1980, at least two known laboratories in the U.S. and Russia control small quantities of it. While considered a category A pathogen (highly infectious with a thirty percent death rate in humans), it was deemed important to keep it from extinction as a matter of national security against potential future bioterrorism (a world war). What is applauded in one society may be anathema to some of its residents, and equally condemned in other societies.[5] Human consumption of coal, dogs, palm oil, horses, turkeys, chickens, whales, monkeys, etc.: each have their vile proponents (note, for example, the June 2022 Supreme Court case, *West Virginia v EPA*, politically ideological in sync with a repressive Congress all but unaccountable to the American public, and out of tune with the functionality of most courts in other countries). One can essentially count on some level of controversy and opposition to anything and everything, when polls, votes, opinions are taken. Cultural change occurs most readily – not by its science, technology or power, but – by its ethical norms. Later, we will discuss how the principles themselves, in the mind of a Thomas Hobbes, take higher precedence than the fall-out such principles might inflict. This is always the tension built in to any ethical absolute: it fails to account for the actual vicissitudes of human nature, or of rapid evolutionary change.

Yet, by such criteria, humanity has not changed as much as we might like to think. A librarian in Virginia, Matthew White, chronicled "History's 100 Worst Atrocities" and came up with "World War II, the regimes of Genghis Khan and Mao Zedong, famines in British India, and the fall of the Ming Dynasty"[6] as critical bellwethers for ranking human-induced horror. But ecologically – *realistically*, in other words – the year 2020 saw more pain meted out to more animals than in any other year of human history. The "Kill Counter" comes closest to the cumulative tally that we have studied – describing it as the "pain points" – namely, *at least* 2.7 trillion animals slaughtered for human consumption in grotesque and unrepentant conditions.[7] Can we adduce any evolutionary jolt within the purview of such numbers?

But before we even set about initiating the framework for exploring parallel narratives destined to conflict and remain unresolved, consider a few emblematic examples from legal and resulting ethical history.

On December 3, 1792, the same day Washington was elected to a second term, then Secretary of State Thomas Jefferson wrote his "Opinion On Fugitive Slaves." It is an utter mishmash from a most literate writer, that provides for the U.S. Government opting out of the details, the underlying moral realities, and any responsibility towards human beings. To carefully study its two pages is at once to recognize the ruthless proclivity at work of language manipulated, of legal reason abrogated, of all those causes and consequences of deliberate obscurity at work to perpetuate a cruelty by abandonment.[8] Little wonder from the two-time President who "owned" in his lifetime over 600 other people, only ever manumitting 10 of them. And, yes: People "were physically beaten" at Monticello where at least three of Jefferson's "overseers had a reputation for cruelty and violence."[9] Like Washington and James Madison, Jefferson's own cruelty was not some anomaly, a mere product of his times. He was well acquainted with one of Virginia's wealthiest gentlemen, Robert Carter III, who fourteen months prior had freed over 500 slaves, under the legal framework entitled a "deed of gift".[10]

During the period 80 to 90 AD, in Judea, or Roman Syria (possibly Antioch), the Gospel According to Matthew the Evangelist (the Matthean material – the biographical M and Q logia, or purported sayings of Christ, and other sources), was composed in Synagogue Greek by an elusive author, its iconic idealism (encompassing Ebionite vegetarianism and abhorrence of any ritual sacrifice) comprising the first book of the New Testament. "Do unto others as you would have them do unto you"[11] has never ceased since that time to register amongst a universal human conscience, although sections of the Old and New Testaments were altered to eliminate anger, combat, countless other expressions pertaining to aggression by Protestants in the 16th century. But not unlike the inconsistent universe in which a Thomas Jefferson operated, the Bible holds only the most symbolic and erratic sway over a very rarified percentage of our kind, impossible to accurately gauge (with polls from Africa to North America suggesting anywhere between 37% and 90% of attendance at countless churches. Until the early 1790s laws in the U.K. mandated a minimum of twice-yearly church attendance).

Biblical hermeneutics, chronologies, fact finding, are rife with confusion during the period following the life of Jesus. It's not clear who Matthew was, or whether his Gospel was the product of numerous authors, and three languages (Aramaic, Hebrew and Greek). Nothing is unambiguous. Portraits, veneration, the writings of subsequent church fathers and historians resurrect little if any clarity in one's search for a consistently ethical time in human history.[12] Seleucus 1 Nicator who conquered Syria following the death of Alexander and the Battle of Ipsus in 301 BC is said to have built sixteen cities named Antioch. Between that time, the birth of Christ and the conquest of the central Antioch by fighters of the Rashidun Caliphate in 637 AD, archaeology of the Middle East – the Judaic world, the Hellenistic age, Rome, Christianity, and Byzantium, and ultimately the Crusades – leaves bewildering trails of inexactitude and deepening, horrific ethical contradictions. Antioch was ultimately overrun by the Mamluk Sultanate in 1268.[13] At that point, the city had already been ransacked multiple times throughout its history. When the Commander Baibars (fourth Mamluk Sultan of Egypt) invaded, it was similar, but on a far vaster timescale, to European forces pulling out of Afghanistan in August 2021. Historians note that "fourteen thousand Christians were slaughtered and a hundred thousand dragged away into slavery."[14]

Looking back across the history of warfare, from the First Punic War waged by Rome against Carthage (264-241 BC) – at least 400,000 people killed – to Germany's Operation Barbarossa, initiated against the Soviet Union (June 22 – December 5, 1941) – approximately 1.6 million deaths, and some 6 million Soviets wounded and/or captured – we can site the last 2300 years as a modern era in terms of human-perpetrated mass casualties. No human-to-human atrocities quite escalate to the level of the Stalin dictatorship resulting in an estimated 20-to-40 million people killed[15]. And no word, like that of *Hitler*, has ever evinced such revulsion. But has it changed any demonstrable biological facts? Human death tolls do not come close to mirroring what is going on outside our species. Although human throw-weight, as yet untried in its totality, leaves nothing of its horror to the imagination. We understand only too well what Hiroshima, for example, looked like in the aftermath; or the bullets of an AR-15 piercing a human body.

Moral Inconsistencies

If *moral consistency* is the hallmark of any ethical persuasion, as so many academic and theological philosophers have suggested over time, then we may surmise that the sporadic adherences to both Old and New Testament values and compass bearings incite very little confidence for projecting human behavior, in part because the documents themselves evidence little equilibrium.[16] Every early document, in whatever form, has codified the erratic nature of human history, which has strictly followed an entropic itinerary, randomized chaos. Or, if not entire pandemonium, a predominantly morbid propensity for serious contraindications and vacillations. Energy and biological equilibria purport to more stable data, but less *readable* information. That's because we cannot contextualize history utilizing our own ambience or understanding. Not surprisingly, non-equilibrium studies over time and throughout space are essential to better grasping eco-dynamics, which never achieve true equilibrium, not across any millimeter or nanosecond of even a fraction of the full suite of known biological distributions.[17]

Our understanding of flux in the natural sciences is not *real* understanding. If it were, there would be no zoos, for example. Moreover, when the Antwerp Zoo banned a female visitor to its facility because the woman had formed a strong bond with a chimpanzee who had been trapped at the zoo for 30 years, the rationale (that other chimpanzees in the zoo, seeing their comrade's affection for a human, had allegedly stopped engaging with that individual) collapsed in a sordid, ethical morass, indifferent to cause and effect, and the moral bankruptcy of presuming that transpicuous zoo culture for incarcerated animals could be modeled as if in the wild.[18] And that such perceived "affairs" were unethical. A madness double-fold; or, as we would think of it, inconsistently, non-replicable ecological diseases that are part of the human expressive exponent. In the Matthean dictum, no heuristic closure will every come for that animal, any more than the kamikaze, suicidal nature of the aviation Japanese Special Attack Units could be described as an undivided psyche with no thought of the reciprocal nature of anger, self-obfuscation and their sum total as expressed by warfare.[19] The opposite of the disingenuous paradox of the war to end all wars.

In his penetrating chapter entitled "The Meaning of the Meaningless Question" Joseph Wood Krutch asked "can human nature adapt and adjust to anything?" and "what kind of world would best accord with his nature?"[20] Writing five years earlier, Lewis Mumford had declared, "When man lives for purposes beyond his limited self or his generation, beyond those of his group or his tribe, these universal purposes command subjective energies comparable to those within the atom…"[21] Krutch (1893-1970) – the ecological pantheist, and Mumford (1895-1990) – the critical humanist, both responded to the inconceivable horrors of World War II in ways that typified their respective critiques of human nature. In each instance, a global view was predicated upon a vision of what humanity *should* be if it were to be livable. Both men regarded human nature as *the* nature; rough, worn down, but theoretically malleable enough to be modified from within. In other words, they retained some level of optimism about the future, our future, despite Auschwitz, Dresden, Hiroshima and Nagasaki.

Philosophers of the coming two generations following Krutch and Mumford, Jonathan Schell,[22] Elizabeth Kolbert[23] and David G. Campbell[24] had the same reasons to be hopeful, or not, about the future. But this time, not the human future so much as any future, given the utter destruction that must follow upon nuclear war, climate change and the ecological ruination of such biomes as the Amazon. Campbell rather summed up the syndrome when he wrote, in his Epilogue, "By the early 1990s, most of the settlers of Santa Luzia had fled their homesteads and dispersed into the favelas and gold-mining camps of Amazonia, forgotten and dispensable."[25] Metaphors, speech, data sets, baselines, the very matrix of metrics had all come of a new age of destruction. An era beset by indelible anxieties. Our focus on the atom had shifted to its parts. If not the very laws of physics, then their nuances and consequences had already been altered in our minds, along with the purported age and speed of the universe. Time and space were now subject to the material causes of quantum entanglement. Most apparent, in the space of two generations, hundreds of human languages had gone extinct. Far more importantly, "more than two-thirds" of all life on the planet had been pushed over the brink.[26] How must such information, that single statistic, affect all future thinking? If it had been inserted into consciousness at the time of Aristotle, Spinoza, Hegel, they would likely have re-imagined humanity's proper role; the nature of deities and their causes and effects. Who knows *what* they would have thought.

Most cerebral idle time is not linguistically driven. It is an easy test. To glance around and not think of a single word. To look upon a garden and contemplate without utterance, or the slightest configuration that would lead to a word. At first, one can become dizzy, frightened, as if some cloud of consciousness is verging upon a stroke, or black-out. Pure vertigo. Without words, even for a few seconds, we are happily, or nervously upside down. Perpetuating that grey area of a state tempts "11 million bits per second" of "the creative, intuitive, non-verbal brain processes…"[27] The implications of this condition of meditation are severe, leading one to imagine that other forms of communication require some level of non-thought that is completely opposite, or contrary to that which has largely galvanized our solidarity as a species. But this is not a novel reading of the senses, which have in so many ways been described within the social sciences literature as somehow transcending both the fact of and need for language. Reasoning may have nothing whatsoever to do with language. Any more than it does with physics or calculus or medieval Bohemian poetics (a favorite, as it turns out, of Sir John Bowring [1792-1872] who may have known as many as 200 human languages to various degrees).

Reasoning

Reasoning remains an utter metaphysic, as elusive as all pre-etymologies, continental or genetic drift. It has no characteristic correlations other than to ascribe it to something physical as Henry Moore once said of his sculptures. Ideas, by whatever means they have evolved and arrived on point, exist inside a braincase. The ideas, comprised of neurons and excited electrons, move as congealed atoms at their own bequest, but beholden to the movement of the brain itself. Like a restive Giant Robber fly confined within a jar it rightly perceives to be a predator. The topography of the brain provides a first order mapping of regions in various ways connected between axons and the neurotransmission between areas of inhibition and excitation. English neurologist John Hughlings Jackson (1835-1911), studying epilepsy, arrived at a theory pertaining to cerebral "Concomitance" by which so much was happening at once, a doctrine of simultaneity that is now a centerpiece of most brain research. The architecture is given to any possibility, and neither time nor space dependent. If there is a constant neural calculus, every brain models every nerve ending. A jellyfish, on average, contains at least 5,600 neurons in its entire nervous system; a hedgehog 24 million. A human brain contains at least 21 billion within its iso- and allocortex portions of the grey and white areas of the pallium, sheltered in a fragile cerebrum.

Thus far, neuroanatomy is nowhere close to explaining explanations, of itself; or accounting for reasoning. The morphology are so many mute stones. As much as electron microscopy has shined a light on portions of a hydrogen atom, a single idea remains isolated from any other idea, or instrument of ideas (e.g., the Golub Collection of several centuries of microscopes at the University of California Berkeley) that tracks it. Perhaps the most isolated, if lonely element on the atomic chart is yet to be catalogued, numbered, revealed: an idea. One that stands alone in an ether of commanding but utterly inaccessible, inexplicable space or time or some other dimension. The fact that 178 million years of mammalian cortical presence does not as yet reveal a window on that dimension says much. It empowers our belief systems, no matter what they are, to hang upon the cusp of dimensionless faith in the service of ideals that also remain uncommitted to matter, scientifically pre-contextualized. We simply have no idea from whence our ideas originate; or how to comprehend the power they exude, the measurements they eschew, the connections with other ideas that may be their shelf-life long after neurons have moved on. We know nothing.

So, we are stuck upon, but far removed from that idea. Whatever it is. Perhaps it succeeds in galvanizing our entire breath and spirit. Certainly, this was the case for a Shakespeare, a Cervantes or Fra Angelico. It could not have been less for Johannes Brahms' "Piano Concerto No. 2 in B♭ major, Op. 83. But, such manifestations aside, by the time an idea of such strength reaches ideation, billions of years of life have necessarily had a hand in the concept. That all precedes expression, speech, behavior, the endless modes of relation between ideas that may occupy one or more organisms. The moral of this enigma spanning the full ontogenetic web of connections neither informs or excludes constants and non-constants of meaning. Meaning as attributed within energy transform space. Elsewhere we have referred to this area of commingling as the "quantum biosemiosphere." An area that sits silently like any other in space. Where interruptions spell doom or imagination. Ideas graze, sleep, wake up, even drown within their own sovereignties. What we say about them is a repetitive exercise in digging towards the center of creation, a place we have been before, as T.S. Eliot trenchantly observed in famed lines from his "Little Gidding," the last of his *Four Quartets* (1941). How well do we, can we, know such places?

While the origins of human language may well be tied to active, targeted thought, there are huge gaps in what we reflect upon and what we say. These are not readiness potential (Bereitschaftspotential), programmatic consequences of a cause tied to reflex, as might be construed in the case of physiologist Benjamin Libet's (1916-2007) famous experiments of the 1980s utilizing an electroencephalogram to measure the activity of neurons in the brain associated with a person's volitional amplitude. Works of art are presumed to have been massaged, gone over, deliberated; whereas speech, daily speech, mirrors a continuum of singularly unimpressive reflex responses that serve a variety of community and expedient purposes, even when such chatter is compulsive. We don't harbor expectations of common parlance. Common hostilities. Common kindnesses. The most important qualifier, the one that dictates unchanging rules and precision, is time as it collides with volition. That collision intimates a force that connects with other forces. That, in turn, leads to every cliché both in quantum physics and popular cultures. Separating the two in a way that can alter worldviews, individual behavior, cultural norms, from the human year 2022 seems all but impossible. All our efforts, to whatever end, must confront their inherent ephemerality, a fact we forever resist, until we cannot any longer do so. Throughout this mortal struggle are ecological correlates that provide our only hope of understanding anything. The great temptation of the natural sciences is to glean something of the Other – the sum totality of biodiversity (and/or all the other hundreds of billions of its designations).

This irresistible, but impossible quest struck home with lasting, revelatory power just yesterday, in our case. When reflex spawns contemplation in real time, and worlds of consideration swirl with a fantastic set of experiential contact points.

We went into our studio, which is a modest library facing a garden; a library with books all asking questions and pointing to human-alleged facts about nature. And there, on a carpet staring at us was a long, gorgeous, curled snake, the *Thamnophis proximus*, or western ribbon snake (bush snake, like a garter, as from the original Latin). All of the books – by the likes of Buffon, Dostoevsky, Darwin, Nietzsche, Ovid, Kierkegaard, Virgil, and so forth – were facing out from their shelves towards this remarkable Other, each book dumb and mute, confined the way most books are – all that learning, trapped between covers. He had clearly gotten in the way insects and spiders and the occasional rodent do. A crack in the universe of our house. A house that is not strictly *our* domicile, to be sure. We live here at the good graces of weather gods and social phenomena. The snake glided with its most elegant circuitousness to a corner, and then with our gentle directional urging headed right outside the door, into *its* home, the green sward, the forest, the riverbanks, the free air universe.

Jane had lullingly lured the snake with enchanted vocables – a snake who seemed without question to recognize her voice and intent – throughout this little ordeal which, in twenty years we will probably have forgotten, or not. But the event does speak to the quintessential divide that marks all speculation, separating our minds from the minds of those Others. Inside that distance is what Emmanuel Levinas described as "immanence" in his masterpiece, *alterity & transcendence*.[28] In that gap, "we remake the making" and "wake out of silence, out of potential absence," as George Steiner has written.[29] Yet, as William James has said, "Philosophy is at once the most sublime and the most trivial of human pursuits…It 'bakes no bread'…"[30] Yet, in some version of a perfect world, it *can* break bread, neighbors and strangers, snakes and crickets, together. Sentimentality, said Albert Schweitzer, is a critical aspect of being human.

There is a fantastic geographical coordinate to any pulse of thought. Reliant, or self-reliant, that locus bespeaks of both random luck (a seedpod blown hither, at last alighting), or a hummingbird hawkmoth or bumblebee intent on its corollae or nectaries specific to that outward combination of co-symbiotic elements: borage, echinops and at least 180,000 other life-sustaining flower species pollinated expressly by at least 20,000 species of bees. If there can be reason in numbers, it is this biologically infinite series of connections.

Biologically Infinite Series

In sloths, colonies, rookeries, grists and voleries, so assemble the interdependent hives, sounders, clutters, dules, convocations, herds, schools, gaggles, prides, troops, litters, rhumbas, families, drays, nests, pods and pledges, packs and descents of vertebrates and invertebrates upon some ὄρεξις (órexis) = appetite or desire) and compulsive, or necessary nervosa. The ecological frissons that penetrate the veils of human obfuscation. To each there is not only a season and a mood, but a specific identity belying the sphere that cannot be mathematically calculated. A geometry with no history of proven theorems. These are spaces with which every known nuance of the philosophical predilection has flirted. But because these spaces are inhabited by Others, the probability of understanding interactions is ordained as irrational, or suborned by the human fascination with cetacean "clicks," "whistles," and acoustical "pulses." They will remain as elusive as Euler's infinite series, or π which offers no ultimate terminus to its endless decimals and, what Aristotle called peripatitikoí (περιπατητικοί), inciting the first scientific odyssey towards the impossible.

From numbers, we naturally turn to the eco-dynamic geographies that must baffle our attempts to comprehend borders, barriers and phylogenetics. We try to make sense of family trees, extrapolating from those closest to us. Again, our Weltanschauung is born of two distinct sides, inside, outside. The fringes are where science, philosophy, the arts probe. These are safe spaces because they remain inside the mind. The dancer is entranced from within. Muscle memory is cellular memory. Any extreme adventure – e.g., the remarkable endeavors of a Reinhold Messner, Tomaz Humar's nine-day solo ascent of the 13,100-foot South Face of Dhaulagiri, or Captain John Franklin's "lost expedition" throughout the Arctic in 1845 – suggests a physicality that is *known*, it is human. It derives all things from its humanness. Geographical contact is impossible to qualify because human experience is fundamentally anthropic. We can only move so far, granting our senses, meditations and choices their fair exchange and fullest prowess. We take our insights seriously, often to the point of implacable belief, and inevitably, subsequent debate or outright conflict. Beyond that we grope in both darkness and the full glare of daylight, devolving in mind and in communities to silly dyads like, optimism versus pessimism, problems and solutions. If all of human evolution appears presented by problems that must be solved, the obvious first question for philosophy is this: is all of Nature equally so confronted? Or are the proposed solutions to each specific test or challenge inherently resolved for the Others by dint of their soupçon of Being and connectedness?

All of our metaphors and allegories are ecological at their core. Yet there is no human kinship that can equate with the forces we label geology, or biology. There is a fallow disconnect that summons, on our part, a combination of nostalgic longing, terror, and armchair equivocations. We were, once, "il figlio selvaggio disperato senza speranza," "the desperate wild child without hope." But there was clearly a line near our origins that resembles a mathematical Verma module, a null vector referring to that point where the impossible becomes possible, the abstract turns physical, by whatever degree. An idea gains traction. What was infinite and unreachable, attains to the finite. Fonds devolves into sub- and sous-fonds. The hierarchies attenuate internally, as an idea back to an atom that has its own completed agenda, every time.

If evolution is viewed according to such transcended boundary lines and areas, then we can assert that the specific contours and epicenters of geography offer us a most useful argument in securing a process, the narrative structure for grappling with the changes everywhere occurring. Those permutations are within our bodies, our minds, all around us. The grand volition is to grasp a foothold that provides evidence, empirical or intuitive, that we are somehow intimately involved. That we can capably exert meaning that is not inflictive but collaborative. For all of our increasing urgencies to find *solutions* to everything, societally and crucially, we don't know how, but in the most amateurish and basically distracting and irrelevant realms. When multiplied simplistically by the number of contemporaneous, large bipedal cohorts, we are not even close to breaking out of, or into the idea(s) that would put us on even the least footing with an ant, or the giant vertebrates, i.e., the largest of them all – *Argentinosaurus* – of Jurassic and Cretaceous lore.

Our collective teamwork with natural forces matters, or, at the very least, will not be in violation of what clearly is a pact the earth has conjured through trial and error. If we *are* an error, then we shall recognize it in time. If not, that time, too, shall come. Clearly, we are on the edge of one way or the other way. Still building unbreachable fences and walls, in either case.

A good place to begin (any geographical marker or golden spike [Anthropocene-pivot] will do) the effort to analogize our condition in light of one of the supreme forces on this planet, is the ecology of ice. Take, for example, the termini of glaciers. They continually shift as numerous forces, principally the rate of ice melting, aggress upon the rates of fluctuation.[31] Climate change gives us a current and plentiful rationale for trying to come to terms with what is, quintessentially, a human-born crisis, a philosophical chasm. It is readily accessible, point to point, the correspondence of cause and effect. Consequentially, it is known, for example, that the Gangotri Glacier, near the wellspring of the Ganga (Ganges), has been retreating since 1780; and started rapid recession in the early 1970s, 76 meters between 1996 and 1999.[32] In Icy Bay, Alaska, beneath Mount Saint Elias, the Guyot Glacier has retreated over 50 kilometers since 1904.[33] We've tracked, in part, the ecological successions that have resulted there, particularly with respect to the life histories of one of North America's rarest bird species, the Kittlitz's Murrelet.[34] "Wherever there were glaciers, the world was in a constant state of creation," wrote John Muir of his 800 mile canoe trip throughout Glacier Bay in 1879.[35] Rejuvenation was also on the minds of ancient Romans in their obeisance to the God Terminus during the annual February 23rd festivals known as Terminalia. Terminus marked a physical place, the border of a property, noted by an implacable stone placed upon a hole wherein the remains of a sacrificed animal would be dumped.[36] Little doubt, then, that termination of a life has been juxtaposed with geological confusion and deification.

According to Plutarch, Terminus was originally considered a God of peace, and no bloodshed or sacrifice ever occurred during homage to him.[37] A profound change occurred in the political winds of Rome, as they always do amongst humans. By February 23 in the year 303 AD, the Emperor Diocletian chose that precise date to begin Rome's systematic oppression of Christians, thereby attempting to elicit the support of a God that would mark the physical boundary of the spread of Christianity.[38] Ukraine's boundaries offer yet more proof of the currency of lines, numbers, artificial measurements and the ensuing chaos that arises when the slightest challenge to such borders occurs. Put a tiny piece of anything atop an ant pile, or in the line of marching ants, and observe the ensuing quantum chaos, not unlike that discovered by Max Planck, researchers using rubidium atoms and "electromagnetic fields."[38a]

The terminus is the beginning and/or end, whether on a glacier, at a bus station or within the labyrinths of philosophical speculation. But biological history guarantees nothing with respect to borders, or of the simple notion that good fences make for good neighbors. Time, and its physical consequences, remains as unclear as it ever did. Every living being carries within a god terminus, who is as unrelenting as the hopes which nevertheless are nurtured in those blind moments where we can see, feel beyond our own mortality. In William Wordsworth's 1804 "Ode: Intimations of Immortality from Recollections of Early Childhood" (in which a child made for the "best philosopher") time acted to wear down the early mystical truths made so readily clear to some youths. But that fledgling spirit can still be remembered, as Wordsworth so tellingly relates at the poem's conclusion:

"Thanks to the human heart by which we live, /Thanks to its tenderness, its joys, and fears, /To me the meanest flower that blows can give /Thoughts that do often lie too deep for tears." (Lines 203–206)[39]

While the poet's closure, line by line, hinges on the rhyme and its encoded pictures of thought, the philosopher in the poet has no true closure, not in mind, only in his language. The transitions are a constant, not unlike gravity, but equally, the helium balloon of consciousness; those perpetually mesmerizing horizon line beyond(s), where the God Terminus has both purchase, but exerts no precise constraint on what is possible, as in Ovid's (43 BC – 17 AD) "Fertilior seges est alenis semper in agris" (the harvest is always more fruitful in another man's fields).

Physical Quanta

The movement in mind from words and images to after-words and afterimages may be meta-regarded. That is, from an outlying, apperceptive vantage. Such a physical quantum, both geographical and sentient, harbors both hopes and ill-bodings. It is infused with an explicitly physical and unwanted domain of redundant, conscious mediation; but an intersect incapable of sifting through its archaeological layers. We might moderate ourselves into an enlightened state (whatever one takes that to mean). Or a depressed, or static, or distant gaze of a place. Every spiritual tradition of which there are records rallies around this ecstatic trance, even defined by the American Psychological Association. Endless concepts of letting go, surrendering to an altered state, achieving unqualified bliss. Et cetera.

"Synaptic transmission" of roughly 1 millisecond,[40] the nerve impulses traveling at approximately 288 kilometers per hour (156-270 miles),[41] are road trips in a deep fog. The speeds do not take into account the actual number of neurons involved in complex thinking. The more neurons, presumably the slower the transmission of electrical impulses. Indeed, "quantifying a single 'speed of thought' may never be possible," writes Beth Daley.[42] It also appears to be irrelevant, because nothing of substantive or dramatic effect has changed in human thought or human nature, ever. Of course, painters over time improved upon their ability to more realistically (even photo-realistically) convey perspectives with regard to the human face, biological realism, perspectives in a landscape or trompe-l'oeil. From the late 20th to the early 21st century, demographic transitions have occurred in dozens of countries. Ideas of race, equality, fairness, and egalitarian justice have struggled forward (note the time involved following Lincoln's "Emancipation" (Order Number 3)– two and a half years – for some 2,000 Union soldiers to reach Galveston Bay and announce the emancipation of nearly quarter-million slaves – Juneteenth), confirming time and again the irrepressible, if repetitive notion that there *is* a forward for humans. Although in the case of Texas, which never changes, it took an army of rifles planted firmly at the faces of slave holders to persuade.

But that same idea, multiplied by more than 17.668 net births per thousand people annually (140 million net births in 2021) undermines its translation given the brute force with which so large a living amalgam fulfills its appetites. Too many faces.

There were nine human species over 300,000 years ago, it is believed. By the end of the Pleistocene epoch, at the height of Quaternary megafaunal extinctions which saw at least 38 mammalian genera erased just from North America, eight of those hominid species had been exterminated by the *last hominin* (still) *standing*.[43] The upheaval ended roughly 11,700 years ago.[44] But we can argue that the terminus post quem of this tumult commenced coevally with the combining powers that *Homo sapiens* first enlisted to exact insensible confrontation, arrogation, and revenge. The qualities empowering conquest came together like an anatomically functioning fuse, but were detonated by distinctly human consciousness. We may rhapsodize 365 poetic angles on what that detonation, had there been distinctive ideas about how to defuse it, might have looked like. But for certain it would have been different than those results we now live with, repeating whole or in part every day.

Wisconsin-born diplomat and philosopher George Kennan (1904-2005), perhaps the most influential American foreign policy pundit of the 20th century, was the author of "A Modest Proposal" (1981, after Jonathan Swift's 1729 anonymously published essay by the same title – very different motif) in which he stated, "Adequate words are lacking to express the full seriousness of our present situation."[45] The tactician who advised numerous presidents with a formula for containment of Soviet expansionism (clearly, it hasn't worked), had early on – in his "Long Telegram" of 1946 – warned of coping with an enemy in a way that would ultimately merge friend and foe, blur cause and consequence, commingle with a lethal complacency before an ultimate horror that shall have passed into our midst without our having ever really reckoned on so sinister and permanent an outcome.[46] Kennan had briefly been the U.S. Ambassador to the Soviet Union for four months in mid-1952 and sensed that atomic conflagration was inevitable.[47] Thirty years later, he was certain of it.[48] The hydrogen bomb was the absolute end of the sapient and sentient lays, an emblem of humanity's "final folly" and he wrote a 79-page memo to then Secretary of State Dean Acheson arguing about "the vague and highly dangerous promise of 'decisive' results, of people 'signing on dotted lines,' of easy solutions to profound human problems."[49]

Annihilation was, for Kennan and the rest of us, the true termination. Unlike Ovid's belief in the Roman god, this marker, the absolute finish line, was the last of the evolutionary sequence of events. There could be no fertile vineyards, feasts drenched in honey after a nuclear war. There would never again be the mythic re-vivification once presumed by the architects of the Temple of Jupiter on the Capitoline Hill in Rome. That is where Terminus was consecrated, looking out over the city and providing security, a symbol of Roman rule forever which was Gibbon's ultimate tease, preparing for the perpetual burst of barbarians at the gate of time. This was the similar geopolitical and cultural intent when George Washington and eight fellow freemasons laid down a cornerstone of the U.S. Capitol, September 18, 1793.[50]

All of these contradictions of topophilia thus far, embroider the impossible *aletheia* (ἀλήθεια) full disclosure, as it was conceived by ancient Greeks (as opposed to oblivion, or lethe). This equivalent to electrical impedance was revived by Martin Heidegger's (1889-1976) restless search for truth, to which the word refers, in the supposed state of being that transcends all obstacles to verisimilitude, as Heidegger suggested in his essay on "the end of philosophy".[51]

Like "the death of nature," the end of philosophy has all the romance of mildew, offering no alternative narrative, perhaps because it cannot. That is the whole point. In our search for the logical conclusion of thought through that same transcendence, we recognize at once the profound difficulty. It is the first cause for humanity, this right and compulsion to think, whether freely or not. But it does underscore the fragility of the act of ponderation in terms of its ability to construct an original framework in which to reside; a fluid, gas or liquid, or some other metaphysical composite of voids, through which to move. There is no solidity to thought. It is always in a state of change, although if its medium is consciousness, then consciousness itself must have a secondary, tertiary, ad infinitum, dynamic state.

Heideggerian Dialectics

Heidegger's controversial center stage right, *Sein und Zeit* ("Being and Time", 1927) elicited severe critiques that spanned comparisons with *Mein Kampf* (1925) as well as the best elucidation of Jean-Paul Sartre's *version* of existentialism.[52] The book's endless iterations of that which is present in the world, the authentic connectivity of object and subject, are undermined, in the end, by the fact Heidegger himself, the man, was a member of the Nazi Party. His insights are unwanted ones. Whilst they have been compared by some to the works of Edmund Husserl and Georg Wilhelm Friedrich Hegel, it matters little. Despite Heidegger's stated intent to mystically grasp Dasein, of being-in-the-world, notwithstanding the complete absence of understanding of what precisely, that means, it is difficult ethically to provision his credos with any lasting credibility. The body of Heidegger's work is nothing less than an inconsequential fiction. But why mention it at all, then? Because, as in the case of an Ezra Pound whose embrace of antisemitism continued to his end, Heidegger's dialectics exerted a polarizing effect upon those who utterly dismissed his "language…running riot" (Bertrand Russell), its being *disingenuous* (Theodore Adorno in his 1964 book, *The Jargon of Authenticity*), the work of a "charlatan" (A.J. Ayer), or, simply a "description of a private spiritual journey" (Roger Scruton).[53] Many others praised Heidegger's alleged brilliance. Ultimately, it is impossible to be rational and ethical in the case of Heidegger's ravenously antisemitic *Black Notebooks* (*Schwarze Hefte*). There, he committed to posterity nearly 1,000 pages of notes written between 1931 and 1959.[54] They represent a summation of hatred and racism espoused in the false consciousness of philosophical deflection by Heidegger himself, as he casts Judaism into an eternal purgatory of "wordlessness," as analyzed by Emmanuel Faye.[55]

Given that every wedge of Heidegger's argument hinges upon the conscious merging of subject and object, of being in the world, to be in exile, as he duly commands of Judaism, is equivalent to eternal damnation. Coming from an ardent member of the Nazi Party from May 1, 1933, just several days after he became Rector of the University of Freiburg, such a calculated purge of Jews was most welcome to the infectious Hitler germ throughout German culture. This has its place in the topology or mapping of what philosophy can and cannot do. It may stifle reason, by betraying the limitations of reasonable conductivity. If it is humanity's principal goal to find solace and social well-being within the protective umbrellas of diverse thought, then there is no place for hatred, none. That *no place* may be allegorically ascribed to a geographical no-man's land, a place of desolation and disease. We know too well the history of this matrix and quiddities, where every war has been fought, each crusade into egomaniacal madness waged.

The message here, as with Gandhi and Jefferson and so many others is the infuriating, contradictory nature of paradox as it applies to humanity's very presence in an all-vulnerable biosphere. Consciousness, and the underlying human conscience, are our markers for recognizing the points of the compass in this push towards open space of thought, as we might understand it. Territory without imperatives. Clearance henceforth. Latitudes and capacity wherein some new nature deploys and explores.

This insuperable intersect, getting beyond the terminus, has harbored, thus far in human history, only infliction; with a self-effacing species that flaunts humility as its default when, in place of that, at the population level, our zealous expressions and behavior have manifested only collective disaster or, conversely, the hubris of back-breeding as a form of penance. Of continued reliance upon dead forms, bodies, generalized destruction as an expedient distraction from the actual graveyards we instruct. Why are we suddenly surprised, in nation after nation? Why, for centuries, but particularly during the past fifty years, has our species been so loath to accept its singular role in the Anthropocene? Our admission of culpability has come not only with a price, but a piercing insight into our cowardice. Until recently, we thought nothing of splitting atoms. Now, we see that *we* are the atom. But even such revelations, in the context of this age, a doubtful renaissance devoted to instantaneity without substance, provides no lens, no hope of processing immediacy, or the schisms it evokes at every biochemical level.

To quote Plato's "Statesman," "Every one of us is like a man who sees things in a dream and thinks that he knows them perfectly and then wakes up to find that he knows nothing."[56] Arendt attributes the origins of the word/meaning, "Being" to Parmenides, connoting duration, a concept at the heart of all philosophy. Time itself; not just the time that marks birth and death, but the quintessence of being in all her iterations.[57] For Sartre, in *Being and Nothingness*, there is no rational integrative function that can reliably separate the nothing which underlies the something. Given this perennial dyad, this binary possibility, everything is capable of anything. Such that "it is almost impossible for us to believe what is true about ourselves".[58] Truth and belief are human luxuries, fantastic scenarios which – were they to exert what evolutionary biology has come to regard as "reciprocal causation" – might find mirror neurons, reversibility of paradox, unlikely co-symbionts, spanning the enormous gulf separating individuals from communities and their populations. These dualities have always represented core dilemmas for all philosophy.[59] As Erik L. Svensson writes in his Evolutionary Biology abstract, "cause-effect relationships are bi-directional," going on to say that this "calls for a revision of standard evolutionary theory (SET)…"[60]

Applied to philosophy generally, bi-directionality replaces one failing of concept with another. "Bi" is a conservative estimate of probabilities, conceptual, moral and linguistic. An effect that triggers a cause implies precursor causes and other effects. Conceptuality itself can neither account for a fickle human nature, or multitaneous perception. Subject and object are equally tainted with the Beingness that human beings consign to their own dominion. This sovereignty is non-existent in the original world, that biological set of truths which registered fully adequate presences before our awkward cue. In other words, there *was* a world prior to our perception of it. The lasting importance of that simple note must empower the reasoning for a foundational succession of ideas, with or without us. But to engineer such a trajectory under the umbrella possibility of human extinction, calls for a level of truth-values and truth-telling examples for which our history resists. Consider Edward Gibbon's (1737-1794) wonderful confession having, by midnight of June 27th 1787, completed his life's great endeavor, twelve years writing the momentous *The History of the Decline and Fall of the Roman Empire* (1776-1788), only to declare: "whatsoever might be the future fate of my history, the life of the historian must be short and precarious."[61] Therein concluding his twelve-volume leviathan with these words, "Of these pilgrims, and of every reader, the attention will be excited by an history of the decline and fall of the Roman empire; the greatest, perhaps, and most awful scene, in the history of mankind."[62]

Biochemical Flux

Elsewhere, we have examined the a priori conditionals that cumulatively made for a world before *H. sapiens*; a planet for which biochemical flux had always translated into systems of equipoise.[63] Balance rather than equilibrium. A sagging line between ambiguous As and Bs. Not a fixed tightrope with unquestioned endpoints. We might prefer to fall back upon a logic that hosts petards as the normal equation of all primordial electrons on earth in the name of violence. But reliance upon an unimaginable chaos is no self-starter; it does not help us resolve conflicts today or tomorrow. When we reckon upon systemic change we fall back on historiography as a means toward some prosaic, Hegelian finale. But what is it, these prime numbers that fall in to step after step in the disagreements that preoccupy a doomed species on an eventually fated planet? The question, like most philosophical questions, is far too ambitious, of course. This is why science, mathematics and physics remain concerned only at the finite scale. On minutiae that can be worked into a theory. Philosophy cringes on the eve of a solid detail. It fears circumspection, combats falling oxygen levels, swearing oaths to infinite, unanswerable truths. Thereby granting to truth a value, which is then part of a series of values, the propositional functions that gives to deliberation a wide berth in which to continue to debate inculpatory, or ex situ, or in vivo, or any number of hypothetical situations. All in accordance with a plausibility paradox. In this latter stage of building an insight, there is no proof between independent models. The modeling itself strikes out between bubbles of alleged fact. But a value is not a fact. It is not subject to any one premise. A premise is a conditional at all times. It is not an independent component, but one connected to other propositional elements. This makes any judgement an artifice because thought cannot dissuade connectivity, or rally disparate entities to converge. The entire history of science is burdened by this inescapable plausibility gap. Every connection is vulnerable. Hence, the story telling is always a series of false positives. What we'll call a premisetory. Natural history is only *our* natural history; a continuity that we equip, furnish and clothe in genetic timelines and phylogenetic (chain-of-being) metaphors, concluding with ourselves. Think of map of biodiversity in which humans are at the center. That was always the Renaissance, time and again.

Framing any argument or narrative in such a context undermines the rationale for sobriety, courting, instead, a battleground of fools for whom no human outcome matters. This is at the large scale. In the microcosm of it, there exists a philosophical basis for the end of deductive reasoning. We cannot know beginnings and ends. The Jains argue there are none. Left to our own within an interdependent, eternal translocation of atoms, we are governed (*we* meaning the morphological, genetic species that is us) by mass continuity, controls on momentum, divergence and the very energy powering these fluids, gases, laminar and turbulent flows, and the *Boussinesq approximation* of buoyancy, upside down or right-side up, it matters not. The question philosophically as to what actually constitutes a dimensionless number or approximate conservations of mass, momentum and energy all depends upon gravitational fields whose expressions – e.g., a Rayleigh or Richardson number – places us within the metarealms of physical fluid dynamics and the normal course of differing types, sizes and categories of, say, bubbles.

Ecological bubbles, and the ethereal castle that encinctures Mind (children chasing detergent bubbles in a park on a summer's afternoon), any mind, are metaphors, applicable to be sure, but insulated by way of implacable suggestions we cannot shake from our mistaken self-identities. One day we are in Paradise, the next, Hell. Joseph Valentin Boussinesq (1842-1929), propounded uncannily relevant methodologies and allegorical depictions of his KdV (Korteweg-De Vries) equation, which would establish the notion of solitary waves, the great beast of fluid dynamics: the soliton, and the accompanying proofs of cnoidal, surface gravity waves. These are waves with a singular direction. They work in all substances to disperse frequencies, and to manifest low-amplitude, propagation, short wavelengths, and the inverse scattering transform. This happens in the instance of finite superpositioning of a constellation of solitons, inherently contradictory because they move towards a least-action principle in nature. Non-zero. Able to quickly (as in time) get beyond the local. An evolution of biology and physics that holds to a single, anomalous constant, namely, integration, but only as the result of imagined tsunamis.

Biologically, we could liken it (the cnoidal waves atop shallow ideas, thinly veiled reality) to interdependency. But there is no hold on the imagination, certainly not the human abstract thinking coordinates, that mandates anything conceivably precise. So that an idea may exist as the aforecited ecological bubble, but its mathematical fate is tied to biochemistry, which in turn, resists fixation, translation or comprehension. Its derivatives are partial. Micro-premises. The integrals that follow are forever asymptotic – they cannot connect. The evolution of such ideas is enlivened by a situation whereby the distribution of those entities that may be likened to it, are teeming with transition and modification, to the extent that we can only characterize its existence to begin with as not a partial, but impartial differential equation. Not even gravity changes the natures of its self-effacing bias. We are, ultimately, speaking here of the inherent bias of all thought in humans. Whether it is so in other species remains a speculative magnet. But we will never know, not in the sense of actual knowledge. And since there is only premisestory, we will continue to populate those spaces with more and more data, without ever having the one connection that is essential for getting beyond mere truth values, and our idea of what constitutes firm reality, solid being, reconcilable margins of error. In a world where all is approximation, our entire species might add up to zero probability. That is both a comforting, and terrifying concept.

We're speaking of an utter mystery that transitions by nature from our minds to the minds all around us – amongst more than one trillion species. That inescapable translocational journey defies human depiction. We just know instinctively that it is occurring at all times. Buttressing most elegantly or chaotically, or some quality in between, that is crucial and life-affirming within the biosemiosphere.

Now, well in to the 21st century, all of human life, in its systemic co-opting of most agencies of the biosphere, have made life an historic struggle that is qualitatively different than ever before. Historians are no longer the bellwethers of change that a Gibbon might have expected. Indeed, the odds against substantive, cultural alterations that would foster ecological stability amongst our kind are statistically close to nil. How close is a matter of colossal debate. The variables remain largely unaccounted for, in spite of many decades of untoward number crunching at every planetary boundary and incremental biological event horizon. Many scientists at the International Geological Congress in Cape Town in August of 2016, declared the Anthropocene Epoch was globally destructive by 1950 as to justify the new designation at that time.[64]

One could argue that elements of the Western Enlightenment, so called, and 19th century burgeoning interest (at least in the U.K.) in animal rights-related issues, could be traced to the various publications and translations of the writings on vegetarianism and rationality in all animals, by the Roman Syrian philosopher, Porphyry (c.234 – c.305 AD).[65] His book *On Abstinence from Animal Food* (*Περὶ ἀποχῆς ἐμψύχων; De Abstinentia ab Esu Animalium*),[66] in addition to his wide-ranging studies of Plato, Aristotle, Plotinus, Pythagoras and many others, sets Porphyry apart in the history of metaphysics. His idealism, like that of Mahavira and Buddha, Christ and Saint Francis, imprints the sustainability dialogues of our time with a penetrating practicality. Porphyry's pragmatism was authentic, but contextualized within the orbit of real human natures, it was also Quixotic. We can follow his influence easily enough to Percy Shelley's own devotion to a non-animal derived diet, and subsequent legal agitation in England that would result in the first anti-vivisection and natural protection societies.[67] Given sufficient time to be able to reflect, historian to historian, upon the many turns of cultural change and emphasis, we can lay the groundwork and its temporal peripheries for the presumed transformation of a philosophy into a real life.

Such transitions – carnivore/herbivore, violence/non-violence – are differentiated points of a clear enough finality. For example, as early as 2002 it was suggested that "Plant herbivore food webs comprise at least 40% of global biodiversity" (mostly in tropical regions).[68] At least 4,000 known terrestrial mammals are herbivores, 74 of which – the largest among them (> 100 kg) were endangered as of 2015; some "60%" threatened with extinction.[69] In fact, herbivores have been shown to be most vulnerable, despite their multitudinous status among all life forms. One significant study revealed that dietary mediation at the omnivorous level has provided for the most generalist success overall.[70] But that data is entangled in human bias by dint of human presence within the material sciences and psychological algebra. It is clear that 350,000 years ago, prior to the advent of *H. sapiens*, we can expect to have seen a very different pattern of mass, versus diet, vis a vis reproductive success. The vast literature on the evolution of meat eating remains unreceptive to the many ghosts of primordial herbivore success. A thousand footnotes would be insufficient, however, to convince most science communities on that fact.

From a current sociological/transitional perspective, what, then, should this tell us about anthropic-embedded statistics? And is this dietary calibration the most salient and predictive of data sets, in terms of speculation as to species success moving forward?[71] It is certainly a profound indication of a shift that marks the most problematic map of injuries, an all-consuming manifest of mortality and "ecosystem stoichiometry" (chemical reactants and products, ratios and relationships) across the biosphere.[72] Violence is to diet and daily human assault what a Hiroshima or Auschwitz is to the imagination. The core is unstable to the extreme, yet its fringes hold, in the guises of compromise, incremental politics, and polls which ineluctably narrow as any human population verges upon decision making. We'll more fully examine the extremes of politics as they utterly detract from the necessarily central bias of all biology at the conclusion of this treatise.

But to linger, slightly, in the realm of dietary diagnosis using paleontology as our guide. Significant transitions early in evolutionary history have been divined from certain fossil records, and there has been deeply informed speculation as to what a world without predation might look like. 1.9 million years ago, records from rocks along Lake Superior in Canada reveal predation by microbes on a cyanobacterium known as Gunflintia. It may well be among the first known predatory relations, possibly a primeval precursor to today's most successful phylum of parasitic alveolates, namely, *Toxoplasma gondii*. Interestingly, there are coeval, theoretical bases for a non-predative (non-cropping) biosphere, with bacterial actors on the world stage emerging at the same time as Gunflintia that have been considered.[73] Writes paleozoologist Stefan Bengtson, "There would be various kinds of photo- and chemoautotrophs making use of available energy gradients to reduce carbon for energy storage…Leaving aside the question of whether such a Shangri-La for primary producers and decomposers is even theoretically possible, the selective pressures would be very different from those that affect most organisms today."[74] But Bengtson also concludes that "Although predation was a decisive selective force in the Cambrian explosion, it was a shaper rather than a trigger of this evolutionary event."[75]

The Triggers of Conceptualization

What were the triggers? Grasping the difference is essential to any future conceptualizations, noting that the human mind is a vast population, rooted to an individual of populations, some of which are accelerating second per second, others dormant. Interpretation of events are subject to both trigger and shaper diplomacy and reflex. In discussing the fact that "most animal phyla appeared over an approximately 10-million-year period, beginning 541 mya, known as the Cambrian explosion," writes Paleobotanist and deep ethicist Dr. Melanie DeVore, "The most possible explanation for this process is a developmental one." And, in looking at early anatomical data for animals at that time specifically explored by Peter W. H. Holland, and others, DeVore cites "complex coordination of homeobox genes, coding positions along a central nervous system" which in turn over a short amount of time, relatively, articulated specific morphological, energy consuming body parts.[76] "Earth's early ecosystems," she writes, "had producers, algae, providing an immense base for food chains. Why hunt, why waste energy, why risk failure to catch prey, why risk injury and death, just to secure food?... Carnivores never make up a great portion of food webs. What was the awareness of the Others that sparked the need to consume other organisms to meet your own immediate needs and those of your offspring?" DeVore's question taps into a vast non-consensus amongst investigators.[77] But what appears clear is the presence of homeodomain proteins (the sixty known amino acids) that controlled formation of organs in animals, and a level of robust cellular differentiation first discovered in flies,[78] and then deciphered as key expressions between the evolution from prokaryote to eukaryote.[79] This portends of the most important organism thus far discovered in the evolution of animals, plants and fungi, namely, the homeobox genes (e.g., Hox genes) that determine a world of meta-herbivores that was a self-sufficient ecosystem of planetary dimensions. Something else triggered predation. A mystery that cannot easily be explained. A simplistic explanation would consist of something like the insight that the average 100,000 follicles on a human head evolved to produce hair for an organism. The reason for that was probably to moderate the build-up of heat off the scalp, mitigating the amount of sweat that entered the eyes, once an individual moved out into unshaded habitat, for example.[80] That's the easy equation. There is none for predation, certainly not one readily decipherable from the hox-subset of genes responsible for such critical axiomatic, embryologic developments of animals.

Nor does that part of the enlarged cerebral cortex (neocortex) itself recommend predators over herbivores, or even omnivores.[81] A looming question is *time*; the time natural selection works to effect demonstrable change. It is a facile projection for humans to think back a few hundred thousand years and accept that that environmental context anywhere on earth would be similar to those with which we now cope (must cope). This remains one of the biggest questions in the de-extinction movement. We have no idea what the real pressures were on a Tasmanian Tiger, or Saber-Toothed, for that matter. Re-creating them in a void is nonsensical. But some pieces of the puzzle of transition fall into place, as in the remarkable mouse study in Nebraska where body fur color changes amongst survivors was accented within a matter of months, matching that of the soil types upon which their outdoor laboratory setting consisted.[82]

The conundrum of herbivory has seen far more study than the phylogenetics of meat eating, its logic consoling, a world of Bambi's, which incites our imaginative collective in a way that should have forever prevented bloodshed, at least amongst our kind.[83] 300 million years ago, write Hans-Dieter Sues and Robert R. Reisz, "a vast standing crop of herbivores supporting relatively few carnivores" was the essential of most "continental ecosystems," with the plant world having figured out "microbial endosymbionts that produce the enzymes needed for fermentative digestion of cellulose." [84] But, in fact, most tetrapod evolutionary studies reveal the dominance of what is (by most human standards) a non-violent diet and daily behavioral set of characteristics, in a multitude of species starting with the *Lokarchaeum* phylum, thought to be transitional from single to multi-cellular organisms.[85]

Which takes us back to the Stefan Bengtson hypothesis, critical reading for anyone who prefers to imagine a scenario whereby the real precipitates of human, sociological transition today are not so much the catalysts but the modifiers, as culturally mandated by ecological boundaries, constraints and realities. If we can accelerate such shifts, we will also be capable of shaping their outcomes, modestly but with enough suasion to enact what would, otherwise, be described as an impossible, ethical revolution. Triggers in the blind. There have been global cultures, and global shifts at such levels of magnitude. We refer to them by three worn paradigms: the advents of technologies, agriculture and surplus. But those researchers who have endeavored to elucidate advantages of carnivory are hard pressed to explain lower protein consumption among most other primates, and other human groups including the Hadza, a foraging tribe (insects playing a large role in their diet) who inhabit savanna that is little changed from the same Serengeti like grasslands from which the predominate "Environment of Evolutionary Adaptiveness" (the "Serengeti Hypothesis") has long been formulated.[86] There are no selective advantages, including alleged preferential *cognition*, that can be accurately attributed to the fossil or environmental records. Extrapolated rain curtains, shifting ungulate migrations, or forensic taphonomy are all puzzle pieces used in "modeling the edible landscape"[87] with some precision. The underlying flaw is that each methodology dictates a unique human trait abetted by predation. That selection bias includes the study of "reduced gut size", "Increased brain size", "increased body size", "exchange of information about patchy and unpredictable resource distribution" and other correlates.[88]

Metabolic Conundrums

One can easily translate issues of size and metabolism as being of so unequal a measure as to be meaningless. Does a hummingbird expend more energy than the elephant, for example. We cannot infer anything about cognition, either historically or in the present tense, across our own species, let alone in any others. Hence, comparable data has a very marginal role in terms of our actually understanding the past, or looming potentialities. Much of the problem for allometric or psychological extrapolation of past and present, in terms of future events can be deciphered in the research to date that has noted the "multiple traits" conundrum (polyphyly) for high-impact invasive invertebrates, a situation made extremely complex in that invertebrates may comprise as much as 97% of all animal species on the planet.[89] But in absence of a common ancestor, the case can reasonably be argued that their unspecific event horizons make anything possible, between the individual and the swarm.

The same complex uncertainty, perhaps at lower numbers, can be said of terrestrial vertebrates. For example, 270 million years ago, the largest land vertebrate, a caseid, probably evolved from aquatic synapsids, ancient carnivores that lived during the Carboniferous and Permian periods,[90] went on, within approximately 30 million years, to become earth's dominant megaherbivore on land, along with the proto-mammalian Edaphosaurus. This has been deciphered from a footprint of one of a tetrapod, *Eocasea martini* found in Kansas.[91] The discovery represents an early instance of a dietary shift that has all but baffled the easier biological generalizations which hold that such vagaries are all but impossible under normal evolutionary rubrics, and often thought of as de-evolutionary.[92] But such case-mining evokes a sensible wonder, if nothing else, with regard to what is possible between the cracks of evolution.

Biological Numerics

We could also easily ask the wrong question with respect to these ancient, non-violent newborns. For example, the optimal size of their social units, if any? British anthropologist Robin Dunbar's number – 150 – helps qualify the size of military platoons throughout history, or the average size of primate communities. Tribal group sizes vary from 120 to roughly 2500 individuals, as determined during the last 6000 years. Among twenty or so recent tribal clans for whom census data was derived, the average number was 153. And this is said to have had some empirical relationship with the size of the neocortex wherein much thought, culture, behavior and ethical dispositions are assumed to originate, amongst those same member individuals, whether humans or other species.[93] Another question, loaded with theoretic misgivings concerns the old adage of strength in numbers, and what that means ecologically? Possibly something entirely other than the defensive strategies asserted by the cliché. 153 *competing* individuals present an entirely different scenario than cooperative ones. Moreover, one person can push a button, any button. Or answer 'Yes' to a call by fishermen in the Faroes. A summons to barbarously slaughter 1,400 dolphins in a single day. In this instance, it was an entire pod of white-sided dolphins herded into a trap, where local interspecies vigilantes, scores of members of the community enjoying the show from a nearby beach, stabbed every dolphin to death in a blood-and-guts saturated orgy of hatred. It violates every known European Union code of ethic and law and does so with arrogant impunity. People, including ourselves, from throughout the world emailed outraged letters to the government leaders in the Faroes, as well as to Copenhagen. There was only hateful silence. The incident happened at the shallows of Skalabotnur beach in Eysturoy. In a rare show of outrage, the BBC warned readers of the horrifying story.[94] Just over a century before, the British themselves had committed a similar massacre at Jallianwala Bagh in Amritsar, on April 13, 1919. Over a thousand people, equally trapped, were gunned down upon orders by Brigadier General R. E. H. Dyer.[95] These are not one-off occasions of evil. We know this much from history: humanity can push buttons, make gruesome decisions, defiantly ignore the notion of the larger, ethical community.

Such scenarios are further compounded by dietary templates. Herbivores, insectivores, omnivores, carnivores: their competitive advantages and disadvantages have long been studied, whether among prairie dogs,[96] irruptive insects,[97] the coevolving "grasses and herbivores," whether in both "middle Eocene strata," or other proxy systems found in or Miocene North American grasslands, or contemporary South American pampas.[98] That's just a few out of literally tens-of-thousands of studies on the subject. This latter example, however, is emblematic of the profound intersections of grazing/browsing vertebrates and the vast association of invertebrates on their preferred habitat, wherein a dominant species, e.g., C4 grasses (plants using PEP carboxylase, a four-carbon molecule versus the C3, three-carbon grasses) are found.[99] So widespread were these grasslands during the Cretaceous that one can find tremendous fossil assets for extrapolating corresponding species and their diets. This is no less the case today, where both perennial C3 and C4 grasslands occur over more than 20% of the terrestrial biosphere.[100] Climate changes during the last 100 million years have greatly influenced these grasses, which have so thoroughly impacted all the species associations. Soils below or above the average 50-degree Fahrenheit threshold for chlorophyll compound dormancy or energized (e.g., cool versus warm season grasses)[101] breaks down the meaning biologically of who lived (lives) and what they ate (eat). And it comes down to a 3-versus-4 atom compound in the photosynthetic process. This is particularly interesting because it is a quantum connection where profound causes and consequences hinge upon a few degrees of weather change, or, with equal importance, a slight shift in communication, cultural norms, or, in humans, simply the slightest, albeit invisible, re-consideration.

This is precisely the difficulty we have in embracing any singular trigger or modifier. The tapestry of shifts is too dynamic to simplify, and this holds for the underlying ethical probability zones.

Reversive pairs, like the de-encryption itineraries of elliptic-curve cryptographic algorithms, reverse Hoogsteen RNA bioinformatic schemes, emordnilaps, reversible dyads, bi-directionality as discussed earlier, are each components of a physical reality tied to philosophy by their transactionalities and geography over time, or in an epiphanic instant. Mathematicians speak of "backdoors" within the quantum computing realm. There are always intermediate positions, or stop-gaps. Zeno's Paradox would add additional distance within the space of any expression or choice.

Gandhi ultimately characterized a very different set of tumultuous flow of events as the *Story of My Experiments With Truth.*[102] They may differ from decade to decade but in the ceaseless, exasperating history of contemporary times "the existential threats of nuclear weapons and climate change have intensified in recent years because of a threat multiplier: the continuing corruption of the information ecosphere on which democracy and public decision-making depend," writes John Mecklin, editor of the 2021 Doomsday Clock Statement, which sees humanity as 100 seconds away from midnight.[103] Such cumulative news represents one more step in the final madness, lost in the chatter of humanity inching ever closer to total self-destruction. Species annihilation itself might give rise to some level of ecological rejuvenation. Studies have long suggested just that, at least at a primitive eukaryotic level. But as early as 1983 researchers had calculated that "30 to 50 percent of the total human population could be immediate casualties of a nuclear war" (at "5000 to 10,000 MT yields)". "Extinction of the human species cannot be excluded," the authors concluded.[104]

If this were simply fireside musing in an academic tower, far removed from the gravitas of cause and consequence, there would be nothing philosophically to worry about. Simply intellectual ping pong or a teleological fashion show, or spa in which to massage ideas. But at the only too real portal of sentience and suffering there is an inescapable and brutal reality. We see it most vividly in the ongoing debates concerning animal law. In such quarters, many have argued for a writ of habeas corpus being granted to every animal, starting with elephants, great apes, and any other large vertebrate in zoos (e.g., the New York elephant, Happy), to name just a few of the oppressed/slave species, and types of emergency public engagement. There are at least 800,000 animals confined to zoos, safari parks and aquaria – and that's just those organizations that are internationally accredited.[105] All such facades of education, or protecting endangered species are deliberate undermines that ignore the nature of life, favoring instead protracted torture and death. For the animals, there are no odds of escape from our pathetically narcissistic convolutions, which begin – for animals and habitat – when science itself is invasive, or germinates the technology, data, and engineering to allow for social incursion, then extraction.

Gandhi's Brahmacharya (celibacy test) experiments of the mid-1940s were highly controversial and remain even more so today.[106] But his early autobiographical discussions, as embodied in *The Story of My Experiments with Truth* cover his life through 1921. They were focused upon his struggles with discriminatory practices in South Africa at the Cape Colony; his feelings regarding self-denial, asceticism and spiritual fulfillment (as decreed by "Christ in the Sermon on the Mount"), and his readings of John Ruskin's political and labor theories within the book, *Unto This Last* (1860). These experiments also examined his entry into politics, which would underscore his theories and advocacy back in England during World War I, and then in India where, by 1920, he was calling for "non-cooperation" with the British, the ultimate consequences of which would require more than another quarter century to maturate.[107]

Human travails take time to recognize, more time to work out. Nearly one billion people were chronically malnourished in 2020. It was not until 2021 that a majority – 667 out of 671 members of the European Parliament – came together to agree to a resolution to recommend to the European Commission "to end all experiments on animals," an enormous breakthrough affecting potentially over ten million vertebrates annually.[108] At the same time, symposia and media attention to entomophagy research and dietary options (insect consumption – mostly "caterpillars, grasshoppers [and] slugs" by people, as an environmentally-friendly protein substitute for an overcrowded human world) has been gaining traction, as earlier referenced amongst some indigenous peoples in Africa. The argument, numerically speaking, is potentially sound. Some 80% of all visible species (to the naked human eye) are insects and spiders.[109] The daily RDA (Recommended Daily Allowance/intake) of protein (comprising at least nine naturally unavailable of the 22 amino acids determined to be essential to the human body) is on average 50 grams between each male and women, 1.7 ounces.[110] These are precise markers whose interpretation leads to that same reverse pairing involving quantitative and qualitative mediation that is conscious and tenable.

Of course, there are innumerable ethical breakdowns in these contradictions which are historical and more with us now than ever. Each problem is systemic. Every confrontational deliberation is compounded by the inordinate power of its impositions that have surely defined much of the largely inequitable basis for those muddled corners where philosophy is stumped. Add to these juggernauts the massive pain points described earlier – mindless, callous dietary obsessions. Multiplied by nearly eight billion of us whose increasing per capita and per household consumption makes most intergenerational handshakes an increasingly implausible vision. The concluding reality is ecocidal. It would appear incapable of any deep learning behavior. Moreover, our unfavorable history has not enlightened to much degree, or in any global unison, our self-absorption, today and probably tomorrow. Hence, there is ample reason for misgivings. They are foundational and we are only beginning to take some notice. Philosopher Ludwig Wittgenstein (1889-1951) found this set of sad circumstances the precursor to a rational, or – if you will – irrational, frustrated, deeply bewildered, sacred but perennially hopeful silence, by which he meant, certainly, something that speaks volumes 100 years after his extraordinary book was published.[111]

The post-modernist ecological saga now encinctures us. We have perilously closed in upon 196.9 million mi^2 (509.9 million km^2) which is earth. How does one species commandeer such a size, 29.2% of which is land, the rest ocean? Why would we do that? Can philosophical traditions mean anything against the forefront of this unimaginable swath of pathologies that mark our kind? The convergence of factors driving the Bulletin of Atomic Scientists' "Doomsday Clock" with its three divining rods of the nuclear threat, climate change and "cyber-based disinformation," the "info-demic," may seem arbitrary but we are perilously close to its dreadful conclusions. In 1947, when the clock began ticking, it was all of 420 seconds (not the current 100 seconds) to midnight.[112] As Stanley Olson wrote of the great poet Elinor Wylie (1885-1928), her gorgeous verse, devoted to Percy Shelley, particularly in the nineteen sonnets "One Person" found in her final work, *Angels and Earthly Creatures* (1928) mirrored our current crisis where there is no "protection of subjectivity…"[113] We can't feel ourselves out of this debacle involving the entire planet. If philosophy began in our gazing at the galaxies and other species who we eventually represented on rock walls; then spread to the earliest campfire discussions, before committing to mythic and religious allegorical meanings of life on earth[114], contemporary positions are beyond all narrow gates. Post-structuralist, critical, postmodern, deconstruction, pragmatic, analytical, experimental, quietistic, post-Frankfurt School etc. all conflate on the implacable abyss of ecological junctures. They are urgent and cannot be denied or ignored.

We will examine these gaps and questions in light of the chronic, perhaps most sinister of all plights confronting humanity, namely, biodiversity loss and its inherent, systemic cruelty. Humanity has utterly failed to offer either a philosophical, or psychological explanation or amicus brief that would overturn our ingrained pattern of domination amongst our species, and all Others. Such a condition presents a unique challenge in the history of ideas. While there have been plentiful laudations exhorting humanity's ability to make rapid changes at a cultural level, largely of a technological nature,[115] phenotypic etiologies reveal not one correlative feature with evolution, or none thus far verified within the orbit of our short span of species duration. Whether matters pertaining to domicile or diet, hygiene or meticulousness, random violence, pleasure seeking and pain avoidance: each behavioral trait continues unabated from the first day of our awakening. Nonetheless, those considerable theories involving rapid change have established a metric predicated upon a myriad of "observed shifts in population and community characteristics."[116]

Precursors of Darwin

A current tide of ecological theory recognizes that "evolution is a mindless, plan-free phenomenon, driven into endless possibilities by random mutations..."[117] It is a viewpoint older than Darwin. One corresponding outlook stemming from this stochastic reality is the r/K* trade-off within populations between quality and quantity. It is that basic. The obstacle that would impose this non-deliberated choice (a constellation of choices) are so called trait boundaries and distributions that succeed in transcending genetic or other bottlenecks, or not.[118] Proponents of saltation (sudden evolutionary change), or, alternatively, orthogenesis (progressive evolution), like the French naturalist Georges Cuvier (1769-1832 – the doctrine of repeat catastrophes), Swiss physiologist Rudolf Albert von Kölliker (1817-1905- theories of common descent by means of saltationist large steps) and English botanist John Christopher Willis (1868-1958 – *The Course of Evolution by Differentiation Or Divergent Mutation Rather Than by Selection*, 1940) defy the linear retrospection of human history with their theories, but have never persuaded those who view gradualism, versus punctuated equilibrium, as the more plausible explanation.[119] Do we live only in the interstices of disaster, or calm? Is our heritage one of plasticity or narrow tenacities? Which is the more steadfast, stubbornness or moderation, aggression or restraint, mind or, in the true Zen sense, no-mind?

To invite consideration of human cultural change as familiar a probability as volcanism, or seismology, hurricanes and tornadoes, is to cultivate a slippery slope. That is to say, the daily events of any given morning might involve a customary series of routine actions, or a devastating tsunami. Simple probabilities favor the former. Chances of being struck by lightning are literally approaching one per million. Complex probabilities favor human manipulation of numbers to encompass a motivation that, presumably, is rational, but inevitably biased.

Hence, the glaciation on Jakobshavn Isbræ in Greenland was recorded at 98 feet of loss per day (nearly 7% annually of the entire Greenland ice shelf).[120] During any number of massive events, speciation at sympatric and allopatric alter-regional levels might, and have occurred at speeds consistent with greatly accelerated mutation rates of "less than 10^{-3} per generation per individual."[121] At least 17 "cataclysmic events"[122] have altered this planet, the most recent being climate change and its biological fall-out. But 17 events out of hundreds of trillions of happenings in biological time does not even compute. It is statistically zero, unless the lens has been altered to encompass an exponent rule (i.e., product, quotient or power of powers) that allows a rational motivation to meet an expected metric range (as in the dependent versus independent variables of the invented null hypothesis). If the motivation is irrational, the bifurcation point draws its clear red line over a paradox target that we can track, but not measure. A motivation to measure an irrationally-motivated metric has been the plight of human history. Whereas, we see no reason to impute irrational motivation amongst ecosystems or their component layers (organisms and the entirety of their connections, which is entirely unknown). This poses a supreme dilemma for philosophy, as it does for all the sciences and social sciences. It also undercuts any notion of free will, divine intervention, assumptions regarding behavior, predictions of cultural change, even our reading of our own histories. We cannot assume anything about the independent variables shaping our premises, operating systems, parameters and conclusions.

If we presume that the differing theories connoting evolution of *Homo sapiens* have been predicated on flimsy premises, it leaves us nowhere, in terms of Mind. Feelings, however, may react differently to such a verdict. And, in turn, will question with different expectations all issues pertaining to mathematical strategy, laws and constants, economic exchange, cultural banter, legalese, dates, facts, figures, nouns and pronouns, semantics, identity, ethological exchange, cultural norms, values, ethics and every facet of civilization, so called. In such an irrational universe, we will still recognize beauty, refrain from self-injury, hopefully empathize even more so with others. But we will do so free of the brutality that we have branded our own perceptions with, generation after generation.

Strategically, geopolitical *pivots* have obvious global impacts that can be immediate, protracted, or in other emphatic ways consequential. English geographer Halford John Mackinder proposed just such a metric of expansive reactivity at the Royal Geographical Society in 1904.[123] Out-migration, various periods of rapid human industrialization, and the "persistence of traditional values,"[124] have obviously wreaked their ongoing results. Other species' equivalents have certainly been intimated, either through changing migration patterns (in humans as well)[125] or their own cultural and technology-related alterations. This would include the recently witnessed events of chimpanzees in the wild applying insects to wounds of themselves and their compatriots.[126] It was reported in 2017 that an estimated "half of all species are on the move" resulting from climate change.[127]

There is enormous taxonomic debate regarding the emergence of chimpanzees, and when the last common ancestor of chimps and humans was alive. 13 million years ago, 4 million years, etc.[128] And for many years field researchers (the phrase itself outrightly rude and intrusive) have recognized Sumatran orangutan culture, a combinatorial prowess including gestures, language, tool use, and countless other forms of behavior, both inherited and learned.[129] Their ancestral taxonomic divergence occurred roughly 12 million years ago.[130] Primate lineages in general date back approximately 65 million years.[131] The *tempest in a teapot* analogy, when thinking of primates, becomes less befuddled when we consider that genetically we share some 98% of our DNA with the Chimpanzees and Bonobo, and nearly as much with Gorillas and Orangutans.[132] Bonobo DNA sequences suggest their divergence from Chimpanzees about 2 million years ago,[133] Gorillas 8.5-12 million years ago (from a common ancestor with humans).[134] Orangutan personalities and inward, philosophical expressiveness are the closest to us.[135] But let us not deceive ourselves: What we have in common with the Orangutan is only during the moment we see or dream ourselves, wishfully, in their eyes. The eight remaining great ape species, four genera, all Hominidae family members, cannot, by our throw-weight alone, defuse the taxonomic bomb configured in our species' hands. What went wrong with us? How did it happen?

Is there a learning process with timely probability of resolving the discord we alone have created during our briefest of all lineages, a mere few hundred thousand years? Is this colossal problem not the most essential question for philosophy? If so, what then? What are the most appropriate questions?

Jain ethics for at least 2,500 years has shined a prolific light on the fact that all life forms are unto themselves of total and uncompromising value. That human utility is irrelevant to that value. Mid-20th century environmental activism in India and the U.S. was re-awakened to these biospheric calls for justice. The Bishnoi of Rajasthan in India's Tar Desert have for centuries called upon the necessity of legal, not just moral rights for all of nature.[136] Currently, that would most certainly include lake Mary Jane, and other contiguous riparian and wetland "parties" to a lawsuit over a proposed development some 14 miles southeast of Orlando International Airport. Mary Jane, with the help of human lawyers, is suing to save her own ecosystem.[137] Whether the case is won or not, it does summon a compelling variation to Shakespeare's otherwise definitive line from "Hamlet," that "There are more things in heaven and earth, Horatio, /Than are dreamt of in your philosophy."[138] Perhaps, with slow juridical progress and decisive, imaginative flashes of activism, philosophy in rare moments *is* capable of catching up with nature. But we are unlikely to ever absolve, or re-engineer the horror of a pack of wolves bringing down a bison, or a brown bear gorging on a live caribou calf. Such images conjure forth the impossibility, or near unlikelihood of making salient connections in the service of a desirable outcome. We don't have any plausibility data to enable us to alter the premise that we are equal and unequal to nature's methodologies, in the same species, either in real- or philosophical-time.[139] There are even more complications.

Remote Sensing, Feeling, and Post-Cognition

Our species' intellectual timeline is receding, with data to suggest that this generation harbors an IQ approximately "13 points" lower than that of those living in the 1970s. Julian Cribb credits this decline to a current generation of "chemically-damaged brains," and Cribb's research to that effect is harrowing.[140] But the central challenge is not the level of intelligence, given the preferential power of self-reference; the abdication of our actual role in the realm of ecological flux. What is of most concern are the separation of ideas and feelings. One rightly experiences lonely misgivings in recognizing that the lexicon of current biological studies can address every conceivable detail of observed nature, but cannot fix anything involving ourselves. We can manage a heart transplant or measure "altered biogeochemical cycling" and "sedimentation rate[s]".[141] Our remote sensing has engendered cognitive upheavals that skim surfaces in pointillist detail: "energy fluxes through ecological food webs" across archipelagos in northern Sweden;[142] algal community responses that affect "concentrations in dissolved organic carbon (DOC)" in "homogeneous [as distinct from]...heterogeneous metaecosystems;"[143] flux measurements throughout entire ecosystems;[144] convection-diffusion equations (e.g., physiologist Adolf Fick's Diffusion Laws, Henry Darcy's hydraulic flow law, French physicist and mathematician Jean-Baptiste Joseph Fourier's law [which anticipated the revelations of climate change] regarding the movement of heat, etc.);[145] "complexity" and "general systems" theories as they apply to our attempting to make sense of the ecologically incomprehensible, and so forth.[146] But we remain foreign to the actual class of *ourselves*, incapable of, at best fecklessly lost in the attempts to, alter our collective moral character, or plot a tenable pathway in such direction.

Every topographical point on earth is subject to human theorizing, and with it the wild swings in our perception between stability and dynamism, but to what ends?[147] "Cell to ecosystem"[148] deliberations have engaged the concept of "deep-time biodiversity changes,"[149] particularly in response to local parameters that seem to influence eco-dynamics, as in the case of climate change. Numerous case studies have sought to translate complexity into "quantum transition state theory" involving "classical dynamics from reactants to products in multi-dimensional systems."[150] No matter the ecosystem studied, a similar currency of metaproducts within language are predictable, as is their distribution according to the underlying logic of human communication. "Pulses," drought-sensitivity, "functional group strategies," scalar flux, feedbacks, etc. are all conceptual semantic components throughout natural history.[151] "Meaning" in and of itself has come to constitute a major problem for evolutionary ecology, and many researchers are involved in endeavors to fathom how biology copes with information.

In 1948 mathematician Claude E. Shannon published his "A Mathematical Theory of Communication" in a Bell System Technical Journal.[152] He selected the most obvious categories of logic to detail the basic transmission of information that have since come to be fundamental components of any biosemiotics model. Hence, we see the linguistic underpinnings in biology and molecular biology at the level of probabilistic correlation. Is the necessity of maximum information – whatever that could possibly mean – a valid threshold for understanding, in any species? At what point does communication actually become meaningful and in what proportions between transmitter and receiver? Such questions go on endlessly into the great unknown that is the biosemiosphere. Because it is a constellation of unknowns relevant at the quantum functions, seeking any meaning at all requires not just the remote sensing agency, but remote *feeling*. This devolves to communication signals that are unlikely to be apparent, particularly when dealing with microbial scalar whorls, or, for example, "invertebrate functional feeding groups."[153] In addition, it begs the question of what constituent thought experiments (as in the case of amalgamations and chemical reactants) are actually fundamental to self-awareness in the force fields, waves, points, vectors and all planar dimensionality and field gradience that connects self to other selves; references points to other points; context to context, bubble to bubble; worlds to worlds. The connections go on forever, our species having entered the force field with a single, apparent goal: to get beyond the constraints otherwise crucial to ecological borders. As if we might be the first organismic system in biological history to achieve liberation, transcendence, biotic nirvana.

Our communication signaling is equally restive, higher dimension branes or phase spaces, in relativity. It is the domain of S^3, the topologically connected spheres and manifolds that were the basis for solving one of the elusive algebraic conundrums of the last 150-years, the Henri Poincaré (1854-1912) conjecture.[154] That riddle, in ecological terms, is one more attempt to mathematically correlate symbolic structures with a through-story that can be identified as biospheric. The field of "rupture-dynamics" is bound to the phase transitional theories stemming from a mathematical language that has inevitably come around to ecodynamic spaces[155] and what is known as "conformity invariance," one of three, probably many more symmetries that occur during a major physical transition in nature (e.g., Antarctic ice shelves melting).[156] Percolation theories provide other insights into the density of nodes – a mesh of clusters – necessary for the connectivity of a physical property to effect and/or abet the phase shift.[157] In no other spaces are anthropic biases more prone to seeing what they want to see. This is not to refute the theories proposed by various symmetries, but to point out our inescapable involvement in the perceptions. When Japanese "inter-universal geometer" Shinichi Mochizuki allegedly solved the "abc" conjecture, he created his own mathematical language (in some 600 pages comprising his proof) to counter the conventional a+b=c syndrome with a "square free part" possessing a "minimum value greater than zero" and so on.[158]

The goals and usefulness of the application of such seemingly obscurantist numbers fiddling may ultimately assist restoration ecologists, in as much as "connectivity" is a key to biodiversity conservation. The Everglades is just one of hundreds of thousands of case studies where contiguous patches of habitat are core to robust genetic fields and thus species rarity or abundance.[159] Ecological fate maps include the number and diversity of wading birds, fish migrations, Everglade landscape changes over time, hydrological perturbations and their impact on water depths and slopes, variations in sawgrass and spikerush.[160] In other similarly oriented mathematical/ecological studies, researchers have examined a "forest-savanna model" using the so-called "Lyapunov function," a scale-dependent set of equations for analyzing landscapes with specific respect to equilibrium.[161/162] In addition, we have seen recent "urgent" studies, reflecting the rapidly escalating magnitude of climate change and impacts on, for example, the variance of ecological flux of the Taizi River in the Liaoning province of northeastern China, and "insect-mediated contaminant flux" as described in the ecological literature dealing with sites of "potential risk", to name just a few out of thousands of such investigations.[163/164]

Pulsed lasers have become critical tools for geographers, ecologists and historians seeking to dig deeper with remote sensing, particularly, utilization of Lidar technologies ("light detection and ranging").[165] Whether for use in robotics or sphere detection as measured within the remote sensing capabilities of the most recent iPhones from Apple, such AI-based tools are expanding the biological and social data bases enormously. One intriguing outcome of the use of Lidar was the discovery in the Bolivian Amazon of numerous sites from AD 500 to AD 1400 that were clearly Casarabe culture economic and agricultural epicenters loosely described as the first known pre-Hispanic interconnected semi-urban settlements in all of the Amazon. As the Authors of the paper propose, there is definitive evidence of "an anthropogenically modified landscape" of "low-density urbanism."[166] In such a case, the information adds to our conception of just how intensively our ancestors were involved with the landscape. The extent to which they became actors on the stage of ecological flux. We've known this about our species' actions over tens-of-thousands of years, from the estimated 45,000 year old Pedra Furada hearths of Brazil, particularly the Nordeste (Northeast) Serra da Capivara site with its "1,150 images and thousands of artifacts,"[167] to the earliest discovered Clovis hunting cultures in North America over 13,000 years ago (e.g., the El

Fin del Mundo site in Sonora, Mexico where remains of two elephant-like extinct gomphotheres were found in 2011),[168] and their successor Younger Dryad cultures, Folsom and Paleo-Indian peoples, who were more accustomed to post-glacial climatic conditions.[169] Around the planet, these ancients each contributed to the "Late Quaternary megafaunal extinctions" that dramatically changed the world as a result of one species.[170] But, again: we are speaking of intellectual impact of remote sensing versus, and/or in accord with, remote feeling.

In his chapter, "An Age of Extinction," Tim Flannery notes the "soul-destroying task" that must come from the documentation of the hundreds of extinct species, just in the past five centuries, not to mention the past 45,000 or more. Flannery's colleague, the brilliant artist Peter Schouten has had the disconcerting task of trying to draw and paint the lost creatures, from what data and remains exist. Flannery writes of his encounters with the life-sized paintings and, in the case, for example of the eight-meter long Steller's sea cow, declares how to see it "in intricate detail – makes one aware as nothing else can just how terrible a loss its extinction was."[171] This is the vortex of thought that does not go extinct, not yet; but lingers in all those disciplines – like mathematics – that struggle to rationalize distance, the enigmatic happenings that have been our history, our present, perhaps our destiny as it involves the Others. Such thought embraces a degree of mythopoesis, stoically or in the realm of post-stoicism.

We communicate in the most simplistic words within stifling constraints, but insist that clarity, even tacit evocation should be sufficient to overcome the combinatorial fragility of language and meaning. With a one and a zero humanity has fashioned a digital world unto its own. Moreover, we have expected these ones and zeros to know it all; to mirror stepladders into the Cosmos, and nanotechnological descents into the microspaces of a "butterfly's proboscis" or "shelled amoeba". In 1995, the electron microscope scanning capacity was approximately 300,000 times. Today, it is over 1,000,000.[172] Compared with the woodcuts illustrating Christopher Columbus' "official report of his first voyage"[173] and 14 years later, the 1507 map of Martin Waldseemüller, the first to mention "America"[174] the biological sciences have been supercharged by techniques of exposure, perspective at distance and neutrality, light spectra penetration, and a revolution in imaging. Whether with respect to "mechanisms of ventilation and perfusion in respiration heterogeneity and regional lung mechanics"[175] or those new star systems being discovered by the James Webb astronomical observatory, discerning nearly 14 billion years back into time,[176] the ecologist's dilemma is humanity's last opportunity to save itself, at least in real-time. By that, we refer to the full circumspection of images, ideas, languages, codes and technologies we might yet bring to the tribal conversations in order to liberate, by our will power, creativities, and not a little luck, the life force on earth which we are killing.

How does one destroy a force, like evolution, or presume to somehow restore it? We don't know such questions or answers; indeed, we don't know the answer to anything. Even asking about evolution reveals a grim window on our species' hubris and the ultimate idiocy it translates to.

Gravity is gravity. Change is predictable. We just can't grasp in what ways our predictions are likely to meet our hopes and dreams, if ever. Philosopher Michael Strevens wrote a strenuous treatise on macro and microdynamics, the components for which, he suggested – *enions* (his term) – were, if we understand his work, the same, whether in population ecology, physics or economics. That the complex variables of these arenas become more and more *simple* as laws (constants) the further out we move from the minutiae.[177] But there is nothing *simple* about arrogance. In humanity's case, it springs from the meteorologic equivalent of a blocking omega high in our self-importance. A pressure to change the world, make it "better"; make our gods join us, commend us, empower us.

In the meantime, our hope is vested in our schizophrenia, a word we use advisedly given that there are at least some people who are not perpetually craven, crass and tyrannical. These are people who truly endeavor to save lives, every life; to impound all that which kills, if we can, and seek transformative modes of being that are not hostile, or inane, but co-symbiotic. Our human forms of language, as far as can be gleaned, will never be able to accomplish such modes. Instead, our ideas will have to become working blueprints. It is not clear from our histories if we have anywhere near the facility as a species trapped by its own populations and fertility successes, so to speak, to manage anything like the migration of ideals into food on the table, gentle and fair collaboration, international congruence of bioculturalism[178]. We have seen incumbent indigenous deifications of the earth, rituals inciting every version of tree hugging. Such efforts, while laudable, have not re-invented antidotes to the absolute disasters of modern strangleholds, the real bastions of implacable power and reach. How we are likely to come by the stability of Dunbar's number in a fragmented amalgam of nearly eight billion strong is neither an arm's length distillation of disinterested theory, nor an enmeshed self-sacrifice to the ideal of ethical ecology. Somehow, from the contested and confangled inner trappings of humanity there is a quiet answer awaiting all of us, not in due course, but either sooner or never.

"In The Heart of the Amazon," Photo © by M.C. Tobias.

Endnotes

[1] See "Gandhi's 1939 Rosh Hashanah Greeting to the Jewish People," by Zack Rothbart, *The Librarians*, September 24, 2019, https://blog.nli.org.il/en/gandhi/; See also, "Gandhi Writes Letters to Hitler: "We Have Found in Non-Violence a Force Which Can Match the Most Violent Forces in the World," (1939/40)," by Josh Jones, in *History, Letters*, February 3rd, 2016, https://www.openulture.com/2016/02/gandhi-writes-letters-to-hitler.html; See also, ""You Are Today the One Person in the World Who Can Prevent a War.' Read Gandhi's Letters to Hitler," by Tridip Suhrud, September 25, 2019, *Time Magazine*, https://time.com/5685122/gandhi-hitler-letter/

[2] See "When Mahatma Gandhi chided Hitler and called his actions monstrous," by Prabhash K Dutta, India Today, October 2, 2019, https://www.indiatoday.in/news-analysis/story/when-mahatma-gandhi-chided-hitler-and-called-his-actions-monstrous-1605346-2019-10-02. The second letter, writes Dutta, was "shot off out of frustration at the expansionist behaviour of Hitler." Ibid.

[3] See "Gandhi's View on Judaism and Zionism in Light of an Interreligious Theology," by Ephraim Meir, *religions*, June 30, 2021, https://www.indiatoday.in/news-analysis/story/when-mahatma-gandhi-chided-hitler-and-called-his-actions-monstrous-1605346-2019-10-02, file:///Users/michaeltobias/Downloads/religions-12-00489-v2.pdf

[4] Shmuley Boteach, "Repudiating Gandhian pacifism in the face of mass murder," *The Jerusalem Post*, March 31, 2016, https://www.jpost.com/opinion/repudiating-gandhian-pacifism-in-the-face-of-mass-murder-449885. A Google search of this

specific controversial subject, as of August, 2021, reveals over 1.2 million articles and references.

[5] See the section on ethical irreversibility, *On The Nature Of Ecological Paradox*, by M. C. Tobias and J. G. Morrison, Springer Nature, New York, NY 2021, p. 795. For some basics on the variola virus see, "Smallpox," Centers for Disease Control, https://www.cdc.gov/smallpox/index.html

[6] See *The Great Big Book of Horrible Things: The Definitive Chronicle of History's 100 Worst Atrocities*, by Matthew White, W. W. Norton & Company, 2011, as reviewed by Randy Dotinga, Christian Science Monitor, February 24, 2012, https://www.csmonitor.com/Books/chapter-and-verse/2012/0224/Encyclopedia-of-evil-a-catalog-of-history-s-100-worst-atrocities

[7] See "Kill Counter-Anonymous for the Voiceless," https://www.anonymousfor thevoiceless.org/kill-counter; See also, Chapter Nine, "The Industrial Fate of Animals," in *God's Country: The New Zealand Factor*, by M. C. Tobias and J. G. Morrison, A Dancing Star Foundation Book, Zorba Press, LA and Ithaca, NY, 2011, https://dancingstarfoundation.app.box.com/s/st72okcdfn

[8] *The Writings Of Thomas Jefferson*, Collected And Edited by Paul Leicester Ford, Volume VI, 1792-1794, G. P. Putnam's Sons, New York, NY, 1895, p. 141. See also, "Opinion On Offenses Against The Law Of Nations, 3 December 1792, National Archives, "Founders Online," https://founders.archives.gov/documents/Jefferson/01-24-02-0681; See also, "The Dark Side of Thomas Jefferson," by Henry Wiencek, *Smithsonian Magazine*, October 2012, https://www.smithsonianmag.com/history/the-dark-side-of-thomas-jefferson-35976004/

[9] "Slavery FAQs - Property," *The Jefferson Monticello*, https://www.monticello.org/slavery/slavery-faqs/property/

[10] See Entry – "Deed of Gift, Robert Carter III's," *Encyclopediavirginia.org*

[11] Matt. 7:12. Streeter, Burnett H. *The Four Gospels. A Study of Origins Treating the Manuscript Tradition, Sources,* Macmillan and Co., Ltd., London, 1924.

[12] See Boris Repschinski, *The Controversy Stories in the Gospel of Matthew: Their Redaction, Form und [sic] Relevance for the Relationship Between the Matthean Community and Formative Judaism*. Vandenhoeck & Ruprecht, Göttingen, Germany, 2000.

[13] See Jean Richard and Jean Birrell, *The Crusades, c. 1071-c. 1291*, Cambridge University Press, Cambridge, UK, 1999.

[14] See Joseph Michaud, *History of the Crusades*, Wm. Robson, trans. 3 vols., Routledge, London, UK, 1881.

[15] See "Operation Barbarossa: A Deadly Turning Point in WWII," Smithsonian Associates, January 30, 2014, https://smithsonianassociates.org/ticketing/tickets/227352; See also, https://www.britannica.com/event/Operation-Barbarossa; See also, "Operation Barbarossa And Germany's Failure In The Soviet Union," https://www.iwm.org.uk/history/operation-barbarossa-and-germanys-failure-in-the-soviet-union. For deaths during the Stalinist era, see Anton Antonov-Ovseyenko, *The Time of Stalin,* NY Harper & Row 1981. p. 126.

[16] See "Consistency and Ethics," Markkula Center for Applied Ethics, January 1, 1988, https://www.scu.edu/ethics/ethics-resources/ethical-decision-making/consistency-and-ethics/

[17] See, for example, "Ecological Non-equilibrium in the Anthropocene," by Giovanni Rapacciuolo, Andrew J. Rominger, Naia Morueta-Holme and Jessica L. Blois, *Front. Ecol. Evol.*, 08 November 2019. https://doi.org/10.3389/fevo.2019.00428, https://www.frontiersin.org/articles/10.3389/fevo.2019.00428/full; See also, "AI turned a Rembrandt masterpiece into 5.6 terabytes of data," by Purbita Saha, January 11, 2022, https://www.popsci.com/science/rembrandt-night-watch-restoration-artificial-intelligence/

[18] See "Zoo Bans Woman Having 'Affair' With Chimpanzee From Seeing Him," by Sara Santora, Newsweek, August 23, 2021, https://www.newsweek.com/zoo-bans-woman-having-affair-chimpanzee-seeing-him-1622129?amp=1

[19] See Albert Axell, *Japan's Suicide Gods,* Pearson Education, London 2002.

[20] Joseph Wood Krutch, *Human Nature And The Human Condition*, Random House, New York, NY, 1959, p. 165.

[21] Lewis Mumford, *In The Name Of Sanity*, Harcourt, Brace And Company, New York, NY, 1954, p. 220.

[22] In *The Fate Of The Earth*, Alfred A. Knopf, New York, NY 1982.

[23] In *Field Notes from a Catastrophe – Man, Nature, And Climate Change*, Bloomsbury, New York, NY 2006.

[24] In *Land Of Ghosts – The Braided Lives of People and the Forest in Far Western Amazonia*, Houghton Mifflin Company, Boston and New York, 2005.

[25] ibid., p. 211.

[26] "The World Lost Two-Thirds Of Its Wildlife In 50 Years. We Are to Blame," by Nathan Rott, *NPR*, September 10, 2020, https://www.npr.org/2020/09/10/911500907/the-world-lost-two-thirds-of-its-wildlife-in-50-years-we-are-to-blame#:~:text=We%20Are%20to%20Blame,-Facebook&text=Human%20activities%20have%20caused%20the,threatens%20human%20life%20as%20well, Accessed September 1, 2021.

[27] See "Happiness Tip: Cultivate Wordlessness," by Dr. Christine Carter, https://www.christinecarter.com/2014/10/happiness-tip-cultivate-wordlessness/; See also, a French documentary featuring American ecological philosopher and musician, Dr. David Rothenberg playing the clarinet beside humpback whales in the wild and lending exquisite commentary to the interspecies wordlessness that achieves the pure merging of art, science, humanity, and cetacean spirit. Even the frequencies are allied, clarinet and whale. https://www.youtube.com/watch?v=d-n_uZ_IYi4

[28] Columbia University Press, New York, NY, 1999, p. 4.

[29] See *Real Presences*, by George Steiner, The University of Chicago Press, 1989, p. 210.

[30] "Lecture 1: The Present Dilemma in Philosophy," originally published as *Lecture 1 In Pragmatism: A new name for some old ways of thinking*, Longman Green and Co., New York, 1907, pp. 1-16, https://brocku.ca/MeadProject/James/James_1907/James_1907_01.html

[31] See, for example, the NASA image of Bhutanese glacial termini, http://visibleearth.nasa.gov/view_rec.php?id=2876

[32] https://nsidc.org/cryosphere/glaciers/questions/climate.html

[33] See "Guyot Glacier Retreat, Icy Bay Alaska," by Mauri Pelto, October 29, 2012, https://blogs.agu.org/fromaglaciersperspective/2012/10/29/guyot-glacier-retreat-icy-bay-alaska/

[34] See *Sanctuary: Global Oases of Innocence*, by M. C. Tobias and J. G. Morrison, A Dancing Star Foundation Book, Council Oak Publishers, Tulsa OK & San Francisco, CA, 2008, pp. 1-12.

[35] See "As glaciers disappear in Alaska, the rest of the world's ice follows," by Jonathan Watts, May 1 2021, *The Guardian*, https://www.theguardian.com/environment/2021/may/01/as-glaciers-disappear-in-alaska-the-rest-of-the-worlds-ice-follows

[36] See H. H. Scullard, *Festivals and Ceremonies of the Roman Republic*. Thames and Hudson, London, UK, 1981, pp. 79–80. See also Ovid, Fasti 2.639-684.

[37] See Plutarch, *Roman Questions* 15; *Numa* 16.

[38] J. H. W. G. Liebeschuetz, *Continuity and Change in Roman Religion*, Oxford University Press, Oxford, UK, 1979, p. 247.

[38a] See "Quantum Chaos," Physical Review Letters, Contact, Dr. Gernot Stania, Max-Planck-Gesellschaft, https://www.mpg.de/510817/pressRelease20051103

[39] By William Wordsworth, Poetry Foundation, https://www.poetryfoundation.org/poems/45536/ode-intimations-of-immortality-from-recollections-of-early-childhood

[40] See "Why Is the Human Brain So Efficient?" by Liqun Luo, Nautilus, April 12, 2018

[41] "It feels instantaneous, but how long does it really take to think a thought?" by Beth Daley, *The Conversation*, June 26, 2015, https://theconversation.com/it-feels-instantaneous-but-how-long-does-it-really-take-to-think-a-thought-42392

[42] ibid.

[43] See "Overkill, glacial history, and the extinction of North America's Ice Age megafauna," by David J. Meltzer, *PNAS* November 17, 2020 117 (46) 28555-28563; first published November 9, 2020; https://doi.org/10.1073/pnas.2015032117, https://www.pnas.org/content/117/46/28555; See also, "300,000 years ago, nine human species lived on Earth. Did homo sapiens exterminate the others?" By Nick Longrich, The Conversation, November 23, 2019, https://scroll.in/article/944558/300000-years-ago-nine-human-species-lived-on-earth-did-homo-sapiens-exterminate-the-others; See also, "Why are we the last hominin standing?" By the Museum Of Anthropological Archaeology, University of Michigan, (n.a.), August 16, 2018, https://lsa.umich.edu/ummaa/news-events/all-news/search-news/why-are-we-the-last-hominin-standing--.html

[44] See "International Chronostratigraphic Chart," *IUGS*, https://stratigraphy.org/ICSchart/ChronostratChart2017-02.jpg

[45] https://www.nybooks.com/articles/1981/07/16/a-modest-proposal/; See also, https://www.gutenberg.org/files/1080/1080-h/1080-h.htm

[46] See "February 22, 1946 – George Kennan's 'Long Telegram'", Wilson Center Digital Archive, https://digitalarchive.wilsoncenter.org/document/116178.pdf; See also, 'A Guest of My Time' by Fareed Zakaria, The New York Times, February 21, 2014 (on The Kennan Diaries), https://www.nytimes.com/2014/02/23/books/review/the-kennan-diaries-by-george-f-kennan.html

[47] See "The Compromise That Never Was: George Kennan, Paul Nitze, and the Issue of Conventional Deterrence in Europe, 1949-1952, by Jerald A. Combs, Diplomatic

History, Vol. 15, No. 3 (Summer 1991), pp. 361-386, Published By: Oxford University Press, https://www.jstor.org/stable/24912120

48 "George Kennan on the Bomb," By Michael Krepon, Stimson, March 18, 2019, https://www.stimson.org/2019/george-kennan-bomb/

49 See "George Kennan's 30-Year Nightmare Of Our 'Final Folly'", by Don Oberdorfer, May 24, 1981, *The Washington Post*, https://www.washingtonpost.com/archive/opinions/1981/05/24/george-kennans-30-year-nightmare-of-our-final-folly/1c90c056-73c9-4804-9b52-f9e07ad33512/

50 *Capitolium* in Charlton T. Lewis and Charles Short, *A Latin Dictionary*, Oxford: Clarendon Press, Oxford, UK, 1879. See also, "History of the U.S. Capitol Building," https://www.aoc.gov/explore-capitol-campus/buildings-grounds/capitol-building/history

51 "The End of Philosophy and the Task of Thinking," in *On Time and Being*, by Martin Heidegger, Martin Heidegger, *On Time and Being* (New York: Harper and Row, 1972), p. 70, translation amended. The original in *Zur Sache des Denkens* (Tübingen: Max Niemayer, 1969), p. 86. Cited in Nikolas Kompridis, *Critique and Disclosure: Critical Theory between Past and Future,* (Boston: MIT Press, 2006), p. 188. page 10 in https://grattoncourses.files.wordpress.com/2016/12/22the-end-of-philosophy-and-the-task-of-thinking22.pdf

52 See George Steiner, *Martin Heidegger*, The University of Chicago Press, Chicago, Ill., p. 5, 1991.

53 Roger Scruton, *A Short History of Modern Philosophy*, Routledge, London, pp. 269–271, 274, 2002.

54 See Free Indexes: Ferrer, D. F. (2016). *Heidegger Schwarze Hefte (1931-1948): An Index* https://archive.org/details/HeideggerSchwarzeBlackNotebooksIndex Ferrer, D. F. (2016). *Martin Heidegger Esoteric Writings: An Index* https://archive.org/details/HeideggerEsotericIndex Ferrer, D.F (2017). *Heidegger Anmerkungen I-V (Schwarze Hefte 1942-1948): An Index* https://archive.org/details/HeideggerGA97Index Ferrer, D. F. (2016). *Heidegger Überlegungen XII-XV (GA96): An Index.* https://archive.org/details/HeideggerGA96Index; See also, the edited texts, by Peter Tawny, 2014-2020, Verlag Vittorio Klostermann, Frankfurt, Germany; and "And now the apologists for Heidegger's anti-Semitism get to work," by Brian Leiter, March 22, 2014, Leiter Reports: A Philosophy Blog, https://leiterreports.typepad.com/blog/2014/03/and-now-the-apologists-for-heideggers-anti-semitism-get-to-work.html

55 See "Why Does It Matter If Heidegger Was Anti-Semitic?" by Richard Brody, March 27, 2014, *The New Yorker*, https://www.newyorker.com/culture/richard-brody/why-does-it-matter-if-heidegger-was-anti-semitic; see also, "The End of Philosophy and the Task of Thinking," Heidegger lecture, 1969, http://www.naturalthinker.net/trl/texts/Heidegger,Martin/heidegger%20-%20The%20End%20of%20Philosophy%20and%20the%20Task%20of%20Thinking.htm

56 See Opening of Hannah Arendt's *The Life Of The Mind*, Volume One, "Thinking", Harcourt Brace Jovanovich, Inc., New York and London, 1978

57 ibid., p. 135,

[58] See the discussion about Sartre in *Agency and Alienation – A Theory of Human Presence*, by Jerome M. Segal, Rowman & Littlefield Publishers, Inc., Savage, Maryland, 1991, p. 169.

[59] See "On Reciprocal Causation in the Evolutionary Process," by Erik L. Svensson, in *Evolutionary Biology, Evol Biol.* 2018; 45(1): 1–14. Published online 2017 Sep 19. doi: 10.1007/s11692-017-9431-x, PMCID: PMC5816131, PMID: 29497217, https://www.ncbi.nlm.nih.gov/pmc/articles/PMC5816131/, Springer.

[60] ibid.

[61] John Murray (ed.), *The Autobiographies of Edward Gibbon*. Second Edition (John Murray, London, UK, 1897, pp. 333-334.

[62] *The History Of The Decline And Fall Of The Roman Empire*, by Edward Gibbon, In Twelve Volumes, London 1821 edition, Volume 12, p.427.

[63] See *On The Nature Of Ecological Paradox*, by M. C. Tobias and J. G. Morrison, Springer Nature, New York, NY 2021; and *The Quantum Biosemiosphere*, by M. C. Tobias and J. G. Morrison, NOVA Science Publishers, New York, NY 2021.

[64] See, for example, "Approaching the Ecological Event Horizon," by Stephen Mulkey, PhD, Natural Resources Council of Maine, September 19, 2016, https://www.nrcm.org/blog/approaching-the-ecological-event-horizon/; See also the Anthropocene Working Group consensus that the exact year was 1950. https://education.nationalgeographic.org/resource/anthropocene; See also, https://2021anthropocene.iasc-commons.org/#:~:text=IASC%202021%20Commoning%20the%20 Anthropocene%20Virtual%20Conference%2C%20April%2021%2D23, and http://quaternary.stratigraphy.org/wp-content/uploads/2022/03/AWG-Newsletter-2021_final.pdf

[65] See, for example, *Renaissance Vegetarianism – The Philosophical Afterlives of Porphyry's On Abstinence*, by Cecilia Muratori, MHRA, Cambridge University, Cambridge, UK, 2020, Italian Perspectives 46, Legenda, http://www.mhra.org.uk/publications/Renaissance-Vegetarianism. See also, *Porphyry's Launching-points to the realm of mind: an introduction to the neoplatonic philosophy of Plotinus*, Translated from the Greek by Kenneth Sylvan Guthrie, With an Introduction by Michael Hornum, Phanes Press, Grand Rapids, MI, 1988.

[66] See *Select Works of Porphyry; Containing His Four Books On Abstinence From Animal Food…* Translated From the Greek by Thomas Taylor, London, 1823. See also, *Romanticism and Animal Rights*, by David Perkins, Cambridge University Press, Cambridge, UK, 2003.

[67] See Note # VIII, pp. 161-182, in Percy Shelley's "Queen Mab," London, 1821. See Timothy Morton, "Joseph Ritson, Percy Shelley and the Making of Romantic Vegetarianism." *Romanticism*, Vol. 12, Issue 1, 2006. pp. 52–61; See also, Shelley, Percy Bysshe, "A Vindication of Natural Diet;" London: Smith & Davy. 1813, pp. 1–36. See also, *on The Nature of Ecological Paradox*, by M. C. Tobias and J. G. Morrison, Chapter 39, "Shelley's Ecological Exile and His Utopia of Animal Rights," Springer Nature, New York, NY 2021; See also, *God's Country: The New Zealand Factor*, by M. C. Tobias and J. G. Morrison, Introduction by Ingrid Newkirk, A Dancing Star Foundation Book, Zorba Press, Ithaca, NY, 2011.

[68] See "Guild-specific patterns of species richness and host specialization in plant-herbivore food webs from a tropical forest," by Vojtech Novotny, Scott E. Miller, Leontine Baje, et al., *Journal of Animal Ecology* 2010, 79, 1193-1203, doi:10.1111/j.1365-2656.2010.01728.x, British Ecological Society, citing P.W.Price, "Resource-driven terrestrial interaction webs," Ecological Research, 17, 241-247, https://besjournals.onlinelibrary.wiley.com/doi/pdf/10.1111/j.1365-2656.2010.01728.x

[69] "Collapse of the world's largest herbivores," by William J. Ripple, Thomas, M. Newsome, Christopher Wolf, et al., *Science Advances*, 1 May 2015•Vol 1, Issue 4, doi:10.1126/sciadv.1400103, https://www.science.org/doi/10.1126/sciadv.1400103.

[70] "Herbivores at the highest risk of extinction among mammals, birds, and reptiles," by Trisha B. Atwood, Shaley A. Valentine, Edd Hammill, et al., *Science Advances*, 5 Aug 2020•Vol 6, Issue 32, doi: 10.1126/sciadv.abb8458

[71] "Diet mediates the relationship between longevity and reproduction in mammals," by Shawn M. Wilder, David G. Le Couteur, and Stephen J. Simpson, *Age (Dordr)*. 2013 Jun; 35(3): 921–927. Published online 2012 Jan 12. doi: 10.1007/s11357-011-9380-8, PMCID: PMC3636383, PMID: 22237559, https://www.ncbi.nlm.nih.gov/pmc/articles/PMC3636383/

[72] See "Predator-driven elemental cycling: the impact of predation and risk effects on ecosystem stoichiometry," Shawn J. Leroux and Oswald J. Schmitz Ecol Evol. 2015 Nov; 5(21): 4976–4988. Published online 2015 Oct 15. doi: 10.1002/ece3.1760, PMCID: PMC4662303, PMID: 26640675, https://www.ncbi.nlm.nih.gov/pmc/articles/PMC4662303/

[73] See David Wacey, Nicola McLoughlin, Matt R. Kilburn, Martin Saunders, John B. Cliff, Charlie Kong, Mark E. Barley, and Martin D. Brasier. Nanoscale analysis of pyritized microfossils reveals differential heterotrophic consumption in the ~1.9-Ga Gunflint chert. *PNAS*, April 29, 2013 doi: 10.1073/pnas.1221965110. See also S. M. Stanley, "An ecological theory for the sudden origin of multicellular life in the Late Precambrian," *Proceedings of the U.S.National Academy of Sciences*, 70:1486-1489. See also, S. M. Stanley, "Ideas on the timing of metazoan diversification," *Paleobiology*, 2:209-219.

[74] See "Origins and Early Evolution of Predation," by Stefan Bengtson, Chapter 11, p. 291, http://citeseerx.ist.psu.edu/viewdoc/download?doi=10.1.1.333.7374&rep=rep1&type=pdf; See also, https://natureecoevocommunity.nature.com/users/38194-stefan-bengtson

[75] ibid., p. 289. See *Virtual Paleontology, The Paleontological Society Papers*, Cambridge University Press, 21 July 2017. See also, "The fossil record of early eukaryotic diversification," by Susannah M. Porter, *Virtual Paleontology, The Paleontological Society Papers*, Cambridge University Press, 21 July 2017.

[76] See "Did homeobox gene duplications contribute to the Cambrian explosion?" by Peter W H Holland National Library of Medicine, https://pubmed.ncbi.nlm.nih.gov/26605046/, 2015 Jan 13;1:1. doi: 10.1186/s40851-014-0004-x. eCollection 2015, PMID: 26605046, PMCID: PMC4604119, doi: 10.1186/s40851-014-0004-x

[77] Personal communication with Dr. DeVore, Sep.23 2021. See also, "Earth science. Causes of the Cambrian Explosion," by M. Paul Smith and David A. T. Harper, Science, 20

September 2013, Vol. 341, Issue 6152, pp. 1355-1356, doi: 10.1126/science.1239450, https://www.science.org/lookup/doi/10.1126/science.1239450

[78] See "Evolution of herbivory in Drosophilidae linked to loss of behaviors, antennal responses, odorant receptors, and ancestral diet," by Benjamin Goldman-Huertas, Robert F. Mitchell, Richard T. Lapoint, Cécile P. Faucher, John G. Hildebrand, and Noah K. Whiteman, *PNAS* March 10, 2015 112 (10) 3026-3031; first published January 26, 2015; https://doi.org/10.1073/pnas.1424656112, https://www.pnas.org/content/112/10/3026

[79] See Corsetti MT, Briata P, Sanseverino L, Daga A, Airoldi I, Simeone A, et al. (September 1992). "Differential DNA binding properties of three human homeodomain proteins". *Nucleic Acids Research.* 20 (17): 4465–72. doi:10.1093/nar/20.17.4465. PMC 334173. PMID 1357628. See also, bio-techne, R&D Systems, "Homeodomain (Hox) Transcription Factors," https://www.rndsystems.com/research-area/homeodomain--hox--transcription-factors; See also, Bürglin, T.R., Affolter, M. Homeodomain proteins: an update. Chromosoma 125, 497–521 (2016). https://doi.org/10.1007/s00412-015-0543-8; and, Fraser, P; Bickmore, W. (2007). "Nuclear organization of the genome and the potential for gene regulation". *Nature.* 447 (7143): 413–7. Bibcode:2007Natur.447..413F. doi:10.1038/nature05916. PMID 17522674. S2CID 4388060. See also, Holland, L. Z.; Ocampo Daza, D. (2018). "A new look at an old question: when did the second whole genome duplication occur in vertebrate evolution?". *Genome Biology.* 19 (1): 209. doi:10.1186/s13059-018-1592-0. PMC 6260733. PMID 30486862.

[80] See "How to be Human: The reason we are so scarily hairy," by the New Scientist, n.a., October 4, 2017, https://www.newscientist.com/article/mg23631460-700-why-are-humans-so-hairy/

[81] See "The evolution of mammalian brain size," by J. B. Smaers, R. S. Rothman, et al., *Science Advances*, 28 April 2021, Vol. 7, Issue 18, doi: 10.1126/sciadv.abe2101, https://www.science.org/doi/10.1126/sciadv.abe2101

[82] See "The Wild Experiment That Showed Evolution in Real Time," by Ed Yong, *The Atlantic*, January 31, 2019, https://amp.theatlantic.com/amp/article/581521/; See also, Howard, H. C., van El, C. G., Forzano, F. et al. "One small edit for humans, one giant edit for humankind? Points and questions to consider for a responsible way forward for gene editing in humans." *Eur J Hum Genet* 26, 1–11 (2018). https://doi.org/10.1038/s41431-017-0024-z

[83] See "Origins and early evolution of herbivory in tetrapods," by Hans-Dieter Suesab, and Robert R.Reiszc, Trends in Ecology & Evolution, Volume 13, Issue 4, 1 April 1998, Pages 141-145, doi:10.1016/S0169-5347(97)01257-3, https://www.sciencedirect.com/science/article/abs/pii/S0169534797012573; See also, "'Bambi' Is Even Bleaker Than You Thought," by Kathryn Schulz, January 17, 2022, *The New York Magazine*, https://www.newyorker.com/magazine/2022/01/24/bambi-is-even-bleaker-than-you-thought

[84] ibid., from the authors' Abstract. See also, https://blog.everythingdinosaur.co.uk/blog/_archives/2014/04/29/fossil-find-provides-information-on-the-evolution-of-herbivores.html; See also, "The origin of tetrapod herbivory: effects on local plant diversity," by Neil Brocklehurst, Christian F. Kammerer and Roger J. Benson,

Proceedings Of The Royal Society B, Biological Sciences, 10 June 2020, https://royalsocietypublishing.org/doi/10.1098/rspb.2020.0124; See *Evolution of Herbivory in Terrestrial Vertebrates: Perspectives from the Fossil Record*, Sues H.-D (ed). Cambridge University Press, Cambridge, Mass., 2000, as reviewed by John W. Hermanson, in *Journal of Mammalogy*, Volume 82, Issue 4, November 2001, https://doi.org/10.1644/1545-1542(2001)082<1124:>2.0.CO;2, November 1, 2001. For "continental ecosystems," see "The Establishment of Continental Ecosystems," by J. Minter, Luis A. Buatois, Gabriela Mángano, Neil S. Davies, Martin R. Gibling and Conrad Labandeira, in *The Trace-Fossil Record of Major Evolutionary Events*, Edited by Gabriela Mángano and Luis A. Butaois, Springer, New York, NY, 2016, pp. 205-324, https://link.springer.com/book/10.1007/978-94-017-9600-2

[85] See Spang, Anja; Saw, Jimmy H.; Jørgensen, Steffen L.; Zaremba-Niedzwiedzka, Katarzyna; Martijn, Joran; Lind, Anders E.; van Eijk, Roel; Schleper, Christa; Guy, Lionel; Ettema, Thijs J. G. (2015). "Complex archaea that bridge the gap between prokaryotes and eukaryotes". *Nature*. 521 (7551): 173–179. Bibcode:2015Natur.521.173S. doi:10.1038/nature14447. ISSN 0028-0836. PMC 4444528. PMID 25945739.

[86] See *Meat-Eating & Human Evolution*, Edited by Craig B. Stanford and Henry T. Bunn, Oxford University Press, New York, NY, 2001, Chapter 1, "Deconstructing the Serengeti," by Martha Tappen, p 15. And Chapter 9, "Meat-Eating by the Fourth African Ape," by Margaret J. Schoeninger, Henry T. Bunn, Shawn Murray, Travis Pickering, and Jim Moore, p. 182. See also, "Eating insects has long made sense in Africa. The world much catch up," by Saliou Niassy and Sunday Ekesi, *The Conversation*, January 10, 2017, https://theconversation.com/eating-insects-has-long-made-sense-in-africa-the-world-must-catch-up-70419 - the Authors point out that Africa "is home to the richest diversity of edible insects – more than 500 species" anywhere on earth, and they refer to such other tribes as the Mofu (between Cameroon and Nigeria), the Nganda of the DRC, and "Bushmen in Namibia and South Africa."

[87] ibid., the title of Chapter 4, by Jeanne Sept, pp. 73-98.

[88] ibid., Chapter 15, "The Evolutionary Consequences of Increased Carnivory in Hominids," by Robert Foley, pp. 316-317.

[89] See "Evolutionary history predicts high-impact invasions by herbivorous insects," by Angela M. Mech, Kathryn A. Thomas, Travis D. Marsisco, et al., *Original Research, Ecological and Evolution*, Wiley, 21 August 2019, doi: 10.1002/ece3.5709, https://www.dartmouth.edu/~mpayres/pubs/Mech.etal.2019.pdf

[90] Lambertz, M.; Shelton, C.D.; Spindler, F.; Perry, S.F. (2016). "A caseian point for the evolution of a diaphragm homologue among the earliest synapsids". *Annals of the New York Academy of Sciences*. 1385 (1): 3–20. doi:10.1111/nyas.13264. PMID 27859325.

[91] See "The Oldest Caseid Synapsid from the Late Pennsylvanian of Kansas, and the Evolution of Herbivory in Terrestrial Vertebrates," by Robert R. Reisz and Jörg Fröbisch, PLOS ONE, April 16, 2014, https://doi.org/10.1371/journal.pone.0094518, https://journals.plos.org/plosone/article?id=10.1371/journal.pone.0094518

[92] See, for example, "For Most of Human History, Being an Omnivore Was no Dilemma," by Nancy Shute, *NPR*, April 20, 2012, https://www.npr.org/

sections/thesalt/2012/04/20/150817741/for-most-of-human-history-being-an-omnivore-was-no-dilemma

[93] See *How Many Friends Does One Person Need? Dunbar's Number and Other Evolutionary Quirks*, by Robin Dunbar, Harvard University Press, Cambridge Mass., 2010, pp. 24-34.

[94] https://www.christinecarter.com/2014/10/happiness-tip-cultivate-wordlessness4 "Faroe Islands: Anger over killing of 1,400 dolphins in one day," by Joshua Nevett, *BBC News*, September 14, 2021, https://www.bbc.com/news/world-europe-58555694

[95] *The Butcher of Amritsar: General Reginald Dyer*, by Nigel Collett, Continuum Books, New York, NY 2006.

[96] See *Prairie Dogs – Communication And Community In An Animal Society*, by C. N. Slobodchikoff, Bianca S. Perla and Jennifer L. Verdolin, Harvard University Press, Cambridge, Mass. and London, UK, 2009, p. 127.

[97] See "Herbivory and plant species coexistence: community regulation by an outbreaking phytophagous insect," WP Carson, RB Root - Ecological monographs, 2000 - Wiley Online Library, https://esajournals.onlinelibrary.wiley.com/doi/abs/10.1890/0012-9615(2000)070%5b0073:HAPSCC%5d2.0.CO;2. Consider "Albert's Swarm" in 1875 (named after Dr. Albert Child). A cloud of locusts stretching from California to Minnesota. See Jeffrey A. Lockwood, *Locust: The Devastating Rise and Mysterious Disappearance of the Insect that Shaped the American Frontier*, Basic Books, New York, NY, 2004, p. 21.

[98] See "Coevolution of Grasses and Herbivores," by G. Ledyard Stebbins, JSTOR and Missouri Botanical Garden Press, *Annals of the Missouri Botanical Garden*, https://www.fws.gov/southwest/es/documents/R2ES/LitCited/LPC_2012/Stebbins_1981.pdf

[99] See "C3, C4 the difference is…" GRDC -Grains Research & Development Corporation, https://grdc.com.au/resources-and-publications/groundcover/ground-cover-issue-35-wa/c3-c4-the-difference-is

[100] See "Humanity's Grassroots: How Grazing Animals Shaped Evolution," by Charles Q. Choi, April 4, 2011, *LiveScience*, https://www.livescience.com/13550-grazing-animals-shaped-human-evolution.html; https://www.livescience.com/13550-grazing-animals-shaped-human-evolution.html

[101] See "Understanding C3 & C4 Grasses," by Russ James, November 4, 2020, AgriGro, https://agrigro.com/understanding-c3-c4-grasses/

[102] Mohandas Karamchand Gandhi, Desai, Mahadev H. (ed.), *Autobiography: The Story of My Experiments With Truth*, Dover Publishers, Mineola, NY, 1990.

[103] See "This is your COVID wake-up call: It is 100 seconds to midnight," Bulletin of the Atomic Scientists, https://thebulletin.org/doomsday-clock/; As of January 20, 2022, the clock remained at 100 seconds, "…closer to midnight than ever in its [75-year] history… the Clock remains the closest it has ever been to civilization-ending apocalypse because the world remains stuck im an extremely dangerous moment." See "At doom's doorstep: It is 100 seconds to midnight, by Lorene Yue, 1/20/22, *Bulletin of the Atomic Scientists*, https://thebulletin.org/2022/01/press-release-at-dooms-doorstep-it-is-100-seconds-to-midnight/

[104] See "Long-Term Biological Consequences of Nuclear War," by Paul R. Ehrlich, John Harte, et al., *Science*, New Series Vol. 222, No. 4630 (Dec.23, 1983), pp. 1293-1300, American Association for the Advancement of Science, https://www.jstor.org/stable/1691640, https://www.jstor.org/stable/1691640

[105] See the story about Happy the "Bronx Zoo's Loneliest Elephant," in *Earth. Org*, https://earth.org/a-case-for-freeing-happy-the-elephant-to-be-heard-by-the-new-york-court-of-appeals/; See also, "World's First Habeas Corpus Order Issued On Behalf Of An Elephant," by Lauren Choplin, November 19, 2018, *Nonhuman Rights Blog*, https://www.nonhumanrights.org/blog/first-habeas-corpus-order-happy/. The first such case was won for two chimpanzees – Hercules and Leo – who obtained their true personhood following what was the first, historic hearing on habeas corpus in 2015. It was a successful suit by the Nonhuman Rights Project, led by Steven M. Wise. The two chimpanzees were relocated to a sanctuary in Georgia. Happy is now 50 years old and – by imposition of the court, had to prove self-awareness looking into a mirror, for a judge. The idea for this obviously controversial requirement derives from studies in 1970 by Gordon Gallup Jr. whose test depended upon an animal looking at itself for a pre-determined duration lending sufficient confidence to the human observer that that observation by the animal merited significance. See Gallup, GG Jr. (1970). "Chimpanzees: Self recognition". *Science*. 167 (3914): 86-87. Bibcode:1970Sci...167...86G. doi:10.1126/science.167.3914.86. PMID 4982211. S2CID 145295899. For a very different opinion, see https://protecttheharvest.com/news/habeas-corpus-humans-not-animals/ See also, "The Elephant In The Courtroom," by Lawrence Wright, *The New Yorker Magazine*, February 28, 2022, March 7th issue, https://www.newyorker.com/magazine/2022/03/07/the-elephant-in-the-courtroom; and see "Interesting Zoo and Aquarium Statistics," by Karlyn Marcy, May 26, 2021, Association of Zoos and Aquariums, https://www.aza.org/connect-stories/stories/interesting-zoo-aquarium-statistics?locale=en#:~:text=There%20are%20approximately%20800%2C000%20animals,accredited%20zoo%20and%20aquarium%20professionals. Sadly, the case on behalf of Happy lost in court, "Bronx Zoo's Happy the elephant is not a legal person, court rules," by Andrea Salcedo, June 15, 2022, *The Washington Post*, https://www.washingtonpost.com/nation/2022/06/15/happy-elephant-person-bronx-zoo/

[106] See "Experiments with Celibacy, Comments on Rape: Gandhi's Controversies," by STP (SheThePeople) editor, October 1, 2019, https://www.shethepeople.tv/home-top-video/controversies-mahatma-gandhi-women/

[107] See Mahadev Desai's translation from the original Gujarati, *An autobiography : or the story of my experiments with truth* (reprint. ed.). Penguin Books, London, UK, 1987.

[108] See "Victory! The European Parliament Votes YES to a Future Without Animal Experiments," September 16, 2021, PETA.Org. See PETA's *The Research Modernization Deal 2021*, https://www.peta.org/wp-content/uploads/2020/12/peta-2021-research-modernization-deal.pdf

[109] See "Grub," by Dana Goodyear, *The New Yorker Magazine*, September 6, 2021, pp. 32-40.

[110] "How Much Protein Is Simply Too Much?" n.a., SCL Health, https://www.sclhealth.org/blog/2019/07/how-much-protein-is-simply-too-much/; See also, "What Happens

To Your Body When It Doesn't Get Enough Protein?" by Alexandra Phelan, October 12, 2015, *Independent*, https://www.independent.co.uk/life-style/health-and-families/features/what-happens-your-body-when-it-has-too-much-or-not-enough-protein-a6690721.html

[111] "Whereof one cannot speak, thereof one must be silent," *The Tractatus Logico-Philosophicus* by Ludwig Wittgenstein, With an Introduction by Bertrand Russell, Harcourt, Brace & Company, Inc., New York and London: Kegan Paul, Trench, Trubner & Co., Ltd., 1922, p. 189.

[112] See "It Is Now 100 Seconds To Midnight," by Gayle Spinazze, Press Release of the Bulletin of the Atomic Scientists -75 years and counting, January 23, 2020, https://thebulletin.org/2020/01/press-release-it-is-now-100-seconds-to-midnight/; In this Press release, executive chair, former California Governor Jerry Brown declared, "Dangerous rivalry and hostility among the superpowers increases the likelihood of nuclear blunder. Climate change just compounds the crisis. If there's ever a tome to wake up, it's now." See also, "Doomsday Clockwork," by Kennette Benedict, January 26, 2018, Bulletin of the Atomic Scientists -75 years and counting, https://thebulletin.org/2018/01/doomsday-clockwork/

[113] See "Elinor Wylie," Poetry Foundation, https://www.poetryfoundation.org/poets/elinor-wylie114 See Carl Olson, *The Theology and Philosophy of Eliade: A Search for the Centre*. St. Martin's Press, New York, NY, 1992. See also, Forrest E. Baird (Ed.), *Philosophic Classics: Ancient Philosophy Vol.1)*, 6th edition, Routledge, London, UK, 2010. See also, Robin Waterfield, *The First Philosophers: The Presocratics and the Sophists.* Oxford University Press, New York, NY, 2009.

[115] See, for example, "Replacing animal agriculture and shifting to a plant-based diet could drastically curb green- house gas emissions, according to new model," by Ker Than, Stanford News Service, February 1, 2022, Stanford News Service, https://news.stanford.edu/press-releases/2022/02/01/new-model-explore-climate-change/; See also, *21st Century Technologies – Promises And Perils Of A Dynamic Future*, Organisation For Economic Co-Operation And Development, OECD, 1998, https://www.oecd.org/futures/35391210.pdf; and *The Great Convergence: Information Technology and the New Globalization*, by Richard Baldwin, Belknap Press, Harvard University Press, Cambridge, Mass., 2019; and, *A World of Three Zeros: The New Economics of Zero Poverty, Zero Unemployment, and Zero Net Carbon Emissions*, by Muhammad Yunus, Hachette Audio, Google LLC.

[116] See "Eco-evolutionary partitioning metrics: assessing the importance of ecological and evolutionary contributions to population and community change," by Lynn Govaert, Jelena H. Pantel and Luc De Meester, *Ecology Letters*, (2016) 19: 839-853, https://bio.kuleuven.be/highlights_eeb/eco_evo/2016-eeb-govaert-et-al-ecology-letters-2016.pdf; See also, *The Hypothetical Species – Variables of Human Evolution*, by Michael Charles Tobias and Jane Gray Morrison, Foreword by Melanie L. DeVore, Springer Nature, New York, NY, 2019.

[117] "These 'useless' quirks of evolution are actually evidence for the theory," by Ben Garrod, December 11, 2018, *The Conversation*, https://theconversation.com/these-useless-quirks-of-evolution-are-actually-evidence-for-the-theory-107395

[118] See, for example the excellent essay, "An Eco-evolutionary System with Naturally Bounded Traits," by Roger. Cropp and John Norbury, *Theoretical Ecology*, 12(4), doi:10.1007/S12080-019-0419-2, June 14, 2019, file:///Users/michaeltobias/Downloads/Cropp164822.pdf, https://www.researchgate.net/publication/331761252_Correction_to_An_eco-evolutionary_system_with_naturally_bounded_traits

[119] See Dele Ogunseitan, *Microbial Diversity: Form and Function in Prokaryotes*, Wiley-Blackwell, New York, NY, p. 13, 2004. See also, J.C. Willis, "The Origin of Species by Large, rather than by Gradual, Change, and by Guppy's Method of Differentiation," *Annals of Botany*. Vol. 37, No. 148. 1923, pp. 605-628.

[120] See "Which are the fastest and slowest moving glaciers on Earth?" AntarcticGlaciers.org, https://www.antarcticglaciers.org/question/fastest-slowest-moving-glaciers-earth/

[121] See "United theory of biological evolution: Disaster-forced evolution through Supernova, radioactive ash fall-outs, genome instability, and mass extinctions," by Toshikazu Ebisuzaki and Shigenori Maruyama, *Geoscience Frontiers*, Volume 6, Issue 1, January 2015, pp. 103-119, https://doi.org/10.1016/j.gsf.2014.04.009, https://www.sciencedirect.com/science/article/pii/S1674987114000681

[122] See "17 Cataclysmic Events That Changed the Earth Forever," by Michael B. Sauter and Thomas C. Frohlich, 24/7 Wall St., January 6, 2020, https://247wallst.com/special-report/2019/11/15/17-cataclysmic-events-that-changed-the-earth-forever/5/

[123] H.J. Mackinder, "The Geographical Pivot of History," The Geographical Journal, Vol. 23, No. 4, April 1904, pp. 421-437. See also, Suban Kumar Chowdhury and Abdullah Hel Kafi, "The Heartland theory of Sir Halford John Mackinder: Justification of foreign policy of the United States and Russia in Central Asia," *Journal of Liberty and International Affairs*, 1 (2): 58-70, 2015.

[124] See "Modernization, Cultural Change, And The Persistence Of Traditional Values," by Ronald Inglehart and Wayne E. Baker, American Sociological Review, 2000, Vol. 65, February: pp. 19-51.

[125] See weather, climate change and poverty related shock displacement commentary in "Rapid evidence assessment on the impacts of climate change on migration patterns," CC By NC-ND 4.0., ODI, UK AID, 07 September 2021, https://odi.org/en/publications/rapid-evidence-assessment-on-the-impacts-of-climate-change-on-migration-patterns/; See also, "Arctic Animals' Movement Patterns are Shifting in Different Ways as the Climate Changes," by Sofie Bates, NASA's Goddard Space Flight Center, November 23, 2020, https://www.nasa.gov/feature/goddard/2020/arctic-animals-movement-patterns-are-shifting-in-different-ways-as-the-climate-changes

[126] "Application of insects to wounds of self and others by chimpanzees in the wild," by Alessandra Mascaro, Lara M. Southern and Tobias Deschner, *Current Biology*, Volume 32, Issue 3, 7 February 2022, pp. R112-R113, https://doi.org/10.1016/j.cub.2021.12.045, https://www.sciencedirect.com/science/article/pii/S0960982221017322. The video accompanying this essay is testimony to a casual interaction that is both decisive and likely millions of years old in practice.

[127] "Half of All Species Are on the Move – And We're Feeling It," by Craig Welch, National Geographic, April 26, 2017, https://www.nationalgeographic.com/science/article/climate-change-species-migration-disease

[128] Bradley, B. J. (2006). "Reconstructing Phylogenies and Phenotypes: A Molecular View of Human Evolution". *Journal of Anatomy.* 212 (4): 337–353. doi:10.1111/j.1469-7580.2007.00840.x. PMC 2409108. PMID 18380860.

[129] See "Culture," https://www.sumatranorangutan.org/

[130] See "Evolution," https://www.orangutanrepublik.org/learn/orangutan-specifics/evolution/

[131] ibid.

[132] See *Handbook Of The Mammals Of The World, 3. Primates*, Chief Editors Russell A. Mittermeier, Anthony B. Rylands and Don E. Wilson, Lynx Ediciones, Barcelona, Spain, 2013, p. 24.

[133] See "The bonobo genome compared with the chimpanzee and human genomes," by Kay Prüfer et al., Nature. 2012 June 28: 486(7404): 527-531, doi: 10.1038/nature 11128, PMCID: PMC3498939, NIHMSID: NIHMS419861, PMID: 22722832, https://www.ncbi.nlm.nih.gov/pmc/articles/PMC3498939/#:~:text=It%20is%20known%20that%20whereas,around%20two%20million%20years%20ago.

[134] See "When humans split from the apes," by Darren Curnoe, The Conversation, February 21, 2016, https://theconversation.com/when-humans-split-from-the-apes-55104#:~:text=Surprisingly%2C%20this%20date%20is%20remarkably,and%2012%20million%20years%20ago[135] A feeling augmented by the work and observations of Dr. Biruté Mary Galdikas. Personal communications. See also, https://orangutan.org/about/dr-birute-mary-galdikas/, as well as a chapter devoted to her work in *Sanctuary: Global Oases of Innocence*, by M. C. Tobias and J. G. Morrison, A Dancing Star Foundation Book, Council Oaks Books, Tulsa OK and San Francisco CA, 2008.

[136] See "Desert survival by the book," by M. C. Tobias, *New Scientist*, Vol. 120, No. 1643, December 17, 1988.

[137] See "Testing The Waters – Should the natural world have rights?" by Elizabeth Kolbert, *The New Yorker Magazine*, April 18, 2022, pp. 16-20.

[138] "Hamlet," (1602) by William Shakespeare, Act 1, Scene 5, ll's 167-169, *The Complete Works Of William Shakespeare*, Edited with a Glossary by W. J. Craig, Oxford University Press, London, UK 1947.

[139] See Benner, S.A. Prebiotic plausibility and networks of paradox-resolving independent models. *Nat Commun* 9, 5173 (2018). https://doi.org/10.1038/s41467-018-07274-y

[140] See "The Age of Deceit," by Julian Cribb, Surviving C21, February 14, 2022, https://juliancribb.blog/2022/02/14/the-age-of-deceit/. Cribb cites Bratsburg B and Rogeburg O., Flynn effect and its reversal are both environmentally caused. *PNAS* 26 Jun 2018. https://www.pnas.org/content/115/26/6674.short. See also, *Earth Detox*, by Julian Cribb, Cambridge University Press, Cambridge, UK, 2021.141 See "Ecosystems: the flux of energy and matter," https://www.blackwellpublishing.com/cotgreave/pdf/Chap12.pdf, in *Introductory Ecology*, by Peter Cotgreave, John Wiley & Sons, New York, NY 2002.

[142] "Energy flux Through ecological networks," The Community Ecology Group @ Unibern, May 2022, https://allanecology.com/projects/energy-flux-through-ecological-networks/ and https://allanecology.com/about-us/

[143] "Ecosystem flux and biotic modification as drivers of metaecosystem dynamics," by Romana Limberger, Julia Birtel, Daniel d. S. Farias, Blake Matthews, First published: 23 January 2017, https://doi.org/10.1002/ecy.1742, ESA -Ecological Society of America, https://esajournals.onlinelibrary.wiley.com/doi/abs/10.1002/ecy.1742

[144] See "Pools and fluxes in ecosystems," by Saurab Babu, Eco-Intelligent, May 5, 2020, https://eco-intelligent.com/2020/05/05/pools-and-fluxes-in-ecosystems/; See also, "Material Transport & Energy Flux In Ecosystem," by Amulas Shomrat, *Plantlet*, May 13, 2022, https://plantlet.org/material-transport-energy-flux-in-ecosystem/

[145] See Fick, A. (1855). "Ueber Diffusion". Annalen der Physik (in German). 94 (1): 59–86. Bibcode:1855AnP...170...59F. doi:10.1002/andp.18551700105. Fick, A. (1855). "V. On liquid diffusion". Phil. Mag. 10 (63): 30–39. doi:10.1080/14786445508641925.; See also Ward, A. F. H.; Tordai, L. (1946). "Time-dependence of Boundary Tensions of Solutions I. The Role of Diffusion in Time-effects". *Journal of Chemical Physics*. 14 (7): 453–461. Bibcode:1946JChPh..14..453W. doi:10.1063/1.1724167. See also, Henry Darcy, *Les fontaines publiques de la ville de Dijon.* Dalmont, Paris, France, 1856. See also J. R. Fleming, "Joseph Fourier, the 'greenhouse effect', and the quest for a universal theory of terrestrial temperatures". Endeavour. 23 (2): 72–75, 1999, doi:10.1016/s0160-9327(99)01210-7.

[146] See Turner, J. R.; Baker, R. M. Complexity Theory: An Overview with Potential Applications for the Social Sciences. *Systems* 2019, 7, 4. https://doi.org/10.3390/systems7010004, https://www.mdpi.com/2079-8954/7/1/4/htm

[147] See Xu L, Zhang F, Zhang K, Wang E, Wang J (2014) The Potential and Flux Landscape Theory of Ecology. *PLoS ONE* 9(1): e86746. https://doi.org/10.1371/journal.pone.0086746, https://journals.plos.org/plosone/article?id=10.1371/journal.pone.0086746

[148] "Flux control at the ecosystem level," by Ernst-Detlef Schulze, *Trends in Ecology & Evolution*, Volume 10, Issue 1, January 1995, pp. 40-43, https://doi.org/10.1016/S0169-5347(00)88966-1, https://www.sciencedirect.com/science/article/abs/pii/S0169534700889661?via%3Dihub; See also "Ecosystems in Flux: Accurately defining stream nutrient concentration and stream health," https://ecology.duke.edu/ecosystems-in-flux/

[149] Gilles Escarguel, Serge Legendre, Bernard Sigé, "Unearthing deep-time biodiversity changes: The Palaeogene mammalian metacommunity of the Quercy and Limagne area (Massif Central, France)," *Comptes Rendus Geoscience*, Volume 340, Issues 9–10, 2008, pp.602-614, ISSN 1631-0713, https://doi.org/10.1016/j.crte.2007.11.005. https://www.sciencedirect.com/science/article/pii/S1631071307003884

[150] See "Quantum Transition State Theory," by Dr. H. Waalkens, Engineering and Physical Sciences Research Council (EPSRC Reference: EP/E024629/1, https://gow.epsrc.ukri.org/NGBOViewGrant.aspx?GrantRef=EP/E024629/1

[151] See, for example, "An experimental forest ecosystem drought," Christiane Werner, et al., *Science* 16 Dec 2021, Vol 374, Issue 6574, pp. 1514-1518, doi: 10.1126/science.abj6789, https://www.science.org/doi/10.1126/science.abj6789; See

also, "Inferring the contribution of advection to total ecosystem scalar fluxes over a tall forest in complex terrain," by K.Novick, S. Brantley, C. Ford Miniat, J. Walker and J. M. Vose, Forest Service, U.S. Department of Agriculture, https://doi.org/10.1016/j.agrformet.2013.10.010, https://www.fs.usda.gov/treesearch/pubs/46133

[152] https://www.science.org/doi/10.1126/science.abj6789, https://people.math.harvard.edu/~ctm/home/text/others/shannon/entropy/entropy.pdf

[153] See Corominas-Murtra, B., Fortuny, J. & Solé, R. Towards a mathematical theory of meaningful communication. *Sci Rep* 4, 4587 (2014). https://doi.org/10.1038/srep04587, https://www.nature.com/articles/srep04587#citeas. For a superb overview, see "20th Century Mathematics," by William Smith et al., n.d., https://www.storyofmathematics.com/20th.html/; See also, "Flux of Matter," by Lewis Doty, *Ecology Center*, May 10, 2022, https://www.ecologycenter.us/population-dynamics-2/flux-of-matter.html

[154] See "The Poincaré Conjecture—Proved," by Dana MacKenzie, *Science*, 22 Dec 2006, Vol 314, Issue 5807. pp. 1848-1849, doi: 10.1126/science.314.5807.1848, https://www.science.org/doi/10.1126/science.314.5807.1848. The "conjecture" regarding three- and four-dimensional space boundaries was not solved until 2003 by Grigori Perelman.

[155] See "Phase Transition," Complex Quantum Systems Science and Risk Mathematics, https://sites.google.com/site/quantumcomplexity/n-risk-science-hypertext/phase-transition; See also, "20th Century Mathematics," by Luke Mastin, *Story Of Mathematics*, © 2020, https://www.storyofmathematics.com/20th.html/

[156] @misc{https://doi.org/10.48550/arxiv.2012.11672, doi = {10.48550/ARXIV.2012.11672}, url = {https://arxiv.org/abs/2012.11672}, By Duminil-Copin, Hugo and Kozlowski, Karol Kajetan and Krachun, Dmitry and Manolescu, Ioan and Oulamara, Mendes, "Rotational invariance in critical planar lattice models," {arXiv}, 2020. For easy explanation, see https://www.quantamagazine.org/mathematicians-prove-symmetry-of-phase-transitions-20210708/

[157] See "The Mathematics of How Connections Become Global," by Kelsey Houston-Edwards, *Scientific American*, 324, 4, 22-29 (April 2021), https://www.scientificamerican.com/article/the-mathematics-of-how-connections-become-global/, doi:10.1038/scientificamerican0421-22

[158] "Mathematical proof that rocked number theory will be published," by Davide Castelvecchi, *Nature*, 03 April 2020, Publications of the Research Institute for Mathematical Sciences, https://www.nature.com/articles/d41586-020-00998-2

[159] See "High connectivity of sloughs a goal of Everglades restoration," in *Connectivity: A Critical Component of Hydrological and Ecological Flux Assessments*, by Laurel Larsen, Jai Choi, Martha Nungesser and Jud Harvey, US Geological Society, p.7.

[160] See Childers, D.L., Iwaniec, D., Rondeau, D. et al. Responses of sawgrass and spikerush to variation in hydrologic drivers and salinity in Southern Everglades marshes. *Hydrobiologia* 569, 273–292 (October 2006). https://doi.org/10.1007/s10750-006-0137-9, http://www.chesapeake.org/stac/presentations/210_Larsen%20Healthy%20Watersheds.pdf

[161] See "Unifying deterministic and stochastic ecological dynamics via a landscape-flux approach," by Li Xu, Denis Patterson, Ann Carla Stave and Jin Wang, *PNAS*, June 11, 2021

[118] (24) e2103779118, https://doi.org/10.1073/pnas.2103779118, https://www.pnas.org/doi/10.1073/pnas.2103779118, https://www.semanticscholar.org/paper/Unifying-deterministic-and-stochastic-ecological-a-Xu-Patterson/e61d373ca38bc515b9635b7312f41e930ad512b9

[162] "Stochastic Lyapunov Functions and Asymptotic Stability in Probability," by Robert D. McAllister and James B. Rawlings, *Technical report number 2020-02*, TWCCC, October 22, 2021, https://sites.engineering.ucsb.edu/~jbraw/jbrweb-archives/tech-reports/twccc-2020-02.pdf

[163] See Xu, W.; Shen, Q.; Wang, X.; Wang, Q.; Yao, Y.; Huang, W.; Wang, M.; Li, J.; Zhang, F.; Chen, X. Sensing Images for Assessing the Minimum Ecological Flux by Automatically Extracting River Surface Width. *Remote Sens.* 2020, *12*, 2899. https://doi.org/10.3390/rs12182899

[164] See "Practical considerations for the incorporation of insect-mediated contaminant flux into ecological risk assessments," by Ryan R. Otter, Gale B. Beaubien, Connor I. Olson, David Walters, and Marc A. Mills, USGS, https://doi.org/10.1007/978-3-030-49480-3_9, https://pubs.er.usgs.gov/publication/70216153

[165] See https://oceanservice.noaa.gov/facts/lidar.html#:~:text=Lidar%2C%20which%20stands%20for%20Light,variable%20distances)%20to%20the%20Earth.

[166] Prümers, H., Betancourt, C.J., Iriarte, J. et al. Lidar reveals pre-Hispanic low-density urbanism in the Bolivian Amazon. *Nature* (2022). https://doi.org/10.1038/s41586-022-04780-4, 25 May 2022, https://www.nature.com/articles/s41586-022-04780-4#citeas

[167] See "The Rock Art of Pedra Furada," by Niède Guidon, UNESCO, Bradshaw Foundation, https://www.bradshawfoundation.com/south_america/serra_da_capivara/pedra_furada/index.php

[168] See Sanchez, G.; Holliday, V. T.; Gaines, E. P.; Arroyo-Cabrales, J.; Martínez-Tagüeñ, N.; Kowler, A.; Lange, T.; Hodgins, G. W. L.; Mentzer, S. M.; Sanchez-Morales, I. (14 July 2014). "Human (Clovis)–gomphothere (*Cuvieronius* sp.) association ≈13,390 calibrated yBP in Sonora, Mexico". *PNAS*. 111 (30): 10972–10977. Bibcode:2014PNAS..11110972S. doi:10.1073/pnas.1404546111. PMC 4121807. PMID 25024193.

[169] See Teller, James T. (16 November 2012). "Importance of freshwater injections into the Arctic Ocean in triggering the Younger Dryas cooling" (PDF). *PNAS*. 109 (49): 19880–19881. Bibcode:2012PNAS..10919880T. doi:10.1073/pnas.1218344109. PMC 3523840. PMID 23161906

[170] See "Late Quaternary megafaunal extinctions on the continents: a short review," by Anthony John Stuart, Sanchez, G.; Holliday, V. T.; Gaines, E. P.; Arroyo-Cabrales, J.; Martínez-Tagüeñ, N.; Kowler, A.; Lange, T.; Hodgins, G. W. L.; Mentzer, S. M.; Sanchez-Morales, I. (14 July 2014). "Human (Clovis)–gomphothere (Cuvieronius sp.) association ≈13,390 calibrated yBP in Sonora, Mexico". *PNAS*. 111 (30): 10972–10977. Bibcode:2014PNAS..11110972S. doi:10.1073/pnas.1404546111. PMC 4121807. PMID 25024193, https://www.researchgate.net/profile/Anthony-

Stuart/publication/269820457_Late_Quaternary_megafaunal_extinctions_on_the_continents_A_short_review/links/5708d87308ae8883a1fa49fb/Late-Quaternary-megafaunal-extinctions-on-the-continents-A-short-review.pdf; See also, roc Natl Acad Sci U S A. 2012 Mar 20; 109(12): 4527–4531. Published online 2012 Mar 5. doi: 10.1073/pnas.1113875109, PMCID: PMC3311372, PMID: 22393004, "Quantitative global analysis of the role of climate and people in explaining late Quaternary megafaunal extinctions," by Graham W. Prescott, David R. Williams, Andrew Balmford, Rhys E. Green, and Andrea Manica, National Library of Medicine, NIH, https://www.ncbi.nlm.nih.gov/pmc/articles/PMC3311372/; and "Global late Quaternary megafauna extinctions linked to humans, not climate change," Christopher Sandom, Søren Faurby, Brody Sandel and Jens-Christian Svenning. Published: 22 July 2014 https://doi.org/10.1098/rspb.2013.3254, The Royal Society Publishing, *Proceedings Of The Royal Society B*, https://royalsocietypublishing.org/doi/10.1098/rspb.2013.3254

[171] *A Gap in Nature – Discovering The World's Extinct Animals*, by Tim Flannery and Peter Schouten, Text Publishing, Melbourne, Australia, 2001, p. xii.

[172] See *Journeys In Microspace – The Art Of The Scanning Electron Microscope*, by Dee Breger, Columbia University Press, New York, NY 1995.

[173] See *The Mapping of America*, by Seymour L. Schwartz and Ralph E. Ehrenberg, Wellfleet Press, Edison, New Jersey, 2001, p. 17.

[174] See *Universalis Cosmographia Secundum Ptholomaei Traditionem et Americi Vespucii Alioru[m]que Lustrationes,* St. Dié, 1507, Geography and Map Reading Room, Library of Congress, https://www.loc.gov/rr/geogmap/waldexh.html

[175] See some of the spectacular work of Dr. Eric A. Hoffman at the University of Iowa Medical School, https://medicine.uiowa.edu/radiology/profile/eric-hoffman

[176] See "NASA releases stunning images from James Webb Space Telescope in final stage of testing," by Marcia Dunn, The Associated Press, May 11, 2022, https://www.usatoday.com/story/news/nation/2022/05/10/nasa-images-james-webb-space-telescope/9720272002/

[177] See *Bigger than Chaos – Understanding Complexity through Probability*, by Michael Strevens, Harvard University Press, Cambridge, Mass, 2003. See particularly, Strevens, Chapter 1 – "The Simple Behavior of Complex Systems," pp. 1-37. As well as his superb analysis of "complex systems," and "simple probabilities," pp. 355-360.

[178] See, for example, "A critical perspective on the concept of biocultural diversity and its emerging role in nature and heritage conservation," by Peter Bridgewater and Ian D. Rotherham, *People And Nature*, 19 July 2019, https://doi.org/10.1002/pan3.10040, British Ecological Society, https://besjournals.onlinelibrary.wiley.com/doi/10.1002/pan3.10040; See also, "Defining bicultural approaches to conservation," by Michael C.Gavin, Joe McCarter, Aroha Mead, Fikret Berkes, John Richard Stepp, Debora Peterson, and Ruifei Tang, Trends in Ecology & Evolution, Volume 30, Issue 3, [/140-145, *Science Direct*, 23 January 2015, https://doi.org/10.1016/j.tree.2014.12.005, https://www.sciencedirect.com/science/article/abs/pii/S0169534715000026#!

Chapter 2

Biosynthetic Constants

Ecodynamics

The First Law of Thermodynamics, among many other variants on power, motion and their definitions, also may be characterized as that tendency within isolated systems of energy to be variously transferred, with no cost ultimately to the environment. No loss, only temporary gains. Rudolf Clausius (1822-1888) was the man who essentially formulated the rationale for fostering an obsession with these physical constituencies, which in itself invites the question of, why? He theorized that it must be a fundamental reality of the universe. Do possums and minnows, gorillas and trees ask such questions? We actually don't know (and frankly, take pleasure in not knowing). Of course, by extrapolating from the biosphere to the cosmos, Clausius was betting on a principle, which always verges on the implausible. He left seven children to ponder their father's remarkable contributions to a field that seemed remote from what he actually did with his far-reaching intellect. He tried to explain to himself and others why the sky is blue. How energy and heat are related. Why cold is cold and hot is hot. And the nature of entropy. He would precondition our basic understanding of the Second Law of Thermodynamics, as well as electromagnetism, kinetic gas theories, electrolysis, and so much more.[1] Perhaps most intriguingly, he gave to the lexicon of physics the demonstrated ideas of constraints, of questions pertaining to reversibility and irreversibility, and the notion and/or parataxic (unrelated but consequential events) reality of *constants* in nature, a topic enshrouding all of the major laws (or rules) of physics.[2] Parataxis was the stumbling block, that butterfly basic to biology whose fluttering wings somehow conjure the unexpected, coincidental or transient effects which continents removed.

We accept energy constants, gravity representing a negative energy field; mass; propulsion; stasis, and so on. We question but cannot alter our fate within these cosmological certitudes. It need not be elaborated upon, it simply is a set of conditionals for living on this planet that we have submitted to, even if we would like to disagree. Living, itself, posits an equally puzzling but nearly incontestable vital sign of what can and does systemically occur here.

Only death, or what we think of as the end of a life, can assist us in balancing the idea of life, its celebrations and lamentations. We are never quite prepared for the life experience, particularly of species suddenly emerging before us, any more than we can confidently speak of death. Both of these phenomena must strike of an uncertainty field, a force in which, when thinking clearly, we are actually lost. Our thought has no antecedents that can truly give us clarity. All is tenuous. Every mortal wonders whether death might not give an answer, or break through the seemingly implacable laws of physics that we object to, particularly as our bodies wear down, or the second we fall off a cliff.

Then there is the physics within biology, that would at some level like to contest the tumultuous examples from other domains, like the surface of the Sun which nurtures the biosphere, but only from a narrow range of distance, to which other localized planets within our vague reckoning attest. We lack an archaeology of the Cosmos, as Avi Loeb of Harvard has pointed out,[3] in speculating upon the likelihood of humanity going extinct in the next few centuries. Lacking any baseline other than that confined to earth and, thus far, our earliest known remains coming from roughly 315,000-to-350,000 years ago at a site in Morocco known as Jebel Irhoud,[4] our infancy appears to know no bounds other than its adamantine superego. There is simply not enough time to spur new conscience neurons at a species-distributed level. To counteract the vast disparities within our species at every tangible point of important intersections of thought and matter. These are expressed as *survival needs* but must yield to a vivid picture of broken promises upending any long-term plans.

This latter idea, survival at all costs, harbors pronounced queasiness, as we recognize the many biological ideals that might otherwise have calmed our worst nightmares were it not for the odd character of human scheming, calculating, dreaming of better days ahead. Could there ever have been a time in biological history when there was truly an Eden, of sorts?[5]

Chemical Catalysis and Equilibrium Distribution

Biosynthesis, all natural catalysis that chemically transforms one thing into another, suggests that change is ever present and a clear signal of equilibrium distribution ("EQD"). We should not be too impressed by this latter phrase (EQD). It argues for evolution that is not guided, but shepherded. Not purposefully distorted or swayed, or not that we can decipher or reasonably argue. But shaped in ways that are unbiased, the outcomes almost universally co-symbiotic or mutualistic. If that represents bias then it is a condition that would argue emphatically for something we imagine but fail to engage. Of course, it does not change the fact of mortality, of suffering, unto suicide which, as Albert Camus suggested, may be the only worthwhile topic for philosophy. But EQD posits both Clausius and St. Matthew. A Newton and Hippocrates in the same test tube.

A neutral state of nature is only manifested to the extent of the word we employ. Politically, neutrality has always posed a *problem*. Neutrality is lost on a shelf of inherent bias, or inaction. This was the case of both Switzerland and Belgium during World War II, though Belgium reversed course after the war and Switzerland joined NATO and the European Union in sanctions against Russia during its 2022 assaults on Ukraine, as did most other sane leaders. In the early weeks of that slaughter, however, it was clear that neutral choices were largely akin to degrees of self-preservation. Hence, a No Fly Zone or No Boots On the Ground approach, the non-violent modalities, appears to evince the utter tragedy of human selfness in the face of population peril. Three months in to her open-door policy for Ukrainian refugees, mostly women and children, Polish authorities began to limit the number of months such victims were welcome, as the government calculated long-term costs/benefits of her humanitarian largesse.

It is the same essential negative energy inherent to the assumption that a lack of choice is not, in fact, a choice itself. The calibrated choices by those proffering reason against the prospect of nuclear weapons being used by a vicious and inaccessible opponent, a madman, binds the nature of choice in a way that cannot be correlated with any other situation. Peace never reigns in human collectives, not large ones. It can only resort to incremental diplomacy, which is never enough, not ultimately, not even in time.

Anthropic linguistics, the word-tied thoughts we wield as humans, prevents us from ever accurately identifying the nature of the underlying problématique. We will never see the world as a King Scallop (*Pecten maximus*), with its 200 mirror-encompassed eyes, can do. The fundamental issue calls upon philosophy to step down, knowing that every human psyche and perspective is fortunately missing from, and unable to access every other known species. A world inaccessible to humans would be the only Utopia worth idealizing.

We might speak of a system that in part derives from the best things, or the worst things. In both cases, all are out of our control; the one driving the mechanisms of viral spread, bacterial vectors and phagocytic invasions. The other, a Louvre. However, we manage the metaphors of medical, aesthetic or metaphysical narrative, we are quite trapped within the langues of our solitary group, at an uncrossable bridge separating those abstractions from the individual of both our own species and every other; comprehensively addicted to human distractions wherein the community and the Self find themselves at forever unmollified odds. The differences defining those odds are both mental and physiological. They are vast worlds apart, separated by every passing birth and death, our lack of fortune, faith and love therein to find.

This strikes of a pessimistic note, certainly, impugning our immunity to ourselves. Addicting us to this preposterous idea of progress, success. But these are biological cross-purposes of which our renown is to have been here for all of a moment, and then to have vanished, leaving millions of Morgan and Vatican-like Libraries, all the human artifacts in the world, locked away in the palm of a fingerless, shapeless, idea-free hand that floats through a great and mighty nothing of ethers. The absolute neutral discharge, where even the vacuum is an umbegungian (local) paradox of paradoxes, tunnels of lost qualia absolving all, abhorrent to the physics that made it so.

These are fibers of ideas, neither in space or in time, that have no connection, and never will, to all those within range of themselves. Where every Self undermines its own Umwelt (what an individual perceives of the world).

If anything, the millions of books do us an inestimable disservice by promising something that will exist no more. We cannot help ourselves, but to indulge in their fortune-telling romance; their adventures heading into what is simply thought of as infinity, pausing before a time-out that is forever. The free reigns of blue. Every experience of white light dimming upon a distant planet in our field of view, where spectra of thought devolve to sleep.

At times of artistic and scientific expression, we approach the philosophical asymptotes that nearly escape the black holes of our self-importance. As when Einstein produced his general theory of relativity, connoting the unfortunate misinterpretation of warps in gravitational lensing and populist space-time. Or in the exhuberant and hallowed writing by Felix Salten (1869-1945), eliciting exquisite simulacra in the guise of other species communications, as in his novels *Bambi* (1923), *Fifteen Rabbits* (1929) and *The City Jungle* (1947). Or, during all those other majestic transports that have stilled by beauty the human condition. One comes round to Handel's "Messiah," (1741), Beethoven's "Ninth" (1824) or the van Eyck's "Altarpiece of Ghent" (1432), among a myriad of such extraordinary ecological releases and resolutions by which the one and the many discover a concord of mutual adoration. Their time together may be the brutality of nature and her ephemerality, but the love is worth all of our attention. After all, we have nothing else to do, to hope for, to give.

Physiolatry

That physiolatry, or love of, reverence for nature, ordains an ecology that harbors the power of shared subjectivism. Such deep feelings might, at their initial suggestion, preclude the rage for ratchetting up targeted mutations, designing mutagenic re-shuffling of proteins so as to exploit enzymes not previously assumed to be working in nature, or not working to human ends. Later on, we shall explore whether, for example, industrial farming, medical breakthroughs and other human dominated machinations would persist in a neutral, collectively subjective world where bias was fully quashed by absolute –and fair-boding- restraints, like physiolatry.

To cease all rendering of rigorous biochemical designs, both within and without living organisms and to embrace a great diminution of technological reliance would represent an alluring, but thus far empty fiction. Are we inclined to specify? A mirroring of very real preludes to a Jain or Buddhist biological suasion: the renouncing of so much wanton prepossession? The ramifications for acquisition of human knowledge without end have more than shown their true self; conclusions that are nothing less than desperate for the planet. No one is unaware of this escalation of indignity, an insanity in our collective gut. Could we have acted differently? Are there remaining hamlets of human deliberated constraint upon which the anthropological record, both historic and contemporary, have confirmed the possibility? Unambiguously so. Jain Digambara monks are as clear an assertive proof as we are likely to ever witness in our lifetimes.

The monastic records of soft handprints, and those now rarified cultures like the Tasaday (Mindanao, Philippines), Bishnoi (Rajasthan, India), Todas (Tamil Nadu, India) and others thoroughly reverse the logic of greed and endlessly devolving manufacture. Of insinuating our species and expressing the worst of its misappropriations. That most certainly would include the genetic modifications and massive military forces that are core to current directed socio-economic, political and evolutionary initiatives. We celebrate antibodies. Are enthralled by anti-matter. But fail to head the reactivity of antithesis which we represent.

The five-year Luddite Movement that started among textile workers in Nottingham (1811-1816) did nothing to dissuade the advent of automated equipment that would undermine handweaving jobs. The rebellions were finally put down by the British Government with the Pentrich rising, as it is recalled. The leaders of the uprising were hung and beheaded. One of the other few documented endeavors to halt implacable forward motion came about in 1636 when Japan's Tokugawa shogunate passed its Act of Seclusion, that would stay in effect for some two centuries. Bhutan had similarly shut itself off from the rest of the world for much of the early 20th century. These political choices were bound to change, and they did. But it is impossible to argue or anticipate human events. Students of history, like all archaeologists, can only speculate upon the forensics. We compound our difficulties by assuming that learning is a genetic process above all others. That learned behavior is inherently successful. Our image of other species calls out maternal and paternal instincts, looks to encephalization factors of intelligence to which it accords the greatest of significance.

Yet, all of these delineations are imagined.

Is it true that some such mechanisms as have played out in the sciences, geopolitics, and the history of cultural technology have resulted in environmental tools and connections that obtained more than merely curious usage? In the case of physics, new elements of the Periodic Table have been created. So what, one might ask? Nature knew of 94 atomic numbers. The other 24, to date, have been synthesized in laboratories, beginning with Americium in 1944, discovered by Glenn T. Seaborg (1912-1999) and colleagues. It was one of the products of the Manhattan Project.[6] In the mid-1980s I (mt) once spent a day with Seaborg, touring his lab at UC-Berkeley. I asked him whether he felt any compunctions about human synthesis (or derivation) of substances otherwise unknown in nature, or at least not for billions of years. *No*, he said. Seaborg found 9 other elements (including #106-Seaborgium), and some 100 isotopes. Americium and Curium were patented. No other chemical elements have ever been. Americium proved useful in some smoke detectors. The Plutonium-239 discovered in 1941 required Uranium-235 (element #92) to be hit with vast numbers of deuterons (found in Hydrogen) resulting in a decaying element, Plutonium-94, something new that was expressed by the Manhattan Project. That secret endeavor has since become an infamous namesake of the 20th century. It was the Pu-239 that found its way into the bomb that destroyed Nagasaki, killing at least 39,000 people, injuring another 25,000 and unknown numbers of other life forms. None of the atomic numbered elements between 95-118 occur naturally.

Synthesis requires bombardment of a nucleus with protons lower than 95 on the Periodic Table.

I found the notion astonishing: intellectual copyright on products or byproducts of nature. At that time controversies were raging around the growing number of ownership claims in a different (but, nonetheless nature-based) realm, namely, the U.S. Supreme Court ruling that genetically modified organisms could be patented. (*Diamond v. Chakrabarty*, 447 U.S. 303 {1980}, filed by General Electric the following year). That same U.S. Supreme Court that would ban *Roe v Wade* on June 24, 2022, has shown itself to be criminal, evil while, hopefully, at length obsolete. The slavery into which Republicans in the United States have aspired to trap American women and their daughters and granddaughters; to undermine privacy; to hate and extoll hatred to women, and by openly declared implication, all contraception, as well as the LBGT communities, ultimately comes down to ecological privacy, intergenerational equity, and future sustainability. The United States, like most nations, has never equated pro-choice with pro-life. In other words, old white men have no problem manipulating how the female gender of their species can live and die, in any more or less a manner then their corresponding assault on other species which they condemn, torture, consume, deny, until entrails of pig, chicken, turkey, cow, and the like, end up in their stomachs and then are shat out into the commons. This is the political reckoning as it hits head on upon animal rights, and ecology in general. This is the end of humanity.

Bio-Manipulation

Since 1980, the bio-manipulation and codification avalanche has resulted in a new, and largely embraced landscape of human-ownership of foods, genes, diagnostic tools and animals, including mammals, fish, bacteria, and many thousands of others. Tens-of-thousands of books, lawsuits and hundreds-of-thousands of research papers, editorials and letters later, the last four decades of such human arrogance has only added to the cliff of biodiversity extinctions, habitat mangling, animal cruelty, and the full revelations of what Swedish physicist Svante Arrhenius (1859-1927), Guy Stewart Callendar (1898-1964) and Charles David Keeling (1928-2005) brought to the world's attention regarding global warming. And, coevally, the revelations pertaining to very real extinctions and mass extinctions. That understanding, first intoned in 1796 in a lecture by Georges Cuvier, following his fossil studies in the

Bassin parisien, would slowly turn into a warning by geologists and then, almost two centuries later, impervious proof of five massive extinctions in the earth's history, each resulting in more than three-quarters destruction of all known living beings.[7] Why did it take so long to recognize the signs? Why is the United States the one of only three countries and one sovereign entity, to refuse to ratify the Convention on Biological Diversity – along with South Sudan, the Vatican and Andorra – the most important treaty in environmental history?[8] The Montreal biodiversity COP15 2022 did little.

On the Nature of Critical Thinking

One wishes that the extent of geopolitical and scientific meddling had ended the day the founder of the Royal Society of London, architect, astronomer, meteorologist, surveyor, microscopist, physicist and all-around genius, Christopher Wren (1632-1723), used the first equivalent syringe to inject opium into the bloodstream of a dog in 1656 at Gresham College. Wren was curious, and by at least one eye-witness account, the dog "was alive and well and living in the locale where the injection took place."[9] Wren would be buried in old age in the crypt of St. Paul's Cathedral in London, for which he was the architect, along with some 50 other churches and many other buildings. We're not suggesting (necessarily) an end to all science, politics, and economics. Our species wouldn't know where to begin the process of reverse modernism and deconstruction (although there are a few examples where expensive old bridges have been removed to re-establish a view, as in the case of the downtown San Francisco waterfront, etc.) But to actually change, not in fear, but through compassionate innovation that is mindful? That would require a collective comprehension for which we have no egalitarian rules, or the slightest compass that could function, presently, or in near-enough term, for almost 8 billion, ungainly, mostly carnivorous, large vertebrates. Our collective, the aggregate of humanities, is undeniably a foul ecosystem for which we cannot glibly allege, это тоже пройдёт as they say in Russian (this too shall pass). That's not happening.

But we know that criticism fails on all fronts. *Critical thinking* is self-evident, but not evidence for anything in particular. One cannot solve oneself, having determined that its personal instrument, as measured against the nearly eight billion replicas of itself that are and own the human ecosystem, is incommensurate with the biological planet.

When we speak of the biosphere we are really referring to every substance, from Wren, that dog, and the first known documented dog who lived nearly 32,000 years ago, to the quadrillions of quadrillions of other organisms, including the past lives of over 107 billion people, who all added their ashes and/or nutrients, tissues, liquids and gasses to the soil, and their souls, if such there be, to a biochemosphere. Currently, on the CAS Registry® (Chemical Abstracts Service Registry) there are a known "188 million organic and inorganic substances"[10] on earth. In 2021, researchers found "55 chemicals never before reported in people and 42 `mystery chemicals' in their analysis of pregnant women.[11] As of early 2017, it was reported by the European Chemicals Agency, that at least 144,000 chemicals were "man-made."[12] Writes Julian Cribb, "Earth, and all life on it, are being saturated with man-made chemicals in an event unlike anything in the planet's entire history."[13] Moreover, man-made, or natural, "humans emit more than 250 billion tonnes of chemical substances a year…"[14] As Cribb points out, only 21 of those 144,000 have been banned. Most have not even been studied, or undergone randomized control trials of related risks and direct or indirect environmental impacts. That is but one set of astonishing windows on our knowing recklessness.

A similarly daunting reality concerns those approximately 40,000 remaining eco-juggernauts, toxic federal Superfund sites just in the United States (the wealthiest nation),1,600 of them on the National Priorities List, that have thus far not seen environmental remediation.[15]

But at the same time, re-wilding efforts, particularly those inclined towards the so called "30 x 30" protective methodology[16] have recognized a directed evolution that mimics historic data, without having to engineer it in vitro. Polar bears might not play with canines, wolves befriending sheep (one thinks back to painter/Quaker/preacher Edward Hicks' (1780-1849) more than 62 "Peaceable Kingdoms" deriving from the Prophet Isaiah [Ch. XI: 6-9] "The wolf shall dwell with the lamb, and the leopard shall lie down with the goat…"). But woolly mammoths might yet wander across parts of Scandinavia, where they once roamed en masse. The exceptions to rules, laws and principles are many. Rules are human perceptions of rules. We suspect that Charles Darwin was not certain about anything. Nor was Aristotle, or Lao Tzu. There's evidence that Wittgenstein, who devoted a posthumously published book to "certainty," never even read Aristotle (though apparently liked Plato).[17] That is but one factoid out of a petri dish of contradictions and rampant uncertainties that ultimately must hover over the predicament that has trapped individuals within their own species; allied, like it or not, with all human populations and, as of 2022, a global average Total Fertility Rate of approximately 2.5.[18] But modeling future human population growth remains what one researcher has described as a "kind of an impossible exercise."[19] Projections during the last half-century have seldom been remotely accurate. Means and ends are protean. Calibrations are perpetually tweaked in the face of new kinds of demographic transition. Pro-natalist countries, once one-or-two-child predominate, argue economics over carrying capacity.[20]

Biological Anthropology

But there are even greater challenges to the certitudes humans think of as endemic to their species. Every emphatic is but a moment passing before the sheen of the unobserved realities, sometimes acutely present, other times dull, that is this vague set of vagaries believed to be consciousness. We have no clue what it really is. Physiology and biological anthropology are teeming with numbers, body to mass ratios, brain sizes and the like. But we remain unintelligible on the topic of intelligence. Knowledge does not comport with the energy-dependent act of knowing. There is a metabolic relationship between truth-values, and "service volume," referring to "processing power," and what has been characterized as the "fourth dimension of life."[21] It is a tautological constraint that burrows deep into emptiness, only to re-surface bearing fully delusional standards and qualifications. Hence the famed "Kleiber's Law," "the relationship of metabolism vs body mass" and named after Swiss agricultural biologist Max Kleiber's (1893-1976) work in the 1930s. That construct still lacks for any absolute theoretical explanation and thus "should be considered a rule that allows for exceptions."[22] Certainly a fundamental allometric shift for the ratio of human mass, surface to volume, and metabolism will, and already are confounded by the energy expenditure needed to overcome heat intolerance as the planet's atmosphere and surface warm up.

Such exceptions, as immediately inform the oldest of all human volition, concern the strangest and most frustrating of underlying verdicts: is there some other basis for a future set of relations between species that is not intrusive, violative, predacious? While we can easily imagine it, biological scale immediately sets to work to trample our vision of a happy camp, beginning with the processes within any cell of endocytosis and exocytosis.[23] At its most blatant, the cell employs phagocytotic neutrophils and macrophages to defend itself, as in the case whereby "immune cells engulf and destroy dangerous microorganisms or toxic compounds."[24] In fact, phagocytosis has been dated to between 2 and 3 billion years ago, a giant evolutionary point in time when "single-celled organisms [began to] 'eat' other cells as a means of absorbing nutrients or eliminating pathogens."[25]

If certain vegetative species are considered model organisms (*Phragmites australis*, for example),[26] then a multitude of different cells should be, as well, including the globally pervasive *Parachlamydia* bacteria in amoebae, which actually have served as *model systems* in research at the University of Vienna's Center for Microbiology and Environmental Systems.[27] "Over 500 generations of bacteria" were examined during the course of 14 months to see how "theoretical predictions on the development of infectivity"[28] would correlate with differing host cells and their diverse impacts on the genes of two bacterial groups utilized within the laboratory. The predictions by researchers were accurate.[29] Infection rates within cell hosts were such that bacterial changes and varying "metabolic pathways" boosted survival levels of the bacteria outside the host cells.[30] The importance of such research underscores the realities of real-time evolution, at all scales. It bodes of the possibility that an individual, any individual, might rise to the ranks of model behaviorism. Of course, some will note the equal probability of that same model becoming an infectious organism. Cellular diet, or the work of antibodies, cannot be ethically correlated with the distant dreams of any one hominid whose lifestyle and philosophical injunctions might code one way or other. That much should be clear.

Infinitesimal Domains

Yet, there is total continuity within the short-lived, infinitesimal domains that comprise the evolution of all cellular life on earth. Compared with size, distance and time of those volumes we sense and attribute to the Cosmos, our little pocket of thin-skinned existence is tightly knit, for all of its trillions of individual personages and component parts within any underscored phylogenesis. Herein lies the fantastic dialogue between biochemistry and philosophy. Between aesthetics, the imagination, and our variable conditions as organisms within distinct, but changeable communities. Museums and history afford the luxury of leisure glances. But real-time does not. The hunter's bullet. A madman's choice. So called market fluctuations. Enormous disparities. Hunger. Oppression. All of these conditionals. Which are also to be found within both life's forces and killing fields, have negentropic properties. Namely, varying distances to the ideal of normality, which, in and of itself, correlates with no known number of bacterial or viral generations. These are areas about which we know, or for which apparently care, nothing.

But in quantifying their content, the quality of life is lost to a manufactured statistical realm that is of a humankind, steeped in linear advantages to the perceptual creator of those theories. This, we *do* know.

As much as our introspective faculties ignite various plays on words and ideas, this fantasy or ideation involving a blind faith in a nature that knows best, is precisely obfuscated by the human coefficient. We intercede, we inject our demands, we play a political game that stages its warfare in ways both seen and accumulating. Our unsuspecting outcomes repeat themselves, and have particularly so in the last few hundred years, where the damage of our controls has begun to leave obvious gaps in most other ecosystems. The connectivity of that defacement potently describes a profound truth, certainly with respect to humans, that was the subject of a 2013 exhibition at the Hirshhorn Museum and Sculpture Garden of the Smithsonian Institution in Washington D.C., entitled, "Damage Control: Art and Destruction Since 1950."[31] The dichotomy of irreconcilability embodies a distinct, ecologically incoherent type of species that we have never observed. Even the inherited cannibalism in some spiders, has its own powerful explanations.[32] In some instances, an "aggressive spill-over" has been hypothesized accounting for continuing killing exhibited by grown females where there is no obvious advantage to the species.[33] The hominin might suggest: train the females to be non-violent. We could probably tinker in the laboratory with such behavior, stand back and ask the relevant questions, both of ourselves, and the spiders spared consumption. To do so systematically across those Serengeti's would be both a formidable challenge but also require an ethic ready to justify the re-shaping of the world. It has been tried in one famous instance, the "tame behavior" in the red fox (*Vulpes vulpes*) that highlighted "SorCS1" as part of the very intriguing "Russian farm-fox experiment."[34]

It would also require questions of our ancestors. For example, an ambitious, ethical entrepreneur might have taken up the export trade in *Cyperus papyrus*, the aquatic sedge, also known as Nile grass, and used for many of the earliest manuscripts dating back not only to Papyrus 46, the codex with the Pauline epistles from the New Testament, but to documents from the First Dynasty in Egypt (3100 BCE). No animal killing, only the papermaking from a plant. But by the time of the great four uncials, *Codex Sinaiticus* א,

Vaticanus B, *Alexandrinus A* and *Ephraemi Rescriptus C*, all 4th-5th centuries, parchment (animal skin) had become the primary substance for books, at least in the West. In Asia, however, manuscripts continued to be written on the treated bark of birch trees (*Betula papyrifera* or the Himalayan *utilis* species) or by the popular use of Borassus (*Palmyra palm*) or *Corypha umbraculifera* (tailpot palm).[35] Papermaking was first discovered in China around 25 CE, the technique attributed to Cai Lun, an official of the Eastern Han period.[36] This was not the cast in the West. In fact, until approximately 1450, and the emergence of the 1455 Guttenberg Bible, tens, possibly hundreds of millions of antelope, goat and sheep were slaughtered for their skins. Across Europe during the Renaissance it is approximated that there were at least 2,500 editions of various *Book of Hours* (horae) disseminated by 1550. It was a best-selling genre.[37] Most were completely hand painted, but with the advent of moveable type, at least 1750 were printed on vegetable-derived paper, using both the original wood and later metal cuts.

Collective Mind

So far, humanity has not been able to validate most of its actions. Perhaps a melodious bicycle built for two. But by what metric or conscious barometer do we undertake to *justify* anything? Most of our collective's impact is muted, unvoiced, unlegislated. Our priorities, and the voracious news cycles devoted to them, shift like the unseen breezes of yesteryear. "Most" is as reliable as the mind's peripheries. We cannot ascribe to matter a physique other than through this vague concatenation of drifting ideas and volatile focus points. One day the U.S. Congress is aswirl in vote counts that would, among other things, add prescription eyeglasses to expanded medical insurances. So that, what? We can look out upon a devastated world with greater clarity? More easily distinguish between the 150 million orphans and those children with loving families? Determine who looks to be part of that mass sum of 815 million chronically undernourished humans? Or better gauge the hundreds of billions of animals being slaughtered annually? This cynicism is warranted to the extent that such discrepancies in our culturally shaping ecosystems of mind and politics are intensely frustrating to those who reflect on all the ironies, compromises, incremental assiduousness that, by any calculation will never make it in time.

The incisive paleolithic scholar, philosopher André Leroi-Gourhan (1911-1986) who catalogued so much of European cave paintings, spoke of a phenomenon separate in humans from either neurology or genetics, namely, "technogenesis".[38] By this he meant to challenge any easy speculation, either past, present or future, with respect to where human choices might lead. He knew intimately the origins and diversity of toolmaking as it was represented so prodigiously on pre-paper surfaces, rock walls. Rupestral aesthetics are no less revealing than a "Ginevra de`Benci" or today's media of digital transmissions. The optics are part of a vast mechanism by which we drive underlying principles into iterative Selves, whose voices want to be heard. A participatory engine of daily, social reassessment, where every emotion is elicited. Hence, the more than 230 serious anti-government protests throughout 2020/2021 in more than half the nearly two-hundred countries of the world[39], not including the riot at Ecuador's Litoral prison in Guayacil which resulted in at least 118 deaths, six decapitations, scores injured;[40] the 30+ civil wars currently in progress, and as of 2022, the barbaric escalation of Putin's invasion of Ukraine.[41]

Late one night, a week after the Bush-Putin Slovenia Summit in late June 2001, we were at a private dinner adjoining Putin's little table at a palace outside St. Petersburg. Our involvement in music had brought us to this gathering. Putin, having delivered his trained, duplicitous grin to Bush, had earlier been invited to visit the Bush family at their ranch in Texas. The world thought for a moment, that the autocrat may have softened. Jane walked over toward him and quickly withdrew her small camera to snap a few after-dinner photographs. Black suited goons from every direction reached for their guns, until Putin waved them off. At that time the world had seen his war in Chechnya and destruction of entire towns and cities. The West sent "diapers and water bottles," to help those on the ground, as one astute observer noted. Could we have fathomed a particular syllogism, concluding from the cascade of desperate events following Boris Yeltsin's December 31,1999 handoff to Putin of Russia's presidency, that here was another Stalin, sitting just a few feet away? Everyone knew what then Prime Minister Putin had done to the Chechen capital of Grozny in the Fall of 1999, slaughtering tens-of-thousands of civilians and ordering the complete destruction of the city. As with everyone else, from diplomats over many years, to private citizens in every country, straight into the heart of all his direct victims – children blown up in hospitals where they lay, fleeing elderly and their daughters and granddaughters, shot at – we had no incentive during that dinner to try and forever still the monster that was quickly incarnating, to talk some sense to him. Too little too late. In. retrospect, never too late. We've had acquaintances who have had countless opportunities to do so over the years, with a much firmer database. But the courage of a Claus von Stauffenberg in his attempt to kill Hitler on July 21, 1944, or the absolute belief in one's deepest intuition, rarely translates in real time (though GOP Sen. Lindsey Graham had tweeted in search of a "Brutus in Russia", playing to a policy long banned in the US [Executive Order 11905 issued by President Gerald Ford on February 19, 1976] following alleged attempts decades before to kill Castro in the wake of President Kennedy's assassination).[42] Just last night the world barely averted a nuclear catastrophe thanks to Putin. History, archaeology, astronomy… these are simplistic studies by contrast. In retrospect, should we have attempted to somehow Quixotically attack the windmills before us? It's a pointless game all people indulge at some level: Should I have turned right instead of left? Or even bothered to get out of bed?

What If?

I remember once as a young man I (mt) was in St. Petersburg with my mother. I passed by the high school #281 at Sovetskiy Pereulok, 4. Putin was studying there as far as I understand. A young kid, a year and a half younger than me. Surely, I could have found him and persuaded the young man to change his views? I was an American there to visit Russian relatives I had never before met. My Russian was adequate to the task. Putin's mother was purportedly of Jewish descent, while his grandfather, Spiridon, had evidently been a cook for Lenin. My grandmother had been a part-time editor for Lenin through her friendship with Lenin's wife, Nadezhda Krupskaya, during the tumultuous lead up to the Bolshevik attack, ordered by Lenin, upon the government at the Winter Palace in Petrograd during one night in October 1917. My grandma was there. She probably also worked with the Lenin's during the couple's respite in a flat at the grandiose edifice of the Smolny Institute, at Smolnyi pr-d, 1. This was about the time Lenin had relocated to Moscow.

Should I have sought out the teenager, and somehow inconceivably attempted to change the course of history? My rhetorical skills were surely not up to it. This was the height of James Bond mania and, while in the country on my first trip, KGB agents followed me everywhere, since I kept slipping away from the Intourist services in those days. It was all idiotic. I gave a cone of ice cream to one of the agents trailing me. And who could have predicted that the scrawny, steely nobody would join the KGB at age 23, and go on to revere and model a career after that of Marx and Lenin? Unlike a Lenin, he would come to basically possess nearly 6,000 nuclear weapons, tactical, strategic, atomic, thermonuclear.

But then – and this is how all philosophy is caught up in a fundamental aspect of irreversibility that forever taunts hindsight and undermines any closure that might have followed from it – I would also have had to image countless other events, assassinations, and twists of history. While my grandparents were getting married in the Moscow Synagogue, the savage pogroms in the Ukraine were systematically killing some 1.5 million fellow Jews. Cossacks and various voluntary troops raped and massacred nearly every last Jew in Skvyra, Justingrad, and the Ivankiv districtss (raions) in Kyiv.

In Kyiv (Kiev then), I later walked along the piles of dirt at the Babyn Yar ravine near Dorohozhychi. I remember having an overwhelming visceral reaction to the fact of some 33,000+ Jews – many relatives of my own – having been murdered and dumped anonymously beneath the dirt hillside I there stood upon.

The same Ukrainian descendants, many Jews among them, now together fleeing to NATO countries, other than males aged 18 to 60, while their country was being devastated, crimes against humanity, mass torture, strict violations of all Geneva Conventions and Accords codified between August 22 1864 and those charters signed in 1949.

Back to St. Petersburg. That little ferine Putin, aged 13 years old, skipping (probably marching) across those heavy stones laid down by the proletariat, coming out after school. That would have been a perfect time to transform something with dramatic effects. Yes, maybe I could have made a friend in him, altered his world view, somehow. We all have some sort of ability within us to do so if we but try. And doubtless, such interplays through time have happened before. We just don't always have personal, parallel stories to contextualize an ethic in the service, presumably, of saving history from another person, we don't even know. This is the fate of consciousness, held hostage before every coming moment. The accumulating toll of all subsequent intention and action obliterates every second that preceded this one, then the next one, and so on. Essentially, lacking any predictive certainty, we are useless at such potentially world-altering instants. With enough hindsight, we *all* might have put the little bastard out of his misery.

It is utterly foolhardy to play out such scenarios in one's mind, depressing, But, we do learn, if we so choose to, from the coordinates that were near misses; planetary retrogrades as we perceive them. That dinner at the Summer Palace was for me an elusive calling, ever since; the salient latitude on either side of wars, holocausts, human-induced disasters that with a single action on my part – just some kind words to a foreign head of state – might cascade an entirely different reading, retroactively, of history. He might have thought: All westerners are really nice people. I'd love to join the European Union, etc. No absolute theory of non-violence could condone the murder of one man. But against the massive tragedy of Ukraine? Hardly a moral equivalency.

It's not simply an idle wish for a crystal ball, but the goal of deciphering a pattern of personal, learned behavior that finds the language of restraint well suited to the as yet unwritten histories through which all of life is journeying.

Ecosystem histories are entirely about biological anthropology, eco-psychiatry, the myriad mechanisms of epiphany that move mountains, if we are willing to listen and learn, in the biosemiospheric sense. This is a pillar of personal scaling, like reading a Ouija board whose numerologies or alphabetical circumference does not merely seek to conjure a mysterious apparition from the movements of a chicken or cow – alectryomancy – as was frequently done throughout the late Middle Ages in Europe. Rather, a divination that gains by every virtuous inflection. Each transcendental point in time that witnesses the passing landscape, crowds moving in all directions, huddled throughout the streets, shuffling between pointless errands. A consciousness grounded in its forward control of the past that has lost all control, except in the mind of that future-headed instinct. Of a personage who accepts what was possible, then; but now must absolutely become in him/herself the instrument of historical redemption. This, too, is an aspect of essential human evolution, like it or not.

How does an individual break step with inevitabilities? Can we posit, then inhabit alternative realities that are the outcome of one choice multiplied by the free will of collectives? The relations between these clauses of sanctuary and hope have their own gravity. They manifest.

Citius Quam Postea, Omnia Paratus (Sooner or later, ready for all things) is a warning that takes us back to the earlier (in Ch.1) referenced conundrum (polyphyly) of multiple traits. It is *the* human condition: an assemblage, fast evolving, endless ancestral lineages having converged and reconverged – πολύς = meaning "multitudinous", and φῦλον = "genus", or species, as conceived by the Greeks. In no greater medium of life are there such numbers, lineages, potential evolutionary guides as were proposed in a critical paper in May of 2016 by Kenneth J. Locey and Jay T. Lennon, "Scaling laws predict global microbial diversity."[43] Utilizing "a unified scaling law that predicts the abundance of dominant species across 30 orders of magnitude to the scale of all microorganisms on Earth" they predicted that there are "as many as 1 trillion (10^{12}) microbial species."[44] Such "local- to global-scale predictions"[45] is historically fascinating in lieu of the fact that Linnaeus documented just over 12,000 species, Aristotle just over 500. Of special allometric importance, the authors of the paper note that their scaling exceeds the Kleiber "3/4 power scale of metabolic power to mass" by 3 orders of magnitude, in terms of comparable species numbers. This, in turn, will challenge all laws of volumetrics, as well as the fundamental nature of genetic translation machinery from mRNA, protein synthesis and codons to a far greater realm of cellular communication, sustenance and architecture.[46]

Ecological Scaling Laws

Four years after the publication of their groundbreaking "Scaling laws..." paper, Lennon and Locey published a follow-up, "More support for Earth's massive microbiome,"[47] their Abstract for which makes poignantly clear that "global biodiversity has been greatly underestimated and, in some cases, completely overlooked." They re-examined the use of the data compilation "Global Prokaryotic Census," as well as searching for sampling discrepancies or misuse (by others) that appeared to be plausible and important errors, and, ultimately, again arrived at their one-trillion prediction. It is a stunning realization.

Near the turn of the 21st century, practical biology noted that some bacteria could live hundreds of years (e.g., the spores of anthrax bacteria).[48] That hydridae (Hydrozoa) were essentially immortal, given their recycling life histories.[49] And that "four unknown strains of bacteria from the Permian Period" (250 million years old) had been revived, and thus were considered "the oldest living organisms ever discovered".[50]

In July of 2021, researchers reported fossil filaments, life, dating back 3.42 billion years from a rock in today's South Africa.[51] This mirrors the 3.5-billion-year-old stromatolites first found in western Australia in 1956.[52] Fossilized remnants hint at another complexity related to modern cellular longevity: the discovery within "supramolecular complexes" of a baseline for "age mosaicism," populations of widely differing cellular ages within specific species of individuals.[53]

In 2015 the first octopus's genome was decoded and perhaps the most striking illumination from that research was the fact that the remarkable invertebrate's nervous system appeared to have been acquired within its short lifespan, day by day, not simply inherited, within the average one-to-two-year lifespan.[54] This suggests a new meta-formation of consciousness as a driver, not merely a shaper, in the generic parlance of what behavioral roles in a biosphere are actually supposed to express. That *supposedly* may strike of a problem for most, who are not keen to think of evolution as purposeful (e.g., the organisms re-configuring for one another, but subsumed by the prevailing bias against "intelligent design" in nature), a force translatable to a god, any god.[55/56] And in no less a testable duration than day by day.

Turn it around, forgetting the translation, conceptual bias, or underlying statistical probability of any one truth prevailing on this or any other planet; or leaving it to natural selection to define its own constructs along-the-way, and a basic biosynthetic principle arises. Real-time, or ancient time, the cumulative process of behavior cannot be explained. Neither chemical prehistory nor the instantaneous can capture probability. Our statistics are dim within the same instant it takes to give birth to an idea. If this is the situation with humans, imagine the case-by-case complex of sublime interactions amongst that one-trillion species (of which only some 30,000 are formally identified).[57] The so called "Earth BioGenome Project" is trying to expand that identity to encompass/sequence all eukaryotic species on the planet[58]. But within that impossible reach are impossible questions and obvious (with a modicum of hindsight) rebellions against human meddling. One case in point: the behavior demonstrated by magpies in which they help one another rid ("rescue") themselves of and from attached tracking devices that weighed less than a single gram.[59]

If we concentrate our thoughts around the 13.8 billion-year old alleged Universe, and the Cosmic Microwave Background fluctuations deciphered in the wake of Einstein's theories to that effect by George Smoot III and others[60] the timeline provides neither comfort nor instruction. Only ecological closure, in the form of substance and interaction before us, can do that. Our minds are liberated from real time, our bodies less so. As we have often reiterated, evolution neither condemns nor liberates us. Only our choices can do that.[61] The calendars of human courses of action, given to mayhem and entropy, are reflections of the violence of the post-ground state. That refers to excited states, wherein superclusters, hydrogen collapse and the formation of star systems and their points of inflationary chaos all express similar preconditions of biochemical constants. These are the prevailing second-by-second states of neurological awareness of any organism confronting any other sentient, partially sentient, or non-sentient structure here on earth. That would include self-consciousness. That, too, is a constant, but one which, as with the example of magpies, has a forever aspect of self-liberation. We don't know how far it is capable of reaching. In one celebrated instance, the 12,500-year old rock art among the tepuis limestone cliffs in modern-day Columbia, Serranía de la Lindosa, particularly at Cerro Azul hill, we are living witness to some of the oldest expressions by human hands of the contiguous consciousness between species, certainly in the Amazon. Therein, a sprawling, reverential proliferation of images of many now extinct species whose existence at that time co-mingled in mind with our ancestors.[62] Nestled in the jungle, these original depictures, without authorship, identities of all concerned as outspoken as the likeness of God and Adam along the Sistine Chapel ceiling, inform our individual destinies. Some have likened this revelatory moment during the late Pleistocene as humanity's "last journey".[63]

East Coker, 1939

Beyond the suggested 100- billion-year mark of the future Universe, cosmologists remain no less clear than those Early Holocene Late Quaternary Stone Age indigenous artists who acquitted any doubts as to their keen, observatories on rock. The *cosmic time* means little to us, who are not ordinarily given to grappling with the authoritarianism that is earth time, any time.[64] The comprehension of incomprehensibility was beautifully described by Constantin François de Chassebœuf, comte de Volney (1757-1820) in his memorable tome, *Ruins, Or A Survey Of The Revolutions Of Empire* (1796), most of which was translated into English by Thomas Jefferson just prior to his campaigning for President in 1800.[65] The book was Volney's meditation on the ghosts of ruins, the passage of time, and the infinitesimal life on earth versus that among the stars. No religion, he said, could explain any of it. He was a Deist, albeit a Romantic one, convinced that nature, even the humblest insect, should be our rational guide to realism. "Man is governed," he wrote, "like the world of which he forms a part, by natural laws… inherent in the nature of all terrestrial beings, identified with their existence, they are at all times and in all places present to the human mind…Let man study their laws, let him understand his own nature, and the nature of the beings that surround him, and he will know the springs of his destiny…"[66]

Jefferson, who had cut and pasted versions of *The Life and Morals of Jesus of Nazareth* (1804) and *The Philosophy of Jesus of Nazareth* (1820) admired Volney but feared the *threat* of his atheism. After all, Jefferson vehemently opposed the notion, propounded by Georges Couvier, that extinctions could occur. The man who would enact the Louisiana Purchase in 1803 was pragmatic. He saw waves of immigrants coming to the U.S. and knew that the Lewis and Clark Expedition had opened the way to make a population boom possible. But he, like Volney, also was assured that humanity could know it all, command and control, with the heavens above looking down at our wondrous ways. This was purposeful evolution, he imagined, and it was woven into the Declaration of Independence, the U.S. Constitution, theology and the natural sciences. To this day nothing has really changed. Our penchant as a species for experimentation cannot be stayed. Similarly, our consumer patterns, self-awareness, arrogance and indifference to the rationale of intellectual and spiritual redemption are a vague, at best temporarily curious phenomenon with no obvious outcomes. Not all beavers build impoundments. Not all birds fly.

It is by the most remote of probabilities that every human on the planet now has access to viewing images from Serranía de la Lindosa. Can we possibly contextualize such art and paleolithic feeling in a manner befitting the amalgams of biological destinies? UNESCO has recognized the site as World Heritage. While wars and suffering escalate, humanity's occupational siege, unlike any other species, is not just a matter of ecosystem dynamics, or of psychoanalysis, although it is both of those.

Levels of stress will alter alert behavior.[67] Current efforts "to recover relationships between individuals and populations" as determined by a sample study utilizing "27 million ancestral haplotype fragments and 231 million ancestral lineages linking [human] genomes"[68] is the most revealing attempt as yet to clarify the picture of our patchwork of migrations and arrivals. Where we now stand in some just less than chaotic medley of self-implosions as a species. If the barometer for being human is something other than physiology, and *humanity* represents the most obvious proxy, then it is clear that our variations are so extreme as to suggest biological latitude. Those Amazonian artisans were philosophers to the core. When we refer to biosynthetic constants we recognize that such a notion embodies all that is unpredictable about humans; our evolution of self-recognition, our hopes, and – broadest of all realms – the thoroughly unknown, even unimagined prospects that elicit an ethological new world view equipped with traction. A history of illustrated paradise imagery makes clear our goal of engendering just such a preternatural setting, as that of times past in those as yet unburnt corners of the Amazon.

"Don Quixote," Illustration by Gustave Doré, Frontispiece, *Don Quichotte De La Mancha*, by Miguel de Cèrvantes Saavedra, Translation by Louis Viardot, Printer Pisan, Librairie d'Hachette et C', Paris, 1863, Private Collection.

An obscure mid-sixteenth century engraving by Bernardo Daddi (also known as 'Il maestro del dado', "The Master of the Dice,"1512-1570) entitled, "Gathering Of The Animals"[69] was, in its time a popular image and concept. An escape into the world of spiritual communion. It was, regardless of denomination, an iconic perspective of a lost world, at a time of near constant war and revolution, the tendencies in which the last few thousand years of human history have specialized. We see its incarnation in the use of fireworks to create a most poignant and ironic ephemerality in the guise of a ladder to heaven, on fire, dissipating almost as soon as it is erected hundreds of feet high, by Chinese artist Cai Guo-Qiang.[70] And we feel the tension of that mechanical brace clinching every word we speak, in whatever language, confining us to lexical autocracies: the derived, inflectional and cranberry morphemes that are forever breaking their boundaries, as with arbitrary roots that seek out linguistic ties to seemingly incompatible relations, allomorphs, cases and genders, allophones, and the ever changing syntactic trees.[71] The historic obsession with Asparagus, Blue Passion Flower, Fever Few, Egyptian Waterlily and the great visions of perfect life by German artist/explorer Carl Friedrich Philipp von Martius (1794-1868), particularly in his three-volume *Historia naturalis palmarum* (1823-1853) with his multitude of paradise landscapes.[72] What a wondrous mess our minds and words have made of a world, otherwise perfect. We obtain through furthered discussion and research no capable infrastructure for unraveling this miasma of dialectics that comprises humanity's travails. From beauty to suffering. If the linguistics are viewed as not material to the essence of what is going on; and if our artforms signify nothing but a surficial and volitional foundation built on air, as in the case of aforementioned Guo-Qiang, a very basic question (among questions) arises: What is human reality, and what is *real* reality?

If we cannot disassociate the two plenaries, can we as individuals walk away from the question, should we choose to?

Where do we walk to? How do we live? Without *believing* in what we perceive, full of feeling for somethings and not for others, making those choices, insisting upon certain dreams, excoriating those we abhor, we exist not by purpose or even chance (though both elements come into play), but by tenacity. If that is the personal through-story of every organism then we can suggest that absolute vagaries dictate evolution, leaving a plus+1. The rules we deduce are adjudged and managed to the extent of our own sovereignties. We have no actual authority to make our presence meaningful. By meaningfulness to ourselves we invent cues, then argue for their rule-making priority. But, not surprisingly, the logic gets tangled, like the so-called "social impact credit trap" cited by solar expert Daniel Waldron in describing the problems associated with bringing energy to some of Africa's poorest communities.[73] These are intricate coils of capitalism that find out sooner or later the cost of a penny, the value of anything in denominated terms. Terms that can be financial, political, medical, technical at any scale, or philosophical. In other words, "the inevitability of knotting".[74] That includes malice, the punitive motives that enable ground troops to blast craters with missiles into large groups of citizens. It is the World War, Chernobyl red forest, the endless assaults – in one war, in all abuse – that engenders what T.S.Eliot described as that moment, that condition, "And you see behind every face the mental emptiness deepen/Leaving only the growing terror of nothing to think about".[75] Eliot started "East Coker" in 1939. The horrors of war were beginning. He knew in his core that such destruction to come was human destiny. This section of "Four Quartets" and the landscapes of Somerset were clearly waiting for the poet who was there two years prior to writing the section. Eliot's ashes are buried there at St. Michael and All Angels' Church, in East Coker.[76]

The priority-thinking Being is one case of pre-linguistic, historical portraiture of *H. sapiens*. But, alas, it is without meaning by definition. A prelude to the meaningless intent of what is otherwise thought of as content. This strange crisis of bed-fellows augers for place, time, and egoless involvement in that which, 1) we don't understand, 2) we are part of, 3) we perceive by whatever means at our discretion, 4) is a world, 5) are multiple worlds, and 6) connected worlds. Beyond ascribing to our inclusion in that interconnectedness, it is for now best to leave it for a more in-depth reaction to the notion of interdependence.

Endnotes

[1] See, "On the Nature of the Motion we call Heat," Philosophical Magazine, Published by *London and Edinburgh Philosophical Magazine And Journal of Science*, Volume 14, Fourth Series, 1857. See also, *Entropic Creation: Religious Contexts of Thermodynamics and Cosmology*, by Helge S. Kragh, Taylor & Francis Ltd., London, UK 2008.

[2] See, for example. "Introduction to the Major Laws of Physics," which include -as described by Andrew Zimmerman Jones, ThoughtCo, July 3, 2019 (https://www.thoughtco.com/major-laws-of-physics-2699071), gravity, Newton's laws of motion, conservation of mass and energy, electrostatic laws from Coulomb and Gauss, etc. Add to this such other primaries as Jagran Josh's list, "Important Laws of Physics," https://www.jagranjosh.com/general-knowledge/important-laws-of-physics-1513943551-1, April 8, 2019: "Archimedes Principle, Avagadro's Law, Ohm's Law… Pascal's Law, Hooke's Law, Bernoulli's Principle, Charles's Law, Kepler's Law… Tyndall effect [and] Graham's Law."

[3] "How Much Time Does Humanity Have Left?" By Avi Loeb on May 12, 2021, https://www.scientificamerican.com/article/how-much-time-does-humanity-have-left/; See also, "How big a change in the Earth's orbit would be required to destroy all life?" by Britt Scharringhausen, Ask an Astronomer, June 27, 2015, http://curious.astro.cornell.edu/physics/39-our-solar-system/the-earth/other-catastrophes/58-how-big-a-change-in-the-earth-s-orbit-would-be-required-to-destroy-all-life-intermediate. Regarding the earth's orbit, Scharringhausen estimates that the planet has a biosphere-sustaining orbital differential around the Sun from a "decrease by 4,5000,000 miles or increase by 34,000,000 miles [to] still be in the habitable zone."

[4] Callaway, E. Oldest *Homo sapiens* fossil claim rewrites our species' history. *Nature* (2017). https://doi.org/10.1038/nature.2017.22114

[5] See "'The only uncertainty is how long we'll last': a worst-case scenario for the climate in 2050," by Christiana Figueres and Tom Rivett-Carnac, The Guardian, February 15, 2020 https://www.theguardian.com/environment/2020/feb/15/worst-case-scenario-2050-climate-crisis-future-we-choose-christiana-figueres-tom-rivett-carnac, Excerpted from the authors' book, *The Future We Choose: Surviving the Climate Crisis*, Knopf Doubleday Publishing Group, New York, NY, 2020.

[6] See Still, B. The unveiled states of americium. Nature Chem 9, 296 (2017). https://doi.org/10.1038/nchem.2733, Issued March 2017.

[7] See Jablonski, D. Extinction: past and present. Nature 427, 589 (2004). https://doi.org/10.1038/427589a; See also, "Mammal diversity will take millions of years to recover from the current biodiversity crisis," Matt Davis, Søren Faurby, and Jens-Christian Svenning, *PNAS* October 30, 2018 115 (44) 11262-11267; first published October 15, 2018; https://doi.org/10.1073/pnas.1804906115, https://www.pnas.org/content/115/44/11262; In addition, see "Mass Extinctions in the Marine Fossil Record, by David Raup and J. John Sepkoski, Jr., Science, 19 Mar 1982, Vol 215, Issue 4539•pp. 1501-1503, doi: 10.1126/science.215.4539.1501, https://www.science.org/lookup/doi/10.1126/science.215.4539.1501; and, *The Annihilation Of Nature – Human Extinction of Birds and Mammals*, by Gerardo Ceballos, Anne H. Ehrlich, and Paul R. Ehrlich, Johns Hopkins University Press, Baltimore, MD, 2015.

[8] See "Joining The Convention On Biological Diversity: A Legal And Scientific Overview Of Why The United States Must Wake Up," by William Snape, III, *Sustainable Development Law & Policy*, Spring, 2010, https://www.biologicaldiversity.org/publications/papers/SDLP_10Spring_Snape.pdf; See also, "Why the US won't join the single most important treaty to protect nature," by Benji Jones, Vox, May 20, 2021, https://www.vox.com/22434172/us-cbd-treaty-biological-diversity-nature-conservation

[9] See "The first intravenous anaesthetic: how well was it managed and its potential realized?" by K. L. Dorrington and W. Poole, *British Journal of Anaesthesia*, Volume 110, Issue 1, January 2013, pp. 7-12, Elsevier, https://doi.org/10.1093/bja/aes388Get, https://www.sciencedirect.com/science/article/pii/S0007091217328428

[10] https://www.cas.org

[11] See "Evidence of 55 new chemicals in people," *Science News*, March 17, 2021, University of San Francisco, https://www.sciencedaily.com/releases/2021/

03/210317094621.htm, Cited from Aolin Wang, Dimitri Panagopoulos Abrahamsson, Ting Jiang, Miaomiao Wang, Rachel Morello-Frosch, June-Soo Park, Marina Sirota, Tracey J. Woodruff. Suspect Screening, Prioritization, and Confirmation of Environmental Chemicals in Maternal-Newborn Pairs from San Francisco. *Environmental Science & Technology*, 2021; doi: 10.1021/acs.est.0c05984

[12] See "Scientists categorize Earth as a 'toxic planet,'" *SciNews*, February 7, 2017, https://phys.org/news/2017-02-scientists-categorize-earth-toxic-planet.html

[13] ibid.

[14] ibid.

[15] See *CERCLA, The Comprehensive Environmental Response, Compensation, and Liability Act of 1980*. See also, the Agency for Toxic Substances and Disease Registry, United States. *Comprehensive Environmental Response, Compensation, and Liability Act of 1980*. Sec. 105(a)(8)(B); 42 U.S.C. § 9605; and ATSDR (2021). Department of Health and Human Services Fiscal Year 2022 Agency for Toxic Substances and Disease Registry Justification of Estimates for Appropriations Committees Report. United States Department of Health and Human Services.

[16] See https://www.campaignfornature.org/news/category/30x30

[17] See "'The Socratic Method!': Wittgenstein and Plato – Connections, Comparisons, and Contrasts, Edited by Luigi Perissinotto and Begoña Ramón Cámara, Springer, New York, 2013, pp. 48-71, https://link.springer.com/chapter/10.1057/9781137313447_3; See Wittgenstein's *On Certainty*, Translated by Denis Paul and G. E. M. Anscombe, Basil Blackwell, London, UK, 1969.

[18] See "Fertility Rate," by Max Roser, December 2, 2017, *Our World in Data*, https://ourworldindata.org/fertility-rate

[19] See statistical modeler at the University of Massachusetts Amherst, Leontine Alkema, as cited in "How far will global population rise? Researchers can't agree," by David Adam *Nature*, 21 September 2021, https://www.nature.com/articles/d41586-021-02522-6

[20] See, for example, *World War III: Population and the Biosphere at the End of the Millennium*, by M. C. Tobias, Bear & Company, Santa Fe, NM, 1994.

[21] See "A general basis for quarter-power scaling in animals," by Jayanth R. Banavar, Melanie E. Moses. James H. Brown, John Damuth, Andrea Rinaldo Richard M. Sibly, and Amos Maritan, *PNAS, Proceedings of the National Academy of Sciences of the United States of America*, https://www.pnas.org/content/107/36/15816

[22] See "Kleiber's Law: How the *Fire of Life* ignited debate, fueled theory, and neglected plants as model organisms," by Karl J Niklas and Ulrich Kutschera, *Plant Signal Behav.* 2015 Jul; 10(7): e1036216, Published online 2015 Jul 9. doi: 10.1080/15592324.2015.1036216, PMCID: PMC4622013, PMID: 26156204, https://www.ncbi.nlm.nih.gov/pmc/articles/PMC4622013/; See also, Glazier DS (February 2010). "A unifying explanation for diverse metabolic scaling in animals and plants". *Biological Reviews of the Cambridge Philosophical Society*. 85 (1): 111–38. doi:10.1111/j.1469-185X.2009.00095.x. PMID 19895606. S2CID 28572410. Kleiber's Law remains greatly debated given the metabolic variables affecting any precise allometric exponent, two/thirds, three/fourths, quadratic, etc.

[23] See "Endocytosis and Exocytosis: Differences and Similarities," by Nicole Gleichmann, April 28, 2020, *Immunology & Microbiology*, https://www.technologynetworks.com/immunology/articles/endocytosis-and-exocytosis-differences-and-similarities-334059

[24] ibid.

[25] See "New Model Predicts Cells That 'Eat' Other Cells," American Museum Of Natural History, n.a., February 2018, https://www.amnh.org/explore/news-blogs/research-posts/new-model-predicts-cells-that-eat-other-cells; recently durophagy was shown to have dramatized the mechanisms enabling Cambrian euarthropods to crush the shells of their prey. See "Biomechanical analyses of Cambrian euarthropod limbs reveal their effectiveness in mastication and durophagy," by Russell D. C. Bicknell, et al., *Proceedings of the Royal Society B*, 27 January 2021 https://doi.org/10.1098/rspb.2020.2075, https://royalsocietypublishing.org/doi/10.1098/rspb.2020.2075

[26] Saltonstall, Kristin (2002). "Cryptic invasion by a non-native genotype of the common reed, *Phragmites australis*, into North America". *Proceedings of the National Academy of Sciences*. 99 (4): 2445–2449. doi:10.1073/pnas.032477999. PMC 122384. PMID 11854535.

[27] See "Evolution in real-time: How bacteria adapt to their hosts," News Release, 18, August 2020, University of Vienna, Eurekalert! *AAAS*, https://www.eurekalert.org/news-releases/664210

[28] ibid.

[29] ibid.

[30] ibid.

[31] See "Doomsday Clock Symposium," Hirshhorn, November 14, 2013, https://hirshhorn.si.edu/explore/doomsday-clock-symposium/

[32] See Andrade, Maydianne C.B. (2003). "Risky mate search and male self-sacrifice in redback spiders". *Behavioral Ecology*. 14 (4): 531–38. doi:10.1093/beheco/arg015.

[33] Johnson, J.; Andrew Sih (August 2005). "Precopulatory Sexual Cannibalism in Fishing Spiders (Dolomedes triton): A Role for Behavioral Syndromes". *Behavioral Ecology and Sociobiology*. 58 (4): 390–396. CiteSeerX10.1.1.630.9443. doi:10.1007/s00265-005-0943-5.

[34] Kukekova, A.V., Johnson, J.L., Xiang, X. et al. Red fox genome assembly identifies genomic regions associated with tame and aggressive behaviours. *Nat Ecol Evol* 2, 1479–1491 (2018). https://doi.org/10.1038/s41559-018-0611-6, https://www.nature.com/articles/s41559-018-0611-6#citeas

[35] See https://web.archive.org/web/20181117104544/http://www.borassus-project.net/; See also, Johnson, D. 1998. *Corypha umbraculifera. The IUCN Red List of Threatened Species* 1998: e.T38494A10118423, https://www.iucnredlist.org/species/38494/10118423.

[36] See *Paper: Paging Through History*, by Mark Kurlansky, W.W. Norton & Company, New York, NY 2016.

[37] Information according to Sandra Hindman, President of Les Enluminures, via personal communication via email, October 18, 2021. See Eamon Duffy, "A Very Personal Possession: Eamon Duffy Tells How a Careful Study of Surviving Books of Hours

Can Tell Us Much About the Spiritual and Temporal Life of Their Owners and Much More Besides." History Today 56.11 (Nov 2006): 12(7); See also, John Harthan - *The Book of Hours: With a Historical Survey and Commentary by John Harthan.* Crowell, New York, NY, 1977.

[38] See "Between The Species – Negotiating the Anthropological Limit: Derrida, Stiegler, and the Question of the `Animal,'" by Nathan Van Camp, *Between the Species*, Volume 14, Issue 1, August 2011, https://digitalcommons.calpoly.edu/cgi/viewcontent.cgi?article=1172&context=bts; See also, "Media Theory," by Mark B. N. Hansen, in *Theory, Culture & Society*, May 1, 2006, *Sage Journals*, https://doi.org/10.1177/0263276406023002 56

[39] "Global Protest Tracker," Updated September 3, 2021, Carnegie Endowment For International Peace, https://carnegieendowment.org/publications/interactive/protest-tracker

[40] "A Riot In A Massive Prison In Ecuador Has Left More Than 100 Inmates Dead," September 30, 2021, *The Associated Press*, https://www.kpcc.org/npr-news/2021-09-30/a-riot-in-a-massive-prison-in-ecuador-has-left-more-than-100-inmates-dead

[41] See "Civil Wars & Global Disorder: Threats & Opportunities," edited by Karl W. Eikenberry and Stephen D. Krasner, *Daedalus*, Fall 2017, https://www.amacad.org/daedalus/civil-wars-global-disorder-threats-opportunities

[42] See "Why Twitter won't remove Lindsey Graham's tweet about assassinating Putin," by Ariel Zilber, *New York Post*, March 8, 2022, 1:15pm updated. See source at: https://twitter.com/LindseyGrahamSC/status/1499574209567199235?ref_src=twsrc%5Etfw%7Ctwcamp%5Etweetembed%7Ctwterm%5E1499574209567199235%7Ctwgr%5E%7Ctwcon%5Es1_&ref_url=https%3A%2F%2Fnypost.com%2F2022%2F03%2F08%2Ftwitter-wont-remove-lindsey-graham-tweet-about-assassinating-putin%2F; See also, "Lindsey Graham Asks Twitter If It Knows Anyone Willing to Assassinate Putin – A lot of people think thisw was very bad idea," by Bess Levin, March 4, 2022, *Vanity Fair*, https://www.vanityfair.com/news/2022/03/lindsey-graham-vladimir-putin-assassination. See "Executive Order 11905," United States History, Brittanica, https://www.britannica.com/event/Executive-Order-11905

[43] *Proc Natl Acad Sci U S A.* 2016 May 24; 113(21): 5970–5975. Published online 2016 May 2. doi: 10.1073/pnas.1521291113, PMCID: PMC4889364, PMID: 27140646, https://www.ncbi.nlm.nih.gov/pmc/articles/PMC4889364/

[44] ibid.

[45] ibid.

[46] ibid. See also their supporting information at: www.pnas.org/lookup/suppl/doi:10.1073/pnas.1521291113/-/DCSupplemental. As well as: https://github.com/LennonLab/ScalingMicroBiodiversity.

[47] Lennon, J.T., Locey, K.J. More support for Earth's massive microbiome. *Biol Direct* 15, 5 (2020). https://doi.org/10.1186/s13062-020-00261-8, Received 26 September 2019, Accepted 26 February 2020, Published 04 March 2020. See also, Sweetlove, L. Number of species on Earth tagged at 8.7 million. *Nature* (2011). https://doi.org/10.1038/news.2011.498, Published 23 August 2011. See also, "How Many Species Are There on Earth and in the Ocean?" by Camilo Mora, Derek P. Tittensor, Sina Adl, Alastair G. B. Simpson, Boris Worm, Published: August 23, 2011,

https://doi.org/10.1371/journal.pbio.1001127, *PLOS Biology*, https://journals.plos.org/plosbiology/article?id=10.1371/journal.pbio.1001127

[48] See "How long do microbes like bacteria and viruses live on surfaces in the home at normal room temperatures?" *Popular Science*, August 22, 2002, https://www.popsci.com/scitech/article/2002-08/how-long-do-microbes-bacteria-and-viruses-live-surfaces-home-normal-room-tem/, Researchers Reed Albergotti and Emily Bergeron, Edited by Bob Sillery.

[49] See Eldra Solomon, Linda Berg, and Diana W. Martin, *Biology* (6th ed.). Brooks/Cole Publishing, Pacific Grove, CA, 2001.

[50] See "Permian Bacteria," in "Oldest Living Organisms in the World," Oldest.Org, n.a. https://www.oldest.org/nature/living-organisms/#:~:text=Permian%20Bacteria&text=In%20late%202000%2C%20scientists%20reported,ever%20discovered%20in%20the%20world.

[51] "3.42-billion-year-old fossil threads may be the oldest known archaea microbes," by Carolyn Wilke, July 26, 2021, *Science News*, https://www.sciencenews.org/article/oldest-archaea-microbe-fossil-fillaments-life-evolution

[52] http://www.fossilmuseum.net/Tree_of_Life/Stromatolites.htm

[53] See Rafael Arrojo e Drigo, Varda Lev-Ram, Swati Tyagi, Ranjan Ramachandra, Thomas Deerinck, Eric Bushong, Sebastien Phan, Victoria Orphan, Claude Lechene, Mark H. Ellisman, Martin W. Hetzer. Age Mosaicism across Multiple Scales in Adult Tissues. *Cell Metabolism,* 2019; doi: 10.1016/j.cmet.2019.05.010

[54] See *Other Minds – The Octopus, The Sea, and The Deep Origins of Consciousness*, by Peter Godfrey-Smith, Farrar, Strauss and Giroux, New York, NY 2016, p. 196.

[55] See, for example, "Was Moral Evolution Purposeful?" by Christopher Boehm, Center For Humans & Nature, January 9, 2017, https://www.humansandnature.org/was-moral-evolution-purposeful

[56] See "Intelligent Design: An Ambiguous Assault on Evolution," by Ker Than, *LiveScience*, September 21, 2005, https://www.livescience.com/9355-intelligent-design-ambiguous-assault-evolution.html

[57] See Louca S, Mazel F, Doebeli M, Parfrey LW (2019) A census-based estimate of Earth's bacterial and archaeal diversity. *PLoS Biol* 17(2): e3000106. https://doi.org/10.1371/journal.pbio.3000106

[58] See https://www.earthbiogenome.org/. See also "Will Earth BioGenome Project Vindicate Darwin?" Evolution News@Discovery CSC, February 22, 2022, https://evolutionnews.org/2022/02/will-earth-biogenome-project-vindicate-darwin/; See also, "A unified genealogy of modern and ancient genomes," by Anthony Wilder Wohns, et al., *Science* 25 Feb 2022, Vol 375, Issue 6583. doi: 10.1126/science.abi8264, https://www.science.org/doi/10.1126/science.abi8264

[59] See "Scientists Attached Tracking Devices to Magpies. But Nobody Asked The Magpies," by Dominique Potvin, The Conversation, 22 February 2022, *The Coversation*, https://www.sciencealert.com/scientists-attached-tracking-devices-to-magpies-that-s-when-things-got-weird

[60] See "George Smoot: We mapped the embryonic universe," by Zoe Corbyn, *The Guardian*, April 19, 2014, https://www.theguardian.com/science/2014/apr/20/george-smoot-we-mapped-embryonic-universe-nobel-winning-big-bang-cosmos; See also,

Quantum Eco-Dynamics, Unpublished MS by George Smoot III, Michael Charles Tobias and Jane Gray Morrison, 2020/2021.

[61] See, for example, "The 'Ahimsa Factor': Ecological Non-Violence Process Analysis in China and Its Implications for Global Paradigmatic Shifts," by M. C. Tobias and J. G. Morrison, https://www.sociostudies.org/books/files/evolution_en_4/pdf/179-190.pdf

[62] See "These ancient rock paintings are unlikely to be about what was for dinner," by Joanne Pillsbury, *Apollo Magazine*, December 15, 2020, https://www.apollo-magazine.com/colombian-rock-art-serrania-la-lindosa/

[63] See "Last Journey – ERC," https://lastjourney.exeter.ac.uk/the-project/

[64] See Bruce, Dorminey "The Beginning to the End of the Universe: The mystery of dark energy". Astronomy.com, February 1, 2021. See also, Adams, Fred C.; Laughlin, Gregory (1 April 1997). "A dying universe: The long-term fate and evolution of astrophysical objects". Reviews of Modern Physics. 69 (2): 337–372. arXiv:astro-ph/9701131. Bibcode:1997RvMP...69..337A. doi:10.1103/RevModPhys.69.337. S2CID 12173790. See also, Chaisson, Eric J. (2013). "Cosmic Evolution: From Big Bang to Humankind". Cambridge, MA: Harvard–Smithsonian Center for Astrophysics; and, Barkana, Rennan; Loeb, Abraham (July 2001). "In the Beginning: The First Sources of Light and the Reionization of the Universe". *Physics Reports*. 349(2): 125–238. arXiv:astro-ph/0010468. Bibcode:2001PhR...349.125B. doi:10.1016/S0370-1573(01)00019-9. S2CID 119094218.

[65] The final portions of the manuscript were translated by Joel Barlow. A. Seale Printers, London, 1802.

[66] ibid., Volney, pp. 33-34.

[67] See "Behavior Change in Urban Mammals: A Systematic Review," by Kate Ritzel and Travis Gallo, Front. Ecol. Evol., 16 November 2020 | https://doi.org/10.3389/fevo.2020.576665, https://www.frontiersin.org/articles/10.3389/fevo.2020.576665/full

[68] op. cit., Anthony Wilder Wohns, et al., *Science.*

[69] See Adam von Bartsch (1757-1821), XV.227.76, Le peintre graveur, dl. 15, pp.227-228, cat. No 76. See also the 100+ volumes of *The Illustrated Bartsch*, Edited by Walter L. Strauss, Abaris Books, Norwalk, CT, and The Council on Library and Information Resources, 1978.

[70] See https://www.netflix.com/title/80097472

[71] See Baerman Matthew, *The Morpheme*, Oxford University Press: Oxford University Press, New York, NY, 2015.

[72] See *Garden of Eden – Masterpieces of botanical illustration*, by H. Walter Lack, Project Management, Petra Lamers-Schütze, Editorial coordination, Julia Krumhauer, English translation, Martin Walters, Taschen GmbH, photographs from Österreichische Nationalbibliothek, Vienna, 2008, p. 405. See also, http://projects.bebif.be/enbi/martius/home

[73] See "Tesla-Backed Startup Made Cheap Power a Debt Burden for the World's Poorest," by David Kocieniewski and Gavin Finch, Bloomberg, April 7, 2022, https://www.bloomberg.com/news/features/2022-04-07/how-pay-as-you-go-solar-made-the-world-s-cheapest-new-energy-unaffordable

[74] See the discussion of "lattice models" in, "The inevitability of knotting: Polymers, filaments and surfaces," by Stu Whittington, *APS March Meeting 2017*, abstract id. K17.001, March 2017, 2017APS..MARK17001W, https://ui.adsabs.harvard.edu/abs/2017APS..MARK17001W/abstract; See also, "Transcending the metabolic rift: a theory of crises in the capitalist world-ecology," by Jason W. Moore, *The Journal of Peasant Studies*, Vol. 38, No. 1, January 2011, pp. 1-46, http://pinguet.free.fr/jasonmoore11.pdf

[75] From "East Coker," in *Four Quartets*, by T. S. Eliot, Faber And Faber, London, UK, 1944, p. 19.

[76] See Peter Ackroyd, *T. S. Eliot: A Life*, Simon and Schuster, New York, NY, 1984, pp.254-255. See also Russell Kirk, *Eliot and His Age: T.S. Eliot's Moral Imagination in the Twentieth Century*, ISI Books, Wilmington DE, 2008.

Chapter 3

Metaphorical Stages of Impasse

Irreversibilities

Professor Butts' "Self-Operating Napkin,"[1] engineering comic Rube Goldberg's (1883-1970) most celebrated cartoon prototype, is also, at heart, a challenge to philosophic reflection, the wave/particle duality, as Werner Heisenberg (1901-1976) likened it, prior to the most superficial aspects of math and physics being popularized to the point of no meaning. How does the amusing cartoon revealing a complicated machine that ultimately does a simple thing relate to sub-atomic mysteries? Quantum optics tells us that velocity, slope, position and acceleration remain simply notational until the standard deviations are of such infinitesimal magnitude as to escape any visual or cognitive predictability because of the gaining variables. A grab-bag of mouthfuls that makes for a continuous rash of spectacular headlines, huge Coronal Mass Ejections and grinding, colossal Black Holes. One would think that Cosmic particulars are far removed from anything remotely environmental. Herein lies the philosopher's stone, and it is cold, and verging on irrelevant. Lowering one's sights to beneath the stratosphere, there remains just enough daylight between the utter obsolescence of *H. sapiens*, and the implacable fluxions of the biosphere, to empower the certainty that philosophy, and her annals, have something remarkable to add to the current debacle of our presence on earth. Both certainty, and her oppositional bulwark of maleffects. There is a tensile strength of that arc between these two antipodes. The oscillations are propounded in the mind, where we are condemned to zero by so much severely ill-boding data, or, from sheer weariness ignore all the signs.

But consider one salient through story to this problem: the ecologically disastrous signs have so multiplied by 2022 as to have formed their own tableau, a semiotics of doom calling out for intelligent re-design, a revivification of clear and steady conceptualization.

The whiplash of uncertainty is, itself, like every life and death toll, a natural constant, though physicist Paul Dirac (1902-1984) questioned whether, in fact, constants were actually constant.[2] It might well be an incessance, byproducts of permeability that allow for eco-political circumstances, both in theoretical constructs, but also in consciousness. On the battle fields and in every dwelling. It's here, in the brain, as clearly as if one were to leap out from the summit (25,531') of Namjagbarwa Peak and face the consequences, head on. Obvious, but not entirely. In the conception of acceleration, of the steepness of a slope, the true story of any hypothetical configuration becomes obscured. The mass, whether living or blunt matter, is at once obfuscated in the rubble of stones, glaciers, air, water, and all other elements, en route to an untimed obscurity. If the questions are those of number or distribution, of range and speed, of time and space, there are ample mathematical equations to represent what is occurring. But if the express goal is something other than a position or velocity-time graph; an actual idea-evolution construct, then the burden of seeing it devolves to the nature of the question, and the reality of answerability. We answer to whom? Our corpses have purpose, the ideas that jettisoned oneself especially so.

But to whom, and what? Our communities? Our entire species? Or to some constellation that is the totality of all life forms cohabiting every square inch of the earth's surface? Relations or relationships? Archae-ecological palimpsests? Inferential, incipient and/or explicit communities? Ecology does not psychoanalyze at the level of bipartisan meaning. It cannot. Or not yet. And, if ever it were to presume such cognitive faculties, we have no way to reach that meaning in a quantum sense. We are left out of that which is in us, around us. Whilst we seem to want, to want more and more, that more has long been substantiated in every view, each setting in which an individual finds itself. We are coming ever closer to a world of interspecies reckoning that may translate, for us, into the most spellbinding epiphanies our species has ever been granted. It is possible.

The very plurality of settings infinitizes minutiae in a propagation that has no boundaries, certainly between life forms. Yes, perimeters exist – 62 miles above the earth's surface, approximately, for the upper level of oxygen molecules; few inches of compressed perspective behind Leonardo's Ginevra de' Benci; and, reaching back in time, all those exploratory organic networks that were self-catalytic and projected memory into their chemical reactions, providing for the alleged earliest conditionals for life to originate. Similarly, we can comment upon the spate of current irreversibilities with respect to planetary limits. When a lake dries up, or one ecosystem turns into another. But there is nonetheless a biological continuity that follows upon every limit, opening up the illimitable (the word itself conjures subjectivity run riot from language to language, English to Chinese, Telugu to Aramaic).

By that liberation ontology, one can imagine an ocean with no shores; such a body of water as to defy the laws of reversibility, breaking the dramatic fourth wall to such a degree that knowledge has neither roots nor endpoints. An infinite dimensional space (think Hilbert topology) bifurcating contact and non-contactual vectors of interaction are also communication spaces. They are intuitive, but thinking in such terms, one can easily imagine layering communication space within any derivative of the biosphere. This would comprise a geographical information system that, as previously intimated, encompasses GFSs (geographical feeling systems). Landsat and Ikonos earth-observing satellites have helped connect on-the-ground data points with actual individuals, not least, those in the tragic *rarity* categories, where the premise of endangered species, and its realization through the accumulation of marked selective sampling, exposes a pattern of human behavior that is, by its second nature, utterly, perhaps irreversibly, tainting the idea, first liberated by Milesian philosopher Anaximander (610 BC – 546 BC) in the sense of the apeiron, or indefiniteness. Milesian philosophy (6th century BC) generally speaking can be said to have been credited with systematic philosophical methods. Such imagined machinations in the world are not the obvious targets of reflection with which we were once familiar. That is the result of methodology being empirically stripped of its metaphysical necessity, so that strict logic prevails. But what is logic that should demand of any organism the "validity" of its thoughts?

In strange tidings we wend through a labyrinth that offers no clues to its purposes, beginning or end. Weight, weightless; current, past; floating ideas. Imagery that emerges instantaneously without the least explanation for its origins or itinerary lend to the restless cortical domains something akin to actual recklessness, uncharted neural triggering. Chlorophyll with no surcease. We read a corollary of such yarns and "poses" in Jean-Paul Sartre's (1905-1980) autobiography, *The Words* (Les Mots, 1963). [3] Every recollection of youth, as *invented* by the 59-year-old philosopher, swivels towards evanescence. No two objects of reality, living and unliving, can pair up because of the irreconcilable truths within our shattered mirrors. We posit that these fundaments are shadowed by the gravitas of contraries. Whether we say "yes" or "no" a similar chain of events will unfold, cascade. All devolves to frailty of mind, metaphors at an impasse, views without a view. What does that mean? The invention of a view that assays to take full advantage of the tangle of images. Elsewhere we have categorized such feral, jungle elicitations as quantum entanglement.

The illogic breathes, divulging imaginative powers of which we were, until the moment, unaware. A full stop, impossible for those still alive, remains as much a mystery as a quest, like forever and a day.

The point to such rhetoric and rambling is this: What is the most potent argument in favor of the blind alley? Where theories of uncertainty yield to stark re-consideration. Where gridlock liberates the idea of freedom in a way no actual freedom herself can manage? Heisenberg would never have attempted to measure freedom. Unlike uncertainty, we know it when we lose it. But the mind is sluggish in recognizing it once regained. John Milton could not find reason enough to grasp it but through Christ's more stolid resolve than that of the *Devil.*[4] The place (Paradise) meant nothing. "To feel atoms," writes Felice C. Frankel and George M. Whitesides, "the tip of the finger must be about the same size as they are."[5] Hence, the atomic force microscope. But it has no traction upon psychology, or philosophy. Frederick Turner speaks of a "Boolean logic" driving the addition of one "increment" after another "to our cumulative attitude"; "a sort of default-judgment toward things in general that is about 61.8 percent positive and 38.2 percent negative. This ratio happens, very interestingly, to be that of the golden section…"[6] The proportionate inflection point occurs, then, much like the odd but constant fact of narrow elections that winnow majorities to the point of nail-biting uncertainty. How is it democracies are so divided in near equal measures of counter-anxiety, anger, frustration and compromise? Like the Heisenberg Uncertainty, the (Wolfgang) Pauli exclusion principle declares that the fermion particle (electrons, protons and their "spin-statistics" [1925, and in 1940] cannot occupy the same space simultaneously.[7/8] This is a scaling issue, like that discussed earlier in terms of projecting the actual number of microbial species on the planet. At human scale, ironically, we understand sizes of beds, cans of food, handles, manual tools, the basic shape and weight of bricks, and the like. But not our own impact. Thomas Hobbes (1588-1679), discussing language, mind and imagination, wrote in his *The Elements of Law* that these scales in human usage were necessarily "arbitrarily imposed".[9] Yes, and no. The hand prefers that which scales to the obvious size of a hand, although our eyes are always larger than our mouths. Our fantasies as vast as the universe. All such nuances that have transformed into metrics, involves a topology of spaces that undercut logic, objectivity, the absolute simplistic concept of progress.

What can be adduced by the flip of a coin, or any statistical chance occurrence? Induction and deduction rely equally on inference from a conceptual substrate that may be observable truth, or simply referential assumption. In either case, our logic is not up to the task of resolving anything with near the unambiguity as gravity. As all velocity and mass have come to express for billions of years. Physics works with biology. But ecological rules cannot judge behavior based upon their conjoining amplifications, not with, for example, at least 2x10x25 molecules in an average human; 100 trillion atoms per cell; or the estimated "42 million protein molecules" in one human cell.[10]

Points of Trajectory

Those ancient points of trajectory and impact continue unabated in every act of sentience, or weight of dialectic. Our responses have no meaning outside the languages we wield amongst ourselves. Within the crosshairs of human ratiocinations, we still find the anthropic bias[11] overwhelming in its instant commandeering of all perception and deliberation. No theory has ever undermined this horizon barrier that is both instantaneous and by accumulation lethal to ecosystems at both centrifugal and centripetal topologies. Primary examples include: human agriculture, urban space, roads and traffic, point-and-non-point sources of air, soil and water pollution, animal consumption and all the exploitive and developmental syndromes contributing to the Human Appropriation of Net Primary Production and Products of Photosynthesis.[12] If the earth were to write her autobiography in a language that humans would try to comprehend, which they do not, it would be no love/hate relationship, no relationship at all.[13]

But human self-abnegation is statistically minimal. That most people *want* to live may come as a philosophical surprise, but not a practical one, given that birth and death are painful (for most beings). Whereas living need not be, or not continually so. Still, the ratios of joy to sorrow do not favor the proportion of ideals supporting a life well lived. Struggle and misery dominate most of humanity's existence and what psychologists term "embodied cognition".[14] Such encompassed actions can be correlated with at least 370 "constants" in physics and math.[15] It is a dizzying *computation*, as Hobbes would have likened its collective effect on human thought, and all the after-images that build sensation, reason and unreason. Such constants, as outlined by Stanislav Sykora, "Extra Byte," and Castano Primo, span the "Universal" ones – speed of light, gravitation, "Quantum/Charge ratio" and the like. They involve all known aspects of electromagnetic causes and effects, radiation, "electron and atomic physics," "physico-chemical" mass, charge, volume, etc. As well as the conditions, circumstances and outcomes of everything we think we know about sub-atomic particles ("rest mass," wavelengths, "half-life times"), the "microwave background" and "metrics of the known Universe," with all of its moving objects, spin dynamics; and then the myriad of "conventional engineering constants" and calendrical units.[16]

Correlating math and physics, cosmology and the powering hydrogen fusion of a star, with human emotions, is no science. For centuries philosophers have waxed in light and darkness to find comparable expressions by which to gauge the meaning and derivations of a *state of being*. Some have suggested that the dynamic involving "human flourishing" or not, is a ratio of 2.9 favoring the positive.[17] From bestowing greater attention values, to "cardio-vascular aftereffects," even the change of "front brain asymmetry" each have been attributed to "adaptive and maladaptive" outcomes, depending on the stage and degree of good feelings.[18] The undergirding of this presumed golden ratio abets two distinct layers of our reality, as finely tuned in the thinking of Freud and Kierkegaard. Writes the former, "The evidence of psycho-analysis [sic] shows that almost every intimate emotional relation between two people which lasts for some time – marriage, friendship, the relations between parents and children – leaves a sediment of feelings of aversion and hostility, which have first to be eliminated by repression."[19] Kierkegaard, in turn, references a "multiplicity of categories" when examining, in his stunning meditation, *Either/Or*, the notions of self, of choice, and of the compulsion to "realize" one's own life amongst a universe of others. He declares, "Not until the individual himself is the universal is it possible to realize the ethical. It is this secret which lies within the conscience…"[20] Here we come upon the pluripotentiality of any system. The individual, itself a system of interior biological whorls, forever wrestles with its outward gene pool populations which cannot escape the reality of its species affiliation. The individual is left out.

These embedded, trans-frameworks for grasping relations between evolution and entropy occupy a mind, many minds, at work. What is it they are doing? Why should we think to further involve ourselves? What predictions can be made of an individual, its species and the niches it occupies, for whatever reasons? Daniel R. Brooks and E. O. Wiley, back in the mid-1980s, discussed bio-predictability in general, as differentiated by "a stochastic component" (one randomly determined) that begs the question (they ask) as to all those "novel predictions by other biologists [which] may hinge on what each one requires from a theory." For their part Brooks and Wiley see non-violence as a more fitting narrative to explain "natural efficient causes" than the meting out of harm. This supposition supports the 2.9 generalization.

It suggests that all the constants are predictable, those which are "extrinsic to the substance being observed". This is in stark contrast to the "inherent processes" of an organism's various proximities to energy, efficiency, revelatory ideation (said proximity being of a poetic, not empirical character) and morphological change. These are the traits far more likely to follow the gravity of genetics – that is, the inevitable sum rule leading to a dominant phenotype – whilst yielding to the unpredictability of individuals, communities, species and their rarified or highly populated circumstances that are the true essence of biological interdependency. In other words, the probability of a distributed pleasure exceeds that of pain. A joy taken in life, accepted from birth, propounds more populous pressure on the organism than the corresponding pains and looming demise. Whether the distribution parities of such fertility are the result of outbreeding or inbreeding will lead to similar "genetic drift," and hence, greater population diversity.[21]

Being caught out in what can only be viewed as a spellbinding moment, our lives on earth, warrants consideration of a biochemical theory that holds to no constant assertion. Rather, it is the subject of ongoing qualification. It neither prepares the individual to be part of a community, nor denies unique identity. Lacking any probable cause or consequence in biospheric terms, the languages we wield to awkwardly get at what we mean, let alone what *it* means, are thoroughly insufficient to account for the phenomena we perceive and/or imagine.

The worst forms of insult – nuclear war, ecosystem destructions, animal and habitat cruelty – underscore a species-wide malignancy, much remarked upon. What then -? – is no relevant query. "Finish your sweet, so that they can take your plate away!" wrote Proust in *Swann's Way*.[22] Adding somewhat later on, "…the torment which had forced him to leave his own house had lost its sharpness when it lost its uncertainty…"[23] Our ambiguities are the full fate of philosophy, impossibly exasperating nuances of life in its moment-by-moment duration. Or, as Camus elaborated, "There exists an obvious fact that seems utterly moral: namely, that a man is always a prey to his truths. Once he has admitted them, he cannot free himself from them."[24] He was speaking of existential philosophers intent upon escape. The aspiration for exile from their own creation, perceptions of a Universe that have become their sole rationale for continuing. But also the coy, not unanticipated reception with which they are greeted when the unthinkable escape is eventualized.

Goethe, Kepler, Spinoza, Humboldt and Darwin each had their own half-spin, like an electron gaining and losing steam at the same zeptosecond, on such matters of faith and the eternal question of renewal. One could quote and cite and reiterate endlessly such points of view at any given instant throughout the arduous trek that has been humanity's apparent destiny, until now. To try and save oneself upon a ledge, or between the pages of a book, or from room to room, slow-moving, in any of the grand museums of the world, that, again, by insistent predilections, we have built up to ensure in our time the edifice of logic that is mortality, from cemetery to cemetery. These things matter. They do not matter. They can or cannot hold us like gravity. Rather, our curated experiences and creations cry out in solemn testimony to what we want and know we must give up. This is all a circumambulatory crisis of free-will and dissipating consciousness.

Ecologically, there is no more assured tragedy for us, because we have loved and lost everything at the end of our odyssey. The more we have loved, so much more the difficulties of saying good-bye. Change course, wake up and utter *hello* in any, in every language, and the segue to post-dialectical thinking at once takes charge of our pessimism. George Wilhelm Friedrich Hegel (1770-1831) tried to work out the phases in his investigations into "the naïve unconscious symbolical," "the sublime," "reflective symbolism," "development of classic art," "romantic art," and the "formal independence of character," as pillars of his thesis differentiating the "philosophy of nature" from the "philosophy of spirit."[25] These same phases Immanuel Kant (1724-1804) described as the "fundamental causes of the recognition of multiplicity…"[26] by which he referred to phenomena and noumena, interior and exterior objects that could be grasped by the senses or by reason, or both. The importance of the aesthetic experience to phenomenology must shoulder what both Hegel and Kant knew to be a preternatural expectation that sadness might be transcended in the course of evolution. But we don't know. Passage of time ameliorates certain pangs and not others. Our lives are too brief to dull some degree of continuous suffering that lives and dies within us. Yet, any philosophical courtship of what we think of as *nature* necessarily equivocates on the issue of the human Self. Multiplicity is far easier to capture in mind, than the one, which eludes all constraints by dint of her constancy of self-reference in every thought turned inward. We cannot avoid this law of apperception that multiplies its vainglorious penchant; of a thoughtfulness that beats as tightly as the heart. It reflects upon its own substantiation as a fully contained mystery of selfness, rushing at all times to perceive outside that enigma of Being-in-Itself as allied with being-for-others. That was a crucial distinction for both Heidegger and Sartre, but never came close to elucidating the actual chasm that continues to prevent our ability as humans to grasp, amid multitudes around us, the Other. Even as the interdependencies of these two fundamental determinants of any biome remain steadfast, if totally vulnerable, our own limited spheres of relation devolve to immediate fellowships, inner family ties, a degree of correspondence with acquaintances. The rest is all chance. We can live with that if we can get past what Albert Camus meant when he wrote, "Man is the only creature who refuses to be what he is." What are we?

How we might think of such *strange ones*, these chances, those multitudes out there, correlate with methods of analysis that range across an unfathomable territory. *Topophilia* in the anthropological realm, *biophilia* as an ecological ideal. Yi-Fu Tuan, a central figure in the investigation of sensory mapping from culture to culture, quotes writer Malcolm Cowley, "Almost every work set on paper involves a choice. The writing of one page might involve hundreds of moral decisions."[27] Such pointillism on the constant verge of change, the personification of ambiguity, records nothing less than a forever shifting target, one never known for resolution. Philosophy cannot resolve its placement or meaning. Ingrained ambivalence is the hallmark of all deep history and shallow presence. Our choices are so volatile as to deftly defy the nature of stability. All expression reaffirms our ephemerality, and inability to speak with certitude on any topic, or point of view.

Mapping Pluralities

Science, like the arts, simply moves the imagination from moment, detail and overview to some other fancy. No matter how inspiring or methodical the expression and analyses, imagination is cornered by its human hosts. Einstein was a huge proponent of this awkward truth. The plurality of said mapping is the perverse end game of optionless cultures. Time dependent, that time is running out. It has always been running out, though in the 21st century, the stakes are uniquely terminal. Time shows its nudity. This is a portal upon nihilism which humanity has never before experienced. For us, in this generation, we have no idea what we're doing, what it will look like. We interpolate, deduce, use artificial intelligence or simply caudal materialism in mind to envision the end, a new beginning, and their respective probabilities. As for probability distribution, our ecodynamic forensics are as limited as the brain (human brain) that processes whatever information is gleaned. Our metabolic options are not up to the task of surpassing the ecological liabilities of our humanness. Our most eager energy expenditures, like that of the cheetah, tend to even out roughly 2.5 times our resting rate. We can only run so fast, so far. But at 2.5, our rough-hewn impacts are seemingly unlimited, can go on forever.

This web of familiar and unfamiliar was graphically enshrined in what some have hailed as the, to-date, earliest known human expression/remnants: footprints and handprints beautifully preserved from Quesang, on the Tibetan plateau, dated to between "169,000 and 226,000" years ago.[28] The travertine rock formation has been eroded on all sides so that its surface stands like a parietal pedestal against time, a declaration of anonymity, like some tomb of the unknown philosophers, thought to be two children, whose lives in the middle Pleistocene represent to us one more piece of evidentiary silence that, once, had strived to be heard, to be remembered.[29] Given such adamantine traces of our near original world, our human surface of experiences, the last few thousand years of intellectual debate appear by contrast hopelessly trivial. Think, for example, of a Cartesian versus a Spinozist at the heart of "a decades-long conflict in the upper echelons of postwar French academic philosophy…"[30] A grab-bag bibliothèque of what George Steiner has elsewhere conjured the notion of "real presences."[31] They were there. We are here. The improvisational space between us all invites the ancient Greek ἀπορῐ́ᾱ (aporíā), the impasse no thought experiment can mollify. All the fact finding from cosmology and archaeology to history and today's news cycles provide second-by-second contexts that have changed perpetually. There is nothing to be done for or about it. Our statements do nothing. All the computations lead nowhere. The sum total of philosophical conjectures fill-up almanacs and encyclopedias. To the extent that we can delineate a Moses Maimonides from a Jakob Böhme, Marx from Wittgenstein, is nothing but the cumulative weight we should expect from any idea in the mental landscapes that have been our joy or curse to traverse, notions to gyrate, feelings to pirouette. These defeasible, non-demonstrative conclusions to a dialectical experience have originated the dangling modifiers that are crucial to the perpetuation of philosophy as something relevant. Reasoning that holds out the hope of being inside the discussion. Whereas the dialectics themselves represent the fiction of our trying to remain in any sense, present.

Outside, there is free space to wander. We'll speak more of such space in a moment. But for now, we understand that with no conditionals of logic, the illogical strides. Those children in Tibet 200,000 years ago might well have been our future, cast in identical aspirations towards the ever unknown, unappreciated or respected. How does one respect the future? Everyone inherits a personal database of opinion that renders anything approaching a group mind ridiculous, loathsome at best, except perhaps during reigns of terror that have from century to century stripped a populous of any discourse, provisioning a single tool that is used against itself, what Thomas Hobbes would come to think of as the most important concession possible by human beings: that which brings them to conclude that the "Commonwealth" is the only possible antidote to a state of nature. With the publication in Philadelphia of Thomas Paine's *Common Sense* on January 10, 1776 an American revolution was invoked, directed principally at one man, George III.[32] In France, collective frustration at the preconditions of their misery was targeted nor merely at its most tangible emblems – the *Ancien Régime* and Citizen Louise Capet (Louis XVI) – but, psychologically, at climate change which had all but laid siege to France by one weather disaster after another. In Brazil, a more sophisticated approach placed correlative blame on its 38th President for his alleged *crimes against humanity*. The same should have occurred with America's 45th President. Similar concussions of reason and the angered mob can be mapped in more than half the countries of the world.[33] Democracies are fracturing.[34] How else to explain a system that empowers the role of one right wing senator's ability to undermine – by cause and effect – a nation's desperate efforts to halt climate change?[35] Extrapolate from one individual's political motives to those of "15 major fossil fuel-generating countries [that] will produce roughly 110% more coal, oil, and gas in 2030 than would be necessary to limit warming to 1.5 degrees Celsius above pre-industrial levels…"[36]

Aesthetically and philosophically, these tumults should have been predicted, forsworn and de-implemented. History looks back upon these nightmares and what does it see? Look at the delapidated state of Herstmonceux Manor in East Sussex by 1890.[37] A lovely setting of the wild having overtaken the then 450-year-old castle, and the lives of its countless owners. Unlike a Tintern or Llanthony Abbey, which remain in a similar state[38] (the Romantic passion for ruins) Herstmonceux was rebuilt, every brick, into its present Queen's University. We liken this, the present, to even a recent past, 200 years ago. The comparisons fail across the map. In Paris, hell meted by a guillotine. While across the Channel in the UK, artists like Paul Sandby, John Crome, Edward Pugh, Thomas Garnett, Walter Watts, Thomas Compton, and Philip James de Loutherbourg were engendering a living renaissance of rapturous local landscape paintings. In every human commons, individuals making little histories, history destroys each individual. With few exceptions (immortal cell lines, for example,[39] or large tortoises that scarcely ever grow old when situated in largely stress-free environments) the biological fate of all entities, populations and individuals, is undeviating when scaled to life spans per species. This has always been the case, until about 30,000 years for our kind, when there was "a dramatic increase in longevity in the modern humans of the Early Upper Paleolithic."[40] In addition to what anthropologists Rachel Caspari and Sang-Hee Lee have summarized as the "cultural innovations," of that time period, they also suggest that patterns of "delayed maturation, slower growth, higher fertility, and increased longevity" all worked in favor of the "grandmother hypothesis," separating hunter gathering societies from other great apes. In other words, an investment in intergenerational transfers of knowledge fundamentally served the process of "inclusive fitness" at the grandparent level, a potentially decisive demographic boost in terms of the O/Y (old to young adult) ratios[41] and what we are quick to characterize as the prefigurements of human civilization.

The Massive Fragmentation

But that is no constant. It boasts of no specific mathematical or physical units of measurement other than the "Great Acceleration". We have never witnessed a uniform code of behavior specific to *H. sapiens*. Has the rate of negative drift sped up, since the 3.3-million-year-old date generally assigned to our first use of tools (the Old Stone Age)? All that we may adduce is a massive fragmentation of morals and immorality, by any definition. Calendar years follow our assignations, presumptions, cultural mores. But the numbers, as we have reiterated time and again, are, in fact, fictions. This concept, once absorbed, leaves us, as Saul Bellow wrote, no different than the universal "dangling man" (1944).

The chasm of manifestations that derives from our concepts of paleolithic history is more persuasive than any solid grounding. Our individual fluctuations have no population-level equivalencies, that we know of, across any taxonomic suite other than microbial and viral communities. In other words, we have found a convenience in marking our journey as a species parenthetically by use of those metaphors (midges, microbes, etc.,) at the nadir of philosophical concerns seeking to embrace applicable microcosms and metaphors that mirror the human condition, somehow. This is one way of describing the price we have paid, and the planet has suffered by our alleged evolution. Hence, the metaphors of our growth, laid out in phases of our incredibly short species history, remain a mystery and a terror. No less dependent on our large-scale, landscape-sized contexts of contiguous ecosystems, as the atoms in our molecules in our cells wherein "colloidal-scale physics" are at work.[42] Is there a philosophy of cytoplasm and surrounding membranes that connects meaningfully for us, in real-time, with, say, a Sannazaro or Petrus Christus? Or with the emotions of a lobster about to be boiled alive? We, the entirely biased ones, have no way to answer such general questions. While our minds live in that *general* tone, as individuals we wax between details that suit us. There are no catch-phrases for this series of unkind phase-states. But there are, it would appear to logic, quantum bridges between micro- and macro. Between the one and the many. Such connective areas of the imagination, and the strange attractors[43] meriting their interest, are, indeed, logical. But this is also all of a human bias. We are left, by that reckoning, with the corrosive fringes of cognition and must forever begin anew from those fragments, regardless of their combining particularity or through-stories.

To summarize the foregoing: In every instance, "construction" and "construal" are fundamental to a metaphorical address that has no pre-ordained set of rules or tests by which it either catches the meaning in some secondary or tertiary sense, or elaborates by way of a linguistic bridge which is our way forward and backward.[44] In assessing endings by O. Henry (William Sydney Porter), Anton Chekhov, James Joyce, Katherine Anne Mansfield, Bernard Malamud and others, Charles E. May speaks of "unending endings."[45] By that construct there are rules. By the *construal*, interpretation. As in Gerald Manley Hopkins' (1844-1889) "God's Grandeur," a poem which opens with that legendary continuum: "Generations have trod, have trod, have trod;…"[46] In a purely linguistic guise, the conjured imagery is "open ended and heterogeneous,"[47] notwithstanding semantics that relate to pairing by understood participants whose reasoning rests upon shared basics. That sharing presupposes neither temporality, space or biological unity. There is no rule that holds to a single species reading of the text(s), although we assume there must be something akin to it, and we are its sole incarnation.

Therein exists the logic of a language and its impressions within the textual. But ecologically, the words, stories, and critical exchanges are subject to no such behavioral requirement. More than one species can access any of this, though we presume otherwise. The *presumption* is the metaphor prior to even the first word of a conversation. No matter what we say, or read into it, our behavior can never meet the test of conversion to a different form of the interpretive. By form we invoke no *bridge too far*, shan shui landscape portraiture throughout Chinese history. Pathways we are both capable and incapable of perceiving. Beyond perception, those earlier referenced fringes figure in our options. We divine something that we cannot see, or understand. We grasp the contours of a wind as it passes through a forest, or picks up the spume of a churning sea. Usually, impasse suggests the mediation process, at least legally.[48] In biophysics, one of the most "elusive" and universally interesting impasse pertains to the distribution and ultimate human manipulation of plant cell walls, and pectin, a polysaccharide, the most prodigious of all carbohydrates.[49] In the realms of physics, "mathematical inconsistencies" keep at odds General Relativity and Quantum Mechanics, the large view, the minute view, both resisting a grand unified theory of nature.[50] In politics, as Aristotle so amply descried, management of laws generated by the state are entirely vulnerable, both from within and without. He cites oligarchies and democracies, referencing the Athenians and Lacedaemonians as "proof" of that continuous irresolution.[51] Even ethical utilitarianism (Kantian strict rationality) devolves at times to the fundamental contradiction that "sometimes telling a lie is exactly what should be done to prevent an unmitigated catastrophe."[52]

Such dyads of logic betraying the logical generics in life are further magnified by (one can't say *every*, but the impression is there) scientific methodologies whose typically strict rubrics adhere to anthropic self-propagation. Vertebrates, thought without any cause but the self-serving one to be the most "intelligent" group of organisms on the planet, are also the least successful, certainly in terms of numbers. The non-chordate notochord phylae comprise at least 97% of all organisms.[53] Combining all of these seemingly contradictory sectors of evolutionary growth throughout the phylogenetic legacies of which our species has taken note, has led to some very emphatic dilemmas. Writes Paul Ehrlich, "conservation biologists should stop focusing so much attention and effort on saving endangered taxa. By the time something is endangered, it often is too late to save it…"[54]

Anticipatory Inevitabilia

Anticipatory inevitabilia ("ai"), is the angst abutting post-morality related stasis; all that inertia which is the machine of our mortality as it self-implodes, or recognizes the looming unavoidability. Those with the strength to out-maneuver early onset depression over the intractable knots of our ecological conatus will perform a variety of heroisms. They add up. Do they outweigh their opposition? The question haunts by the force of internal wrangling of one's nature. We do not know of this dualistic condition in any other species. How could we know? Only by more investigative methodological missteps. Pejorative stumbles. To assay a pragmatic resolve to this assertive principle founded on all that is presumed to be inexorable is an endeavor of very mixed content, at least from any historical/archaeological perspective. In discussing all such contradictions, Michel Foucault lent numerous levels of astonishing clarity to "the principle of cohesion" that he believed should act upon "hidden unity" to thereby hinder the futile and unnecessary proliferation of additional contradictions, almost as "a procedural obligation," "a heuristic rule".[55] In their fascinating study of objectivity, Lorraine Daston and Peter Galison acknowledge the contemporary (and by implication, historic) compulsion to manipulate. What we take to mean, again, engaging in a scientific method that is altogether intrusive. They write (in reference to nanotechnology) of "intervention by the scientist, through the image, to make things, to cut, move, combine, weld, or set in operation."[56] These verbs, in turn, mirror the word "take" as defined by the Endangered Species Act of December 27, 1973 (Public law: 93–205): "to harass, harm, pursue, hunt, shoot, wound, kill, trap, capture, or collect, or to attempt to engage in any such conduct." "Incidental take is an unintentional, but not unexpected, taking."[57]

Is this, perhaps, a way of validating one of the fundaments of "buddhahood," as enshrined by the eloquent Mahayana philosopher, Nagarjuna (c.150- c.250 CE) who wrote, "Regarding the internal and external spheres, When thoughts of 'I' and 'mine' have ceased, Grasping too will be arrested…"[58] If we think of that annihilation of volitions as the ultimate biological reconciliatory mode of preferred being on earth, is that a condition we deduce, extrapolate, aspire to, knowing the futility involved? Is it a general prerequisite for life, given how every enterprise of each organism at least appears to adhere to principles of self-preservation? If so, then we must allow that such attempts – more legally futile than not – as the ESA of 1973, came into being on the basis of that still small voice within the legislative maelstrom recognizing an ethic, however incommensurate it has proved to be out in the real world of discriminating altruisms.

If that self is fundamentally preservative, the question arises as to whether *questions* are appropriate for the matter envisioned. If we cease to ask, do we cease to be humans? Are we capable of non-asking? Does that comport with Being, when all intuitive import suggests that such in-Being is inherently what our brains *must* do? Analogies cascade from bias to bias in terms of the traditional scala naturae ("Ladder of Being") human superiority syndrome.[59] Because this goes to the core of what we do, questions, answers, non-answers and choices/decisions frame what, elsewhere, we have described as a compound expressive" totality of any given individual. Pop-psychology describes something like thousands of questions per hour, on average; and the fact that children – at least in one study – appear to ask "73 questions" every day.[60] If these combined elements of human existence translate into method, logic, anticipation, assumption, resignation and compliance, then our framework for the future is fixed, ultimately complacent, even if the data pool keeps changing second by second. Our faculty for awareness has at times derailed apathy, certainly. But the scale always moderates towards inertia at the population level. This is no societal anomaly but an apparent absolute inflection of the status quo.

"Rooster at Gut Aiderbichl Sanctuary, Salzburg, Austria," Photo © J. G. Morrison.

There can be no philosophical status quo, given what we have suggested above. Similarly, there has never been biological unconsciousness. There are interests continually given, some to disorientation, others to precise route-finding. Human heresy of thought, or abundance of enthusiasm, cannot count upon a similar compass reading anywhere but in an individual's mind. The species remains isolated, in our case, amongst like, or un-like- minded members of a community. But their community of communities, speaking at the taxon level, has no comparable aggregate. Not because there might not exist the possibility of such a thing, but, rather, because probability theories have no way of proving anything like a case outside our own referential powers of guesswork, regardless of the intensity, probity, even alleged authenticity of our investment in the ideal of possible breakthrough (interspecies) relations.

That said, we are incapable, perhaps, of forsaking the ideal. If that day should ever come, the conversation will have been sadly completed. In the meantime, the orientation of our ideals may be the only reason our species still exists at all, given the degree to which we have abused the fulcrum of our mechanical powers over all the Others. It is the history of idealism, the matrix of everything we imagine beyond impasse, that gives us to understand something far beyond probability.

Endnotes

[1] By Rube Goldberg, https://www.rubegoldberg.com/artwork/self-operating-napkin/

[2] Werner Heisenberg, *The Physicist's Conception of Nature*. Harcourt, Brace, New York, NY, 1958. See also, Elion, W. J.; Matters, M.; Geigenmüller, U.; Mooij, J. E. (1994), "Direct demonstration of Heisenberg's uncertainty principle in a superconductor", Nature, 371 (6498): 594–595, Bibcode:1994Natur.371..594E, doi:10.1038/371594a0, S2CID 4240085; See also, Huang, Yichen (24 May 2011). "Entropic uncertainty relations in multidimensional position and momentum spaces". Physical Review A. 83 (5): 052124. arXiv:1101.2944. Bibcode:2011PhRvA..83e2124H. doi:10.1103/PhysRevA.83.052124. S2CID 119243096. Lee Smolin, Einstein's unfinished revolution: the search for what lies beyond the quantum, Penguin, London, UK, 2019, pp. 92–93. See also, "How Constant Are The Constants Of Nature?" by Professor Geraint Lewis, Space Australia, May 16, 2020, https://spaceaustralia.com/feature/how-constant-are-constants-nature. In Lewis' essay he argues that "the fine-structure constant" which is "a dimensionless number, without units" is "related" to such other constants as electromagnetism, but its ultimate value remains elusive to the point of proving out "null results".

[3] Gallimard, Paris. English edition in 1964, translated by Bernard Frechtman, George Braziller, New York, NY. See "Jean-Paul Sartre's 'The Words'," George Braziller, *The Harvard Crimson*, December 8, 1964.

[4] See Barbara Lewalski, *Milton's Brief Epic: The Genre, Meaning, and Art of Paradise Regained*, Brown University Press, Providence, Rhode Island, 1966.

[5] *No Small Matter-Science On The Nanoscale*, The Belknap Press Of Harvard University Press, Cambridge, MA, 2009, p. 15.

[6] See *Beauty – The Value of Values*, by Frederick Turner, University Press of Virginia, Charlottesville and London, 1991, p. 75.

[7] Irving Langmuir, "The Arrangement of Electrons in Atoms and Molecules" *Journal of the American Chemical Society*. 41 (6): 868–934, 1919, doi:10.1021/ja02227a002.

[8] See "Violation of Heisenberg's Measurement-Disturbance Relationship by Weak Measurements," Lee A. Rozema, Ardavan Darabi, Dylan H. Mahler, Alex Hayat, Yasaman Soudagar, and Aephraim M. Steinberg, *Phys. Rev. Lett.* 109, 100404 – Published 6 September 2012; *Erratum Phys. Rev. Lett.* 109, 189902 (2012), https://journals.aps.org/prl/abstract/10.1103/PhysRevLett.109.100404

[9] See *The Elements of Law*, in J. C. A. Gaskin (ed.) *The Elements of Law, Natural and Politic*, Oxford University Press, Oxford UK, 1990, 5.2-3.

[10] See "A Cell Holds 42 Million Protein Molecules, Scientists reveal," by Jovana Drinjakovic, Temerty Faculty of Medicine, University of Toronto, January 17, 2018, https://temertymedicine.utoronto.ca/news/cell-holds-42-million-protein-molecules-scientists-reveal#:~:text=Ho's%20analysis%20reveals%20for%20the,between%201000%20and%2010%2C000%20molecules.

[11] See Nick Bostrom's text, *Anthropic Bias: Observation selection effects in science and philosophy*, https://www.anthropic-principle.com/q=book/table_of_contents/

[12] "Human Appropriation of Photosynthesis Products," by Stuart Rojstaczershannon, M. Sterling and Nathan J. Moore, 21 Dec 2001, Vol. 294, Issue 5551, pp. 2549-2552 doi: 10.1126/science.1064375; See also, Paudel S, Ovando-Montejo GA, Lant CL. Human Appropriation of Net Primary Production: From a Planet to a Pixel. *Sustainability*. 2021; 13(15):8606. https://doi.org/10.3390/su13158606, https://www.mdpi.com/2071-1050/13/15/8606#cite. Most recently, however, traditional "terrestrial biosphere models" (TBMs) were examined with respect to what is known as "CO_2 fertilization," namely "the historic increase of photosynthesis as [the] result of increasing atmospheric CO_2 concentrations" and this, say researchers, has to date skewed the extent to which human appropriation has actually intensified its intersect with the terrestrial sinks. See "A Constraint on historic growth in global photosynthesis due to increasing CO_2," by T. F. Keenan, X. Luo, M. G. DeKauwe, et al., *Nature*, Vol 600, https://doi.org/10.1038/s41586-021-04096-9, 8 December 2021, pp. 253-258.

[13] See "One Man's Vision: Learn By Listening To The Earth," by Patricia Brennan, *The Washington Post*, February 17, 1991, https://www.washingtonpost.com/archive/lifestyle/tv/1991/02/17/one-mans-vision-learn-by-listening-to-the-earth/ca9af77d-2477-4857-954f-9bdcf30bb4ca/

[14] Marmolejo-Ramos, F., Correa, J.C., Sakarkar, G. et al. Placing joy, surprise and sadness in space: a cross-linguistic study. *Psychological Research* 81, 750–763 (2017). https://doi.org/10.1007/s00426-016-0787-9, 18 July 2016, https://link.springer.com/article/10.1007/s00426-016-0787-9#citeas

[15] See "Constants of Physics and Mathematics," compiled by Stanislav Sykora, Extra Byte, and Castano Primo, *CODATA* 2019, doi: 10.3247/SL2Phys07.001, http://www.ebyte.it/library/educards/constants/ConstantsOfPhysicsAndMath.html

[16] ibid.

[17] Empirical evidence, with a sample size of N=188, over a duration of 28 days, was described by Barbara L. Frederickson and Marcia F. Losada in their research paper, "Positive Affect and the Complex Dynamics of Human Flourishing," *Am Psychol.* Author manuscript; available in PMC 2011 Jun 29, Am Psychol. 2005 Oct; 60(7): 678–686, doi: 10.1037/0003-066X.60.7.678, PMCID: PMC3126111, NIHMSID: NIHMS305179, PMID: 16221001, https://www.ncbi.nlm.nih.gov/pmc/articles/PMC3126111/; See also other research in this realm at the National Library of Medicine, https://pubmed.ncbi.nlm.nih.gov/?cmd=link&linkname=pubmed_pubmed&log%24=relatedarticles&logdbfrom=pmc&from_uid=16221001

[18] ibid, Frederickson and Losada.

[19] Freud cites Schopenhauer's story of the porcupines who have crowded together to keep from freezing in winter, only to eschew their chosen proximities because of the irritation of each other's quills. See *Group Psychology and the Analysis of the Ego*, by Sigmund Freud, Translated by James Strachey, No. 6, The International Psycho-Analytical Press, London and Vienna, 1922, p. 54.

[20] See Søren Kierkegaard, *Either/Or*, Abridged Edition, Edited by Steven L. Ross, Translated from the Danish by George L. Stengren, Perennial Library, Harper & Row, Publishers, New York, 1986, pp. 206-207.

[21] See *Evolution as Entropy – Toward a Unified Theory of Biology*, by Daniel R. Brooks and E. O. Wiley, University of Chicago Press, Chicago, Ill., 1986, pp. 306-307. See also, "The Genetic Variation in a Poopulation Is Caused by Multiple Factors," n.a., Scitable, *NatureEducation*, https://www.nature.com/scitable/topicpage/the-genetic-variation-in-a-population-is-6526354/; See also, Plomion, C., Chancerel, E., Endelman, J. et al. Genome-wide distribution of genetic diversity and linkage disequilibrium in a mass-selected population of maritime pine. *BMC Genomics* 15, 171 (2014). https://doi.org/10.1186/1471-2164-15-171; and see Abadía-Cardoso, A., Hernández-Guzmán, R., Varela-Romero, A. et al. Population genetics and species distribution modeling highlight conservation needs of the endemic trout from the Northern Sierra Madre Occidental. *Conserv Genet* 22, 629–643 (2021). https://doi.org/10.1007/s10592-021-01388-5

[22] *Swann's Way*, by Marcel Proust, Translated by C. K. Scott Moncrieff, With An Introduction By Justin O'Brien And Illustrations By Bernard Lamotte, The Limited Editions Club, New York, NY 1954, p. 270.

[23] ibid., Proust, p. 283.

[24] Albert Camus, from, *The Myth of Sisyphus and Other Essays*, Translated from the French by Justin O'Brien, Alfred A. Knopf, New York, NY, 1955, p.31

[25] See *The Philosophy of Art: Being The Second Part of Hegel's Aesthetik, In Which Are Unfolded Historically The Three Great Fundamental Phases Of The Art-Activity Of The World*, Translated by Wm. M. Bryant, D. Appleton & Co., New York, NY, 1879.

[26] See *Kant's Critical Philosophy*, Vol. II, *The Prolegomena To Any Future Metaphysic*, Translated, With Notes And Appendices by John P. Mahaffy and John H. Bernard, Macmillan And Co., London and New York, 1889, p. 177.

[27] In *Passing Strange and Wonderful – Aesthetics, Nature, And Culture*, by Yi-Fu Tuan, Island Press/Shearwater Books, Washington, D.C., Covelo, CA, 1993, p. 219.

[28] See "Chinese Scientist Hopes to Conserve What May Be the World's Oldest Art," by Chad De Guzman, *Time Magazine*, October 18, 2021, https://time.com/6107313/oldest-prehistoric-art/

[29] See "Earliest parietal art: Hominin hand and foot traces from the middle Pleistocene of Tibet" by David D. Zhang, Matthew R. Bennett, Hai Cheng, Leibin Wang, Haiwei Zhang, Sally C. Reynolds, Shengda Zhang, Xiaoqing Wang, Teng Li, Tommy Urban, Qing Pei, Zhifeng Wu, Pu Zhang, Chunru Liu, Yafeng Wang, Cong Wang, Dongju Zhang and R. Lawrence Edwards, 10 September 2021, *Science Bulletin.* doi: 10.1016/j.scib.2021.09.001

[30] See "Descartes, Spinoza, And The Impasse Of French Philosophy: Ferdinand Alquié Versus Martial Gueroult," by Knox Peden, MIH, Cambridge University Press, 28 July 2011, https://www.cambridge.org/core/journals/modern-intellectual-history/article/abs/descartes-spinoza-and-the-impasse-of-french-philosophy-ferdinand-alquie-versus-martial-gueroult/E62498A67B8E860AA9FF99B25001BC40

[31] *Real Presences*, by George Steiner, The University of Chicago Press, Chicago, Ill., 1989.

[32] See Robert A. Ferguson (July 2000). "The Commonalities of Common Sense". *William and Mary Quarterly*. 57 (3): 465–504. doi:10.2307/2674263. JSTOR 2674263.

[33] See the Carnegie Endowment For International Peace, "Democracy, Conflict, and Governance Program," https://carnegieendowment.org/programs/democracy/

[34] Writes Thomas Carothers, "The U.S. political system is indeed beset by a high degree of polarization and a low sense of common purpose. Should we blame democracy itself, or should we blame ourselves for the pathologies of our own politics?" from *American Interest*, January 16, 2019, https://carnegieendowment.org/2019/01/16/is-democracy-problem-pub-78137.

[35] See "Key to Biden's Climate Agenda Likely to Be Cut Because of Manchin Opposition," by Coral Davenport, *The New York Times*, October 15, 2021. He "strongly opposes the clean electricity program…" https://www.nytimes.com/2021/10/15/climate/biden-clean-energy-manchin.html\

[36] See "The world plans to produce far more fossil fuel than it should to stay under dangerous climate limits, UN says," by Rachel Ramirez, October 20, 2021, *CNN Business*, https://www.cnn.com/2021/10/20/business/fossil-fuel-production-gap-climate/index.html

[37] Views of the British Isles, in the Photochrom print collection, http://hdl.loc.gov/loc.pnp/pp.pgz; Print no. "10316".; Title from the Detroit Publishing Co., Catalogue J-foreign section, Detroit, Mich.: Detroit Publishing Company, 1905.

[38] See "Llanthony Abbey," in the "retired vale of Ewias," Photo by F. Bedford, from *Ruined Abbeys and Castles of Great Britain*, by William and Mary Howitt, A. W. Bennett, London 1862.

[39] See Kaur G, Dufour JM (January 2012). "Cell lines: Valuable tools or useless artifacts". *Spermatogenesis*. 2 (1): 1–5. doi:10.4161/spmg.19885. PMC 3341241. PMID 22553484.

[40] See "Older age becomes common late in human evolution," by Rachel Caspari and Sang-Hee Lee, *PNAS* July 27, 2004 101 (30) 10895-10900; https://doi.org/10.1073/pnas.0402857101, *Proceedings of the National Academy of Sciences of the United States of America*, https://www.pnas.org/content/101/30/10895

[41] ibid.

[42] See Roseana N. Zia comment in, "A Journey To The Center Of Our Cells – Biologists are discovering the true nature of cells – and learning to build their own." By James Somers, *The New Yorker*, February 28 (in March 7th issue, p. 20), 2022, https://www.newyorker.com/magazine/2022/03/07/a-journey-to-the-center-of-our-cells

[43] See "Strange Attractors," by Juan Carlos Ponce Campuzano, *Dynamic Mathematics*, August 15, 2018, https://www.dynamicmath.xyz/strange-attractors/

[44] See Davidson, Donald. "What Metaphors Mean." *Critical Inquiry*, vol. 5, no. 1, The University of Chicago Press, 1978, pp. 31–47, http://www.jstor.org/stable/1342976.

[45] See "The Literary Formula of the Unresolved Impasse," by Charles E. May, Mashstories, August 14, 2014, http://www.mashstories.com/index.html@p=7469.html

[46] See "Nature as Metaphor," by Freya Latona (quoting from Hopkins' 1877 sonnet), Images by Daniel Shipp, *The PlantHunter*, Issue 45, November 10, 2017, https://theplanthunter.com.au/culture/nature-as-metaphor/

[47] See "The Impasse of Metaphorical Essentialism," by Yicun Jiang, Philosophy, December 3, 2016, doi: 10.1515/css2016-0049, Corpus ID: 1712944491, https://www.semanticscholar.org/paper/The-Impasse-of-Metaphorical-Essentialism-Jiang/6ea0fe99e8350d91134aed1ef2fa53d8510731fb, from the *Journal Chinese Semiotic Studies*, https://doi.org/10.1515/css-2016-0049, De Gruyter Mouton, https://www.degruyter.com/document/doi/10.1515/css-2016-0049/html

[48] See "How to Get Past Impasse in Mediation," by Stewart Edelstein, American Bar Association, March 14, 2017, https://www.americanbar.org/groups/litigation/committees/young-advocates/practice/2017/how-to-get-past-impasse-in-mediation/

[49] See "Breaking an impasse in pectin biosynthesis," by Antony Bacic, *PNAS*, April 11, 2006, 103 (15) 5639-5640 | https://doi.org/10.1073/pnas.0601297103, https://www.pnas.org/doi/full/10.1073/pnas.0601297103

[50] See "The Mystical Impasse in the Unification of Dualistic Physics," by Bryce Haymond, n.d., https://www.thymindoman.com/the-mystical-impasse-in-the-unification-of-dualistic-physics/

[51] *A Treatise On Government*, Translated by William Ellis. T. Payne, London, 1776, p. 270.

[52] See *Conscience – The Origins of Moral Intuition*, by Patricia S. Churchland, W. W. Norton & Company, New York, NY, 2019, p. 159.

[53] See *Brain and Intelligence in Vertebrates*, by Euan M. Macphail, Clarendon Press, Oxford, UK, 1982, p. 20.

[54] See "Practical Goals," in *A World of Wounds: Ecologists and the Human Dilemma*, by Paul R. Ehrlich, Edited by O. Kinne, Ecology Institute, Oldendorf/Luhe, Germany, 1997, p. 90.

[55] See *The Archaeology of Knowledge*, by Michel Foucault, Translated from the French by A. M. Sheridan Smith, Pantheon Books, New York, NY, 1972, p. 149.

[56] See *Objectivity*, by Lorraine Daston and Peter Galison Zone Books, New York, NY, 2007, p. 414.

[57] "What does take mean under the Endangered Species Act and what is incidental take?" NOAA Fisheries, National Oceanic And Atmospheric Administration, U.S. Department of Commerce, https://www.fisheries.noaa.gov/node/8051#:~:text=

Take%20as%20defined%20under%20the,%2C%20but%20not%20unexpected%2C %20taking.

[58] See *The Wisdom Chapter – Jamgön Mipham's Commentary On The Ninth Chapter Of The Way of the Bodhisattva,* Translated by the Padmakara Translation Group, Shambhala, Boulder CO, 2017, p. 147.

[59] See Michael Ruse, *Monad to man: the Concept of Progress in Evolutionary Biology*, Harvard University Press, Cambridge, MA, 1996, pp. 432-433. See also, Edward P. Mahoney, "Lovejoy and the Hierarchy of Being," *Journal of the History of Ideas* Vol. 48, No 2, pp. 211-230.

[60] See "Curious children ask 73 questions each day – many of which parents can't answer, says study," by Emma Elsworthy, 03 December 2017, *The Independent*, https://www.independent.co.uk/news/uk/home-news/curious-children-questions-parenting-mum-dad-google-answers-inquisitive-argos-toddlers-chad-valley-tots-town-a8089821.html. See also, "How Many Decisions Do We Make Each Day?" by Eva M. Krockow, *Psychology Today*, September 27, 2018, https://www.psychologytoday.com/us/blog/stretching-theory/201809/how-many-decisions-do-we-make-each-day

Chapter 4

Post-Modernist Personage Paradox

Non-Paradoxical Certitude

Para-dox, etymologically *distinct from opinion.* A world subjected to the proposition of constants, all of which are *our* opinions, has resulted in what is the most paradoxical crisis in our entire biological presence. That fiasco may be characterized in a multitude of disciplines and moods. There is no grand design upholding or circumventing the distinctions that freely range across the topology of our species' behavior. Its sciences waffle like politics. The only known non-paradoxical certitude is that, regardless of disposition at any moment, no organism wants to suffer. Our reflexes reject pain. Our compulsion to think about its ramifications for Others, is the only relevant story in this or any other time. But in confronting mortality at any instant catapults reckoning into unknown space. What is paradoxical about our own avoidance at all costs of pain, is how easily we are willing to ignore it, or, worse, encourage, collaborate with and profit by it. We do this through the very mechanism of population distributions, in others; from so called farm animals to all of the victims of war and oppression, each of whom carries to their grave a philosophy that has been horribly intercepted, leaving neither a sense of doomed kin, nor something approaching assimilable trace. We give up on pain by rejecting its locus, retreating in the face of it, leaving it for others. To argue that humanity is a coward before the menace of all pain greatly understates how we have vouchsafed all that succors us in our manifest exits, whilst turning our backs on the trillions of organisms who, by our indifference and laziness, have died in pain. Few facts stand out on earth with such brutality, willful stupidity. This has laid the groundwork for an ethic that is at once inconsolable, and fully corrupted. We simply, when it comes down to the roots of our destructive tendencies, do not care, or certainly not for very many. The degree of our kindnesses is utterly bankrupt within instants of its proclamations. In Jain, and Hindu Vaishnav traditions, the period of Chaturmas, also known as "Rainy Retreat," settles monks and nuns during monsoon(s) to the extent that they will not roam during those months, emphatically unwilling to risk stepping on a hapless insect or frog or other in the mud. Moreover, they will not eat at night, again fearing that such a creature could inadvertently fall into a water-filled gourd (e.g., of the Cucurbitaceae family), or be accidentally consumed within a bowl of soup.

The irony that steeps an individual human in an all-out endeavor to avoid pain inevitably causes it to others. Personal identity that is dispersed out to every conceivable coordinate of that paradox, vanishes to the near terminal zeros of infinity, speaking in terms of the sheer multitudes of near invisible invertebrates that co-habit our same zones of life. There is conflict. We are gargantuan, a flea, a mite, a stick insect, not. Such disproportionate sizes propound a condition of allometric challenges with regard to our smaller colleagues who cannot look out for one another against the onslaught of giants upon the land. The Jains, and some other adherents of other ethical traditions, know that the landscapes exploding with harm and human indifference are given, at a fundamentally moral ground to a life of circumspections, fences, the pantheistic hope born of the theory that none should ever suffer. They literally attempt to encincture themselves in every possible restraint. Their restraining orders derive from a devotion to ahimsa, absolute non-violence.

All those biomes about which our knowledge has proved useless; our passions incapable of promoting ecological renascence, at the same time share in a majority of good people who want to exhibit virtue. What stays their hand is not so much the hand but the collective. This, as we have reiterated, poses a near constant beyond Dunbar's Number.

While that basal dysfunction is taking place, our personal coordinates, the geography of the individual, exponentially increases due to interactivity with other personages, willingly or not. Therein lies the most profound liability stemming from trophic cascades. This is not simply an urban space, the number thresholds of 10,000 (a micropolitan) or 50,000 (statistical metropolitan) area. Our cumulative experience of death, seeing it, feeling it, knowing it firsthand through perished loved ones and friends, widens its mystery in terms of numerical contacts. Here we look to the contagion of any disease as it statistically spreads through a population, or zoonotically between species. With unanticipated variables, the so-called *poisson autoregression* (Siméon Denis Poisson, 1781-1840, French mathematician who specialized in variations and thermodynamics, but particularly in gravitational, magnetic and electrical *potentials*) models the contingencies that everywhere surround us. In the case of Covid-19 its applications provide a kind of landscape across which observations accumulate into a *probability mass function* and its contacts/cases $R_c\ (t)$ reproduction rate. That, in turn, recognizes basic structures of contagion, both physical and emotional. Interdictions include, of course, the very history of inoculations and vaccines; of all research attempting to preserve the medical autonomy of a life form. But they also have resulted in the deliberate manipulation of species into exploitable breeds, or thousands of genetic combinations that help destroy (what science and most communities think of as) "pests" like harlequin ladybirds, cane toads, or Africanised honey bees.

Unstressed combinations, versus those that are in some state or version of disease, at any level of its advance, argues strictly in favor of biomanipulation, if your perspective is human. If it is not human, then it is the machination of a consciousness run awry.

It is too simple to lay the blame of our collective manipulative franchises on our languages and tool use, dating back millions of years. If we philosophically engage in the opinions magnified by our singling out of some specific individual, or breeding pair dating back to mythical Eden, our metaphors, particularly the Biblical ones, are painfully ignorant, serving only to highlight good and evil. The transitions are soft, totally lost on our ability to imagine modalities that bypass the old cliches involving territory, competition, survival of the fittest, etc. These analogies that have gained so much traction in simplistic thinking that we have no obvious mental antidotes to them. We have carried with us, from anthropology to science, the same narrow-minded view of biology.

But, again, we have not lost the most important of baselines: The distinction between a few and the many that is likely to find unity only in the most common themes, of which pain ranks foremost. Without it, and preoccupations upon which it insists, we could stand amid a formidable crowd and feel nothing. Mob actions register the benumbed and overwhelming sense that our population dynamics are without any recourse to the individual. That we are utterly powerless in the play of odds. Consider those who attended the Kumbh Mela on the Ganga at Prayagraj in India in 2013, an estimated 120 million people squeezing into a few hundred hectares. In addition to the unprecedented onslaught of urine and feces, there were over 400,000 people treated for everything from dysentery to burns, as has been described by Indian Armed Forces researchers led by M. P. Cariappa in 2015. An estimated 60-80 million came to Haridwar three years prior to that. Annually, some 45 million people visit Karbala in Iraq during the Arba'ein tradition of mourning the loss of a family member. Festivals, funerals, other peaceful gatherings from a Rolling Stones concert of half-million people at Hyde Park in the late 1960s to marches of over one million at the National Mall in Washington all put into perspective our species' bizarre gregariousness.

Numbers en masse convey superficial pictures, like the 110,000 estimated soldiers within Albrecht Altdorfer's 1529 painting of "The Battle of Alexander at Issus" (where Alexander conquered Darius in 333 B.C.) commissioned by Duke William IV of Bavaria, later stolen by Napoleon, eventually donated to the Alte Pinakothek in Munich. Therein lies the sunset contradicting a victory; an aesthetic orgy illuminating a human horror. We know nothing of all those individual's crises (the moment of death for each of them). Altdorfer commemorates our inability to resolve the reality of a violent rabble. It easily segues to China's largest standing military which once numbered at over 4.8 million. Whilst the largest documented battled was that of Stalingrad in 1942-1943, with 2 million combatants killing each other. To the French Revolution beginning May 5, 1789, and the U.S. January 6th 2021 insurrection.

These are infant numbers compared with some 50 separate locust swarms in Kenya in 1954, each one covering some $100km^2$ and numbering 10^{9th} individuals, according to the work of British entomologist Reginald Rainey. The largest supercolony of ants has been found to stretch from northern Italy to the coast of Spain, thousands of miles. And as Bert Hölldobler and Edward O. Wilson made clear in their masterwork, *The Ants* (Harvard University Press, 1990) some ant species are deliberate in their efforts to wipe out an "enemy"; to commit genocide, and not just against one species of ant, or termite or other insect. Ants in general are acutely aware of their dead colony members and have primordial rituals for dealing with the decomposing insects, that includes, among others, cannibalism.

To the extent that we perceive or respond to the masses of numeric realities that comprise nature, ethically immune to our captions and opinions, we are nothing less, as a species, than a mirror image of everything going on around us. With one colossal exception: our said ecological costs/benefits schemas are fully insulated from perspective or even the self-image test. While the odd expletives – ultimately in the form of self-analysis – have burdened our literature with doomsday probability equations, we are feckless in the end, reduced to four-letter words and name calling. A finale that occurs every day, when humanity is tallied in total. The trillions of ants, all those water drops and grains of sand, do not give rise to humanity's insights that are capable of drawing effective parallels. To epiphanies even close to the humility necessary to curb our global-wide intrusions, unique in biological annals by cubic meter, column of air, particulate matter, and so many other physical and epidemiological indicators.

As with the continuing increase in deduced numbers of planets, stars and galaxies, these abstract multitudes (an estimated 7.5×10^{18} grains of sand and

$1.2 \times 10^{17+}$ leaves on earth), the many faiths that are aligned to the vagaries of hope, must contend with these conjurations: but do not. Abstracted ideals endlessly caught out between the biologic past, posed in any number of historical versions, and the daily prospect of a utopia in future times, our collective psyche is torn in the mesials. A social paradise that could somehow work for every personage, together or in social isolation, remains a mournful delusion.

While we have no other choice but to cope with our circumstances, all of them, there is a profound element in ourselves that must envy the dead, because we eventually grow incapable of full attachment, reckoning instead with the relief of detachment. Those who have already passed the full measure of their selves, have succeeded in reaching a place, a condition about which we can only speculate. The horror of every familiar death hits us hard. Regardless of that empathy for those who have disappeared, paid the full price for being born, we remain in a grayish zone of what it means, each and every one of them. The paradox of their pain invalidates any cult of personality, were that to ever matter, which is does not. Julius Caesar, Napoleon Bonaparte, who are they, now? Death only leaves us that much more stranded, one by one, as their numbers queue up in our own direction. Some hands behind their back, lying in the snow and the mud. The weary, unimaginable gasp of the stricken; by all those named in its weary travails and travels toward loss; there within the very anhydrous religion of anonymous zeros that once were zeros plus one. Both in the pivotal point the zero plays in negative and positive exponents, its efficiency in light of the powers of ten, but also its persistent reminder that we are indeed living on the borrowed time of our hopes and dreams, gives to nullity a specific purpose.

As ecologists we can suggest any number of worthy trajectories for insectivores, carnivores. But we really have no actual idea, other than the recent studies on flying biomass, revealing an absolutely atrocious diminutions of population sizes. Overall, amongst both invertebrates and vertebrates, the world is losing close to 45,000 populations of organisms every day. At the same time, any such speculation as to human/biospheric comparables, with the pivot point hinging upon the manner of death, is shattered by the barbarisms of a mass grave in Bucha (Ukraine), of every thoroughly abhorrent, unnatural selection involving human behavior. That we even go so far as to demarcate the natural from the unnatural is predicated entirely upon pain. The pain at our peril of thinking not through but around occurrences in the world that demolish the idea of our pre-existence, mocking the future we give but scant attention to. Is there any credible argument that can effectively counter our personal ephemerality? Not one.

Zero

That the numerative and abstracted zero has represented so full an imagined construct – embodying every process we engage in as a species – should come as no surprise. Mathematician Robert Kaplan's remarkable study of the zero (*The Nothing That Is – A Natural History of Zero* (Oxford University Press, 1999) opens with an uncanny, nagging assertion: "If you look at zero you see nothing; but look through it and you will see the world." A readily relatable metric can be followed in real time.[1] By mid-afternoon, there were over 104,000 deaths today, 246,000 births. Each of these individuals passes through instants of what we call *free space* en route to interactions with others. Like atmospheric rivers[2] dumping trillions of raindrops in passing storms. The lifetime of an individual 5 mm sized droplet of water is approximately 23 minutes. Then it disintegrates.[3] Its lifespan is comparable to Miyake events,[4] solar energetic particles that induce spikes on earth of ^{14}C. These are among the infinite other magnitudes of sub-atomic particle dispersion. They are measured in dimensionless units such as milli- and micro-steradians (μsr).[5] They can be geometrically captured. By that we mean conceptually. A world of various angles, caps, points-to-polygons, degrees of freedom, spheres and Hilbert Spaces or areas beyond the Euclidean finite leading us to the infinite. Even their theoretical boundaries comprise free space. In optics, that freedom is nothing more than the expansion and concomitant dispersion of photons. The free space of a landscape painting offers the ultimate paradox of such diffuse light: the particles are contained within the layers of paint, confined (at least conventionally) to the perimeters of its frame, or expressive structure. Whatever the material relevance, the exponent that is the imagination of the viewer cannot be counted, not for lack of intent, but due to the very existence of the world, which we view as some kind of eternal entity. It is our own sense of forever, the fact that that background over Mona Lisa's right shoulder reaches endlessly in mind. The image of a 23-year-old Van Gogh sitting, bored, in a bookshop in Dordrecht writing out translations from the Bible in the Autumn of 1876, when his real heart lay out in the illimitable fields.

As Samuel Beckett wrote in his brief *Imagination Dead Imagine* (Les Lettres Nouvelles, 1965) the character who is each one of us, the lives separating one from the next all but incomprehensible, is an ever-present ghost, reminding our internal affairs of a perpetual simultaneity that echoes both birth and death. We have no empiric understanding of when beginnings and ends actually sign in or sign out. Continuities, contiguities, confirmations, they do not separate into their portions. Life is a flow without our design. Designs there are, without doubt. But not ours. We do not, we cannot know. Science is no comfort in this blurred wake of connections. Indeed, if anything, the details of natural history, to date, have reconfirmed the peril of birth, the inevitability of failed morality, and our species' proffered chicanery as it attempts to defraud biology with its hubris, megalomania, and conspiracy theories rewarding humanity with false apex credentials. Our power over other species is a measure of our indelicacy, our stubbornness, and recklessness.

Those connotations mark the same infinite arena of Zeno's Dichotomy Paradox, and Aristotle's analysis of the mistake of thinking in fractional space/time when contemplating the motion and line of an arrow.[6] These assertions and logical remonstrations remain stuck, like the equivalent concept of those infinitesimal beings (fairies) on the tip of a pin. The raindrops do add up, of course. But the sums are beyond our ken. Like proverbial grains of sand on every beach, snowflakes in every storm, or the estimated $10^{57\text{th}}$ atoms of hydrogen in the Sun, $10^{80\text{th}-82}$ in the Universe[7], we think in generality terms of 100 billion galaxies each with 1 trillion stars and should be as humbled, both as an individual, and as a species. Human populations have periodically stopped and looked up collectively at Haley's Comet in 1910 and any number of other fantastic celestial events.[8] The net effect of these intermittent mesmerizing incidents (barring an asteroid like that of 66 million years ago, the Cretaceous-Paleogene extinction of some 75% of life on earth)[9] has not been one of human humility, at least not discernibly. Nor has the fact of nearly 700 million malnourished "hungry" fellow humans – "8.9 percent of the world population" and "a quarter of a billion people potentially at the brink of starvation";[10] – moved us, despite tenacious efforts by various organizations to lower chronic undernourishment.[11] Indeed, noble endeavors by half-dozen major international donors, like the World Health Organization, UNICEF and the International Fund for Agricultural Development (IFAD), as well as by the Food and Agriculture Organization of the United Nations (FAO), have not made much of a dent on the disheartening truth: a healthy diet is inaccessible to at least 3 billion people.[12] Such enormities cloud any kind of focus because of the role the zero plays in allowing us to describe in an instant that which can neither be internalized or identified with.

We glance off eternities unscathed. Stare into all kinds of an abyss without flinching. This is part of the post-modernist dilemma. Our psychological grasp of causes and consequences has been distended, is diseased. Here, beside so many artistic and social giants of pure empathy like France's incomparable composer and master of the viol, Marin Marais (1656-1728); Charles Dickens (1812-1870) who, perhaps more than any writer understood poverty and a vicious class system (like the NGO, Oxfam, which originated to combat famine in Greece in 1942); Roman Syrian philosopher Porphyry (c.234 AD-305) who fully grasped the importance of vegetarianism; the 24th Jain Jina, Mahavira (c.599 BCE-c.540 BCE), the older teacher of Buddha and a truly enlightened magnet for human non-violence; one of China's greatest landscape (shan shui) painters Guo Xi (1020-1090); Ludwig van Beethoven (c.1770-1827), the inconceivable voice within his Ninth Symphony (1824). Choose your hero. Seize your inspiration in a person, a picrolite, chalcolithic Cypriot from 5,000 years ago, staring vaguely towards eternity; a stenciled handprint from a cave in Sulawesi from nearly 40,000 BCE, as if to render a first but final declaration. We cannot help but wonder, in the presence of all the fragments, guises, nuances, touches of a real personage from every continent. Such are the critical links between the world and our own personal sanity, that has been so nearly exhausted and circumscribed by the misery of so many. By the horrors of nature.

Does our individual empathy matter? It is impossible to compare astonishments or the depauperate; to reason between cemeteries or logically address crimes against humanity, crimes against nature. We are, for every modern reason, stunned and trapped. And by *modern* many will think in terms of that span of time demarcating the imagined millennia far behind us, a period and a place prior to the Late Paleolithic (50,000 to 11,600 BP), when we began to collectively weaponize our tools; and to the barbarous post-modernist epochs of the Holocene and Anthropocene.

By post-modernist we're here referring to the cynical self-questioning political and economic realities wrought by world systems that are systemic, punctuated by a variety of selection biases favoring wealth over people who are hungry, poor, disenfranchised, and the most vulnerable in society. We're not concerned with graphic arts, literature, architecture or philosophy for that matter, where debates concern style and nostalgia for specific contexts, as well the underlying anger promulgated by change.[13] Rather, we focus on the post-modernist ecologies (a phrase first given loft in 1997 by Daniel R. White).[14] White endeavors "to map…ecological territories of the twenty-first century…"[15] This sociological inquiry hovers over the word *territory*. The etymology of *tory* figuring appropriate behavior stemming from the land, *terra*, pivots now upon the most critical correlation, the suite of activities exerted and imposed upon the earth. The added record of deeds in law and in action perpetuate the underlying call for an ethical set of characteristics defining any parcel of land, or water measurement (i.e., volume and flow units).[16] The UN Watercourses Convention (August 2014)[17] suggests a *human right* to water. And by implication, to land.[18] All the legal covenants to these two fundamental life-sustaining properties of earth are entangled by ancestral ties, and modern economic polarizations. The geography designated by these charged antecedents, even across Antarctica which, prior to the 1959 Antarctic Treaty[19] was thought to be *free* of these conflations of human hubris, is an obsolete map of 61 colonies and 195 nations; or, by other definitional methods, 253 countries including "194 independent nation-states, 55 dependencies, Antarctica and three other areas" (that could number as large as 20 such regions).[20]

The ethical overlay of this earthly cartography represents the most thorough post-modernist ecosystem. It is either endergonic or exergonic, namely, the chemical machinations that either produce negative or positive energy in terms of any spontaneous reaction. From the non-human perspective, everything we do is spontaneous, notwithstanding the patterns we ourselves (our species) recognizes.[21] Just as we have described free space, the Second Law of Thermodynamics refers to the downward-moving release of free energy (negative energy) as a universal principle, $\Delta G = G_{final} - G_{initial}$ (the transition or release of the so called Gibbs free energy, named after the American mathematician, Josiah Willard Gibbs [1839-1903]) during a reaction or metabolic process. Such "conditions", with their "forward and reverse reactions" are thought to "hold roughly true for cells and other living systems" that are always excited, outside any possible equilibrium. Equilibrium translates to stasis, death for a cell, like that of granular matter (everything larger than 1micrometer (1 x $10^{-6\ \mathrm{metre}}$).[22]

The Anthropocene is unambiguously the dominant mathematical operator between and within spaces, such that a topological analysis would always be behind (in time) any *ecosystem logic*. By this we summon the language of embedded *knots* that may be harmonic, tame or wild, for example.[23] Each knot, or tied problem translates into a domain, a type of space that is a representative topos or place, in which continuous or non-continuous functions are occurring. When the function entails a deformation it is known as a homotopic. Double the functions and added levels of ambience become part of the geometrical complex, such as an ambient (or "h") isotopy. These are as much properties of the imagination – manifolds and submanifolds of space in perpetual unions – as they are actual behavioral identities within the natural world, objects like the three-leaf clover (the trefoil knot). Ecological systems are homeomorphic in that a circle and a square can be continuously morphed from one to the other and back again.[24] Every conceivable configuration of space has been mathematically mapped.[25] There exists an infinity of such maps, just as Cosmology is embedded in every point, line and ambient space. In manifold theory, there are three principal embeddings: "smooth, piecewise-linear or topological". These are categories representative of what mathematicians call "non-trivial" paths of embeddedment.[26]

Are such arcane and seemingly twisted language points of mathematics even relevant to the ecological dilemmas faced by real organisms in real time?

Knots and Straight Lines

For every knot there is a straight line that can be resolved. A pathway, one might prefer to interpret it. For every line, there exists a set of points. Every space and meeting of spaces is a penultimate vertex or surface. Considering the incomprehensible variety of biological surfaces in nature, little wonder that perhaps the most *relevant* concordance of meeting places, spelled out in Euclidean geometry, are those concerned with such informatics as "precision agriculture," "life cycle assessments," "applied geography," "nano convergence," "biophotonics," and other focal points of human related activities that penetrate, occupy, or exploit the subsets and templates of the natural world.[27] So, yes: there is absolute relevancy to these collision courses and equations. The most useful set of interfaces are those brought forward during the combined ecological modeling of multiple categories of natural change and behavior. *Post-modern topologies* have as baselines the greatly accelerated deformations throughout every space. So whether the applications are to "next-generation ensemble"{s}, "nutrient-plant interactions," or "general decline" in sync or counter-sync with various "future climatic scenarios,"[28] the histories of math and physics now face the same thresholds of natural despoliation. It is thematic and systemic. The singular all-pervasive vertex that is biodiversity posits those connectomics capable, for example, of mapping the approximately 100,000 neurons in the brain of a fruit fly, or 100 billion neurons in an average human brain.[29] The needed overlay that would explain anything, or validate a comparison, mentor with reasonableness, tutor all totemics, devolves to *human ethics*.

Thus far, that overlay has been intensely erratic. We can, in varied ways, track its absence. For example, consequences of unmitigated greenhouse gas emissions represent the wholesale business-as-usual track. A continuing rise in animal consumption, or tropical deforestation, manifest their own inherent cause-and-consequence incoherencies. But they too are grasped easily enough by the same mathematical desires that would contest infinity with the poignancy of a lovely moment in human time; or, conversely, the desperate gaze of a captured and caged fox on U.S. Capitol grounds, on her way to be euthanized.

The application of a virtue ethic to a Eulerian or semi-Eulerian trail, so called;[30] or to the improvisational free space of socio-economic and political maps of cultural change is an imaginary human margin that struggles in every season to make of itself. Something tangible and good for the commonweal, as exemplified by the late sixth century BC Cleisthenes (the "father of Athenian democracy").[31] How rare, indeed. It was Aristotle (384-322 BC) who forcefully articulated democratic principles, writing: "…in a Democracy the Poor ought to have more power than the Rich, as being the greater number; for this is one mark of Liberty, which all Framers of a Democracy lay down as a criterion of that State; another is, to live as every one [sic] likes…"[32] The fox? Taken as an ecological injunction, we can readily trace those legal and governmental milestones that encompassed the integration of human politics with other species. It is, at best, a fragile and scarce shortlist. Extrapolating from the 1964 U. S. Civil Rights Act, or the Thirteenth, Fourteenth, and Fifteenth Amendments of the U.S. Constitution, does not come close to meeting a test, or proof of concept in terms of nature. There has been no attempt to do so, but with simplistic teases like *climate optimism*, *hopes for the future*, "effective altruism" (Scottish philosopher William MacAskill, et al.), "intuitive ethics" (Walter Sinnott-Armstrong) and socially responsible investing (Blaine Townsend, et al.) Phrases enshrining wishful thinking.

Elsewhere we have discussed the limitations of such concepts as animal welfare or animal protection.[33] Other wish-lists by a minority of humans. Welfare, as embodied in laws from country to country typically seeks the lowest common denominator of care, the minimal standards. The kinds of incremental compromises that serve the largest continents of expediencies. How different a paradigmatic concept than that of the Jain monk who would seek for a standard that is all inclusive. One that inculcates a sovereign oath of never stepping on, or even touching, a living organism, or exploiting (with regret) any but one-sensed beings. Such a modest suggestion has seen no traction in the cultural mores of any confederation, community, or collection of them at the national level. That foremost abnegation most assuredly counts India among ecology's most ironic of contradictory signals. A country that has comprehensively ignored such ideas, making them into politically inconvenient ideals. Even India's failure to condemn Russia's attack on Ukraine bears exacting scrutiny. These silent players in the fellowship of global greed and energy and wealth gluttony can never bode but entirely ill for that Aristotelian democratic Utopia, if the majority simply will not concede such basics. Even male aggression amongst the more than 900 known species of crickets concedes, steps back, recognizes dominance, or, stated differently, what's what. Humans are incapable of that. We can only gaze upon such parities in our private reveries. Jan Breughel the Elder, Roelant Savery, Edward Hicks and a few other masters of the paradise prerequisite come to mind. But to-mind only. How to transform *only* into an ethic, the ethic into a practice, the practice by turns distributed without negative probability or the contradictory enthusiasms of aesthetic achievements.

Math and neurophysics can point out the directions and define the mass and duration of our energy and ethical expenditures; topologists will map boundaries and specific points and blockchains of consumption and impact, from edge effects of roads in the Amazon to household carbon footprints across the planet. Biogenetics can decipher Sitting Bull's DNA from a lock of his hair, or that of Abraham Lincoln from the sweat on his handball, which is at the Smithsonian Institution, as its 12th Secretary, Dr. Gerald Wayne Clough has explained. Philosophy can summarize the debacles, whilst psychiatrists try to assess dichotomies of human natures. All are left with the only paradox, a problem of distribution, and precursors of multiplying through a culture, any collective, a single idea that can be placed into the hands of unknown, but effective human forces. The only mechanism universally recognized is the dominance of power and its many threats, over fear.

There will always be the rare diplomat or movement for animal and habitat liberation, the end-spaces or event horizons of ecological sequences from a moral perspective. But presently, these modest gains, the traction of eloquence or stubborn inspiration, are trapped by ways and means, by all that is politically intransigent, magnified by the persistent demands of every human community in their power and comfort grabs, at home or beyond their borders. And cornered by what we think of as time, notwithstanding the current so called *physics crisis*, models showing vibrating sub-atomic strings and loop quantum gravity, but under the universal aegis of causation rather than time.

We can re-create the evolution of all those components of a comfortable way of life; and take careful note of the hundreds of millions of humans for whom existence, from the moment of birth, is anything but comfortable. Because of the enormous disparities within our one species (one standard measurement of total wealth accumulation and distribution is the Gini ratio or coefficient)[34] we have to peer through a labyrinth of causes to understand how such inequalities arose. We have ample evidence to understand the converging basket-case civilizations that nurtured mass violence, inequality, slavery and countless other forms of exploitation by the few.[35] The Gini Index puts at near opposite distribution scenarios the Faroe Islands and Greenland, both regions of the Kingdom of Denmark. One (the Faroes) is economically socialized – an economic success story – the other, Greenland, revealing significant discrepancies of wealth and poverty. Similarly, Nogales in Arizona and the Mexican (Sonoran) side of Nogales show enormous differences in quality of life and income generation. According to economists Acemoglu and Robinson, *institutional inclusiveness* is a key factor in distinguishing successful communities and countries, from failed powers. For Diamond, it would appear that inclusiveness is all but meaningless if natural capital (that perception of the environment as providing services for humans in and of itself) is not a fundamental part of that equation. Here, any index of quality is purely anthropic. Take, for instance, estuary (transitional) water quality measurements (EcoQS). Every change, particularly those subject to the BOPA index (Benthic Opportunistic Annelida Amphipod), involve pre-existing "anthropogenized systems,"[36] a control data base of bias, in other words. Since all measurements are calibrated by previous measurements, there is no objective starting point, even with the lowest energy equivalent at -273.15 °C (-459.67 °F), numbers that scale along with 3.14159265359… or pi. In other words, there is only an imagined absolute zero. It does not exist in the Universe we perceive.

Other incompatibilities of human quantum speculation exist in the humanities with a fervor. In his *Questions de méthode* (Search [Problem of] for a Method)[37] J-P. Sartre sees existentialism as a compatible, ideological response to Marxism. Their unlikely juxtaposition highlights the difficulty with any expatiation of the proletariat. What is it? Who are they? What fatalistic intersection of civilizations engendered in Marx so dour and downtrodden a vision of humanity? Four of his seven children died before reaching their teens, three of them at the small, cramped freezing one room apartment at 28 Dean Street in London. In an earlier century the young Mozart once gave a concert down the street. We've sat on the sagging bed where Jenny

Eveline Franziska Frances Marx (1851-1852) took her last breath. Barely supported for several years by Engels, Marx used to wear mittens while devouring every economic and political text available at the British Museum Reading Room. Sartre (1905-1980), a century later turned down the 1964 Nobel Prize and with it, a lot of money, as well as most royalties in his life. He never lived as uncomfortably as Marx, however; he enjoyed his skiing vacations, international celebrity and, like Marx, was a heavy, almost delirious drinker. Dead at 75. Marx at 64. Both had their favorite (and famed) cafés in Paris (de la Régence and Les Deux Magots), their literary *Critiques*, manifestos, promises of coming revolution, and ill-health, which Marx (1818-1883) described as "the wretchedness of existence".[38] Whereas Marx had numerous children, Sartre by most accounts had women. His family tree ended in 1980. Whereas Marx, as of 1954, still had 13 living descendants.[39] Their two centuries are gone and whatever else we may fumble to exhume about their respective careers, it is clear that philosophy – burning furiously in their furnaces – could save neither of them. But this is obvious. Each were the unconscious victims of their own best ideals and implacable species. Gift either of them $300 billion dollars and it wouldn't matter: They would complain, and rightly so, about its motives, vast inequity, and most sinister underlying value in light of a hemorrhaging world.

From the perspective of work, of thermodynamics and energy expenditure, philosophy can never win.

Just walk out of Plato's Cave. Banish, like Beethoven's Leonore, the demons that had incarcerated her Florestan in the composer's single opera, "Fidelio" (1814). See the proverbial *light of consciousness* shining on Mars, or the Las Vegas strip. Marx attested to the violent history of this routine in tracking the mournful history of the Highland Celts in Scotland, culminating at that time in a thorough examination of one woman, the Duchess of Sutherland, who had resolved to appropriate "794,000 acres of land that had from time immemorial belonged to the clan." How, "From 1814 to 1820 these 15,000 inhabitants, about 3,000 families, were systematically hunted and rooted out. All their villages were destroyed and burnt, all their fields turned into pasturage. British soldiers enforced this eviction, and came to blows with the inhabitants…"[40] An old woman burned to death rather than leave her cottage, reported Marx.

These passages regarding the expropriation of traditional agricultural lands are emblematic of Marx's entire vision and career. Whereas he reacted personally to his own poverty and sought to make it an example of the human condition, Sartre was sufficiently buffered throughout his life, so that rather than concentrating on those matters germane to survival, he was at leisure to speculate on the psychology and imagination, the loneliness and displays of vanity that had perpetuated the post-modernist absurdities. So did English poet Dante Gabriel Rossetti (1828-1882) when he wrote, "Hence came his feet into my field, and why? How it is that he sees it all so drear? How do I see his seeing, and how hear The name his bitter silence knows it by? This was the little fold of separate sky…"[41] This is part of that tradition of obscure shepherd songs of early 16th century Portugal, particularly by the likes of the great Gil Vicente[42] or the many tales of Margaret of Navarre[43] and Cervantes[44] in whose collective veins flowed the song and action linked to a biosemiosphere. These were landscapes in which all hear, all know, all feel for one another, the pristine purity that has been alluded to and analyzed by philosophers for all time. Yet, arising from their contemplations are only questions pertaining to an obscure but beautifully familiar sensation, common to us all. The mulling moods and airs of every season, clandestine pasts, anonymous, that lie buried here and there, without the least fanfare. Marx and Sartre were agencies of philosophical turns that mirrored neither biodiversity nor the multitude of nature's rubrics. Their quite varied obsessions amounted to basically the same theme of human self-interest and its pejorative place in the world.

Theirs were worlds of human wars, human suffering, scorched earth policies. But, by comparison with today's abysmal ecological crises, on the every edge of utter ruination, Marx and Sartre were the lucky ones.

The scientific community is unambiguous regarding the sixth mass extinction.[45] Some, like Alison Goldwyn, founder of Synchronistory[46] have wisely re-labelled this event, "the sixth mass evolution".[47] Scientifically provocative, none of us alive today will know how the post-Anthropocene will look, though there has been ample speculation.[48] Over half of the earth's terrestrial surface is used for human agriculture. Without intensive, high human population densities appropriating the products of photosynthesis, we could expect a massive insect and spider rebound, and with them, a microbial and viral renaissance.[49] With systematic reductions in global greenhouses gasses, the biochemical re-establishing balance provided by ocean depths, natural rewilding and rapid real-time species re-evolution, would combine to trigger forces that would be noticeable (if even a single human were left to observe the changes) within minutes. That state of affairs would constitute what we have termed a straight line.

On the Nature of Impacts

But with a continuing human population explosion, and its corresponding, escalating consumer impacts[50] peak fossil fuel use will likely be reached even before 2030,[51] prior to the likelihood of energy sufficiency supplied by zero greenhouse gas-emitting technologies, particularly in those 24 low-income, high impact countries, like Somalia.[52] By *high impact*, we refer to local impacts on biodiversity and ecosystem services.[53] That is where the *conceptual challenge* to a non-violent ecological ethic is most precarious, because of its vulnerability index. By that we infer a ground zero reality for human comfort zones that differ radically from the existing urban syndromes, or fully rural and economically tenuous circumstances. As Joy S. Clancy writes, "At an aggregate level, African countries have the lowest ecological footprints in the world. However, there is little available data for individual cities…"[54] EF (ecological footprint) models in China have been analyzed according to rural production.[55] A Swiss study suggests that "the rural footprint is about 20% larger than the urban one" but this is differentiated between "transportation and home heating" in rural sectors, versus "food, clothing, cultural activities, and air travel" in the urban setting. And that is strictly within the realm of Swiss households as determined by the government's "Household Budget Survey".[56] In other words, the pre-existing connective links that sustain a 21st century way of life for people is a jumble of habits, addictions to services, technologies, and efficiencies that have been centuries in the making, and provide a view towards counter-intuitive energy use intensities between rural and urban populations. It must also be pointed out that we do not understand the energy expenditures, life expectancies, and environmental impacts and changes amongst those wild animals who have migrated into human conurbations.

While it is true that impoverished family lives vary less from region to region than those families of high income, the EF models almost entirely focus upon greenhouse gas emissions, not animal and habitat rights or conservation biology.[57] Moreover, with so much of the world given to using pesticides, and to the exploitation of cloven-hooved herbivores – with well over 1,000 recognized breeds worldwide[58] at 80 degrees F (26.6 Celsius) (a normal global temperature throughout much of the world in 2021), these bovines do not have the sweat-glands to sustain normal metabolic processes that would –ultimately – perpetuate the industries supporting their slaughter. That's the good news, except that the overall metabolism of the animal industries themselves represents a massive amount of suffering by tens-of-billions of vertebrates that will be slaughtered, regardless of the degree of their suffering prior to slaughter.[59]

The countering response to climate change may well occur in the biotechnology realms where cross-bred bovines will be developed to produce less than their average 200 pounds per year of methane; and animals that can tolerate heat stress better than their near ancestral livestock. It is an unseemly vision, but one that is inevitable as humanity itself feels the stress with increasing resolve to outsmart human behavior by inducing more and more invisible destruction in the name of smart farming, smart technology, smartness that is actually more inhumane and sinister than ever. Most technological advances typically cover-up heightened abuse at some trophic level. Deep sea mining, unregulated, unmonitored is an obvious example, with its many disruptions of the sea floor and aquatic biodiversity throughout the water columns that are contaminated. Given a World Economic Forum Report in 2014 suggesting that just one seabed metal, gold, may be worth $150 trillion, exposes the degree to which human greed will blindly follow the numbers.

But at the same time, we can look forward to antidotes that are non-violent: from the current surge in economically viable non-animal derived food and other products[60], even vegetarian apartment complexes like the Veda Village on the outskirts of Russia's St. Petersburg[61], vegan friendly universities[62], entire towns that have borrowed from the preliminary models of such cities as Pushkar and Palitana (as of 2014 officially) in India, Ghent in Belgium, and Amirim in Israel.[63] We might further extrapolate from Jain, Bishnoi, Toda and Brahmanical Hindu communities (all vegetarian – for the most part) in seeking to better imagine an evolved future. We exclude the nearly 20 million Seventh Day Adventists from this group because, as has been documented, the motivation for meat abstinence is human health, not animal compassion. At some point the ethics have to be core.

But food consumption is not humanity's only preoccupation, as primary as it is for us, and all other species. Our other needs may not easily be singled out (from greed, excess, countless extractive industries). Nor is it merely a Gedankenexperiment to think through what it would take to adopt to a life not dissimilar in cumulative impact from the monks of Mount Athos.[64] Thc history of monasticism – with its sketes, eremites, lavritic and coenobitic versions, as well as the occasional soloist, a "52-hertz whale" (unidentified, presumably blue-whale sub-species) of an anchorite– all argue for the legacy of the 4th century AD Egyptian Saint Macarius, Pachomius the Great and Melitius of Lycopolis; of the Judaic Therapeutae, Essenes and Elkasites.[65] And of course, the earliest Ebionites.[66] In Buddhist and Jain traditions, the *sangha* encompassed similarly monastic community traditions.

Each of these thought experiments integrate our current psychic landscape of epiphenomena with our practical positioning on any given moment, in any assorted place. Great distractions, like the reading of books, the partaking in communications with other humans, are reversible thrusts towards community. The ecological received wisdom is that all life necessitates communities. Even the definitive history of *The Paradise of the Holy Fathers*[67] finds connections with other people essential, although *some* of the monks would become true solitaires, their companions strictly other-than-humans. The derivative characterizations of such affinities, involving going farther and farther afield from other humans, are perhaps best fitted to the character of Saint Jerome (341-420) and his perpetual companion, a lion who had entered a monastery where Jerome proceeded to remove a thorn from the animal's paw with "delicate gold tweezers," thereby gaining an inseparable friend for life. Their relationship has been beautifully depicted by hundreds of artists, particularly Jan van Eyck, Hans Memling, Leonardo, Lucas Cranach the Elder, Vittore Carpaccio, Giovanni Bellini, Albrecht Dürer and Rogier van der Weyden.[68]

The communal properties of an information system deriving from human companionship with Others is a far more ancient sociology than that simply concerning human-to-human relations. Consider that there was a time when the human population worldwide was a few thousand pairs. But surrounding life forms with whom this nascent humanity would have had conceptual and daily contacts numbered some illimitable count and variety. We accept the notion that there are currently one trillion or more species on earth[69] (though we know of fewer than 99.999% of them all); and that each of those species remains a mystery in terms of the actual average number of individuals per species. With the exceptions of those few species that have been counted (e.g., most known rare and endangered species are relatively understood quantitatively) the best guess for that magic number of living individuals other than humans has been computed in terms of the earth's approximate 550 gigatons of Carbon, with some 80% of it distributed amongst the planet's terrestrial flora, embryophytes (multicellular eukaryotes); and 15% locked into bacteria.[70] The rest is to be found in vertebrates and invertebrates. It is a distributive conundrum in terms of today's other-than-human survivors. There may be billions of red billed sub-Saharan weavers (*Quelea quelea quelea*) and hundreds-of-millions of starlings; over 30 billion chickens, untold trillions of ants. But the most likely human contact species 350,000 years ago, given the largely African common denominator geographically, can only be vaguely surmised from the few tens-of-thousands of known examples of rock paintings, the majority of which date to less than 40,000 years ago. The mystery of interspecies communications involving human participants remains the same, unflinching enigma.

Synanthropospheres

What can be adduced is the fact that 55% of today's human population is urbanized.[71] The numbers of other species contacts with us is unquestionably rising again. Central Park in Manhattan is a kind of Serengeti or Lamar Valley in Yellowstone, unique to its setting. But as Brooke Jarvis has written, there is a "subset of wild animals" which are quasi-urbanized alongside humans. Jarvis highlights possible long-term evolutionary changes such urbanization has invoked, whether amongst mice genes within Central Park ("that allow them to metabolize fatty foods and rancid peanuts") to other significant species dietary changes elsewhere among mountain lions and certain bird species which have discovered that the nicotine in cigarette butts are useful for nest building because it seems to diminish the number of invasive mites).[72] This transitional synanthroposphere, in which rock doves and cockroaches, coyotes and cougars, black bear (a very few brown bear), deer, raccoons, skunks, foxes, rat and mice species and any number of companion animals co-occupy diverse portions of cityscapes, presents a rich comparison to that ungraspable past during and before the Paleolithic between 3.3 million and 11,650 years BP.

One of the most compelling visions of the "Synanthropic Suburbia" comes from Sarah Gunawan, who has architecturally described "new synanthropic suburban typologies," reinventing a system of homebuilding "which subtly blurs the spatial definition between human and non-human to maximize the mutual benefits of cohabitation" and thus "enabling more hybrid conditions to emerge."[73] A group of organizations in New York have assembled "The Synanthrope Preserve" website to encourage and inform such collaborative multi-species experiences within Central Park.[74] In Toronto, biologist Suzanne MacDonald is among those who are studying the interplay of urban planning, biology and psychology. Her focus on urban racoons has led her "to theorize that the demands of the urban habitat are creating a type of 'uber raccoon' that is more intelligent and resourceful than its country cousins."[75] One wonders about the more than 210 avian species in New York's

Central Park: how their behavior had moderated the human impact on their behavior? But we must add, we don't subscribe to "uber" intelligence as a reality. That is a role that has been performed, much like literally hundreds of known forms of self-serving mimicry throughout the natural world, whether wielded by African Gray Parrots, and Red-Capped Robin Chats, mimesis amongst Heliconius butterflies (e.g., the Zebra Longwing), bluestreak cleaner wrasses, or entire biomes, such as coral reefs.

Clearly, social media and density of populations conflate to exert mimetic lures, most readily characterized in such modes as the theorized defensive flocking behavior of dark-eyed juncos, studied back in 1980 by Peter Goldman. Starling murmurations are among the most celebrated. There is every reason to assume that one culture after another (human and Others) mimic their predecessors through the ordeal of naturally selecting the best forms and values, and discarding the "worst." This has certainly been key to our understanding of genetics and mutation rates towards a goal. Some, like astrophysicist Adam Frank and NASA Goddard Institute Gavin A. Schmidt have posited the "Silurian hypothesis" which suggests the interesting notion that perhaps an earlier industrial civilization existed on earth. We might find backtraces of it in the records of fertilizer, plastic, rare metals and other possible footprints. We just haven't yet.[76] Such an archaeological discovery would help us possibly prepare for our own coming obsolescence in a more philosophical light, whatever solace that might convey.

In the meantime, our biological analgesics are likely not to come from freeways and frenzied airline schedules; from the natural selection of robots or nanotechnology; from densely packed high-rises or solar arrays spanning hundreds of square miles, all of it subject to the erratic nature of hacking, or the sheer obesity of grids, tools, apps, manipulations and fundamental crowding. It is all of an ugly, teeming, strident vision. Our future urbanized realities will find their heart and soul in the bubbles of commingling between species whose fringes are countryside, not city. And even those will have struggled to improvise somehow around the distinct, inexpressible forlorn for what is assuredly to be glaringly absent from the puzzles of true nature, true conscience.

In those species-convergent spaces other topologies have endeavored to come to the rescue. In the same vein that has catapulted the work of cartographers for centuries drawing maps of paradise and attempting to interpret its physical location (somewhere in the East, from the Book of Genesis 2: 8-15),[77] so too, today, optimism emerges, and rightly so, in the cataloguing (and mapping) to-date of over 75,000 eco-restoration projects around the world;[78] as well as the World Protected Areas Database with its more than 260,000 regions within 245 countries and territories.[79]

As much as the physical properties of protection designated through "21 action-oriented targets" between now and the year 2030 by the Secretariat of the Convention on Biological Diversity ("CBD")[80] a complex of additional circumstances are projected and entangled. These stem from the U.N.'s 17 Sustainable Development Goals[81] as well as the Aichi Target 11 initiatives designed to have been implemented by the year 2020 (they weren't). Those included "at least 17 per cent of terrestrial and inland water, and 10 percent of coastal and marine areas, especially areas of particular importance for biodiversity and ecosystem services" be "conserved through effectively and equitably managed... well connected systems of protected areas..."[82] While the world has reached one of its targets [out of 20], the protection of 10% of marine areas,[83] as of 2022 the planet enjoys only 15% of territorial areas under some aegis of protection[84]. It is worth considering that the first Rio Earth Summit, in 1992 (United Nations Conference on Environment and Development) produced three central pillars of focus for the past three decades of human ecological commitment. They were concentrated on climate change (the UNFCCC), desertification (UNCCD) and biodiversity loss (the CBD). In most cases, humanity has failed to come even close to its anticipated benchmarks, particularly Target 12 involving "conservation of species".[85]

We have three ultimate metrics for measuring human impact and the success and/or failure of its remedial endeavors: the survival and quality of life of individuals, of species populations, and of connected ecosystems. The philosophy of these metrics must surely comprise an ambivalence that wants to ask: Who are we? What are we doing to the rest of the world? Why can't we see clearly, feel with unprejudiced and biologically undifferentiating pathos, submit to our extraordinary sentimentality, offer of ourselves the full throw-weight of our emotions in the face of Others who need our immediate love? What is the problem? Why can't we easily solve this predicament of human nature that is stifling the world with its superegos and hostility? It should be easy to do so. If we can't, or will not, is self-destruction the only blessing we can offer the world?

There have been numerous approaches to answering such questions. One includes the "entropy considerations" where "when conflicts occur, pick the solution that maintains the closest value for constant divergence from equiprobability."[86] Another, also posed by Brooks and Wiley, consists of using German biologist Will Hennig's (1913-1976) proposed syntax, what Brooks and Wiley describe as "surface structure justifications,"[87] that might include "empirical justification of a consistent syntax based on some general principle such as information density or parsimony as well as consistency with a causal theory."[88] Wittgenstein deepens the conundrum when he questions a statement such as, "Now I understand the system" but proceeds to enumerate the contingent meanings, descriptions, and very process of elaboration.[89] Each step may well invalidate our assumptions. In German language philosopher Rudolf Carnap's (1891-1970) work with colleagues of the "Vienna Circle" in the early 1930s, he too questioned process with a methodical challenge to his colleagues in math, physics and philosophy that they stay within "bounds of proper logical syntax and experience" which would necessarily preclude "unshareable experience," "absolute ontological commitments," "dogmatic values and politics," among others.[90] Carnap's *Der Raum* (the space) and *Aufbaum* (construction) endeavors in the 1920s would subject every epistemological, scientific and philosophical order of knowledge to a process of induction whereby everything (read: the biosphere, all knowledge) existed within a single space. Hence, all objects of knowledge, and in a real sense were relatable. What tied all things together – one may easily read, all species into this – was the human capacity and need for deductive knowledge.[91]

"White-Crowned Hornbill Trapped for Life," Photo © M. C. Tobias.

So that the entire history of philosophy would come down to deducing facts from a single space, utilizing a simple, but implacable logic, premises leading to the inference of reasonable reasoning; of the self-generating validity of human thought. Here again, the post-modernist paradox, of a person so convinced by her/his/and every other pronoun's point of perspective, that nothing external to the inner command of a voice, a pitch, an amplitude could be deemed to be plausible. Rules of inference are human rules. The notion of *natural deduction* is a human notion. Neither Wittgenstein nor Carnap presented a boundless space, one in which humans did not reign supreme.

It is not *our* space. The realization of this should certainly be troubling, given the extent to which our species has breached someone else's space; invaded their territory; appropriated that which is not ours to take. We may seek forgiveness, redemption, proffering pleas on behalf of ourselves and our friends and loved ones. If such appeals and prayers are inaudible, unanswered, left exposed and scorned upon the same earth that gave them their birth, what then? How to continue when we cannot, should not, continue?

Endnotes

[1] Kaplan's line cited is from page 1 of his book (the very opening first sentence). It is a phenomenal read we recommend to everyone. For the relatable metrics, see https://www.worldometers.info/; for Kumbh Mela see https://www.youtube.com/watch?v=D_ACyQy5bq0; See also, Med J Armed Forces India, 2015 Juol; 71(3): 278-281, M.P.Cariappa et al, doi: 10.1016/j.mjafi.2014.08.001, PMCID: PMC4534537. PMID: 26288497, National Library of Medicine, https://www.ncbi.nlm.nih.gov/pmc/articles/PMC4534537/; for Arba'ein, see "From Iraq, an Intimate Glimpse of the Religious Holiday of Arbaeen," by Andrea DiCenzo, November 18, 2020. *The New York Times*, https://www.nytimes.com/2020/11/09/travel/arbaeen-karbala-iraq.html; for Chinese standing army numbers see "Top 10 countries with the highest active military personnel," by Vaamanaa Sethi, February 28, 2022, *BI India*, https://www.businessinsider.in/defense/news/top-10-countries-with-the-highest-active-military-personnel/slidelist/89892321.cms; for Battle of Stalingrad numbers, see Alec Luhn, "Stalingrad name may return to city in wave of second world war patriotism". *The Guardian*, June 8, 2014; for Kenya locust swarms, see "Chapter 27: Book of Insect Records," University of Florida, Hussein Sanchez-Arroyo, April 15, 1997, https://entnemdept.ufl.edu/walker/ufbir/chapters/chapter_27.shtml#:~:text=In%20early%201954%2C%20air%20reconnaissance,2%2C%20approximately%2010%20billion%20locust; for Wilson and Hölldobler, see pp. 219-220, 288, 296, 398-399, 462; for grains of sand, see "Which Is Greater, The Number Of Sand Grains On Earth Or Stars In The Sky?" by Robert Krulwich, NPR, https://www.npr.org/sections/krulwich/2012/09/17/161096233/which-is-greater-the-

number-of-sand-grains-on-earth-or-stars-in-the-sky; for number of leaves, see "How many leaves are in the world," Lisbdnet.com, November 27, 2021.

[2] See Zhu, Yong; Reginald E. Newell (1994). "Atmospheric rivers and bombs" (PDF). *Geophysical Research Letters*. 21 (18): 1999–2002. Bibcode:1994GeoRL..21.1999Z. doi:10.1029/94GL01710.

[3] See "Scientists Record World's Largest Raindrop," by James Gleick, *New York Times*, Orlando Sentinel, December 7, 1986.

[4] See, "A Single-Year Cosmic Ray Event at 5410 BCE Registered in 14C of Tree Rings," by F. Miyake, I. P. Panyushkina, A. J. T. Jull, F. Adolphi, N. Brehm, S. Helama, K. Kanzawa, T. Moriya, R. Muscheler, K. Nicolussi, M. Oinonen, M. Salzer, M. Takeyama, F. Tokanai, L. Wacker, First published: 01 June 2021 https://doi.org/10.1029/2021GL093419, https://agupubs.onlinelibrary.wiley.com/doi/10.1029/2021GL093419

[5] See "Steradian", *McGraw-Hill Dictionary of Scientific and Technical Terms*, fifth edition, Sybil P. Parker, editor in chief. McGraw-Hill, New York, NY, 1997.

[6] W.M.Itano; D.J. Heinsen; J.J. Bokkinger; D.J. Wineland (1990). "Quantum Zeno effect" (PDF). *Physical Review A*. 41 (5): 2295–2300. Bibcode:1990PhRvA..41.2295I. doi:10.1103/PhysRevA.41.2295. PMID 9903355.

[7] See "How Many Atoms Exist in the Universe?" by Anne Marie Helmenstine, ThoughtCo., August 9, 2019, https://www.thoughtco.com/number-of-atoms-in-the-universe-603795

[8] "Rarest And Amazing Astronomical Events!" by Fred Schaaf, *The Farmer's Almanac*, July 9, 2020, https://www.almanac.com/content/greatest-eclipses-and-sky-events-history; see also, for numbers of galaxies see "How many galaxies are there?" by Elizabeth Howell and Alisa Harvey, February 1, 2022, Space.com, https://www.space.com/25303-how-many-galaxies-are-in-the-universe.html.

[9] See Pope KO, d'Hondt SL, Marshall CR (1998). "Meteorite impact and the mass extinction of species at the Cretaceous/Tertiary boundary". *PNAS*. 95 (19): 11028–11029. Bibcode:1998PNAS...9511028P. doi:10.1073/pnas.95.19.11028. PMC 33889. PMID 9736679.

[10] U. N. Sustainable Development Goals," "Goal 2: Zero Hunger," https://www.un.org/sustainabledevelopment/hunger/; See United Nations (2015) Resolution adopted by the General Assembly on 25 September 2015, Transforming our world: the 2030 Agenda for Sustainable Development (A/RES/70/1

[11] See "World Hunger: Key Facts And Statistics 2021," https://www.actionagainsthunger.org/world-hunger-facts-statistics; See also, "As more go hungry and malnutrition persists, achieving Zero Hunger by 2030 in doubt, UN report warns, UNICEF, 13 July 2020, https://www.unicef.org/press-releases/more-go-hungry-and-malnutrition-persists-achieving-zero-hunger-2030-doubt-un-report

[12] ibid.

[13] "Postmodernism Glossary". *Faith and Reason*. https://www.pbs.org/faithandreason/gengloss/postm-body.html

[14] See White's book, *Postmodern Ecology-Communication, Evolution, and Play*, SUNY Press, Excelsior Editions, State University of New York Press, Albany, New York, 1997, https://www.sunypress.edu/p-2665-postmodern-ecology.aspx; See also "The

Re-construction of Nature: Postmodern Ecology and the Kissimmee River Restoration Project," in *From Virgin Land to Disney World – Nature and Its Discontents in the USA of Yesterday and Today*, Critical Studies Volume 15, pp. 229-250, Brill, 2001, https://brill.com/view/book/edcoll/9789004333932/B9789004333932-s013.xml; See also "Inhuman(e) Subjects: Postmodern Theory and Contemporary Animal Liberation Fiction," by Nicholas Spencer, in ibid, pp. 187-208, doi: https://doi.org/10.1163/9789004333932_011, https://brill.com/view/book/9789004333932/B9789004333932-s011.xml?rskey=xZ0OJa&result=2

[15] ibid.

[16] "Water Measurement Units and Conversion Factors," by Saleh Taghvaeian, OSU Extension, October 2016, https://extension.okstate.edu/fact-sheets/water-measurement-units-and-conversion-factors.html;

[17] See "UN Watercourses Convention," https://unece.org/environment-policy/water/un-watercourses-convention

[18] See "The Impact of a Human Right to Water on the Sustainable Balance of Water Uses under the UN Watercourses Convention," by Antoinette Hildering, Utrecht Law Review, October 30, 2020, 16(2), pp.7–17. doi: http://doi.org/10.36633/ulr.562, https://www.utrechtlawreview.org/article/10.36633/ulr.562/

[19] See https://www.ats.aq/e/antarctictreaty.html

[20] Peakbagger.com 1987-2021, https://www.peakbagger.com/pbgeog/countries.aspx

[21] See IUPAC, *Compendium of Chemical Terminology*, 2nd ed. (the "Gold Book") (1997). Online corrected version: (2006–) "exergonic (exoergic) reaction". doi:10.1351/goldbook.E02262

[22] See "Free energy," Khan Academy, https://www.khanacademy.org/science/biology/energy-and-enzymes/free-energy-tutorial/a/gibbs-free-energy; See also, Nagarajan, U., Beaune, G., Lam, A.Y.W. et al. Inert-living matter, when cells and beads play together. *Commun Phys* 4, 2 (2021). https://doi.org/10.1038/s42005-020-00506-y, https://www.nature.com/articles/s42005-020-00506-y; See also, https://www.springer.com/journal/10035

[23] See Charles Livingston, *Knot Theory*. Cambridge University Press, Cambridge, UK, 1993, p. 11.

[24] See Jan J. Dijkstra, 1 December 2005, "On Homeomorphism Groups and the Compact-Open Topology", *The American Mathematical Monthly*. 112 (10): 910. doi:10.2307/30037630.

[25] See, for example, James R. Munkres, *Topology* (2nd ed.), Prentice Hall Inc., Upper Saddle River, NJ, 2000.

[26] See "The Manifold Atlas Project," "Isotopy," http://www.map.mpim-bonn.mpg.de/Isotopy

[27] See the *International Journal of Design and Nature and Ecodynamics*," https://academic-accelerator.com/Journal-Abbreviation/zh-CN/International-Journal-of-Design-and-Nature-and-Ecodynamics

[28] See nature portfolio, "Ecological Modelling," https://www.nature.com/subjects/ecological-modelling

[29] See "How to Map a Fly Brain in 20 Million Easy Steps," by Emily Anthes, *The New York Times*, October 26, 2021.

[30] See Herbert Fleischner, ("X.1 Algorithms for Eulerian Trails", Eulerian Graphs and Related Topics: Part 1, Volume 2, Annals of Discrete Mathematics, 50, Elsevier, pp. X.1–13, 1991. See also, Brendan McKay and Robert W. Robinson, Asymptotic enumeration of eulerian circuits in the complete graph, *Combinatorica*, 10 (1995), no. 4, 367–377.

[31] See R. Po-chia Hsia, Lynn Hunt, Thomas R. Martin, Barbara H. Rosenwein, and Bonnie G. Smith, *The Making of the West, Peoples and Cultures, A Concise History, Volume I: To 1740*, Bedford/St. Martin's, Boston and New York, 2007, 44.

[32] See Aristotle, *A Treatise On Government*, Translated by William Ellis, London, UK, 1776, pp. 312-313. See also, *Aristot. Pol.* 6, 1317b, https://www.perseus.tufts.edu/hopper/text?doc=Perseus:text:1999.01.0058:book=6:section=1317b

[33] See *God's Country: The New Zealand Factor*, by M. C. Tobias and J. G. Morrison, A Dancing Star Foundation Book, Zorba Press, Ithaca, New York, 2011.

[34] See Corrado Gini's (1884-1965) "GINI index (World Bank estimate) | Data". data.worldbank.org. See also, "The latest data on global inequality and a look into the future," within "Global Economic Inequality," by Max Roser, *Our World In Data*, https://ourworldindata.org/global-economic-inequality, Accessed October 27, 2021. See also, "What is the Gini Coefficient?" n.a., CFI, https://corporate financeinstitute.com/resources/knowledge/economics/gini-coefficient/; And, "U.S. Income Distribution: Just How Unequal?" by Inequality.org, February 14, 2012, https://inequality.org/research/unequal-americas-income-distribution/

[35] See, for example, *Collapse – How Societies Choose To Fail Or Succeed*, by Jared Diamond, Viking Press, New York, NY, 2005; *and Why Nations Fail – The Origins Of Power, Prosperity, and Poverty*, by Daron Acemoglu and James Robinson, Crown Business, New York, NY, 2012.

[36] See "The estuarine quality paradox: Is it possible to define an ecological quality status for specific modified and naturally stressed estuarine ecosystems?" by Jean-Claude Dauvin and Thierry Ruellet, Elsevier, https://doi.org/10.1016/j.marpolbul.2008.11.008Get, https://www.sciencedirect.com/science/article/abs/pii/S0025326X0800533X

[37] *Les Temps Modernes*, September 1957, pp. 338-417.

[38] Werner Blumenberg, *Karl Marx: An Illustrated Biography.* Translated by Douglas Scott. Verso, London, New York, 2000, p. 98. See also the devastating portrait of Sartre near the end of his life in "The Last Days of Jean-Paul Sartre," by Webster Schott, *The Washington Post*, May 20, 1984, https://www.washingtonpost.com/archive/entertainment/books/1984/05/20/the-last-days-of-jean-paul-sartre/3f75987e-69af-43f7-a2ff-a386b7947c6c/. Schott quotes from Simone de Beauvoir's book *Adieux- A Farewell to Sartre* (Pantheon, New York, 1984) and it is a devastating account. https://www.washingtonpost.com/archive/entertainment/books/1984/05/20/the-last-days-of-jean-paul-sartre/3f75987e-69af-43f7-a2ff-a386b7947c6c/ https://www.washingtonpost.com/archive/entertainment/books/1984/05/20/the-last-days-of-jean-paul-sartre/3f75987e-69af-43f7-a2ff-a386b7947c6c/3

[39] See "Burden" by Janet Flanner and Brendan Gill, *The New Yorker Magazine*, September 17, 1954, https://www.newyorker.com/magazine/1954/09/25/burden-2

[40] See *Capital – A Critique Of Political Economy*, Volume 1, Book One, The Process of Production of Capital, Translated from the third German edition by Samuel Moore and Edward Aveling and edited by Frederick Engels, Progress Publishers, Moscow, USSR, 1978, pp. 682-683.

[41] Dante Gabriel Rossetti, *The House of Life*, Arthur L. Humphreys, London UK, p. 53, 1912.

[42] *The Lyrics Of Gil Vicente*, by Aubrey F. G. Bell, Second Edition, Basil Blackwell, Oxford, UK, 1921.

[43] *The Heptameron Of The Tales Of Margaret, Queen of Navarre*, Five Volumes, With An Essay Upon The Heptameron by George Saintsbury, The Society Of English Bibliophilists, London UK, 1894.

[44] *A Dialogue Between Scipio and Bergansa, Two Dogs belonging to the City of Toledo, Giving on the Lives, Humours, and Employments of the Masters They Lived With, To Which Is Annexed the Comical History of Rincon and Cortado, Both Written By The Celebrated Author of Don Quixote*, Foreword by Hal Stebbins, S. Bladon, London UK, [First Printed, 1767], new edition published in Collaboration with the Huntington Library, San Marino, CA, 1967.

[45] See, for example, Ceballos, Gerardo; Ehrlich, Paul R.; Dirzo, Rodolfo (23 May 2017). "Biological annihilation via the ongoing sixth mass extinction signaled by vertebrate population losses and declines". *PNAS*. 114 (30): E6089–E6096. https://doi.org/10.1073/pnas.1704949114. PMC 5544311. PMID 28696295.

[46] See synchronistory.com

[47] Podcast with Erwin Laszlo and Michael Tobias, moderated/hosted by Alison Goldwyn, Munich, November 9, 2021.

[48] See, for example "What would happen to Earth if humans went extinct?" by Emma Bryce, LifeScience, August 16, 2020, https://www.livescience.com/earth-without-people.html; See also, "Half of the world's habitable land is used for agriculture," Hannah Ritchie, November 11, 2019, Our World in Data, https://ourworldindata.org/global-land-for-agriculture

[49] See, for example, https://www.documentarymania.com/player.php?title=Aftermath%20Population%20Zero

[50] See "2021 Global Consumer Research Reveals Escalating Concerns about Climate Change and Threats to Forest Biodiversity," by the Forest Stewardship Council, Bonn, Germany, 21 October, 2021, https://fsc.org/en/newsfeed/2021-global-consumer-research-reveals-escalating-concerns-about-climate-change-and-threats; See also, U.S. Energy Information Administration "Analysis & Projections," https://www.eia.gov/analysis/; and, "The Anthropocene: a conspicuous stratigraphical signal of anthropogenic changes in production and consumption across the biosphere," by Mark Williams, et al., AGU – Advancing Earth And Space Science, Earth's Future, Volume 4, Issue 3, March 2016, pp. 34-53, 03 February 2016, https://doi.org/10.1002/2015EF000339, https://agupubs.onlinelibrary.wiley.com/doi/full/10.1002/2015EF000339

[51] See "World to reach peak oil demand before 2030 – TotalEnergies," Reuters, September 27, 2021, https://www.reuters.com/business/energy/totalenergies-expects-rise-use-renewable-energy-future-2021-09-27/

[52] Those countries are measured by GNI – Gross National Income – which is less than $1,026 (in US dollars). But even the so called "high income countries are ranked by the World Bank at a minimum of per capital $12,476, which is well below the poverty line in most "developed" nations." World Population Review," https://worldpopulationreview.com/country-rankings/low-income-countries; See, "Global poverty: Facts, FAQs, and how to help," World Vision, https://www.worldvision.org/sponsorship-news-stories/global-poverty-facts

[53] See "The Economics Of Biodiversity Loss And Agricultural Development In Low Income Countries," by Charles Perrings, University of York, https://www.fao.org/fileadmin/templates/soilbiodiversity/Downloadable_files/agriculture_2.pdf; See also, "Environmental degradation at different stages of economic development," by T. Panayotou, in Ahmed I., and Doelman J. A. (eds), Beyond Rio: the environmental crisis and sustainable livelihoods in the Third World, Macmillan Press, London UK, 1995. See also, "Final Report – The Economics of Biodiversity: The Dasgupta Review", 2 February 2021, https://www.gov.uk/government/publications/final-report-the-economics-of-biodiversity-the-dasgupta-review

[54] "Urban ecological footprints in Africa," by Joy S. Clancy, October 22, 2008, https://www.fao.org/fileadmin/templates/soilbiodiversity/Downloadable_files/agriculture_2.pdf, https://onlinelibrary.wiley.com/doi/pdf/10.1111/j.1365-2028.2008.01041.x

[55] See "Estimation of China ecological footprint production coefficient based on net primary productivity," by Liu Mou-cheng and Li Wen-hua, www.cnki.com.cn, https://en.cnki.com.cn/Article_en/CJFDTotal-STXZ201003031.htm; See also, "Progress and Implication in Domestic Research on Ecological Footprint Model," and Zhang jin-he and Zhang Jie, www.cnki.com.cn, https://en.cnki.com.cn/Article_en/CJFDTotal-DYYY200702019.htm

[56] See "Your carbon footprint may have more to do with your wealth than your location," by Sarah DeWeerdt, Daily Science, February 11, 2020, https://www.anthropocenemagazine.org/2020/02/the-unexpected-drivers-of-carbon-footprints/

[57] See *World War III: Population and the Biosphere at the End of the Millennium,* by M. C. Tobias, Bear & Company, Santa Fe, NM, 1994.

[58] See Marleen Felius, *Cattle Breeds: An Encyclopedia.* Trafalgar Square Publishing, London UK, 2007.

[59] "A new breed of cattle rancher," by Jaweed Kaleem, *The Los Angeles Times*, November 9, 2021, https://www.latimes.com/world-nation/story/2021-11-09/arizona-cattle-ranch

[60] There are current projections that report "Global Vegan Food Market to Surpass $31 Billion By 2026," by Liam Pritchett, LIVEKINDLY, https://www.livekindly.co/global-vegan-food-market-surpass-31-billion/. In 2019, "FoodNavigator…predicted that 25 percent will be either fully vegan or vegetarian." Ibid. Put into perspective, the 2021 total global agricultural value is estimated at over $5 trillion." See, "Do the costs of the global food system outweigh its monetary value?" by Martien Van Nieuwkoop, June 17, 2019, World Bank Blogs, https://blogs.worldbank.org/voices/do-costs-global-food-system-outweigh-its-monetary-value. Moreover, the projections for global meat consumption/costs in 2025 see a "$1,157.6 billion U.S. dollars," "Meat

industry value worldwide in 2020 and forecast for 2021 and 2025," statista, https://www.statista.com/statistics/502286/global-meat-and-seafood-market-value/; See also, "COVID-19 fueling rise of plant-based diets," n.a., Food & Beverage Insider, February 24, 2021, https://www.foodbeverageinsider.com/vegetarian/covid- 19-fueling-rise-plant-based-diets

[61] "Veda Village in St. Petersburg," *OshoNews*, October 14, 2017, https://www.oshonews.com/2017/11/02/veda-village-in-st-petersburg/

[62] See "The Top 25 Most Vegan-Friendly Universities," College Pads, by Ali Bartmer, June 15, 2018, https://www.rentcollegepads.com/blog/topics/college-life/top-25-vegan-friendly-universities/

[63] See https://www.livekindly.co/israel-vegan-village-800-residents/; https://timesofindia.indiatimes.com/travel/destinations/welcome-to-palitana-worlds-first-vegetarian-city-in-indias-gujarat/as71049380.cms#:~:text=Yes%2C%20that%20is%20right%2C%20India,for%20those%20who%20follow%20Jainism. https://stad.gent/en/city-government/food-strategy-ghent/thursday-veggie-day; and https://theveganword.com/vegan-friendly-cities/; See also the noted transition a few groups of farmers are making, from the UK to Switzerland, to become veganic operations."The meat and dairy farmers who are going vegan," by Suzanne Bearne, BBC News, May 25, 2022, https://www.bbc.com/news/business-61565233

[64] See *Athos – The Holy Mountain*, by Philip Sherrard, Photographs by Takis Zervoulakos, The Overlook Press, Woodstock, New York and Alexandria Press Ltd, London, UK, 1982.

[65] See Attridge, H. W., & Hata, G., "The Origins of Monasticism" in *Ascetics, Society, and the Desert: Studies in Egyptian monasticism*, Trinity Press Intl., Harrisburg, PA, 1999; See also, James E. Goehring, "Withdrawing from the Desert: Pachomius and the development of Village Monasticism in Upper Egypt," Harvard Theological Review 89, 1996; and Harmless, W., "Chapter 5: Pachomius" in *Desert Christians - An Introduction to the Literature of Early Monasticism*, Oxford University Press, New York, NY 2004.

[66] Bauckham, Richard, "The Origin of the Ebionites". In Tomson, Peter J.; Lambers-Petry, Doris (eds.). *The Image of the Judeo-Christians in Ancient Jewish and Christian Literature*. Brill Publishers, Leiden, Netherlands, pp. 162–81, 2003.

[67] By Ernest A. Wallis Budge, two volumes, Chatto & Windus, London, UK 1907.

[68] See *St. Jerome*, by Jean Steinmann, Translated by Ronald Matthews, Geoffrey Chapman Publishers, London UK, 1959. See also, *Saint Jerome*, by Jean Paris, Éditions Du Regard, Paris, France, 1999. See also "Saint Jerome Extracting a Thorn from a Lion's Paw," by the Master of the Murano Gradual, Detached Leaf # Ms. 106, Getty Museum, Los Angeles, CA.

[69] See "Researchers find that Earth may be home to 1 trillion species," National Science Foundation, May 2, 2016, https://www.nsf.gov/news/news_summ.jsp?cntn_id=138446; See also, Li, S., Du, X., Feng, K. et al. Assessment of microbial α-diversity in one-meter squared topsoil. *Soil Ecol. Lett.* 4, 224–236 (2022). https://doi.org/10.1007/s42832-021-0111-5, https://link.springer.com/article/10.1007/s42832-021-0111-5; See also, Bunge, J., Willis, A., Walsh, F., 2014. Estimating the number of species in microbial diversity studies. Annual Review of Statistics and

Its Application 1, 427-445. See also, Rajakaruna, H., Drake, D.A.R., Chan, F.T., Bailey, S.A., 2016. Optimizing performance of nonparametric species richness estimators under constrained sampling. *Ecology and Evolution* 6, 7311-7322; and finally, Colwell, R.K., Coddington, J. A., 1994. Estimating terrestrial biodiversity through extrapolation. Philosophical Transactions of the Royal Society of London. *Series B, Biological Sciences* 345, 101-118.

[70] See "Materials and Methods" in the research article, "The biomass distribution on Earth," by Yinon M. Bar-On, Rob Phillips, and Ron Milo, *PNAS* June 19, 2018 115 (25) 6506-6511; first published May 21, 2018; https://doi.org/10.1073/pnas.1711842115, https://www.pnas.org/content/115/25/6506

[71] See "68% of the world population projected to live in urban areas by 2050, says UN," United Nations Department of Economic and Social Affairs, May 16, 2018, https://www.un.org/development/desa/en/news/population/2018-revision-of-world-urbanization-prospects.html/; See also, "Optimum Population Size Revisited," by Richard Blaber, *SocArXiv Papers*, doi 10.31235/osf.io/bfzfa, April 7, 2022, https://osf.io/preprints/socarxiv/b5zfa, in which the author posits that given the current ratio of "total non-nuclear and non-CO2 emitting renewable energy sources" as part of the total huma global "energy consumption" of "171,240 TWh" that "This would only be enough to sustain a global population of 779.989,242, approximately that of 1750."

[72] See "Deer Wars and Death Threats," by Brooke Jarvis, *The New Yorker Magazine*, November 8. 2021, https://www.newyorker.com/magazine/2021/11/15/deer-wars-and-death-threats

[73] See "Synanthropic Suburbia is a portion of Sarah Gunawan's Master of Architecture Thesis completed at the University of Waterloo School of Architecture," https://activesynth.cargo.site/Synanthropic-Suburbia

[74] See "The Synanthrope Preserve," https://synpreserve.com/

[75] See "Rise of the synanthropes," by Kerry Banks, February 12, 2018, *Canadian Geographic*, https://www.canadiangeographic.ca/article/rise-synanthropes, https://www.canadiangeographic.ca/article/rise-synanthropes

[76] For Peter Goldman's study, see "Flocking As A Possible Predator Defense In Dark-Eyed Juncos, Wilson Bulletin, 92(1), 1980, pp. 88-95, https://sora.unm.edu/sites/default/files/journals/wilson/v092n01/p0088-p0095.pdf. See "The Silurian Hypothesis: Would it be possible to detect an industrial civilization in the geological record?" by Gavin A. Schmidt and Adam Frank, *International Journal of Astrobiology*, April 10, 2018, https://doi.org/10.1017/S1473550418000095, https://arxiv.org/abs/1804.03748v1

[77] See *Maps of Paradise*, by Alessandro Scafi, The University of Chicago Press, Chicago and London, 2013.

[78] See restor.eco

[79] See https://www.iucn.org/theme/protected-areas/our-work/quality-and-effectiveness/world-database-protected-areas-wdpa

[80] Drafted on 5 July 2021, "a 2050 vision and 2030 mission"...See "First Draft of Global Biodiversity Framework Identifies Four Goals for 2050," 15 July 2021, IISD,

https://sdg.iisd.org/news/first-draft-of-global-biodiversity-framework-identifies-four-goals-for-2050/

[81] See https://sdgs.un.org/goals

[82] Convention on Biological Diversity, "Aichi Target Pages," https://www.cbd.int/aichi-targets/target/11

[83] See "World hasn't met a single Aichi biodiversity target: Leaked UN Report," by Ishan Kukreti, 10 September 2020, DownToEarth, https://www.downtoearth.org.in/news/wildlife-biodiversity/world-hasn-t-met-a-single-aichi-biodiversity-target-leaked-un-report-73314

[84] See "World met target for protected area coverage on land, but quality must improve," 19 May 2021, UN Environment Programme, https://www.unep.org/news-and-stories/press-release/world-met-target-protected-area-coverage-land-quality-must-improve

[85] See "Aichi Targets," in "Species," IUCN, https://www.iucn.org/theme/species/our-work/influencing-policy/convention-biological-diversity-cbd/aichi-targets: "UNEP/IUCN Protected Planet Report: great progress since 2010 with over 22 million km^2 of land and 28 million km^2 of ocean protected or conserved and 42% of current coverage added in the last decade; but a third of key biodiversity areas lack any coverage, and less than 8% of land is both protected and connected." See https://www.unep.org/news-and-stories/press-release/world-met-target-protected-area-coverage-land-quality-must-improve

[86] See *Evolution as Entropy – Toward a Unified Theory of Biology*, by Daniel R. Brooks and E. O. Wiley, The University of Chicago Press, Chicago, Ill., 1986, p. 219.

[87] ibid., p. 220. See Hennig's book *Phylogenetic Systematics*, University of Illinois Press, Urbana, Ill., 1966.

[88] ibid., p. 222.

[89] See Ludwig Wittgenstein's *Philosophical Investigations*, The German text, with an English translation by G. E. M. Anscombe, P.M.S. Hacker and Joachim Schulte, Revised 4th edition by P. M. S. Hacker and Joachim Schulte, Wiley-Blackwell, Malden, Mass., 2009, p. 66.

[90] See *Objectivity*, by Lorraine Daston and Peter Galison, Zone Books, New York, NY, 2007, p. 293.

[91] See *Der Raum: Ein Beitrag zur Wissenschaftslehre*, Kant-Studien Ergänzungshefte, Nr. 56, Berlin: Reuther & Reichard. Translated into English in Carnap 2019: 21–208. And *Aufbau*, 1928, [1967], *Der logische Aufbau der Welt*, Berlin: Weltkreis. Second edition, Hamburg: Meiner, 1961. Translated into English as *The Logical Structure of the World*, Rolf A. George (trans.), Berkeley, CA: University of California Press, 1967.

Chapter 5

Eco-Psychologies

Suicide and Ecocide

Every recent discussion of self-destruction is accompanied by the National Suicide Prevention Lifeline: 800-273-8255. But there is no equivalent telephone number for people concerned about planetary devolution. Where to start? How to even fathom the chain of events necessary to curb *the* most pressing and competing issues? There *are* a few biodiversity 911's and 988's.[1] But they scarcely minimize the striking reality that is at the heart of humanity's propensity for suicide, albeit proportionately a de minimis number (excluding the enormous ratio one might surmise of suicidal thoughts). Realistically, there is no 911 for human cruelty to animals, the incremental loss of ecosystems, the global population explosion and with it, vastly inordinate consumer footprints. What is ecocidal highlights that which is suicidal, at a glance. We are, quintessentially, capable of permanent injury to ourselves as we have been habitually to others.

But that is merely a glance that also misses past and looming varieties of self-destructive experiences. The nature of depression in an individual mirrors that of the population; of the fact that the collectivity of life itself, in countless and too obvious guises, is irreversibly sullen, heartsick, desperate. Such is the colossal irony that so much post-traumatic syndrome effects is readily mollified by a companion puppy, a turtle, a dove.

When the biological turns toward itself, attempting to make sense of and capture its own identity within the force fields of annihilation, we are merely describing the systematic pangs of interiorization of an otherwise explicit process of accelerated end-of-life systems. Perhaps self-vindictiveness, hatred of others, and violence in general is endemic. We know that those who are cruel to other animals and plants are more likely to be cruel to other humans. That is one of those points of physics and mathematics that poses a lethal reversibility. Those who see the struggle to survive as the core mechanism in evolution are more likely to prejudice their perceptions of violence as a universal quotient, necessary for all biological equilibrium. Others will entirely disagree, viewing mutualism, symbioses and other collaborative forms of co-existence and existential altruism as the most successful strategies for survival.

Then there are those for whom survival is not even at issue. Not at all. People who care not for themselves, only for Others. What they can give, how much assistance and kindness they can render in the midst of ongoing wars and woes. Indeed, one's own survival is irrelevant. A pledge to be kind to one's neighbors. That is the matrix of the future.

What is most relevant is the fact – as Mahavira, Buddha, Lao-Tzu and Christ so stressed – that there is suffering. The causes and consequences of pain must challenge every philosophy. The promise of amelioration. Or, if none be in sight, the need to die, as painlessly and quickly as possible.

On this latter point, there is no need here to elaborate the many inferred ethics deriving from euthanasia, a fundamental right. *Papaver somniferum,* the opium poppy, is but one of hundreds of known plants that provide therapeutic advantages for millions of humans and other species in pain. Indeed, plants for medicinal purposes are utilized by an estimated "80%" of the global human population.[2] In the U.S., the Harrison Narcotic Act of 1914 sought to curb what had been an epidemic of pain relief for centuries, indeed, millennia.[3] While morphine was first specifically isolated in 1803 by Frederich Sertürner, evidence dating back some 60,000 years suggests that Neanderthal were well accustomed to using medicinal plants for treatment of pain and diseases.[4] By the time of Aristotle and his botanical protégé, Theophrastus, plant usage dominated all treatments. Aristotle himself most likely moderated his own pain prior to death in his early 60s from an intestinal ailment using a powerful plant derivative from a now extinct sub-species of silphium once found in abundance on the coast of Libya.[5] By AD 60, "approximately 500 plants" provided some "1000 simple drugs."[6] But nothing was more powerful than opium. Writes Eric Trickey regarding pain intervention during the U.S. Civil War, "The Union Army alone issued nearly 10 million opium pills to its soldiers, plus 2.8 million ounces of opium powders and tinctures."[7] By 1898, when the Bayer Company initiated production and widespread distribution of commercial morphine, it was deemed by all "a wonder drug."[8]

By utilizing plants to alleviate pain, to help heal, a bounty of data illuminates other species who have been doing just that for hundreds of millions of years, from "pregnant elephants," indeed, every living mammal, to "macaws," "fruit flies," and "lizards."[9]

All thought begins somewhere, by some means whose end is illimitable, as far as we can adduce. But thought which sets out to destroy, or knows of ongoing destruction (whether primary, secondary, tertiary) may be described singularly as psychotic, a word bandied about like never before. Its etymology, however, is a peculiar misalignment between the Greek – "'*psykhē*' mind, life, soul" and Latin, "'osis,' abnormal." Indeed, in Greek "psykhosis meant 'a giving of life; animation; principle of life." Only by 1847 did the noun refer to "mental affection or derangement."[10] Throughout the mid-1800s, psychopathy was viewed as a mental disorder, and by the late 1800s, a "cerebral disease" with legal ramifications. In the 1870s a "psychrolutist" was one who bathed in rivers in the Winter. By the early 1900's, psychotherapy had come of age, whilst "psychopomp" referred to the guide or conductor who took souls to the land of the dead.[11] Ecocide is less ambiguous: 'oikos' or 'oeco'- household, and the Latin 'caedere' – to "cut down" or "kill".[12]

This is not merely a human probability disorder. Other species commit autothysis (self-sacrifice), from insects to marine mammals. A considerable literature has sought to understand the nature suicide in ants, birds, termites, canines, other primates, Hymenoptera, and various parasites, as well as hosts. There is tremendous evidence, not surprisingly, of widespread grief and depression amongst Others.[13] When we interpolate, from any locale where the indigenous flora and fauna have endured human offensives, to larger scales where the human destruction has accumulated for millennia, we are presented with an entirely unknowable quantum of desperate melancholy, which we see at once in the eyes, and emphatic forlorn of all those animals in cages, in zoos and aquaria and pet stores. It was an epiphany of horror that first slammed into my consciousness (mt) when I was three years old, accompanying my father to the San Francisco Zoo, where a wolf was pacing frantically back and forth, a condition generally thought of as stereotypies.

Such general descriptions and approaches hint at the practical person's guide to getting started from the outside. Starting from the inside, however, is a whole different matter. The history of empathy, of pain killers, of legal attempts to remedy war, abuse, cruelty, ecological negligence and outright destruction, all enter into a biochemistry that belongs to every organism, in tandem with every other. The combined effect gives rise to philosophies and systems far beyond our ken. One could argue that it involves philosophy at every level. But when that delicate calibration gets anywhere close to the environment, to sentient Others, the effort, however one might choose to characterize it, quite frequently backfires, and for good reasons.

Our suicides may be evidence for our sheer sadness for having been born. Not failed, or lived up to some expectation – our own or, we interpret, someone else's – but the fact, as Buddha evidently enunciated, that life *is* sadness. In his important study of Buddhism, compassion, ecological and psychological studies, Charles Fisher notes that "phenomenon of genes conferring useful traits on a species but also having harmful side effects.. called in biology antagonistic pleiotropy."[14] The duality of pain and its counterpart in Nature presents to the inquiring mind – any mind, any constellation of instincts – a perplexity: to tenaciously persist, or to relinquish, letting go. In examining word for word ancient Vedic traditions, the great comparative religions scholar, Ananda Coomaraswamy (1877-1947) expatiated upon the famed statement, between humans and non-humans (heavenly Devas), "Who thou art, that am I; and who I am, that art thou ('yo'ham asmi sa tvam asi')".[15] It is this aspect of biophilia in which suicide is part of the ritual leading from one to the other, as understood not as death, per se, but as an exchange that alters the Western view of self-destruction (often deemed illegal during periods throughout European and American history, not that it mattered, for example to the more than 1,800 people who have jumped off the Golden Gate Bridge).[16] That exchange has its roots in the earliest known communions between humans and other species, a form of transcendence that both eliminates pain, but also assures the sufferer of some version of heaven. It may be in a dark cave, or atop a mountain, or simply by closing one's eyes, forever. To some, it is the most unpleasant, indeed loathsome conceptualization. To others, something quite different, ineffable, essential, the key to our mortality, and the meaning of our place on earth. As a species that has proven time and again its lethality to Others, our ending is really a beginning.

Émile Durkheim's (1858-1917) landmark study of suicide[17] has subsequently evinced a debate culminating in the "ecological fallacy" critique that differentiates between populations and individuals. The units of aggregation by which data is assembled and correlated typically concerns environmental only in the sense of ambience, which could be medical, cultural, or counter-inferential.[18] All four of Durkheim's definitive types of self-destruction confirm an aggressive act of individuation arising from one of any number of what amount to separation anxiety response equivalents.[19] Separation itself connotes a fascinating spectrum of species whose natural turn it is to leave the nest, or parental care in general. To go solitary into the world. Whereas for other colonial species, thrips, aphids, Damaraland mole rats, eusociality invokes the fundaments of an educational system that is genetic and instinctive. Those for whom natal philopatry or homing is crucial, i.e., the Atlantic bluefin tuna, salmon, turtles, albatross and penguins, etc., there are imprinting mechanisms that provide a map of chemical and magnetic clues to a birthplace, which becomes the target after however many years of adolescence. For a heavily socialized primate like *H. sapiens*, environmental correlates are certainly most crucial in their supply-chain of hits to the psyche. The real-time impacts of density are impossible to follow, let alone predict, in terms both of violence to oneself or to others. But the image conjured by E. O. Wilson's "social conquest of earth" (2012) certainly conveys the full burden that is humankind's self-obsession; as well as a chilling, underlying qualification of life that is a template for its quantification. The superpositioning biologically leaves an irremediable trace of its crushing presence. A continuing global fertility rate of 2.4 (replacement value would need to be 2.1), or 1.05% overall growth per year, which means approximately 81 million more people every twelve months, nine New York's, or ten Chicago's. Or, if your imagination prefers, a greater Mexico City, Los Angeles, Rio de Janeiro and Tokyo-Yokohama. By whatever ungraspable metaphor one envisions the seething crowd sizes, there can only be queasy fright, uncontrollable dizziness, demographic nausea. The mind waterboarded.

Most suicides are thought to occur during a sleepless night, between midnight and 4 a.m.[20] More suicidal behavior manifest indoors than outside (by a factor of 4) and more frequently in rural rather than urban settings, during Springtime.[21]

At well over one million documented suicide cases annually throughout the world, one suicide every 40 seconds – the numbers are highest across Europe, and then throughout southern Africa[22] – the etiologies can be discussed from all 360 degrees. For Durkheim, it was a simplified formula, in retrospect, a rather crazy notion: More Protestants, he thought, killed themselves than Catholics, for reasons Durkheim believed to be the varying levels of education and stringency of faith.[23]

In a 2010 study, researchers suggested that "the most dangerous form of suicidal desire is caused by the simultaneous presence of two interpersonal constructs—thwarted belongingness and perceived burdensomeness" and they went on to distinguish "capability to engage in suicidal behavior" from the "desire" to do so.[24] Others have suggested that suicide for many is the only "answer" to a miserable life, while some argue that it is the act following upon the most profound of questions: What comes afterwards? While still other investigators have followed a psychological model (particularly for males) proposed by Roy Baumeister in 1990, namely, "six steps" all leading to "escape".[25] Marsha Linehan refers to a "bio-social" precondition for suicide, a suite of symptoms swirling around "hypersensitivity" to all that is personally inclement.[26] In a survey of 56 recent National Library of Medicine research papers[27] the predicates for self-nullification include predispositions for prolonged depression in combat vets, anxiety-ridden teens, various attenuations of the reason to go on living, aging ideations, a vast array of stress forms, suites of anxiety pouring in from family life, eating disorders, and stoicism, to fearlessness in the face of protracted pain.

Only in certain microbes has "ecological suicide" actually been described.[28] We know from centuries of anecdotal data that the totality of environment precariousness is an obvious precursor to lethal morbidity. Suicide itself is *not* considered a disease.[29] But mere ruminations on the world can certainly lead to it, says a recent group of investigators, not to mention U.N. Secretary General António Guterres speaking to ministers from forty countries in Berlin at the Petersberg Climate Dialogue speaking of humanity's "collective suicide."[30] No surprise there. And to that extent, a swath of recent research has led to conclusive relativity between "major depressive disorder" and a "map of environmental factors."[31] Conversely, even exposure to trees on streets within cities can act as a lifeline, a life-or-death anodyne.[32] Hence, an entire field, that goes back thousands of years, of nature therapies.[33]

But they will not remediate language, as adopted by the majority of nations at COP26 in Glasgow, that wavers around vague business-as-usual paradigms. A language of court-imposed increments, country to country, without the slightest metric of obligation. As the political language mingles with the ecological, the effect is a sum of dilutions, obfuscations, denials. This is cut-throat competition to achieve the lowest possible contribution to the already impoverished commons. To insist on separability between nations, only rarely factoring in an intermarriage.

The cycles of environmental refutation, defense, deferral and dilution year by year, decade after decade continues. "For heaven's sake, don't kill this moment. Please embrace this text so that we bring hope to the hearts of our children and grandchildren," pleaded the "frustrated" European Union Vice President Frans Timmermans, near the last few hours of the U.N. conference at Glasgow.[34] To which Aminath Shauna, Minister of Environment for the emblematic Maldives declared resignedly, "I'd like to note that this progress is not in line with the urgency and scale with the problem at hand."[35] It was the ecological equivalent of the "failed" Treaty of Versailles in 1919, which laid down the preconditions for World War II that erupted two decades later.[36] Similarly, in its worst-case scenario outlook, the Politico platform characterized the potential for a "tremendous scale of mass suffering, food system collapse, intolerable heat, multiple and simultaneous extreme weather events, and large-scale, irreversible changes to the climate and ecosystem to come."[37] Little wonder, one should add, reading the draft agreement, with its endless "acknowledging," "recognizing," recalling, stressing, expressing, noting, emphasizing, urging, welcoming, also recognizing, further recognizing, reaffirming, inviting, underscoring, calling upon, also acknowledging, deciding, requesting and resolving, taking note, and finally, encouraging.[38]

As if to further isolate the COP26 linguistic quixotries, the meeting of nearly 200 countries coincided with recognition that the last great hope to stave off deforestation throughout Africa – a Green Wall across the continent for 5,000 miles of planted trees, begun in 2007 – had all but failed, with only 4% completed. And even that paltry sum had been compromised by dying trees. It just wasn't going to happen.[39]

Whether deeply spelled-out thought is the basis for language (for example, the Honorable John Kerry, U.S. Special Presidential Envoy, summing up Glasgow, voicing "I believe…"), or vice versa, no field test is going to look pretty. COP26 and 27 both exemplified a near best case scenario for determined optimism, or reified depression; a renaissance of planetary infidelity and imbecility, or the ultimate self-delusion, expressed in the form of a mask, a cheering on of the Titanic's maiden voyage. Immense crocodile smiles.

All of our best hopes come girded by the underlying, unstoppable devastation, even with a thousand green innovations every day. Nothing about that is ideal. Human natures cannot be corrected by any technology or political leadership. No "leader" has ever succeeded beyond a distinctly finite span, a spasm of futile executive orders in blue ink signatures on fancy paper. Every technology is superseded, each tradition of thought relegated to a divisiveness. Absolutes, fundamentalism, total intolerance always succumb to cracks on the first day. Even the "Hermit of Treig" has a *human* beginning and by his mid-70s, has come to rely on other human assistance. He is an ingenious toolmaker, but also has binoculars, a watch, normal 21st century clothing.[40] His motivations would appear to be not unlike those of Thoreau: just wanting to be in the wild, on his own terms. A man who deserves utmost regard if not outright celebration. But, like the 4th of July, it has become difficult to separate explosions, failed dreams, penultimate exasperations.

Other Factors

Multiplied by over 8 billion of us, other inevitable factors intervene. Mathematics guarantees that once a compromise, *any* compromise, then ensues another division upon division, until the fractions add up to nothing like an ideal, not even the original idea, but some other face of a skewed or entirely watered-down general principle. In the case of the Anthropocene, ruination. Unlike the cooperative nature of most other species, we cannot permutate human nature into human natures. Our plurality ensures inventiveness but not stability, collateral safety, or even margins of peace. The matrix of so many will not abide any entirely eusocial[41] commands or structures to engender smooth policies, or anything remotely like an egalitarian truth function. By that expression we refer to distributions of every good and service that are not merely subject to the whims of a Leviathan nature consolidated in a proto-feudal skirmish. Prosociality is the limited exception, not a norm. Dreamers occupy but a pejorative outlier, or what is called a heavy-tailed distribution, a fabled land – not model or even sample set – perceived dismissively by most. In statistics this is known as Chauvenet's criterion (named after the polymath William Chauvenet (1820-1870); or an inverse cumulative distribution function that treats random variables in a Monte Carlo method orientation. In other words, a reliance on an ecological ergodicity – the apprehension that large systems cannot be replicated or converged into smaller ones. Differential geometry has made great strides since the 1828 publication of German mathematician Carl Friedrich Gauss's (1777-1855) *Theorema Egregium* ("remarkable theorem"), that signaled the field of curved surface analysis, or Riemannian manifolds, which eventually led to the general theory of relativity. As with other outlier tests (by Charles Sanders Peirce, by Robert H. Grubbs, and others) the idea is to prove that there are errors in a distribution. There is no central stable solution, or mean. This is the realm of robust statistics and it fails in every biological sense given the deviations that are the life blood of the biosphere.

At its worst convolution, compromises turn readily with a vengeance that history has all but ordained. There is no mean average war, or probable distribution factor of mortality, other than in pathological terms and the spread of a disease. One recalls the Kellogg-Briand Pact of 1928 (to end all wars); the 1855 General Act of the Conference of Berlin which succeeded in providing the genocidal King Leopold II of Belgium a free hand to decimate the Congolese; or the Treaty of New Echota, 1835 (resulting in the Trail of Tears).[42] As with any philosophical projection, the mathematics of resolution (treaties, pacts, agreements of any kind amongst humans) are explicitly stochastic, the outcome of random trials.

The psychological precedents of despoliation confirm a diagnostic tally. Wrote journalist Jo Confino after learning of the scientific consensus regarding destruction of Australia's Great Barrier Reef, "Why aren't we on the floor doubled up in pain at our capacity for industrial scale genocide of the world's species?"[43]

Thanatologists studying human-devised death across the natural world and its logically converse impact on the human psyche refer to the myriad syndromes in terms of "grieving".[44] In the late Middle Ages, plagues and sheer toll that life would take limited life expectancy at birth across the world to less than half of what it is today, or between 24 and the low 40s.[45] In our time, anticipatory grief has moved from malevolent autocrats and Civil Wars, to the specters of nuclear engagement, melting ice caps, ruinous pollution, pandemics and vast extinction spasms. Dozens of individuals are worth in excess of one hundred billion dollars, whilst billions of people are poor, hundreds of millions of people, untold billions of other animals, starving. Aspiring multitudes all but celebrate the prospect of such wealth, content to ignore the outrageous disparities, let alone overly concern themselves with the very source of these endless toxic disaggregations. Such human systems, or collective staying power for any one target of virtue, are not, possibly cannot, be morally distributed.

Distribution calls immediately into question, Who? What, and, to whom? These are only the obvious points of contact. Culpability follows, at every juncture of ethical disarray and outright deception along the chains of exploitation. This is not a jaundiced overview, but the inherent (Marxist) breakdown of what began simply within the barter systems of early human self-interest and surprisingly generous altruism. Ashley Montague documented that innocence and its consequential cooperative narratives quite compellingly in his fine book, *Learning Non-Aggression: The Experience of Non-Literate Societies*.[46] The (with hindsight, inevitable) avalanche of incremental modernity that followed early Tasaday-like human experience, comports with today's pervasive solastalgiac (homesickness) epidemics, most noticeably climate and extinction anxiety. The ecological rose-tinted glass syndrome. It was always better in the past, goes the formula. But there is no real formula, since the past is always ahead of us, a realization that requires a leap over the relativity portion of the formula: the fast-moving train, the Doppler Effect, their directionality confounds us for the same reason that J.-P. Sartre's starting argument was his famed statement that *man is condemned to be free*. Sartre's point hinged upon our taking "responsibility" for everything we did, thought, dreamt. Intentionality, as in the Jain ethical pantheon, for Sartre held pivotal importance. Hence, the appropriateness of calling our condemned space and time the Anthropocene.

A growing systemic pang of perception prompted by all that is environmentally looming, or disastrous right outside, now. The psychological profile of this most glaring of civilization's discontent has been articulated since at least 2007 when Glenn Albrecht, Gina-Maree Sartore and colleagues published a qualitative and quantitative diagnosis of global cultural changes predicated upon the "large-scale open-cut coal mining [impact] on individuals in the Upper Hunter Valley of NSW" (New South Wales, Australia).[47] Levels of urban instability have been identified as key factors in a psychiatric context termed "the ecology of suicidal behavior."[48] It is not a spinning of reality, but an underscoring pillar of all eco-psychologies that endeavor to characterize a slow ecocide at the species level. Individuals cannot escape it, which ignites a most perplexing aberrance. Can the single psyche circumvent, combat, survive self-destruction at the species level? A donation of twelve dollars per month – "call now" – is, amazingly, a requisite first step, assuming all nearly eight billion people paid $144.00 annually, or one trillion one hundred fifty-two billion. With the most financially fortunate nation in the world, the U.S., allotting 8.849 billion for the EPA in its 2019 budget,[49] even if we make a broad extrapolation multiplying that figure times 193 U.N. recognized nations we arrive at slightly more than 1.7 trillion US dollars. Add the other inputs from biodiversity financing to costs associated with animal welfare regulations, as a total global budget, and it is clear that humanity is nowhere near even modest levels of mitigation.[50] The gaps between safeguarding and failing at a collective level add up to sums neither governments nor scientific institutions even have the means to quantify. One way to offer up a description of just one, albeit widespread, sector, is the impact of climate change on the global economy as measured in three decades or so. At least one report from Swiss Re suggests that by 2050 (thinking optimistically) "annual global economic output" will be reduced by "$23 trillion" or "14 percent".[51] Spending down future deficits requires a moral decision to apply lost future opportunity costs to today's environmental debacles. Like all deficits, we can expect it to be absorbed in the generalized trauma of the everyday, with huge inflationary consequences. Too many immediate problems to deal with. It's one thing to respond locally with sandbags. Quite another to reform the entire workings of a human economy involving trillions of dollars earmarked for immediate remediation, tracked proportionately day by day moving forward.

But this is all lonely nonsense. No government has ever budgeted trillions of dollars to save animals in the future, although this is the vow taken by cohorts working to create new sanctuaries and to rescue endangered or at-risk species from extinction.

Self-destruction is ironic in a population where general attitudes among the young are on the edge of a desperation,[52] a situation not unlike forms of PTSD for which the psychiatric profession has no clear antidotes.[53] In one recent survey, 70% of all Americans are experiencing current "anxiety and depression" over the state of the world's environments.[54] In India, over 10,000 farmers commit suicide every year. The causes are all ecologically related.[55] In 2018, a famed civil rights lawyer in Brooklyn NY committed self-immolation to "call attention to climate change."[56] And as a former Los Angeles Times foreign correspondent has written, "from Brazil to Congo, the Philippines to Tanzania" "Defending the environment has become a suicide mission…"[57] It might be described as a continual onslaught upon self, no matter the small victories, like the U.K. "sentience bill" mandating recognition by all British citizens that cephalopods and decapods feel "pain, pleasure, boredom, excitement, frustration, anxiety, and joy."[58] But in the legislative update there was general agreement that nothing would change, in reality. That "there is no evidence of a 'humane and commercially viable' slaughter method for hyper-intelligent animals like octopuses. They are difficult to euthanize and it is likely that they experience extensive suffering at fisheries."[59] Human compromise, it turns out, is just as lethal in the end, as philosophical sobriety.

Robust Statistics

This collapse of the cause-of-action, in spite of the cartography of well-known, salient pain points, crashes into ecological paradox with every piece of legislation from county to state to nation. Listing an organism as Endangered under the Endangered Species Act ("ESA") of 1973 by the U.S. Fish and Wildlife Service, delisting and listing again mirrors much of the continuing disarray within the conservation and genomic worlds. To what extent might the attenuation of a population, or the aggregation of open pollinated (non-hybrid) seed species qualify as endangered? What constitutes a robust species of "least concern," as according to the IUCN (International Union for Conservation of Nature)?[60] The fluctuating biological opinions regarding the status of the Gray Wolf (*Canis lupus*)[61] in the United States, or debates over the selling of poached ivory[62] are microcosms of a debilitating public window on a biointeriorization complex without egalitarian, meaningful or consistent resolve. What is the worth of ten-million letters to the editor(s)? How did the U.S. Supreme Court become a demonized, fascistic, obsolete instrument of terror and destruction in the allegedly most pervasive democracy among nations?

"Robust statistics" are said to derive from "data drawn from a wide range of probability distributions" that are free of deviations from "model assumptions in a given dataset."[63] A population, never static in time or place, particularly under global stress conditions, loses its stark *model* characteristics that would otherwise lend it to a biological sub-set of the individual who, in turn, might comprise any specific species under investigation. Moreover, computational methodology obfuscates the relations between populations almost by definition, given the inevitability of gaps (stochastic, randomization, or "sequencing techniques" that fail to account for more than a fraction of objects [e.g., genes]) in a data sample.[64] For years it has been understood that overlapping generations of one species presents to natural selection a challenge in terms of the correlative "levels of variation in realistic settings where mutation and drift are also operating."[65] These are just a few of the teases that come back to haunt any ecological philosophy posing as a verity.

The absence of a rigorous continuity in applied methods should concern our general focus upon any matter demanding ethical determinations. The confidence intervals in all scientific investigation, the realm of likely errors, are pre-ordained and error-full in the sense that our own metrics are devised in the orbits of our own abstractions. That conundrum alone makes it an unwinnable strategy. There is no ultimate resolution to such fundamental quirks in cognition or purported equation solving. With a sliding scale inchoate within all deliberation, our ability to obtain any moral status is at best risky and questionable. Multiply it by the population and the distribution functions are further compromised. Ultimately, each individual for whom our scientific method is meant to gently target ecological opportunism in the form of non-violence and an ethical sustainability, turns round and targets the very Self who has eluded any such thought experiment, not out of spite, instinct, or disregard. But by the very nature of the gap blurring the probability functions between the one and the many. The mob transcends science, ethics, philosophy. This is an elaborate no-win scenario.

We humans easily are assuaged by our assignations with respect to nature, selecting phrases that comport with underlying similes. For example, when E. O. Wilson wrote of "Patchy Distributions Of Ant Species In New Guinea Rain Forests" in 1958, the 29-year old biologist was sufficiently impressed by the common feature of continuously changing compositions as to suggest that "the theoretical implications of discordant patchiness" could be correlated with "rapid evolution" within the "great kaleidoscope" that, in turn, exerted its power from the population structures of numerous species, down to "the evolution of individual species of ants." All of this, he made clear, came about through "subjective impressions".[66]

Add to that the insights from those involved in nanosciences. "The Elegance of Simple Animals" involves, in one example, a "blob of a creature [who] builds for itself an intricate, hierarchical cage of silica" in which shrimp become trapped into a symbiotic relationship well "beyond the best that engineers can do." Does nature make mistakes? "Yes," according to Felice C. Frankel and George M. Whitesides, differentiating between "friends" and the "enemy" with respect to antibodies. "Allergies," they write, "are this wonderful system getting it wrong: the cells that produce antibodies can mistake bee venom, pollen, proteins in fish soup, or feces from dust mites as evidence of infection by parasites, with unhappy consequences."[67]

New Guinea ants, microscopic marine creatures, human antibodies and every other living being remain equally elusive when it comes to human descriptive or predictive clarity. More importantly, the degree to which our perception of other species, no matter how scientifically elevated the characterization, remains fixated on the discrimination of being. As Calvin O. Schrag wrote insightfully over forty years ago, "we are in quest of a recovery of the origin" referring to "value". This requires radicalization of value to complement our radicalization of knowledge." This, he wrote, would require "a dismantling of the conceptual scaffolding of traditional value theory through a displacement of the fact-value dichotomy…" This is a contemporary equivalent of "thinking beyond the transcendental-empirical dichotomy," says Schrag.[68]

While an estimated 280 million adults in the world suffer from the depression[69] of which seven primary forms have been described in psychiatric literature,[70] data from 2020 in the U.S. revealed that 34% of all Americans have described their own "symptoms of anxiety, depression or both." "24 percent showed clinically significant symptoms of major depressive disorder…[71] We have no reason to assume medical census numbers yielding any more upbeat data worldwide.

Spccies Depression

Nor do we have the slightest sense of what other species depression, let alone the scope of it, looks like. Utterly fallacious biomedical experiments have utilized models to try and gauge aspects of "helplessness, anhedonia [the inability to feel pleasure], behavioral despair…[and] alterations in sleep and appetite patterns" in some other species, in an effort to divine efficacies of various antidepressant interventions for humans.[72] But imagine the types of depression amongst survivors of "hell on earth,"[73] an attribution lent to Ukraine's city of Mariupol by Ukrainian military, with over 431,000 human inhabitants as of January, 2022, and untold numbers of other animals, following Russia's terrorist assaults. That set of circumstances represents any number of eco-psychological depredations among our kind but cannot begin to fathom the suffering of Others, though several animal rights organizations including PETA have been in Ukraine rescuing companion animals left behind in the rubble and dispatching photographic documentation of the distraught.

Pain Points

To reiterate: The pain points cannot be diagnosed. We have neither the inclination, in most cases, the investigative techniques, nor understanding to fathom what we are doing here in terms of our relation to others. It is no aphasic category of neurophysiological decline. We know enough about our environment to recognize the fundamental signs of our dependencies on air, water, food and sleep. But we do not compute the nature of interdependency. While we celebrate "the hidden lives of pets," and "secret life of pets," laud the intelligence, physical adroitness, spirit of adventure, dance performances, and tool usage of Sulfur-crested cockatoos, African gray parrots, rodents, iguanas, dogs and cats, etc., we do so with the enthusiasm of insulated infants, as if after millions of years of close company with others, we are just beginning to wake up.[74]

Moreover, our oppressive design mechanisms for bearing experimental proof, manifesting our clumsy hypotheses, reveals far more about human beings than the subjects of our investigation. In our opinions, this is very sad. The "wow" factor that pervades most natural history *entertainment* can be deeply offensive.

At the heart of our disconnects are the universality of pain and depression, true distribution functions about which we are largely ignorant. Nor do we have a memory commensurate with our strict indebtedness to nature. That memory, in many families, is virtually immune to any sense of genealogy. Thoreau wrote that "It is in vain to dream of a wildness distant from ourselves. There is none such." But goes on to acknowledge that "It is the bog in our brains and bowels, the primitive vigor of Nature in us, that inspires that dream."[75] Simon Schama writes of Thoreau, "The very idea of culture layered over culture on the same site turned Thoreau's stomach, and he rejoiced that, as he imagined, the three acres Emerson had given him on Walden Pond had never seen any form of human settlement."[76] This ecological misanthropy, opines Schama, pits the barren, mundane and sullen everyday ruins of archaeology against the less dreary, indeed fantastic perimeters of mythology. The two are not remotely the same. Somewhere in the middle is the notion, as some contemporary geographers are employing it, of the transfer of critical, sacred space between overlapping of successive cultures. That is, the attempt to imagine "hidden codes in the landscape" as Paul Devereux has used the expression.[77] The Islamic world that came to occupy the city of Balkh in northern Afghanistan represents a prime example of the fluid power of sacrality in the transference of meaning within a site-specific place. Just as a place like Walden Pond was inhabited and visited long before a singular mid-19th century naturalist would live there and write about it from his particular time in history, with its attitudes and perspectives, so too Balkh had, for at least 4,000 years gone through a multiplicity of complex human orientations. It was previously known as Bactra (Bactria or Tokharistan) to the ancient Greeks; as Zariaspa to the Persians, and so forth. Certain surviving structures were undoubtedly Buddhist. There is even some evidence to suggest that the peoples of this region gave rise to the original Bonpo (pre-Buddhist) Tibetan epicenter. But also to a mayhem of settlements, empires and kingdoms including Achaemenid, Hellenistic, Kushan, and Iranian.[78] Co-occupancies of cave sites like Shanidar in modern Iraq hosted two separate Homo species; Syria's Tell Brak, Sumeria's Uruk, India's Pondicherry, or the Aztec capital of Tenochtitlán have each seen countless cultural visitations at variance or convergence.[79]

If Thoreau got queasy over the idea of living atop a human graveyard, it is a plausible assumption to make that he fervently wanted to discover a theoretically pure, untainted place he called wilderness, as have so many who have been, and are frustrated by humanity's penchant for conurbations, with all the pollution and ill-fitted consequences of their human density. Among those demoralizing repercussions, the inherent ambiguity – often times perverse or pathetic – of ritual, is a subject that philosopher/geographer Yi-Fu Tuan has addressed in terms of its religious but also frequently violent character.[80] One thinks back to the appalling history of sacrificing animals, a practice that still very much persists in some cultures. Or of sipping blood and calling it communion. Tracking history through the lens of historians of the ilk of a Thucydides, Herodotus, Arnold Toynbee, Clarence Glacken, John

Keegan, Will and Ariel Durant, or Jared Diamond, to name but a few, confirms that ritual persistently transmogrifies into our worst collective instincts and the pernicious show of machismo, domination, oppression of Others. Juridical choices are entirely swayed by populist primitivism and utter ecological illiteracy. Consider the overturning of *Roe v Wade* – fanatical biases and tragically revealing rage. The legislatures bow not to central reason, but emergent paranoias from the fringes. Time and again marmoreal custom has been outweighed by the mass and velocity inherent to fear, anger, hatred/envy of women, and the socialization of slavery in some form or other.

"Garden of Eden, Studio of Jan Van Breughel The Elder, ca. 1606," Photo © M. C. Tobias, Private Collection.

Our mental occupation and striking down of the world has no biological parallel. We can't stop it because we cannot stop ourselves. When we march in protest, we are protesting our own species. These are synonymous ventures with identical neurological infrastructures and groundswells. While it is a common current that we do not learn (or cannot imbibe the complex of messaging) from history, our history, anyone's history, it cannot be said that we know ourselves only to the extent of history. As Louis Menand writes in his review of Richard Cohen's book *Making History: The Stortytellers Who*

Shaped the Past, "what do historians want the facts for?"[81] A multiple of reasons but, in the end, he says, the history matters and is filtered through the historian's own person. Citing Cohen, "any author is the prisoner of their character and circumstances yet often they are the making of him."[82] Søren Kierkegaard summed up the deeper dilemma when he wrote about "two sorts of the unhappy" by declaring, "that what prevents him from becoming present in his hope is memory, what prevents him from becoming present in memory is hope."[83]

Endnotes

[1] https://suicidepreventionlifeline.org/faq/ Probably the best numbers to call would include those of the nearest police station or humane society, the EPA Criminal Enforcement hotline – 1-202-564-2480 (https://www.epa.gov/enforcement/forms/enforcement-contact-us), PETA's hotline: 1-757-622-7382 (https://www.peta.org/), U.S. Fish & Wildlife Law Enforcement – 1-703-358-1949 (https://www.fws.gov/program/office-of-law-enforcement/contact-us), the United Nations Regional Enforcement Network (https://www.unodc.org/res/field-offices_html/FO-map2_2500_1560px.png), the World Wildlife Fund's TRAFFIC International call line -+44 (0) 1223-277427, or +41 22 364 91 11, or wwfus.ethicspoint.com, or the scientists at Global Wildlife Conservation at +1-512-686-6062 (hello@rewild.org), or https://www.rewild.org/contact, or the National Audubon Organization which maintains various crime-related task forces, 1-844-4283826; or at Conservation International – 1-800-429-5660 or 1-703-341-2400 (https://www.conservation.org/contact), or the Office of the Inspector General Hotline at the U.S. Department of Interior for filing a classified tip, 1-800-447-8477. Interpol maintains active wildlife and environmental crimes groups, and can be reached at its General Secretariat in Lyon, France, Fax #: +33 4 72 44 71 63, as well as an office in Singapore, https://www.interpol.int/en/Contacts/Contact-INTERPOL, or the Animal Liberation Front-Line Press office – Press@AnimalLiberationPressOffice.org. And so on. If you are calling a local wildlife rescue group or humane society, just pause a moment to determine/enquire whether the animal at risk is likely to be euthanized or saved by the organization you call. Please note: All such contacts are subject to change. For concerns regarding a global meltdown (e.g., Chernobyl or Fukushima), one can always call the International Atomic Energy Agency at the Vienna International Centre, +43 (1) 2600-0, although no one gives guarantees these days. Getting your call put through to the Washington-Moscow military hotline is most unlikely.

[2] "Medicinal Plants of the Family Lamiaceae in Pain Therapy: A Review," Cristina M. Uritu, Cosmin T. Mihai, Gabriela-Dumitrita Stanciu, Gianina Dodi, Teodora Alexa-Stratulat, Andrei Luca, Maria-Magdalena Leon-Constantin, Raluca Stefanescu, Veronica Bild, Silvia Melnic, and Bogdan I. Tamba, *Pain Res Manag.* 2018; 2018: 7801543. Published online 2018 May 8. doi: 10.1155/2018/7801543, PMCID:

PMC5964621PMID: 29854039, *Journal List Pain Res Manag* v.2018; 2018 PMC5964621, National Library of Medicine, https://www.ncbi.nlm.nih.gov/pmc/articles/PMC5964621/

[3] See "Inside the Story of America's 19th-Century Opiate Addiction," by Erick Trickey, *Smithsonian Magazine*, January 4, 2018, https://www.smithsonianmag.com/history/inside-story-americas-19th-century-opiate-addiction-180967673/

[4] "Medicinal Botany," by Susan J. Zunino, Celebrating Wildflowers, U.S. Forest Service, USDA, n.d., https://www.fs.fed.us/wildflowers/ethnobotany/medicinal/index.shtml

[5] Pliny the Elder, *The Natural History*, John Bostock, M.D., F.R.S., H.T. Riley, Esq., B.A., Ed., XXII, Ch. 49, http://www.perseus.tufts.edu/hopper/text?doc=Plin.+Nat.+toc&redirect=true

[6] op. cit.. Susan Zunino.

[7] op. cit., Erick Trickey.

[8] "The History of heroin," by S. Hosztafi, PMID: 11862675, Acta Pharm Hung, 2001 Aug; 71(2):233-42. PubMed.gov, https://pubmed.ncbi.nlm.nih.gov/11862675/

[9] See "Animals that self-medicate," by Joel Shurkin, *Journal List Proc Natl Acad Sci USA* v.111(49); 2014 Dec 9 PMC4267359, Proc Natl Acad Sci USA. 2014 Dec 9; 111(49): 17339–17341. Published online 2014 Dec 9. doi: 10.1073/pnas.1419966111, PMCID: PMC4267359. PMID: 25492915, NIH, National Library of Medicine, https://www.ncbi.nlm.nih.gov/pmc/articles/PMC4267359/#:~:text=A%20wide%20range%20of%20animals,when%20they%20need%20a%20remedy.&text=Bears%2C%20deer%2C%20elk%2C%20and,plants%20apparently%20to%20self%2Dmedicate.

[10] See psychotic, both as adjective and noun, https://www.etymonline.com/word/psychotic#:~:text=psychotic%20(adj.),Related%3A%20Psychotically.

[11] See *The Oxford English Dictionary*, Volume VIII, Oxford and New York, The Clarendon Press and Oxford University Press, 13 volumes, 1961, pp. 1552-1553.

[12] "Ecocide," Young People's Trust for the Environment, FactSheet, https://ypte.org.uk/factsheets/ecocide/what-is-ecocide

[13] See Courtet, Philippe, ed. (2016). *Understanding Suicide*. Cham: Springer International Publishing. doi:10.1007/978-3-319-26282-6. See also, Preti, Antonio (December 2007). "Suicide among Animals: A Review of Evidence". *Psychological Reports*. 101 (3): 831–848. doi:10.2466/pr0.101.3.831-848. ISSN 0033-2941. PMID 18232440. S2CID 40423383. See also, Trail, Deborah R. Smith (1980). "Behavioral Interactions between Parasites and Hosts: Host Suicide and the Evolution of Complex Life Cycles". *The American Naturalist*. 116: 77–91. doi:10.1086/283612. hdl:1808/17548. S2CID 16777324.

[14] See *Dismantling Discontent – Buddha's Way Through Darwin's World*, by Charles Fisher, Ph.D., Elite Books, Santa Rosa, CA, 2007, p. 77.

[15] *Coomaraswamy, 1: Selected Papers, Traditional Art And Symbolism*, Edited by Roger Lipsey, Bollingen Series LXXXIX, Princeton University Press, 1977, 3 volumes, p.474.

[16] See "Golden Gate Bridge suicides: A history of fatalities, and how further tragedies may be prevented," by Justin Ray, Los Angeles Times, March 30, 2022, https://www.latimes.com/california/newsletter/2022-03-30/golden-gate-bridge-

suicides-a-history-of-fatalities-and-how-further-tragedies-may-be-prevented-essential-california

[17] *Le Suicide: Étude de sociologie*, Ancienne Librairie Germer Bailliére, Paris, France, 1897.

[18] See Freedman, D. A., "Ecological inference and the ecological fallacy," International Encyclopedia for the Social and Behavioral Sciences, 6, 4027-30, 2001. See also, "ecological fallacy, epidemiology," by John J. Hsieh, Britannica, https://www.britannica.com/science/ecological-fallacy; See also "disaster epidemiology," by Thomas J. Songer, Britannica, https://www.britannica.com/science/disaster-epidemiology. This latter essay also focuses on humans and the environment, correlating public health, societal mitigation responses, and the extent of disruption and morbidity in the aftermath. Because there is no aftermath from a suicide, and pre-mitigation (psychological preparation by specialists, e.g., therapies) have failed, the most common denominator for self-disaster is generally delineated as an environmental factor, or factors. For the suicide hotline website, see https://suicidepreventionlifeline.org/

[19] See, for example, Redlich, Ronny (February 2015). "Are you gonna leave me? Separation anxiety is associated with increased amygdala responsiveness and volume". *Social Cognitive and Affective Neuroscience*. 10 (2): 278–284. doi:10.1093/scan/nsu055. PMC 4321627. PMID 24752071. See also, *The Taming of Solitude – Separation Anxiety in Psychoanalysis*, by Jean-Michel Quinodoz, Routledge, London UK, 1993.

[20] See "Study finds that suicides are far more likely to occur after midnight," n.a., American Academy of Sleep Medicine, June 1, 2014, https://aasm.org/study-finds-that-suicides-are-far-more-likely-to-occur-after-midnight/

[21] See "Seasonality of Suicidal Behavior," by Jong-Min Woo, Olaoluwa Okusaga and Teodor T. Postolache, PMC, *Int J Environ Res Public Health*. 2012 Feb; 9(2): 531–547. Published online 2012 Feb 14. doi: 10.3390/ijerph9020531, PMCID: PMC3315262, PMID: 22470308, https://www.ncbi.nlm.nih.gov/pmc/articles/PMC3315262/; See also, "A 2-Year Psychological Autopsy Study of Completed Suicides in the Athens Greater Area, Greece," by Atonios Paraschakis, et al., *Psychiatry Investig*. 2015 Apr; 12(2): 212–217. Published online 2015 Jan 20. doi: 10.4306/pi.2015.12.2.212, PMCID: PMC4390592, PMID: 25866522, https://www.ncbi.nlm.nih.gov/pmc/articles/PMC4390592/; See also, Fakhari, A., Farahbakhsh, M., Esmaeili, E.D. et al. A longitudinal study of suicide and suicide attempt in northwest of Iran: incidence, predictors, and socioeconomic status and the role of sociocultural status. *BMC Public Health* 21, 1486 (2021). https://doi.org/10.1186/s12889-021-11527-9, https://bmcpublichealth.biomedcentral.com/articles/10.1186/s12889-021-11527-9; See also, Graetz, N., Preston, S.H., Peele, M. et al. Ecological factors associated with suicide mortality among non-Hispanic whites. *BMC Public Health 20*, 1339 (2020). https://doi.org/10.1186/s12889-020-09379-w; and Martins Junior, D.F., Felzemburgh, R.M., Dias, A.B. et al. Suicide attempts in Brazil, 1998–2014: an ecological study. *BMC Public Health* 16, 990 (2016). https://doi.org/10.1186/s12889-016-3619-3; and Qi, X., Hu, W., Mengersen, K. et al. Socio-environmental drivers and suicide in Australia: Bayesian spatial analysis. BMC Public Health 14, 681 (2014). https://doi.org/10.1186/1471-2458-14-681,

https://bmcpublichealth.biomedcentral.com/articles/10.1186/1471-2458-14-681#citeas

[22] "Suicide: one person dies every 40 seconds," World Health Organization, https://www.who.int/news/item/09-09-2019-suicide-one-person-dies-every-40-seconds; See also, World Health Organization. Public health action for the prevention of suicide: a framework. Geneva, Switzerland: World Health Organization; 2012.

[23] See "Durkheim on Suicide," SOCY 151: Foundations of Modern Social Theory, Lecture 24, Open Yale Courses, https://oyc.yale.edu/sociology/socy-151/lecture-24; See also, "Economics helps explain why suicide is more common among Protestants," by Sascha O. Becker, and Ludger Woessmann, Edited by Sam Haselby, aeon, January 14, 2019, https://aeon.co/ideas/economics-helps-explain-why-suicide-is-more-common-among-protestants

[24] See "The Interpersonal Theory of Suicide," by Kimberly A. Van Orden, Tracy K. Witte, Kelly C. Cukrowicz, Scott Braithwaite, Edward A. Selby, and Thomas E. Joiner, Jr., Psychol Rev. Author manuscript; available in PMC 2011 Jul 6., *Published in final edited form as:* Psychol Rev. 2010 Apr; 117(2): 575–600. doi: 10.1037/a0018697, PMCID: PMC3130348, NIHMSID: NIHMS301351, PMID: 20438238, https://www.ncbi.nlm.nih.gov/pmc/articles/PMC3130348/; See also, Chu, Carol; Buchman-Schmitt, Jennifer M.; Stanley, Ian H.; Hom, Melanie A.; Tucker, Raymond P.; Hagan, Christopher R.; Rogers, Megan L.; Podlogar, Matthew C.; Chiurliza, Bruno (2017). "The interpersonal theory of suicide: A systematic review and meta-analysis of a decade of cross-national research". *Psychological Bulletin.* 143(12): 1313–1345. doi:10.1037/bul0000123. PMC 5730496. PMID 29072480.

[25] See "Why do people kill themselves?" by Robert Olson, Centre For Suicide Prevention, InfoExchange 17, 2014, https://www.suicideinfo.ca/resource/suicidetheories/

[26] ibid. See also, E. Shneidman, "Suicide as psychache: A clinical approach to self-destructive behavior," Jason Aronson, Inc., Northvale, NJ, 1993. See also, M. Rudd, D. Trotter, and B. Williams, "Psychological theories of suicidal behavour," In D. Wasserman and C. Wasserman (Eds), *Oxford textbook of siuicidology and suicide prevention,* Oxford University Press, New York NY, pp. 159-164, 2009.

[27] NIH, PubMed.gov, https://pubmed.ncbi.nlm.nih.gov/?term=Van%20Orden%20KA%5BAuthor%5D&cauthor=true&cauthor_uid=20438238, Accessed November 13, 2021.

[28] See Ratzke, C., Denk, J. & Gore, J. Ecological suicide in microbes. *Nat Ecol Evol* 2, 867–872 (2018). https://doi.org/10.1038/s41559-018-0535-1, https://www.nature.com/articles/s41559-018-0535-1#citeas; See also the authors' essay, Ratzke, C., Barrere, J. & Gore, J. Strength of species interactions determines biodiversity and stability in microbial communities. *Nat Ecol Evol* 4, 376–383 (2020). https://doi.org/10.1038/s41559-020-1099-4

[29] See Turecki, G., Brent, D.A., Gunnell, D. et al. Suicide and suicide risk. Nat Rev Dis Primers 5, 74 (2019). https://doi.org/10.1038/s41572-019-0121-0

[30] See Tang, H., Xiong, T., Shi, J. et al. Global and reflective rumination are related to suicide attempts among patients experiencing major depressive episodes. *BMC Psychiatry* 21, 117 (2021). https://doi.org/10.1186/s12888-021-03119-z; for "collective suicide" remark, see "Humanity faces 'collective suicide' over climate

crisis, warns UN Chief," by Fiona Harvery, 18 July 2022, *The Guardian*, https://www.theguardian.com/environment/2022/jul/18/humanity-faces-collective-suicide-over-climate-crisis-warns-un-chief

[31] See Hullam, G., Antal, P., Petschner, P. et al. The UKB envirome of depression: from interactions to synergistic effects. Sci Rep 9, 9723 (2019). https://doi.org/10.1038/s41598-019-46001-5, https://www.nature.com/articles/s41598-019-46001-5#citeas; See also, Córdova-Palomera, A., Tornador, C., Falcón, C. et al. Environmental factors linked to depression vulnerability are associated with altered cerebellar resting-state synchronization. Sci Rep 6, 37384 (2016). https://doi.org/10.1038/srep37384

[32] Córdova-Palomera, A., Tornador, C., Falcón, C. et al. Environmental factors linked to depression vulnerability are associated with altered cerebellar resting-state synchronization. Sci Rep 6, 37384 (2016). https://doi.org/10.1038/srep37384

[33] See, for example, "'Recovering With Nature': A Review of Ecotherapy and Implications for the COVID-19 Pandemic," by Pouabi Chaudhury and Debanjan Banerjee, Frontiers in Public Health, Front. Public Health, 10 December 2020 | https://doi.org/10.3389/fpubh.2020.604440, https://www.frontiersin.org/articles/10.3389/fpubh.2020.604440/full

[34] See "Nations strike climate deal with coal compromise," by Seth Borenstein and Frank Jordans, Los Angeles Times, November 13, 2021, https://www.latimes.com/world-nation/story/2021-11-13/nations-strike-climate-deal-with-coal-compromise

[35] ibid. See also, "Just Stop Oil," https://juststopoil.org

[36] See "Failed Peace: The Treaty of Versailles, 1919," by Jerry D. Morelock, HistoryNet, (first publisher November 2013, Armchair General), https://www.historynet.com/failed-peace-treaty-versailles-1919.htm

[37] See "The Beat-and Worst-Case Scenarios for the World as COP26 Ends," by Paul Behrens, The Big Idea, Politico, 11/11/2021, https://www.politico.com/news/magazine/2021/11/11/cop-26-climate-future-520817

[38] From "Draft Text on 1/CMA.3, Version 12/11/2021, Recalling Article 2 of the Paris Agreement, https://unfccc.int/sites/default/files/resource/Overarching_decision_1-CMA-3_0.pdf

[39] See "Africa's 'Great Green Wall' shifts focus to hold off desert," by Associated Press, 11/13/2021, in Politico, https://www.politico.com/news/2021/11/13/africa-great-green-wall-521292

[40] See https://www.bbc.co.uk/programmes/m0011hp3; See also, "The man who has lived as a hermit for 40 years," by Steven Brocklehurst, BBC Scotland News, November 9, 2021.

[41] See Batra, Suzanne W. T. (1985). "Polyester-making bees and other innovative insect chemists". *Journal of Chemical Education*. 62 (2): 121. doi:10.1021/ed062p121.

[42] Cited from Benjamin Soloway's "The 5 Worst Treaties the United States Ever Signed," *Foreign Policy*, https://foreignpolicy.com/2015/08/25/the-5-worst-treaties-the-united-states-ever-signed/

[43] Jo Confino, "Grieving could offer a pathway out of a destructive economic system". *The Guardian*, October 2, 2014.

[44] See Ashlee Cunsolo, and Neville Ellis, "Hope and mourning in the Anthropocene: Understanding ecological grief". *The Conversation*, April 4, 2018, https://theconversation.com/hope-and-mourning-in-the-anthropocene-understanding-ecological-grief-88630.

[45] "A brief history of human longevity," AgeUp, n.a. https://learn.age-up.com/blog/a-brief-history-of-human-longevity/#:~:text=1300%2D1400%20%7C%20Life%20expectancy%3A,1500%20%7C%20Life%20expectancy%3A%2048%20years, Accessed November 14, 2021.

[46] Oxford University Press, New York, 1978.

[47] See "Solastalgia: the distress caused by environmental change," by Glenn Albrecht, Gina-Maree Sartore, et al., *Australasian Psychiatry*, 2007;15 Suppl 1:S95-8. doi: 10.1080/10398560701701288. https://pubmed.ncbi.nlm.nih.gov/18027145/

[48] See "The Ecology of Suicidal Behaviour," by J. W. McCulloch, A. E. Philip and G. M. Carstairs, *The British Journal of Psychiatry*, Volume 113, Issue 496, 29 January 2018, https://www.cambridge.org/core/journals/the-british-journal-of-psychiatry/article/abs/ecology-of-suicidal-behaviour/3E834687DC924ABDAF7E37EAE9F0CCDC, *The British Journal of Psychiatry*, Volume 113, Issue 496, March 1967, pp. 313 – 319, doi: https://doi.org/10.1192/bjp.113.496.313

[49] See "EPA's Budget and Spending," EPA, https://www.epa.gov/planandbudget/budget

[50] See "A Comprehensive Overview of Global Biodiversity Finance," Final Report, April 2020, by the OECD, report-a-comprehensive-overview-of-global-biodiversity-finance.pdf

[51] See "Climate Change Could Cut World Economy by $23 Trillion in 2050, Insurance Warns," *The New York Times*, April 22, 2021, by Christopher Favelle, https://www.nytimes.com/2021/04/22/climate/climate-change-economy.html

[52] See "Young people's climate anxiety revealed in landmark survey," by Tosin Thompson, Nature, 22 September 2021, *Nature* 597, 605 (2021), doi: https://doi.org/10.1038/d41586-021-02582-8, https://www.nature.com/articles/d41586-021-02582-8;

[53] See "Climate anxiety and PTSD are on the rise. Therapists don't always know how to cope," by Isobel Whitcomb, 20 April 2021, *The Guardian*, https://www.theguardian.com/environment/2021/apr/20/climate-emergency-anxiety-threapists

[54] "70% of Americans experiencing climate change anxiety and depression, survey finds," by Leslie Brinkley, by Leslie Brinkley, *ABC News*, November 7, 2021, https://abc7news.com/climate-change-depression-anxiety-pre-ptsd/11202847/

[55] See "India has a farmer suicide epidemic – and farmers are protesting new laws thjey fear will make things worse," by Yasmina Hatem, Lisa Desai, and Mark Abadi, *Business Insider*, January 7, 2021, https://www.businessinsider.com/india-farmers-protest-law-suicide-epidemic-2021-1

[56] See "Viewing a Suicide as an Environmental Protest," Editorial, n.a., *The New York Times*, April 18, 2018, https://www.nytimes.com/2018/04/18/opinion/suicide-environmental-protest.html

[57] "Defending the environment has become a suicide mission in many parts of the world," by Robyn Dixon, *The Los Angeles Times*, December 22, 2017, https://www.latimes.com/projects/la-fg-environmental-activists/

[58] See "UK Law Recognizes Octopus, Crab and Lobster Sentience, by Liam Pritchett, LiveKindly, November 23, 2021, https://www.livekindly.co/uk-law-recognizes-octopus-sentience/?utm_campaign=subscribers-octopus-sentience&utm_medium=subscribers_push_notification&utm_source=subscribers

[59] ibid.

[60] "The IUCN Red List in a nutshell," https://www.iucn.org/resources/conservation-tools/iucn-red-list-threatened-species#:~:text=Least%20Concern%3A%20species%20evaluated%20with,assessment%20because%20of%20insufficient%20data.

[61] See "Gray wolf listing reinstated under Endangered Species Act," by Cassie Ferri, The Wildlife Society, February 14, 2022, https://wildlife.org/gray-wolf-listing-reinstated-under-endangered-species-act/

[62] "'Let us trade': Debate over ivory sales rages ahead of CITES summit," by Busani Bafan, July 11, 2019, Mongabay, https://news.mongabay.com/2019/07/let-us-trade-debate-over-ivory-sales-rages-ahead-of-cites-summit/

[63] "Robustness in Statistics," by Courtney Taylor, ThoughtCo., July 11, 2019, https://www.thoughtco.com/what-is-robustness-in-statistics-3126323#:~:text=Robust%20statistics%2C%20therefore%2C%20are%20any,to%20errors%20in%20the%20results.

[64] See "Bayes-optima estimation of overlap between populations of fixed size," by Daniel B. Larremore, *PLOS Computational Biology*, 2019 Mar; 15(3): e1006898, Published online 2019 March 29. doi: 10.1371/journal.pcbi.1006898, PMCID: PMC6440621, PMID: 30925165, https://www.ncbi.nlm.nih.gov/pmc/articles/PMC6440621/

[65] See "Role Of Overlapping Generations In Maintaining Genetic Variation In A Fluctuating Environment," by Stephen Ellner and Nelson G. Hairston, Jr., *The American Naturalist*, Vol. 143, No. 3, March 1994, p. 413, https://ecommons.cornell.edu/bitstream/handle/1813/57250/Role_of_Overlapping_Generations_in_Maintaining_Genetic_Variation_in_a_FluctuatingEnvironment.pdf?sequence=1&isAllowed=y

[66] See "Patchy Distributions Of Ant Species In New Guinea Rain Forests," by Edward O. Wilson, Psyche, Vol. 65, March, 1958, No. 1, Reprinted in *Nature Revealed – Selected Writings, 1949-2006*, by Edward O. Wilson, The Johns Hopkins University Press, Baltimore, MD, 2006, pp. 26-38

[67] See *No Small Matter – Science On The Nanoscale*, by Felice C. Frankel and George M. Whitesides, The Belknap Press Of Harvard University Press, Cambridge, Massachusetts, London, England, 2009, pp. 73-76.

[68] *Radical Refection and the Origin of the Human Sciences*, by Calvin O. Schrag, Purdue University Press, West Lafayette, Indiana, 1908, p. 78.

[69] Institute of Health Metrics and Evaluation. Global Health Data Exchange (GHDx). http://ghdx.healthdata.org/gbd-results-tool?params=gbd-api-2019-permalink/d780dffbe8a381b25e1416884959e88b

[70] See https://www.healthline.com/health/depression/facts-statistics-infographic#prevalence

[71] See "A third of Americans now show signs of clinical anxiety or depression, Census Bureau finds amid coronavirus pandemic," by Alyssa Fowers and William Wan, *The*

Washington Post, May 26, 2020, https://www.washingtonpost.com/health/2020/05/26/americans-with-depression-anxiety-pandemic/

[72] See "Animal Models of Depression: Molecular Perspectives," by Vaishnav Krishnan and Eric J. Nestler, *Curr Top Behav Neurosci.* 2011: 7: 121-147, doi: 10.1007/7854 2010 108, PMCID: PMC3270071, NIHMSID: NIHMS352347, PMID: 21225412, https://www.ncbi.nlm.nih.gov/pmc/articles/PMC3270071/

[73] "Ukraine marine commander tells pope Mariupol is 'hell on earth'," by Kelsey Carolan, *The Hill*, April 18, 2022, https://thehill.com/policy/international/3271990-ukraine-marine-commander-tells-pope-mariupol-is-hell-on-earth/

[74] See, for example, the recent series, "The Hidden Lives of Pets," Netflix, https://www.netflix.com/title/81318943; See also, https://www.google.com/search?q=secret+life+of+pets&rlz=1C5CHFA_enUS893US901&oq=secret+life+of+pets&aqs=chrome..69i57j69i61j69i60.2300j0j7&sourceid=chrome&ie=UTF-8

[75] Henry David Thoreau, *Journal,* August 30, 1856, cited in the beginning of *Landscape And Memory*, by Simon Schama, Alfred A. Knopf, New York, NY 1995.

[76] ibid., pp. 575-576.

[77] See Paul Devereux, *Sacred Geography: Deciphering Hidden Codes in the Landscape*, Gaia, London, UK, 2010, p 9.

[78] See *Sacred Landscape in Medieval Afghanistan – Revisiting the Fada il-i Balkh*, by Arezou Azad, Oxford University Press, Oxford UK, 2013, p. 5.

[79] See *On the Nature of Ecological Paradox*, by M. C. Tobias and J. G. Morrison, Springer Nature, New York, NY 2022, Chapter 42, pp. 377-387.

[80] See *Passing Strange and Wonderful – Aesthetics, Nature, and Culture*, by Yi-Fu Tuan, Island Press/A Shearwater Book, Washington, D.C., 1993, p. 183.

[81] "Gibbon's Left Testicle -What influences the writing of history?" by Louis Menand, The New Yorker Magazine, April 18, 2022, pp. 63-65.

[82] ibid., p. 65.

[83] See Søren Kierkegaard's *Either/Or*, Abridged Edition, Edited by Steven L. Ross, Translated from the Danish by George L. Stengren, Perennial Library, Harper & Row, Publishers, New York, NY 1986, p. 59.

Chapter 6

End User Fallacies

Inevitable Maladies of Historicism

History inevitably relies upon a story that frames our certitudes, invents verities. It has all the recognizable traits of oral tradition, the trappings of individuals we have known or know. Situations familiar to us in our own time. Dante, among so many others, certainly engaged in its perpetuation.[1] The breakdown of facts by our predilections for what has been described as "counterfactual inference"[2] is torn between statistical conclusions absent any clear contextual objectivity and all that has happened since whatever events in question have receded behind us. So many surveys of history offer only insights into the historians whose regard must be understood within its own rootedness. That evolves with all the accompanying fixations, causes of action; obvious approaches toward a subject that are necessarily predicated on selection bias, constellations of the subjective for which there is no test of relations, proof of methodology.[3] One overseer's dementia is another's love affair. Hatreds, personal diet and disingenuities, narratives born of different continents, all suffer massively in translation, like poetry and most certainly in every attempt at biosemiotics, ethological, interspecies interpretation. George Steiner (1929-2020), of all the historians of translation, knew this better than anyone. Steiner revered Greek and Hebraic invention, suggesting that it was Aeschylus who discovered the true tragic vein, marking the original moment in humanity's psychological journey from oral tradition to the written definitive. But a writing that was propounded from past experience. Whereas, continued Steiner, "The grammar of the Prophets in Isaiah enacts a profound metaphysical scandal – the enforcement of the future tense…"[4] By attempting to resolve the staying power of human languages and meaning – notwithstanding the stultifying clichés that could and have routinely arisen from overuse, or linguistic drift – Steiner inadvertently empowered a text that is among those very few works of contemporary monumentality that allows any paragraph, in order, out of order, to be selected with nearly an equal gravity. Indeed, down to the sentence, Steiner's own poetic and hermeneutic gifts enabled him to divine a storyline that can be expressed in any direction or structure. This style accords with his very opening line of the Acknowledgments where he concedes, "Though this book has, to a great extent, had to define and map its own field, it is none the less dependent on a large body of related work."[5] *Its own field*. Herein lies the dilemma he ascribes to the tragedian, Aeschylus; but also to the idea that, in the beginning, there was dialogue between some God and some Adam and Eve, now forever grown cold as stone. That with the evolutionary exuberance of metaphor came the preconditions for a great quiescence. Which the ecological imponderable has now inherited as its fully ordained language of crisis. A development that neatly comports with Steiner's "after Babel" construct, in which the multiplication of many madnesses must result in the silence that is the most fitting commentary on all that chatter that once was human but is no more. Indeed, one of the great discoveries of world literature is that you can start at any page, any sentence, and it won't matter at all. Begin at the ending, or in the middle, or nowhere particular. The language is the same, the story, the information. All that changes in the shuffling of the deck of words is one's personal fitting within the composite. Read between the lines, take account of the vast complexes on either side of any given word, and at once we begin to feel the contours of an ecosystem that far outweighs the trivial little drama, or sequence of events, that a human being has seen fit to jot down. There is the overwhelming realization of its arbitrary concretizing into a thing, with characters, motives, time and place. But none of it really matters. The emotions likely to be elicited will be so, in any case. That biome is what counts. This is where all the human languages combined form a single unit of pleiotropy, the endless variations on a single gene, or being, or place on earth, connected to other pleiotropy. While our bias is a human one, the ecological liberation we can achieve in letting go of the story line, is of enormous import.

To feel for even an instant a certain dizziness when thinking about the changing contours and inevitable mortalities that have preceded this language moment, one might be advised to journey to the Perry-Castañeda Library Map Collection at the University of Texas Libraries at Austin. There, in turn, we gaze upon the wildly crazy cartography that was the map of "The Persian Empire about 500 B.C.", the "Achaemenid empire at its greatest extent."[6] Somewhere hidden in that miscellany of wars, immigration, hubris and widespread suffering is the famed Behistun inscription. It still stands as tumultuous proof, within the vertiginous reaches of a long inaccessible cliff, at the crossroads of a most malevolent history in Western Iran, that the words and imagery from the ruinous and monumental reign of Darius I (522-486) were easily and totally misinterpreted century after century. From slaves, the conquered wretched, obeisant, mindless ghosts, to silly students sidling up to the monster. If this is the inevitability of every translation over human time, we can scarcely imagine the difficulties outside of time, when confronted, face to face, with a curious blue whale, or suspicious grizzly mother with her cubs.

As arrogant and insidious as other vast hegemonies, that massive world of limestone-inscribed Persian conquest, all situated beneath the notorious feet of Darius was fair game for Greece's most illustrious, and modern-like historian, Herodotus (5th century BC). His multi-volume *The Histories* (430 BC) remains as inflective of humanity's deceptive insanity as the 19th century attempt by many to humanize natural selection, and the 20th century's adulation of the physics and chemistry that have come to issue the final antipathies towards life on earth, in the sickening final reckonings that would be nuclear war. And it remains the case that Herodotus' research (the very word in Greek meaning history and vice versa) exposed in the Greek mental world what another great researcher and translator, Aubrey de Sélincourt (1894-1962) would describe, in characterizing "Greek attitudes towards evidence" as a culture of odd if seemingly irrational selectivity that "would make a modern jury gasp."[7] As strange to modern sensibility as the rash, unfathomable cries that emerge from Africa's mythic jungle in the hands of the great Nigerian Yoruba writer, Amos Tutuola (1920-1997).[8] Or that legendary Theodora, a city mobbed by one disaster after another throughout its unfortunate pertinacity, as imagined by Italo Calvino in his *Invisible Cities*, the onslaught of every conceivable predatory invasive.[9] Such are the demons of any history. The dense vulnerabilities of any fixed semiosis.

Whilst we celebrate the newly informed second term of the high school student who fell in love with and would eventually marry his teacher and went on to become 25th and 26th President of France, we also are acutely attuned to the forces bearing down all around Emmanuel Macron's continued calls for a new "revolution" for democracy.[10] As with every alleged major power the same seismic fault lines have always threatened the "politics of sanity,"[11] such as they/it might be. But Macron would not obtain anything like an absolute majority in Parliament, having instead to reconcile with the far right, a model, as with the U.S. Senate, for intransigency and the ineffectual. Macron's predecessor, President François Hollande made clear what, in his mind, made the Darius I's of the new world safe: "'"less than 300"' nuclear warheads, three sets of 16 submarine-launched ballistic missiles and 54 medium-range air-to-surface missiles." This was a precondition for deterrence, said Hollande, and he suggested "other countries" to act with similar "transparency".[12] The short history of MAD – "mutual assured destruction"[13] – is an ecological theory that cannot be sorted out by political treaties, human trust, or human faith. In late April 2022, it was becoming all too clear how close the nine nuclear nations (including Israel) were rapidly verging upon the unthinkable. Noting that one singular lesson regarding nuclear deterrence was the exploitation of that very concept by Russia in its fanatical determination to continue daily war crimes in Ukraine, knowing that Moscow's 6,257 nuclear warheads should all but guarantee its freedom to continue such crimes. The earth will, at length, lose. To date, it has lost by so many cuts. Now, we can easily imagine a near future that has been fortified by all the interpretations of the past. An instantaneous cessation.

Such divagations in the words that frame the loosely organized narrative that is human behavior offer neither hope nor disease, only the cracked mirrors we each know too well. History has its own set of diseases that don't kill, they only leave you miserable. A severely arthritic, poisoned, hungry drought-ridden world. But history also insists on mortality, with only the anomalous exceptions (e.g., the immortal HeLa cell lines, etc.).[14] Paul Ehrlich suggested that "conscious evolution" and the fact of "small scale" discussions by people earnestly concerned about "the massive arsenals of nuclear weapons" throughout the world, might show the way.[15] Fourteen years after Ehrlich spoke of such hopes, he and I (mt) wrote a book together entitled *Hope On Earth: A Conversation*[16] in which the word, hope, had become all but anachronistic. Or, as Kierkegaard described it, "comfortless".[17] During a rooftop interview in Kyiv with Anderson Cooper on April 26 2002, U.N. Secretary General António Guterres, a day after discussions with Mr. Putin, declared that "meetings" would not end the war against Ukraine.

People are meeting, discussing, and more discussing. The "half-earth" proposals[18] and High Ambition Coalition for Nature and People, the latter (to which the Biden Administration signed on) not a 50% but 30% preservation ideology[19] among countless other proffered scenarios throughout the world. To slow down or outrightly nullify the destruction occurring. The "hotspots" methodology is another, with great logic instilled in its overall ambition to save those 36+ terrestrial sites that together share the largest number of threatened and simultaneously endemic species across the planet.[20] And a similar hotspots consideration for ten biodiverse marine areas.[21] As in the case of Kierkegaard, all this high end mumbling, these designs occurring in the midst of such out-of-control, unwanted futures; at the sides of so many unwritten, unheralded tombs. Is the task at hand one of science? Poetry? Miraculous translation of a text yet to be written, or sung? Simply caving into our worst intuitions? What is it? These chatty zones of environmental citizenry are neither regimes nor solutions. As so many have recognized, we cannot solve our own problems. We do not have the phylogenetic gift to spare our grandchildren our own architectures and infrastructures, at least those who still go on choosing to have children in spite of all the evidence which would ordinarily question the wisdom of doing so. Of perpetuating our current history.

Ecospaces

Hence, our interest in what has been described as an "under-filled region of ecospace" by Neil Brockerhurst[22] in his research into evolutionary morphological changes due to dietary shifts in an extinct reptile clade. Researchers have long examined U-versus-V shaped vicissitudes with respect to two key variables: "body size and trophic guild," recognizing, in the case of many vertebrates, a near universal formula that has been in place for at least 66 million years. But the Anthropocene extinction rate at present is likely to re-formulate those relationships.[23] While other similar patterns of past, present and future defense and diversification strategies amongst plants and invertebrates have also seen significant study,[24] there is no absolutism, or town hall meetings in biology. Individual free choice hints at rapid as well as convergent evolutionary forces. But history cannot lend any algorithmic divinations about the future, or even the next five minutes. Or none that ever a George Steiner could translate. While the rate and magnitude of volcanism has not changed in hundreds of thousands of years, individuals can change within seconds.

This phenomenon, what we call *liberated (or freed-up) choice*, is only free, however, unto itself. That is a conceptual and materially-involved conundrum in ecological terms: "correlations" versus "causation".[25] Neither interpolated cause, relation, consequence or potential consequence could be established, for example, with regard to some 3 trillion trees – half of all that once lived within the timeframe of human antiquity – having been destroyed and another third of all remaining trees vulnerable to human destruction.[26] Liberated choice can be linked, never measured, on the individual plane. Consider Buddhist climate activist Wynn Alan Bruce who immolated himself directly before the Supreme Court on April 22, 2022 (Earth Day), an heroic sacrifice, one of deep compassion for the world.[27] But this is precisely the issue before us: How the individual might sway his/her species? Persuasion is an immensely complex task. Even as an idea it suffers from the necessity of contact, wherein surprises of evolution come down to the pico (one trillionth of a) second. In our earlier discussion of suicide the overwhelming attribution stemmed from environmental depression, with at least the hint of ecological necessity. Indeed, there are those who have always imagined a second coming, the end of days. But at the personal level of convictions an act of deep love of the world is almost impossible *not* to translate correctly. We all know precisely what it means. Such self-sacrifice represents one of the most astonishing qualities of the quantum biosemiosphere as it pertains to our humanity.

Loss, either self-willed or self-embraced, has evolutionary connections that accumulate, possibly in the interests of restraint/constraint throughout every life zone, as has been posited in certain herbivorous flies[28] as well as arthropods. For both groups, it appears to have taken two distinct biological innovation pulses. The first occurred between one and some twenty million years to devise their herbivorous diets. This was followed by a span of approximately 18 million years, between the "latest Silurian" ("417" Ma) and "Middle Pennsylvanian (327 to 309 Ma)" for the patterned changes to take hold.[29] Such research also comports with "the evolution of adaptive traits in plants"[30] generally speaking: the timeframes, while of a limited duration within the context of overall time-horizons for the biosphere, comprehensively overshadow human conceptions of personal time and cause. Dinosauria dietary time spans between omnivorous and strictly herbivorous behavior equally reveal enough pulses to explain both imbalance and superimposing phenotypic characteristics.[31] At the metrical center of such incremental shifts is an ecological psyche, in every species. Such broad strokes are relatively easy to assess. Pin-pointing that psyche requires an acceptance of the biological simulacrum, as figured in every individual. This was the original concept of agape, of loving thy neighbor. Extended without limit poses all the same mathematical multidimensionality scenarios. They certainly are real across biological taxa. But for us humans to divine anything of that biochemical sensorium requires a level of analysis and translation for which we have no tools, only blunt concepts.

The most graspable one concerns what we eat, where our food comes from, and how much of the original world has been altered because of our rapacity. At least 70% of the planet[32] has been adversely altered due to our habits; eating habits and other behavioral and occupational styles, primarily agriculture. That, in turn, is the sobering truth behind nearly eight billion people with no humane population policies in place. Not the least ethical ties configured between a fetus and a mob. No understanding that all life forms are equally precious, but that there is a biological relativity that is distribution oriented. As the Jains have so remarkably analyzed in terms of ten vitalities and five senses, consumption whose hope is to soften an individual's presence in a violent world, must constrain her/his appetite to the minimum, to one-sensed organisms. Of course, we recognized that the assessments are human assessments, and to say that a piece of romaine lettuce possesses only one sense, may be pure fiction. But, the alternative is to starve to death. We do have that choice.

Aside from the Jains, and some other cultures, our species is largely indifferent to its own species' numbers, to *any* numbers other than those translatable into money. Remarkably, the "Mesopotamian shekel" (the first such currency) is no more than approximately 5,000 years old.[33] Unlike the pulses of change described above, we know that rapid alterations occur as measured not in millions, or thousands of years, but in less than one human generation. A European rabbit (*Oryctolagus cuniculus*) of the Leporidae family is most familiar to us. It lives on average 9 years, during which time the female may have, on average, 72 offspring, but as many as 168 in a single year. A rabbit's "math can quickly become overwhelming."[34] Not infrequently but one kit per litter survives. Regardless of the number of individual rabbits, and their co-symbiotic competitors, plant survival has always posed a mystery to biology. Do macro- and microevolutionary traits of growth, defense and recruitment differ? One study of an artificially designed experiment involving rabbits and sorrel (*Rumex acetosa L.*)[35] suggests that "contemporary evolution" may be altering feedback loops in ways we cannot yet describe with any definitive or predictive prowess. But that's not to question the legitimacy of certain ecological constants, or (Andrei) Kolmogorov equations used to grasp the probability of "jump processes" in sporadic linear differentiations.[36] In other words, anything can happen, and probably has. The literature of physics, math and philosophy describes this as stochastic. If one imagines the number of pennies contained in all the world's daily financial transactions – Federal Reserve definitions of M0, M1, M2 and until recently M3 – there are trillions of material bills and coinage in circulation, and even more trillions in non-material exchanges and investments. But these are amateurish numbers by comparison with cellular and molecular interactivity. By the tie we reach such enormous size equivalencies as the birth of a rabbit or a human, or the size of a city, we're talking about essentially simplistic numeric values.

Other transactional equivalencies emerge in any fluid where Brownian motion applies to the random diffusions of particles. They also invoke principles and anomalies of modal logic, e.g., Buridan and Barcan formulae and converse formulae (after Ruth Barcan, American philosopher of logic, 1921-2012). These are both ecological and linguistic conditions that logicians use to describe transitions within probability distributions. Modal logic involving such propositions state that "everything that could exist does exist."[37] Hayaki goes on to embrace an "ontology of contingent objects"[38] as the most accessible way to a logical cul de sac wherein "the domains of all possible worlds" are "identical".[39] This is one useful approach to substitution algorithms that are fraught with comparisons. The number of one group of objects versus another. Or the degree to which one individual can sympathize with millions of other individuals. There are no laws or equations to resolve emotional differentials like that. To fathom the nature of such quantifiable extrapolations requires an appreciation of modal logic and implicative physicalism. But it is neither moral nor spiritual in its capacities. That is, systems of values that pivot upon a variety of relations that can be described as any number of frames or narratives, each toying with the idea and the materialism of reality, are inaccessible. Accessible properties of objects and their relations to other objects limit the terms of truth functions to the extent that we begin to take part in the connections. We become party to the relations. Economic systems are the most simplistic of such indicators, as in the case of the one (Indian) rupee note, with Mahatma Gandhi pictured on the little bill. Properties symbolize the extent of other properties. The logic of mathematics and of morality turn upon the same encompassing of sub-sets. In other words, a relativity of reflexive correspondence between entities. This is where analytical logic turns to biology and chemistry for help in solidifying real possibilities. We're not talking of *probabilities*. Those require a field of objects in which to be manifested, whereas possibilities implicate the concrete reality of objects, like that one rupee note, which, in turn, symbolizes 100 paisas.[40]

Probabilities do not observe deterrent postures of politicians or the least political capital on the brink of nuclear war. Nor can they assess boom and bust amongst populations, or rapid evolution in any sense where rapidity lends context to what is happening, at least in the meager human experience of it. The question as to whether micro-community changes can persist uncorrelated with macro-evolutionary alterations has been cursorily examined with respect to plants and arthropods.[41] The relations between all objects lend themselves to the study of logic. But well beyond what is logical are the contingencies of any emergence of a Being that has strayed from mere being. This is the logic of evolution, if such a one can be adduced.

All of the aforementioned combinatory symbols, sets and sub-sets may lend themselves to different forms of logic and usage within human communities. Each entails an ecological correlation, but we would be ill-advised to place monetary value on values, or life forms. This has been one of the most egregious of human assumptions and appropriations.

Cryptic Phylogenetics

It is also the movement between order and disorder, or at least the expression or nuanced appreciation of chaos and the non-chaotic. All the various taxonomic representations of the Tree of Life, or Great Chain of Being – of angels, animals, plants and of humanity etc. – conflates the pan-Asiatic cosmographies, the Socratic, Judeo-Christian, and multiplicity of indigenous hierarchies into a phylogenetics that stems both physics and biochemistry.[42] It touches the origins of life just as it seeks to understand the age and travails of what we humans think of as the Cosmos. Our persistent antecedent here concerns the immanence of eco-dynamics within the mind, presupposing that degree of reciprocity necessary to raise the realism of feedback to the point of prominence, between possibility and probability. All human research moves between these two distinct appetites that are both of life and of human life. Their fields of representation may be described as logical, mathematical, or the domain captured by physics or quantum theories. No matter the translation into human terms (geopolitics, environmental economics, trade, community organization, legislation, or psychology) the rudiments of transition remain structurally the same. Whether monetary, linguistic, or genetic, the translation between entities conveniently assigned a number, or space, involves our species' exercise of choices. Such translation and transactions fix their determinations, nurture moral character, sense of place, goals for a future, upon all those same transitional zones that are emphatically ecological.

The immense network of so many transactions explains why the relatively sudden convergence of so many Anthropocenic inflictions points to so massive and global an undoing. Every human exchange numerically adds to the erosion of a former world, in no different a manner than the enlargement of a garbage dump, where un-recycled plastic and metals and millions of tons of other waste seem to spread beyond the horizon.

It would be unthinkable *not* to suffer as a result of these end-user fallacies, as we will call them. We might turn our inquiry to all those impediments, both in Nature and in Mind, that appear in correspondence to accelerate this most amorphous problem, that of fixing our true interest and capacity so as to slow down and reduce our penchants for all things exponential. The stock market. Rankings. Second-by-second portfolio fluctuations.

None of this cynical commentary is proffered to underestimate all the positive orientations that still inspire the notion of solutions, also catalogued within the realm of accessible numbers. We are awash in technofixes that argue our species' capacity to overcome any inventor paradox, or solution-paradox quandary. Richard Buckminster Fuller (1895-1983)[43] was one of its general proponents, attempting with both neologistic cleverness and tautological rhetoric accessible to popular audiences to engender a kind of innovator culture that could solve every problem of both outer and inner nature. He kept company, historically, with the likes of one of the world's first mathematicians, Archimedes (c.287-c.212 BC), the transport guru of Great Britain, Isambard Kingdom Brunel (1806-1859), the Mesopotamian author of *The Book of Knowledge of Ingenious Mechanical Devices*, Ismail al-Jazari (1136-1206), army engineer Rube Goldberg, best known for his cartoons of his gadgetry (1883-1970), and Utopian architect Paolo Soleri (1919-2013) famed for his Arocsanti community north of Phoenix. It is an odd list of inventors and engineers, each sharing a thirst for a human-addicted visionary reversal of knots and festering lumps best described as snarled traffic in one form or other. A situation that might in its totality be symbolized by nothing more ingenious and simplistic than the Jersey barrier, those 3 and ½ foot high concrete blocks (also known as K-rails) developed in New Jersey and first employed in southern California in the 1950s to try and limit highway fatalities.[44] In 1792 the *Farmer's Almanac* began publishing in New England. By 1818, it had spread deep, daily influence from Lewiston, Maine to the rest of the U.S. In its way, the *Almanac(k)* had its roots in the history of herbals, including the Ebers Papyrus (c. 1500 BCE)[45] and Greek pharmacologist, Pedanius Dioscorides (40-90 AD) whose encyclopedic *De Materia Medica*[46] would provide predictive remedies and recipes for the coming two millennia. These were solutions, undergirded by numbers.

But the snarls, obstacles to understanding, for example, the power of steam, are not to be confused with knurls or knars, the nots in trees. They need no *solution*, obviously. Nor does Mount Everest need to be moved. Lunatical and humorous responses to the insoluble ("don't look up,"[47] "birds aren't real,"[48] the tick that makes people allergic to meat [truer than false], etc.) these are all pieces of the self-imposed cultural puzzles of our times, as carefree as Punxsutawney Phil on groundhog-day. The problem-solving spins dizzyingly across all ecological parameters.

Human Equivalencies

Consider EarthFolio, one of numerous socially responsible investing screens, but one of few directly accessible online.[49] Its numerous funds invoke criteria that no one would fail to applaud from "conservation" and "human rights" to "non-violence" and "animal welfare."[50] It contains an estimated $16.6 trillion in assets invested just in the United States in 2020 (up from "$639 billion in 1995").[51] The organization People For the Ethical Treatment of Animals points out two cruelty-free companies – Karner Blue Capital[52] and Invest Vegan.[53] Philanthropists, including Jeff Bezos, have demonstrated a willingness to deploy billions of dollars to additionally solve ecological problems.[54] Blueprints and pledges by hundreds of corporations to do better in terms of their total gross environmental impacts look impressive on paper.[55] In a 2020 survey of positive environmental stories, mongabay.com categorized them as pertaining to such areas as gains in the recognition of indigenous peoples, particularly women, new strides in conservation technologies and protected areas, more financial commitments towards curbing GHSs, and the like.[56] These sagacious and instrumental advances had to be measured against what the World Resources Institute described in its own set of categorically negative trends and projections in light of the February 28th 2022 report from the Intergovernmental Panel on Climate Change (IPCC), which included "34,000 studies and involved 270 authors from 67 countries". The areas of escalating risk included all of the too familiar negative atmospheric, terrestrial, marine, social and biological flashpoints. "The world needs urgent action now to address losses and damages," read the report."[57] Ultimately, as exemplified in countries like Bhutan[58] and Bolivia[59], nations that equate human happiness with low carbon sustainable economies, all of these various oppositional stakes merely underscore the philosophical impasse that such *combatants* represent, in a world of nearly 8 billion human consumers who are unable to stop. One can both read it and feel it in the numbers games.

Well prior to the conditions our species has imposed by way of the Anthropocene, there has been as much speculation on the merits of philosophy as on its imperiled premises and conclusions. Reviewing Stephen Gaukroger's book, *The Failures of Philosophy: A Historical Essay* (Princeton University Press, 2020) Robert Pasnau exclaims, "The coda to the story leaves us with the dismal words about how philosophy has now 'lost its bearings'…"[60] When on May 2, 2022 the U.S. Supreme Court leaked a Republican, fascistic draft opinion to abolish *Roe v. Wade* after 49 years, Americans, along with those in

24 other countries saw the demise of stare decisis, of a legal precedent basic to any possible amelioration of the human population bomb, as Paul and Anne Ehrlich had called it in 1968.[61] In the same 48-hour period, Putin's inner circle made it clear that the madman would clearly link and invigorate Russia's so-called Victory Day, May 9th, marking Soviet defeat of the Nazis, to the medieval dictator's slaughter of the city of Mariupol and to Russia's incessant escalation of its transparent war crimes on Ukrainian people and their sovereignty.[62] As if these combined sacrilegious jolts weren't enough, Russian Foreign Minister Sergei Lavrov made much of the fact that Jews were the worst anti-Semites and Hitler "had Jewish origins."[63] But, painful as it is to admit the obvious, this is just one of the conjunctions of bad news, horrible numbers, occurring on any given day throughout the human world: Converging variables of planetary doom.

Any reasonably informed human being will at once recognize with a deafening roar, an inward near-collapse, that the earth has become a monumental crime scene, human forensic sciences useful but not more so than our memories, sense of wholesome connection to one another and to other species. Those associations are often shy by nature. Not waning in confidence, but often stupefied with the sheer humility necessarily imparted to one among so many. To a guilty species that has tried for millennia to either justify its means of dismissing Others, not embracing them; assayed to ignore, deny, cover up or celebrate its independence, no evidentiary balance sheet will ever suffice to call it true philosophy. As if philosophy long ago went to sleep. It is simply a list, like the earliest Egyptian and Sumerian tallies of food stocks and surplus. Or of far more recent summaries of economic mismanagement by Bourbon or Habsburg dynasts, or the rankings of deficit-laden nations.[64] Of things gone awry, misconstrued, or outright undermined for purposes that, to date, neither philosophy nor normative ethics has ever been able to elucidate realistically, given the political inveigling that typically pre-ordains attempts at agrarian reform, democratic elections, of ageold balances of power.

Costica Bradatan has argued that such inabilities to solve problems, failure to find reconciliatory success, has been a crucial corollary of what, in fact, is the championing of satisfactory humility, an important element of human life. He cites such people as Rumanian/French cynic E. M. Cioran, as well as Gandhi, Japanese author Yukio Mishima (who ultimately committed seppuku at the age of 45), and Simone Weil, among others mentioned; each of whom appeared to have been therapeutically self-abnegative. Each ultimately prevailed over the intellectual, social and moral obstacles they had dissected throughout their respective careers.[65] In an earlier work, Bradatan had systematically questioned the very nature of intellectual enterprise, and its risks to those who indulge their philosophical passions, whether a Socrates or Giordano Bruno, both martyred for their thoughts.[66]

Raymond Tallis speaks frankly about these ironic performances of great ideas on grand stages. He writes, "Enough already. Yes, even great philosophers can be foolish like the rest of us, while the majority of humanity manages to be daft" or in so many ways carry on with their lives without any burning need to consult, or be guided by, philosophy.[67] As of 2022, 21 countries were self-proclaimed as neutral, though Switzerland renounced Russia's war against Ukraine.[68] The U.S. endorsed three separate neutrality acts between 1935-1937 hoping to use such legislation as a means of keeping America from caving in to Hitler. Senator George W. Norris, however, argued that "Absolute neutrality is an impossibility."[69] Just as silence represents complicity with horror. George Steiner characterized this linguistic collaboration best when he described Auschwitz as "outside speech" and "outside reason".[70] Others have embraced vows of silence, for other reasons than Steiner's deeply concerned challenge to what is rational; or nations that have chosen to remain immune to taking sides. Materially complicit views represent the extreme obfuscation of a daily reality framed by the many narratives of communication. Perspectives, like those in the U.S. dealing with abortion, that have completely abandoned the logic of what pro-life should really mean. How authoritarianism rejects any comparable "new deal" to grapple with any and all assertions from the public meant to redress ecological and social woes. Rejecting the very premise of problems and thereby normalizing solutions that have been invented expediently from within the toxic maelstrom of an unflexing politic. Language itself is held total hostage to the corruption from within. There is little distance from that deterioration to the very capacity of language to be free to formulate ideas that can resonate. Not with a political de facto vacuum usurping, at the very least fully manipulating, the basics – as laid down in the pernicious maxim, "the less said, the better"[71] – of a semiotic relation between people.

Chickens and the Numeric Zenith of Our Destructive Oblivion

Consider our largely silent species as it hourly enshrouds the slaughter of innocents, most prolifically, chickens (*Gallus g. domesticus*). There are well over thirty billion chickens in the world at any one time, at least 55 breeds, all descending from the Red Jungle Fowl approximately 10,000 years ago, and some of them still found in the wild in Vietnam. We have watched them also in the jungles of Brunei. Most of those thirty billion will be replaced by another thirty+ billion, as the human appetite for chicken pieces escalates, and the human population soars.[72] This strictly antithetical ecosystem that is the deep schizophrenia within human meat eaters, is (arguably) not dissipating, despite modest vegetarian/vegan gains in popularity. In 2021 an avian influenza virus outbreak of Eurasian H5N1 resulted in the mass slaughter, by slow, ghastly means, of at least 36 million chickens and turkeys. The world, for the most part, did not notice, or care. Given their forced reproduction rates, at least 70 billion chickens are murdered under human Holocaust-like conditions annually throughout the world.[73]

For a few activists, the method of slaughter – in essentially every country – has invoked endless forms of protest, legal briefs, and numerous opinions by veterinarians, lawyers, dieticians, scientists and journalists who have seen fit to get involved. Particularly given the enormous empirical data revealing the remarkable intelligence of birds like chickens.[74] Many have tried to divine the addiction to flesh that inhabits humanity, tracing its neurobiology in our brain's anatomy which proffers an insula, devoted to a sense of flavor; and the orbitofrontal cortex, where decisions are in part set forth. Then there are taste buds in the throat, the palate, papillae along the tongue, and a combining of the facial, hypoglossal, glossopharyngeal and trigeminal nerves that translate and dispatch various messages of desire or distaste at approximately 220 miles per hour into the brainstem and on to the spinal cord.[75] Notice that we refer to the brain, not the mind. The chicken is the most tortured of all vertebrates, the metacenter of suffering on this planet. And our species, numerically speaking, is unconcerned by the slaughter.

This distinction is not only number-driven, in terms of the sheer multitude of victims and human profiteering. It also recognizes that we humans cannot distinguish either the merits, the meaning, or the criteria relevant to any discussion of intelligence, let alone misery. Humans may possess ten times the number of overall neurons than those quietly roosting within a chicken, but this is only the most-crude of accounts. Any list of encephalization quotients breaks down, at the very least, at two levels: dependence on the cerebellum, and the efficiency with which neurons are configured within the brain. Birds are far more efficient, in this latter sense, than are mammals.[76]

But the overwhelming determinant of so-called *intelligence* should by all accounts accrue by way of a species' ability to alter its course, change its mind, re-shape the vision by which a population's individuals go about their days. Just as those who rally around the pro-life manifesto seem all but indifferent to the massive slaughter earlier referenced. Killing that goes far beyond chickens. Add up all the suffering of some three trillion known vertebrates and invertebrates at human hands. In addition to tire dust, microplastic nurdles, polluted and disappearing ground water. The toxins we emit across and within every square inch of the planet. Yet, many favor the ethical hypocrisy of preserving a fetus at all costs to the mother and the environment. Vegans and pro-choice morality tend to go hand in hand, though non-violence absolutism strays into troubled gray zones.[77] For one of America's premier 20th century statesmen, George Kennan (1904-2005) another gray area had to do with immigration. His theory was a simple one of equivalencies. The pressure by immigrants would cease when the political and economic inferno of the United States had become as bad as the countries from which such aspirants were hoping to flee.[78] We could add to that global equation the hope that environmental refugees would tend to flock from areas of high biodiversity endemism to low endemism, but it might not work out that way. As in the case of 100,000 mothers and their children to Rumania, from Ukraine. The point is that what we deem to be intelligent in human beings has no historical forensics to back up any claims to a priority species. None whatsoever. The numbers we put forth in our favor are utterly meaningless. Our continuing population explosion (a net addition of 74+ million newborns annually as of 2022)[79] shows every sign of continuing well over 11.2 billion by the end of the century, if there is an end.[80] That is no biological success story; only a compulsion with numbers that is deeply rooted and toxic.

Back in 2011 Sir David Attenborough referenced the inbred "taboo" about speaking of the population crisis,[81] providing one more rallying cry amongst a score of outspoken warnings.[82] With one failed U.N. climate conference after another, the strident cautionary tales have only materialized with increasingly transparent inflictions that no scientific or philosophical debate can any longer tackle. The vying headlines are simply too comprehensive and dismal.[83]

Coevally, steady state economists like Herman Daly have assiduously articulated systems of "ecological tax reform" and rational recommendations for international commercial and progressive, egalitarian banking changes.[84] In grappling with the proliferation of opinions (and, hence, choices), in a 2013 revised Negative Population Growth, Inc., forum paper, Michael G. Hanauer suggested that "20 percent of underlying problems cause 80 percent of significant effects."[85]This is one of those mind-bending assertions that leaves more sectors, biophysical ratios, causal relations and ecological dynamics unanswered than can reasonably be envisioned. But clearly the global "underlying problems" require, as conservation biologist Stuart H. Hurlbert has written, that we "drop all the globalist chatter and get to work on a sane population policy…"[86] Following upon Attenborough's invocation of population taboo, Hurlbert points out that "the largest environmental organization in the United States, the Sierra Club, abandoned in 1996 its long-standing advocacy of U.S. population stabilization" with a vote being taken in which an astonishing "85%" of membership "abstained."[87]

Philosophy and politics were conditioned, in Aristotle, by a biological bias that continues to do great injury to this population juggernaut. In his *Treatise On Government* he affirmed unmistakably that civil society, his huddled masses, confirms the "greatest good; for as by the completion of it Man is the most excellent of all living beings, so without Law and Justice he would be the worst of all…"[88] In his *Dialectick* Aristotle addressed the through-story that was the same human odyssey from one disposition to another; from one confirming choice to the absolute concatenation of such decisions. His description for this ultimate resolution which is any politic is rich. He offers a choice overview: "The soul is not Harmony, (a proportionate mixture of contraries)…"[89] But he goes on to clarify Nature and goodness. Nature is all "that is free of madness." And "Good is understood *three* ways. First, for that which is the cause of preservation to all beings; next for that which is predicated of every good thing. Lastly, for that which is expetible [worthy of being] in itself." And such universals apply ultimately, says the philosopher, to the essence of virtue, all of which "consisteth in action".[90]

Light visible to life forms on earth represents one salient form of high energy action. Between red and violet.[91] The rest we cannot see. Similarly, the cave in which philosophy is best suited, remains largely invisible to us. Most unnoticeably are the high intensity gamma rays, charged as much as 459 trillion electron volts, first detected in the Crab nebula, from the ASG amma array in Tibet.[92] Humans are trichromatic, capable of seeing three basic colors, whereas birds see four. A mantis shrimp has "16 color-receptive cones" enabling it to see ten times more color than humans.[93] Hummingbirds perceive multiple "nonspectral" colors in abundance, and it is likely that most other species have the same necessary "extra cone type" that enables them to see such hues as well.[94] But the sensory repertoire of other species is a different category entirely from the underlying premise of rights, morality, and Jeremy Bentham's (1748-1832) famed, "The question is not, Can they reason?, nor Can they talk? But, Can they suffer? Why should the law refuse its protection to any sensitive being?"[95] The conjecture has become something of an animal rights manifesto, but, in fact, Bentham was not as obliging as the theory would suggest. He did not contest animals for human food, or medical experiments if they were not overly subjected to pain. Hence, an Aristotelian contrary of the sort that has, even in its most flattering moments, failed to harken to the purity one would only find in a truly vegetarian/vegan community, where the shared ethic was unambiguously driven. In its human embodiment, we can only imagine the exponentially increased ecological ruin that should result had abortion been illegal for centuries throughout the world. And wonder at the brazen biological outcomes that should result from a doubling of the human population. As it is, the number of annually unborn humans, as a result of their mother's and/or parents' decision to abort is very near the number of net births each, of those surviving. At least 73 million abortions annually, at present.[96] The number rises according to data on multiple births. In the U.S. 31.1 per 1,000 live births are twins, or 112,437 individuals.[97]

Linking consumption of other animals, and the violence such horrors induce in humans is a bioecological feedback that was explored by the Neoplatonic philosopher Porphyry (c.234-305), and in great depth by poet Percy Bysshe Shelley (1792-1822), along with a continuous constellation of others.[98] We have inferential evidence but no proof that the consumption of a lamb will ultimately, step by step, translate into nuclear war. The tendencies, as they accumulate, are there. This is indisputable just as the world is unlikely to ignore the memories of Hiroshima and Nagasaki. Memories accumulate. The truth of souls, as well.

And yet, the conflation of violence has not seen fit – in those nations that forbid termination of pregnancy – to add the numbers up. To perceive the squandering of biocultural capital in debating the rights of the fetus and the rights of future fetuses, while slaughtering trillions of living beings. This gap in thinking represents one of the most galling elements of human psychology. Closing such gaps might not seem like the only way to rid humanity of nuclear weapons and wounded hearts; of bipolar disorders, and the widespread depression earlier discussed, resulting from the general ecological breakdown across the planet. Indeed, it isn't, nor can we herewith offer any clear remedy to this ultimate crisis that is built into human causes and consequences.

However, we can suggest two very distinct pathways that are clearly calling upon this generation of our humanity to make some very decisive choices. Are they philosophical, political, spiritual? The numbers add up, make sense, tell of decisive victories and defeats. But the last thing we should be doing is counting all the missteps, improprieties and lavish disasters in the isolation of safe and congenial historiography. Our memories – the executions of Charles I and Louis XVI aside – do not come even close to comporting with present behavior. But normalization was the first principle, in fact, of the pursuit of outlines in human history. One recalls vividly how Will and Ariel Durant literally made their considerable way on to the shelves of "middlebrow culture," as Joan Shelley Rubin described the eleven-volume cover-to-cover comfort that became of the *Story of Civilization*.[99] How different a saga from, say, Jonathan Schell's study of the *end* of the world, not of our species' so-called progress. There is now human trash on Mars which somehow seems to say it all.

But one does not read history the way we read of the news. Similarly, as the Durant saga pointed out, we have no way of prying beneath the contradictory nature of, say, an Oliver Cromwell. There is simply no objectivity that we can wrestle to the floor of such a personage. But today's moment-by-moment *news* is no different, as we are assaulted by openly described violent sociopaths,[101] endless crisis, apocalypse, deadly cults, Last Judgments and black holes en route to gobble us up. At present, every time we replace ourselves, we culminate an additional confrontation with the one lengthy past we can neither understand nor preserve. That is the course of the earth, in all her moments of tumult, that nonetheless preserved the reality of biodiversity. Our values exceed that preservation, which is to say, we have normalized sub-values, sets of imaginary numbers that are meaningless to daily uncountable workings of a forest, let alone the oceans. But those numbers somehow inconceivably have seeded our minds. We appear incapable of living without them. Our imaginations are teeming with populations of numbers.

Ecological history recalls a wilderness. But like all history does so with the fullest regrets of the present picture of ambivalent proliferations.

"Child of the Eastern Himalayas," Photo © M. C. Tobias.

Endnotes

[1] See Dimaggio, Vanessa, "Uncovering the Sources: Historical Characters In Dante's Divine Comedy" (2019). Publicly Accessible Penn Dissertations. 3486. https://repository.upenn.edu/edissertations/3486

[2] Gary King and Langche Zeng. 2007. "When Can History Be Our Guide? The Pitfalls of Counterfactual Inference." *International Studies Quarterly*, Pp. 183-210. Copy at https://tinyurl.com/y48c9sem

[3] See Alex Rosenberg's *How History Gets Things Wrong: The Neuroscience of Our Addiction to Stories*, MIT Press, Cambridge, MA, 2018.

[4] See Favareau, D. Facing Up to the Hard Problem of Biosemiotics. *Biosemiotics* 14, 603–615 (2021). https://doi.org/10.1007/s12304-021-09461-9; See *After Babel – Aspects of Language and Translation*, by George Steiner, Oxford University Press, New York and London, 1975, pp. 21-22.

[5] ibid., George Steiner, p. vii.

[6] See https://maps.lib.utexas.edu/maps/historical/history_asia.html; See the work by cartographer William R. Shepherd (1871-1934).

[7] *The World of Herodotus*, by Aubrey De Sélincourt, North Point Press, San Francisco, CA 1982, p. 197.

[8] See, for example, Tutola's *My Life in the Bush of the Ghosts,* Grove Press, New York, NY 1954.

[9] See *Invisible Cities*, by Italo Calvino, Translated from the Italian by William Weaver, A Helen and Kurt Wolff Book, Harcourt Brace Jovanovich, New York and London, 1972/1974, p.159.

[10] See "Macron's 'Revolution' Faces a Reckoning," by Lionel Laurent, Bloomberg, April 6, 1922. See also, "'Democratic shock': Macron loses absolute majority in Parliament," by n.a., *Reuters/Business Standard*, June 20, 2022, https://www.business-standard.com/article/international/democratic-shock-macron-loses-absolute-majority-in-parliament-122062000055_1.html

[11] See "The Politics of Sanity Are Within Our Grasp," Opinion, The Conversation, by Gail Collins and Bret Stephens, https://www.nytimes.com/2020/04/21/opinion/coronavirus-biden-trump.html

[12] See "Nuclear deterrent important in 'dangerous world', says Hollande," by Staff Writers, *Space Daily*, France AFP, February 19, 2015, https://www.spacedaily.com/reports/Nuclear_deterrent_important_in_dangerous_world_says_Hollande_999.html

[13] See "Nuclear Deterrence," atomicarchive.com, https://www.atomicarchive.com/history/cold-war/page-15.html

[14] See, for example, abcam, https://www.abcam.com/products?sortOptions=Relevance&keywords=Hela&selected.classification=Cell%20lines%20and%20Lysates--Knockout%20cell%20lines&gclid=Cj0KCQjw6pOTBhCTARIsAHF23fJ6FYvFBJmDO4lZswmgH1KXSspYmvFpy7iS8dascZa6lkh9Sc-7U0AaAp4aEALw_wcB&gclsrc=aw.ds

[15] *Human Natures -Genes, Cultures, and the Human Prospect*, by Paul R. Ehrlich, Island Press/Shearwater Books, Washington D.C., Covelo, CA, 2000, p. 327.

[16] *Hope On Earth: A Conversation*, by Paul R. Ehrlich and Michael C. Tobias, With Additional Comments by John Harte, University of Chicago Press, Chicago, Ill., 2014, https://press.uchicago.edu/ucp/books/book/chicago/H/bo17588109.html

[17] See Søren Kierkegaard's discussion of "the equality of death" in his chapter entitled "At The Side Of A Grave," from his work, *Thoughts On Crucial Situations In Human Life – Three Discourses on Imagined Occasions*, Translated from the Danish by David F. Swenson, Edited by Lillian Marvin Swenson, Augsburg Publishing House, Minneapolis, Minnesota, 1941, p. 100.

[18] https://www.half-earthproject.org/

[19] See "How Conserving 30% of U.S. Land by 2030 Could Work," by Andrea Thompson, *Scientific American*, April 22, 2022, https://www.scientificamerican.com/article/how-conserving-30-percent-of-u-s-land-by-2030-could-work/?amp=true; See also, "What Protecting 30 Percent of the Planet Really Means, by Michelle Nijhuis, Scientific American, March 12, 2021, https://www.scientificamerican.com/article/what-protecting-30-percent-of-the-planet-really-means/

[20] See "*Biodiversity Hotspots Defined*," https://www.cepf.net/our-work/biodiversity-hotspots/hotspots-defined#:~:text=There%20are%20currently%2036%20recognized,as%20%22endemic%22%20species. See also, www. https://www.hotspots-thefilm.org/, and the book on which the film is based, Russell A. Mittermeier, Norman Myers and Cristina Goettsch Mittermeier, *Hotspots: Earth's Biologically Richest and Most Endangered Terrestrial Ecoregions,* Conservation International, CEMEX, 2000.

[21] The areas include the Salas y Gómez and Nazca Ridges, the Costa Rica Dome, the Sargasso Sea and Corner Rise Seamounts, the Gulf of Guinea, the Walvis Ridge, the Arabian Sea, Mascarene Plateau, Emperor Seamount China, Lord Howe Rise and South Tasman Sea. See "The Top 10 Ocean Biodiversity Hotspots to Protect," by Tara Lohan, The Revelator, May 21, 2020, https://therevelator.org/ocean-biodiversity-mpa/

[22] See "Rates of morphological evolution in Captorhinidae: an adaptive radiation of Permian herbivores," by Neil Brocklehurst, *PeerJ*, April 13, 2017, https://peerj.com/articles/3200/reviews/, https://peerj.com/articles/3200/

[23] See Cooke, R., Gearty, W., Chapman, A.S.A. et al. Anthropogenic disruptions to longstanding patterns of trophic-size structure in vertebrates. *Nat Ecol Evol* (2022). https://doi.org/10.1038/s41559-022-01726-x, https://www.nature.com/articles/s41559-022-01726-x#citeas; K-curves are also much discussed in banking (inequality patterns) and environmental economics (the U-shape inversion with reference to growth counterintuitively forcing more marginalized individuals), all in reference to American economist Simon Kuznets. See Kapuria-Foreman V., Perlman M. An Economic Historian's Economist: Remembering Simon Kuznets//*The Economic Journal*, 105 (November), 1995, p. 1524–1547, and "Is There an Openness Kuznets Curve?" by Stephen Dobson and Carlyn Ramiogan, KYKLOS, Wiley Online Library, 14 April 2009, https://doi.org/10.1111/j.1467-6435.2009.00433.x

[24] See Futuyma, D.J. and Agrawal, A.A., 2009. Macroevolution and the biological diversity of plants and herbivores. *Proceedings of the National Academy of Sciences*, *106*(43), pp.18054-18061; See also, "The Evolution of Endophagy in Herbivorous Insects," *Frontiers in Plant Science*, by John F. Tooker and David Giron, Front. *Plant Sci.*,

02 November 2020 | https://doi.org/10.3389/fpls.2020.581816, https://www.frontiersin.org/articles/10.3389/fpls.2020.581816/full

[25] See Reznick, D., Bryga, H. & Endler, J. Experimentally induced life-history evolution in a natural population. *Nature* 346, 357–359 (1990). https://doi.org/10.1038/346357a0, https://www.nature.com/articles/346357a0#citeas

[26] "Arbor Day Post-Mortem: One-Third of the World's Tree Species Face Extinction," by Adrian Newton, FlaglerLive.com, https://flaglerlive.com/168191/trees-exctinction/; See also "Global Tree Assessment," Botanic Gardens, Conservation International, https://www.bgci.org/

[27] See "A man who died after self-immolating in front of Supreme Court was a climate activist," by Rachel Ramirez, CNN, April 25, 2022, https://amp.cnn.com/cnn/2022/04/25/politics/supreme-court-climate-activist-dies-fire/index.html; See also, Silverman, Ellie; Shapira, Ian (April 26, 2022). "Outside the Supreme Court, a life of purpose and pain ends in flames". *Washington Post*, and Brasch, Sam (April 25, 2022). "A Boulder climate activist died after he set himself on fire. His friends remember his talent and compassion". Colorado Public Radio. See also, "Who Was Wynn Alan Bruce, Climate Activist Who Set Himself on Fire on Earth Day?" by Yasmine Leung, April 23, 2022, https://www.hitc.com/en-gb/2022/04/25/wynn-alan-bruce/

[28] See "Evolution in herbivory in Drosophilidae linked to loss of behaviors, antennal responses, odorant receptors, and ancestral diet," by Benjamin Goldman-Huertas, Robert F. Mitchell, Richard T. Lapoint, +2, Cécile P. Faucher, John G. Hildebrand jhildebr@email.arizona.edu, and Noah K. Whiteman, *PNAS*, January 26, 2015 | 112 (10) 3026-3031 | https://doi.org/10.1073/pnas.1424656112

[29] See Conrad Labandeira's fascinating research paper, "The Origin of herbivory on land: Initial patterns of plant tissue consumption by arthropods," *Insect Science* (2007) 14, 259-275, Journal compilation © Institute of Zoology, Chinese Academy of Sciences, doi: 10.1111/j.1744-7917.2007.00152.x

[30] See "Evolution of herbivore-induced early defense signaling was shaped by genome-wide duplications in *Nicotiana*," by Wenwu Zhou, Thomas Brockmöller, Zhihao Ling, Ashton Omdahl, Ian T Baldwin, and Shuqing Xu, eLife, Nov 4 2016, https://elifesciences.org/articles/19531

[31] See "Paleobiology of Herbivorous Dinosaurs," Paul M. Barrett, *Annual Review of Earth and Planetary Sciences* 2014 42:1, 207-230, https://www.annualreviews.org/doi/abs/10.1146/annurev-earth-042711-105515, https://www.annualreviews.org/doi/abs/10.1146/annurev-earth-042711-105515#abstractSection

[32] See "Global Land Outlook," *United Nations Convention to Combat Desertification, GLO2*, April 27 2022, https://www.unccd.int/resources/global-land-outlook/glo2-summary-decision-makers, https://www.unccd.int/resources/global-land-outlook/global-land-outlook-2nd-edition - "Land Restoration for Recovery and Resilience"

[33] See "When – and why – did people first start using money?" by Chapurukha Kusimba, The Conversation, June 19, 2017, https://theconversation.com/when-and-why-did-people-first-start-using-money-78887#:~:text=The%20Mesopotamian%20shekel%20%E2%80%93%20the%20first,gold%20coins%20to%20pay%20armies.

[34] "Breeding Like Rabbits? What Does That Really Mean Anyway?" n.a., June 1, 2020, Morris Preserve, Will County https://www.reconnectwithnature.org/news-events/the-

buzz/cottontail-rabbits-breeding; See also, *Sylvilagus floridanus*, eastern cottontail, Animal Diversity Web, https://animaldiversity.org/accounts/Sylvilagus_floridanus/; and, "Eastern Cottontail (Cottontail Rabbit)," https://mdc.mo.gov/discover-nature/field-guide/eastern-cottontail-cottontail-rabbit

[35] "Contemporary Evolution of Plant Growth Rate Following Experimental Removal of Herbivores," by Nash E. Turley, Walter C. Odell, Hanno Schaefer, Georg Everwand, Michael J. Crawley, Marc T. J. Johnson, and Symposium Editor: David N. Reznick, *The American Naturalist*, Volume 181, Number 51, May 2013, A Critical Look at Reciprocity in Ecology and Evolution, doi: https://doi.org/10.1086/668075, University of Chicago Press Journals, https://www.journals.uchicago.edu/doi/10.1086/668075; See also, Pilson, D. The evolution of plant response to herbivory: simultaneously considering resistance and tolerance in Brassica rapa. *Evolutionary Ecology* 14, 457 (2000). https://doi.org/10.1023/A:1010953714344, https://link.springer.com/article/10.1023/A:1010953714344

[36] See Kolmogorov, Andrei (1931). "Über die analytischen Methoden in der Wahrscheinlichkeitsrechnung" [On Analytical Methods in the Theory of Probability]. *Mathematische Annalen* (in German). 104: 415–458. doi:10.1007/BF01457949.

[37] See Reina Hayaki (2006). "Contingent Objects and the Barcan Formula". Wansing, H. (2000). "A Reduction of Doxastic Logic to Action Logic". Erkenntnis. 53 (1–2): 267–283. doi:10.1023/A:1005666218871. https://web.archive.org/web/20060826180747/http://www.unl.edu/philosop/people/faculty/hayaki/ContingentObjectsAndBF.pdf

[38] ibid., p. 10.

[39] ibid., p. 1.

[40] See Lewis, C. I. (1917). "The issues concerning material implication." *Journal of Philosophy, Psychology, and Scientific Methods*, 14:350–356. See also, Ruth C. Barcan (Mar 1946). "A Functional Calculus of First Order Based on Strict Implication". *Journal of Symbolic Logic*. 11 (1): 1–16. doi:10.2307/2269159. JSTOR 2269159.

[41] See Johnson Marc T.J., Vellend Mark and Stinchcombe John R., 2009, Evolution in plant populations as a driver of ecological changes in arthropod communities," *Phil. Trans. R. Soc*. B3641593–1605 http://doi.org/10.1098/rstb.2008.0334

[42] See *The Great Chain of Being: A Study of the History of an Idea*, by Arthur O. Lovejoy, Harvard University Press, Cambridge, MA, 1936.

[43] https://www.bfi.org/

[44] See "New Jersey Median Barrier History," *Roads to the Future*, by Scott M. Kozel, © 1997-2004, http://www.roadstothefuture.com/Jersey_Barrier.html

[45] See "Herbal History: Roots of Western Herbalism," Herbal Academy, https://theherbalacademy.com/herbal-history/; See also, B. Petrovska, "Historical review of medicinal plants' usage," *Pharmacognosy Reviews*, 6(11), 1-5, http://doi.org/10.4103/09873-7847.95849; See also, https://www.farmersalmanac.com/

[46] See *Pharmakon -Plato, Drug Culture, and Identity in Ancient Athens*, by Michael A. Rinella, Lexington Books, Rowman & Littlefield Publishers, Inc., Lantham, Maryland, 2010.

[47] See "Adam McKay Says He Welcomes 'Don't Look Up' Haters, but Some Outrage Is 'Utterly Ridiculous,' by Zack Sharf, *Variety*, January 13, 2022, https://variety.com/2022/film/news/adam-mckay-dont-look-up-haters-1235153266/

[48] See https://birdsarentreal.com/; See also, "Birds Aren't Real, or Are They? Inside a Gen Z Conspiracy Theory," by Taylor Lorenz, *The New York Times*, Dec. 9, 2021, https://www.nytimes.com/2021/12/09/technology/birds-arent-real-gen-z-misinformation.html

[49] See https://www.earthfolio.net/how-it-works/

[50] ibid., https://www.earthfolio.net/sustainability/esg-screens/

[51] ibid., https://earthfolio.net/top-3-questions/#performance, citing "Report on US sustainable and impact investing trends 2020, U.S Social Investment Forum, 2020". This is a difficult figure to calculate considerining that the total estimated amount of U.S. assets held by investors at the time of 2021Q2 was "34,196." Trillion. See "U.S. International Investment Position, Second Quarter 2021," https://www.bea.gov/news/2021/us-international-investment-position-second-quarter-2021

[52] https://www.karnerbluecapital.com/

[53] https://investvegan.org/; See, https://www.peta.org/issues/animals-used-for-experimentation/cruelty-free-investments/

[54] See "Jeff Bezos names former head of environmental think tank to lead $10 billion Earth Fund," by Annie Palmer, CNBC, March 9, 2021, https://www.cnbc.com/2021/03/09/jeff-bezos-names-andrew-steer-ceo-of-10-billion-earth-fund.html

[55] See https://www.theclimatepledge.com/challengeaccepted; See https://www.theclimatepledge.com/#main-navigation

[56] See "Top positive environmental stories from 2020," by Liz Kimbrough, 30 December 2020, https://news.mongabay.com/2020/12/top-positive-environmental-stories-from-2020/

[57] "6 Big Findings from the IPCC 2022 Report on Climate Impacts, Adaptation and Vulnerability," by Kelly Levin, Sophie Boehm and Rebecca Carter, World Resources Institute, February 27, 2022, https://www.wri.org/insights/ipcc-report-2022-climate-impacts-adaptation-vulnerability?utm_medium=cpc&utm_source=google&utm_campaign=ipcc2022&gclid=Cj0KCQjw37iTBhCWARIsACBt1IzpdU1gwTGKueqvkrXw0faOVVhI2geYsS30Vwzx8sFE9toZNzEany0aAjzvEALw_wcB

[58] *Bhutan: Conservation and Environmental Protection in the Himalayas*, by Ugyen Tshewang, Michael Charles Tobias, and Jane Gray Morrison, Springer Nature, New York, NY, 2021; See also, *Bionomics in the Dragon Kingdom: Ecology, Economics and Ethics in Bhutan*, by Ugyen Tshewang, Michael Charles Tobias, and Jane Gray Morrison, Springer Nature, New York, NY, 2018.

[59] See "The High Happiness-Low Carbon Link – A new study from Bolivia on well-being and sustainability," by William D. Powers, Karina Mariaca de Oliveira and Hilvert Timmer, The Solutions Journal, November 18, 2019, https://thesolutionsjournal.com/2019/11/18/high-happiness-low-carbon-link-new-study-bolivia-well-sustainability/

[60] "The Failures of Philosophy: A Historical Essay, Book Review," by Robert Pasnau, *Australasian Journal of Philosophy,* 14 Nov 2021, https://doi.org/10.1080/00048402.2021.1999281, https://www.tandfonline.com/doi/full/10.1080/00048402.2021.1999281

[61] *The Population Bomb*, by Paul R. Ehrlich and Anne Ehrlich (who went uncredited as co-author), Sierra Club/Balantine Books. See also, "Bombshell opinion leak shows US Supreme Court set to overturn Roe v. Wade," AP, *The Times Of Israel*, May 2, 2022, https://www.timesofisrael.com/bombshell-opinion-leak-shows-us-supreme-court-set-to-overturn-roe-v-wade/; See also, *World War III: Population and the Biosphere at the End of the Millennium*, by Michael Charles Tobias, Bear & Co., Santa Fe, NM, 1994.

[62] See "Putin 'to declare all-out war on Ukraine on Russian Victory Day', officials fear," by Emily Atkinson, *Independent*, May 1, 2022, https://www.independent.co.uk/news/world/europe/putin-could-declare-allout-war-on-ukraine-b2068837.html

[63] "Israel demands apology after Russia says Hitler had Jewish roots," by Crispian Balmer, Reuters, Jerusalem, May 2, 2022, https://www.reuters.com/world/middle-east/israel-denounces-lavrovs-hitler-comments-summons-russian-ambassador-2022-05-02/; See also, "Russia's media propaganda turns to 'spine-chilling rhetoric' to intimidate the West," by Yuliya Talmazan, May 14, 2022, NBC News, https://www.aol.com/news/russia-media-propaganda-turns-spine-083013020.html

[64] See, for example, International Monetary Fund, "World Economic Outlook Database," 86,694,449,453,942,936,961,524,926,298,927,&s=GGR_NGDP,GGX_NGDP,GGXCNL_NGDP,&sy=2019&ey=2021&ssm=0&scsm=1&scc=0&ssd=1&ssc=0&sic=0&sort=country&ds=.&br=1

[65] See *In Praise of Failure – Four Lessons in Humility*, by Costică Brădăţan, Harvard University Press, 2023, as described by Harvard University Press, during pre-press promotion. https://www.hup.harvard.edu/catalog.php?isbn=9780674970472

[66] See *Dying for Ideas: The Dangerous Lives of the Philosophers*, by Costică Brădăţan, Bloomsbury Publishing, New York, NY, 2015.

[67] See "On Failing to be a Philosopher," by Raymond Tallis, Philosophy Now, © Raymond Tallis, 2019, https://philosophynow.org/issues/131/On_Failing_to_be_a_Philosopher

[68] See "Neutral Countries 2022," https://worldpopulationreview.com/country-rankings/neutral-countries

[69] See "Congress, Neurality, and Lend-Lease," https://www.archives.gov/exhibits/treasures_of_congress/text/page20_text.html; See also, "The Problem of Neutrality," C. G. Dehn, Transactions of the Grotius Society Vol. 31, Problems of Public and Private International Law, Transactions for the Year 1945 (1945), pp. 139-149, Published By: Cambridge University Press, https://www.jstor.org/stable/743275, https://www.jstor.org/stable/743275

[70] See "George Steiner, *Language and Silence: Essays on Language, Literature, and the Inhuman*," Atheneum, New York, NY, 1967, Review by Robert S. Leventhal, http://www2.iath.virginia.edu/holocaust/steinerls.html

[71] See "The Less Said, the Better: Interpreting Silence in Qualitative Research," by Makie Kawabata, and Denise Gastaldo, International Journal of Qualitative Methods, Sage

Journals, November 22, 2015, https://doi.org/10.1177/1609406915618123, https://journals.sagepub.com/doi/10.1177/1609406915618123

[72] See "Number of chickens worldwide from 1990 to 2020 (in million animals)," statista, https://www.statista.com/statistics/263962/number-of-chickens-worldwide-since-1990/#:~:text=The%20number%20of%20chickens%20worldwide,14.3%20billion%20chickens%20in%202000. See also, *God's Country – The New Zealand Factor*, by Michael Charles Tobias and Jane Gray Morrison, Zorba Publishers, Ithaca, NY, 2011, A Dancing Star Foundation Book, Los Angeles, p. 447.

[73] See "Yearly number of animals slaughtered for meat, World, 1961-2018," Our World in Data, https://ourworldindata.org/grapher/animals-slaughtered-for-meat; See also, https://animalclock.org, and "Chickens Used for Food," PETA, https://www.peta.org/issues/animals-used-for-food/factory-farming/chickens/

[74] See "The horrific bird flu that has wiped out 36 million chickens and turkeys, explained," by Kenny Torrella, May 5, 2022, Vox, https://www.vox.com/future-perfect/23053296/bird-flu-chickens-turkeys-cull-depopulation-ventilation-shutdown; See also See *Brain and Intelligence in Vertebrates*, by Euan M. Macphail, Clarendon Press, Oxford, UK, 1982, p. 20. See also, for example L. Edinger "The relations of comparative anatomy to comparative psychology". *Journal of Comparative Neurology and Psychology*. 18 (5): 437–457, 1908; doi:10.1002/cne.920180502. hdl:2027/hvd.32044106448244; See also, E. Macphail, ibid., p. 223, citing R. L. Gossette and W. Riddell, "Comparison of successive discrimination reversal performances among closely and remotely related avian species," *Animal Behavior*, 1966, 14, 560-4. See one of the most comprehensive and sensitive essays on the topic, "Cognitive ornithology: the evolution of avian intelligence," by Nathan J. Emery, *Philosophical Transactions B, Philos Trans R Soc Lond B Biol. Sci.* 2006 Jan 29; 361(1465): 23-43, Published online 2005 Dec 7. doi: 10.1098/rstb.2005.1736, PMCID: PMC1626540, PMID: 16553307, The Royal Society Publishing, NCBI PMC, https://www.ncbi.nlm.nih.gov/pmc/articles/PMC1626540/. Accessed May 4, 2020. See "Bird brain? Ounce for ounce birds have significantly more neurons in their brains than mammals or primates," *Vanderbilt University, Science News*, June 13, 2016, citing "Birds have primate-like numbers of neurons in the forebrain," by Seweryn Olkowicz, Martin Kocourek, Radek K. Lučan, Michal Porteš, W. Tecumseh Fitch, Suzana Herculano-Houzel, and Pavel Němec, *PNAS* first published June 13, 2016 https://doi.org/10.1073/pnas.1517131113. Edited by Dale Purves, Duke University, Durham, NC, and approved May 6, 2016 (received for review August 27, 2015), *Proceedings of the National Academy of Sciences of the United States of America*, https://www.pnas.org/content/early/2016/06/07/1517131113.abstract.

[75] op. cit., *God's Country*, p.473.

[76] Herculano-Houzel S, Avelino-de-Souza K, Neves K, Porfírio J, Messeder D, Mattos Feijó L, et al. (2014). "The elephant brain in numbers". *Frontiers in Neuroanatomy*. 8: 46. doi:10.3389/fnana.2014.00046. PMC 4053853. PMID 24971054. See also, Herculano-Houzel S, da Cunha FB, Reed JL, Kaswera-Kyamakya C, Gillissen E, Manger PR (December 2020). "Microchiropterans have a diminutive cerebral cortex, not an enlarged cerebellum, compared to megachiropterans and other mammals". *The Journal of Comparative Neurology*. 528 (17): 2978–2993. doi:10.1002/cne.

24985. PMID 32656795. S2CID 220499352. See also, "Bird brains are dense – with neurons," by John Timmer, ars technical, June 16, 2016, https://arstechnica.com/science/2016/06/bird-brains-are-densewith-neurons/

[77] See, for example, "Vegans and Abortion: Everything You Need to Know," by Tyler McFarland, May 4, 2019, *I Am Going Vegan*, https://www.iamgoingvegan.com/vegans-and-abortion/

[78] See George F. Kennan, *Around the Cragged Hill: A Personal and Political Philosophy*, Random House, New York, NY 1995, cited in "The Environmental Movement's Retreat from Advocating U.S. Population Stabilization (1970-1998): A First Draft of History, by Roy Beck and Leon Kolankiewicz, *Journal of Policy History*, The Pennsylvania State University Press, Vol 12, No.1, 2000, p. 148.

[79] World Population, https://countrymeters.info/en/World; See also, https://www.prb.org/, https://popresearchcenters.org/centers/cpipr-prb/, and https://data.worldbank.org/indicator/SP.POP.TOTL, https://sdg.iisd.org/news/world-population-to-reach-9-9-billion-by-2050/, and https://repository.gheli.harvard.edu/repository/11330/; See also, "Number of births," The World Counts, https://www.theworldcounts.com/populations/world/births

[80] "World population projected to reach 9.8 billion I 2050, and 11.2 billion in 2100," U.N., 21 June 2017, New York, https://www.un.org/development/desa/en/news/population/world-population-prospects-2017.html#:~:text=The%20current%20world%20population%20of,Nations%20report%20being%20launched%20today. See https://www.un.org/development/desa/en/news/population/world-population-prospects-2017

[81] "Planet and Population," Royal Society for the encouragement of Arts, Manufactures and Commerce," London, March 10, 2011.

[82] "World Scientists' Warning to Humanity: A Second Notice," by William J. Ripple, and 15,371 scientist signatories from 184 countries, *BioScience*, December 2017, Vol. 67, No. 12. See also, "A Proposal for a United Nations Framework Convention on Population Growth," by Rob Harding, Rewildingearth, Mary 24, 2018, https://rewilding.org/a-proposal-for-a-united-nations-framework-convention-on-population-growth/

[83] For example, see "Our Overcrowded Planet" A Failure of Family Planning," by Robert Engelman, *environment 360*, June 24, 2013, http://e360.yale.edu/slideshow/our_overcrowded_planet_failure_of_family_planing/205/1/

[84] See "Top 10 Policies for a Steady-State Economy," by Herman Daly, *The Daly News*, October 28, 2013, Center for the Advancement of the Steady State Economy, http://steadystate.org/top-10-policies-for-a-steady-state-economy/

[85] "Overpopulation And Overconsumption: Where Should We Focus?" And *NPG Forum Paper* by Michael G. Hanauer, August 2013, NPG Forum Paper, www.npg.org

[86] See "Critical Need for Modification of U.S. Population Policy," by Start H. Hurlbert, *Conservation Biology*, Volume 27, No. 4, 887-889, doi: 10.1111/cobi.12091 (The Authors thank Dr. Hurlbert for providing us his essay, and several others germane to these issues).

[87] ibid. As recently as September 2019, Dr. Hurlbert has published widely on this taboo syndrome. In September 2019, he authored the essay, "Attempts by scientists to

suppress discussion of overpopulation: A California case that backfired nicely," by Stuart H. Hurlbert, *Eubios Journal of Asian and International Bioethics* 29, September 2019.

[88] *A Treatise On Government*, Translated from the Greek Of Aristotle by William Ellis, T. Payne, London UK, 1776, p. 7.

[89] From *The History of Philosophy Containing The Lives, Opinions, Actions and Discourses of the Philosophers Of Every Sect*, by Thomas Stanley, 2nd edition, Thomas Bassett, London, UK 1687, p. 381.

[90] ibid., p. 388

[91] NASA Hubblesite, "The Electromagnetic Spectrum," May 30, 2019.

[92] "Highest energy light ever seen traced to Crab nebula," by Dennis Normile, *Science*, 8 Jul 2019, doi: 10.1126/science.aay6629, https://www.science.org/content/article/highest-energy-light-ever-seen-traced-crab-nebula

[93] "Which Animals See More Colors Than Humans?" by Jacob Olesen, *Color Meanings*, 2013, https://www.color-meanings.com/which-animals-see-more-colors-than-humans/

[94] "Wild hummingbirds discriminate nonspectral colors," by Mary Caswell Stoddard, Harold N. Eyster, Benedict G. Hogan, David W. Inouye, June 15, 2020, 117 (26) 15112-15122 | https://doi.org/10.1073/pnas.1919377117, *PNAS*, https://www.pnas.org/doi/abs/10.1073/pnas.1919377117

[95] See "Speaking of research," https://speakingofresearch.com/extremism-undone/ar-beliefs/#:~:text=%E2%80%9CThe%20question%20is%20not%2C%20Can,Principles%20of%20Morals%20and%20Legislation. See also, Jeremy Bentham, "Of the Limits of the Penal Branch of Jurisprudence." pp. 307–335 in *An Introduction to the Principles of Morals and Legislation*. London: T. Payne and Sons, London UK, 1780.

[96] See https://www.who.int/news-room/fact-sheets/detail/abortion

[97] See "Multiple Births," National Center for Health Statistics, CDC, https://www.cdc.gov/nchs/fastats/multiple.htm

[98] In tracing the violence toward animals as a societal crisis stemming from distinct philosophical dispositions cemented into the very logic of European social evolution, several prominent voices willing to psychoanalyze at various levels the degrees of insipid human behavior stand out. See Gottfried Immanuel Wenzel (1754-1809), *Neue auf Vernunft und Erfahrung gegrundete Entdeckungen uber die Sprache der Tiere*, Wien, Anton Doll, 1800. Wenzel's work had been anticipated to the extent that there were outstanding critics of Descartes' mechanistic attributions (animals as no more than machines), going back to the pre-Socratics, as well as to most early Asian spirituality. Indeed, one could also invoke the reverence that many interpret from the many Aurignacian and Magdalenian cave paintings of Western Europe. In 1739, Father Guillaume-Hyacinthe Bougeant (1690-1743) had published his own striking refutation of the belief that animals were mere machines. He would be exiled on account of the radical notions propounded in his treatise *A Philosophical Amusement Upon The Language Of Beasts* (London: Printed for T. Cooper) made the case for animal souls and supreme intelligence. He writes, "Two Sparrows will know one another by their Voice among a thousand. I might here allege a hundred like Facts, to prove that all Animals have, in their mutual Correspondence, a Delicacy of

Discernment, which is not within our reach, and which makes them observe Differences among themselves which are altogether imperceptible to us. If then many Birds seem to us always to sing the same Note, as the Sparrow, the Chaffinch, and the Canary–Bird; we must not thence conclude that they are saying the same thing for ever." (p.50) Bougeant later wrote a letter to Abbe Savalette of the Jesuit Council recanting his views, if for no other reason to calm down the turmoil his attack on the Cartesian paradigm had unleashed. Joseph Ritson (1752-1803), *An Essay on Abstinence From Animal Food, As a Moral Duty*, London, Printed for Richard Phillips, St. Paul's Church-Yard, 1802. See also, "The first Europeans were cannibals: archaeologists," by Virginie Grognou, http://news.yahoo.com/s/afp/20090624/ts_afp/spainarchaeology/print, 6/24/2009. "The Speech of Lord Erskine in the House of Peers on the Second Reading of the Bill for Preventing Malicious and Wanton Cruelty To Animals," Taken in Short Hand, Edinburgh, Printed for Alex, Lawrie, Bookseller and Stationer, Parliament Square, 1809. Shelley, *"Queen Mab,"* Printed and Published by W. Clark, London, 1821, p.182. Thomas Taylor (1758-1835), *Select Works of Porphyry: containing his Four Books on Abstinence from Animal Food; his Treatise on the Homeric Cave of the Nymphs; and his Auxiliaries to the Perception of Intelligible Natures...and an Appendix, explaining the Allegory of the Wanderings of Ulysses*, London, Thomas Rodd, 1823. See also, *The Rise and Fall of the Afterlife – The 1995 Read-Tuckwell Lectures at the University of Bristol*, by Jan N. Bremmer, Routlege, UK, 2001. Bremmer examines Parmenides, Empedocles and Pythagoras, among others, in looking at the pan-Orphic philosophies oriented towards the abstinence of flesh in diets. She also provides a superb discussion on the origins of the word "paradise" with its ancient vegetarian connotations, see p. 109 of Bremmer's book. For a comprehensive look at "Some Origins of Ideas Concerning Vegetarianism and Meat-Eating," "Transcending the Violence of the Past," and "The Industrial Fate of Animals," see *God's Country: The New Zealand Factor*, by M. C. Tobias and J. G. Morrison, Dancing Star Foundation, Zorba Press, Ithaca, NY, 2011.

[99] See "The Link Between Cruelty to Animals and Violence Toward Humans," Animal Legal Defense Fund, https://aldf.org/article/the-link-between-cruelty-to-animals-and-violence-toward-humans-2/#:~:text=Research%20Shows%20the%20Link%20Between,abuse%20and%20other%20violent%20behavior. See "Animal cruelty and human violence," https://www.humanesociety.org/resources/animal-cruelty-and-human-violence-faq; See also, "Understanding the Link between Animal Cruelty and Family Violence:: The Bioecological Systems Model," by Brinda Jegatheesan, Marie-Jose Enders-Slegers, Elizabeth Ormerod and Paula Boyden, Int J Environ Res Public Health. 2020 May; 17(9): 3116. Published online 2020 Apr 30. doi: 10.3390/ijerph17093116, PMCID: PMC7246522, PMID: 32365760, PMCID: PMC7246522, PMID: 32365760, NIH, National Library of Medicine, https://www.ncbi.nlm.nih.gov/pmc/articles/PMC7246522/ *The Making Of Middlebrow Culture*, by Joan Shelley Rubin, The University of North Carolina Press, Chapel Hill, NC, 1922. See, *The Story of Civilization*, 11-volumes by Will and Ariel Durant, Simon and Schuster Publishers, New York, NY, 1935-1975.

[100] Jonathan Schell, *The Fate Of The Earth*, Alfred A. Knopf, New York, NY 1982.

[101] See "Further Evidence Emerges That Trump Is A Violent Sociopath," by Bess Levin, May 2, 2022, *Vanity Fair*, https://www.vanityfair.com/news/2022/05/donald-trump-mark-esper-just-shoot-them

Chapter 7

Two Distinct Futures

Mathematical Analogies

It's tempting to reference terminal velocity as having a strange fitting when it comes to philosophy. Both simile and metaphor tracking, since at least 1300 AD (see the etymology of incarnation)[1] invite some semblance in our time to the last years of our lives, and an impetus to seek out all the great fairy tales – "The Princess on the Glass Hill," "Rapunzel," "The Six Swans," "The Colony of Cats," "The Magic Kettle," "Jorinda and Joringel" and so forth.[2] As great flocks of birds gather at length, and the disgruntled remonstrate. The notion of a free state disappears like an angle that never was, a vector imagined as part of some grand equation thought to have worked in the past, but no more. Contrary to Edmund Burke's famed opening lines concerning "The Present State Of The Nation": "Party divisions, whether on the whole operating for good or evil, are things inseparable from free government. This is a truth which I believe, admits little dispute, having been established by the uniform experience of all ages."[3]

Free government, like improvisational free play of ideas, meets its imputed characteristics, or some of them, in an imagined Utopia. The kind that "it seldom chanceth that any stranger, unless he be guided by a *Utopian* can come into this haven"[4] which, as Sir Thomas More endeavored most ironically to elucidate, is anything but a desirable location. So too, in the case of all those theories propounding the conditions upon which terminal velocity is occasioned, including such formulae as, $\|\mathbf{a}\|=a21+a22\overline{\qquad}\surd$ (the magnitude of a vector)[5] and all of the physical paraphernalia that accompany the journey of any such collective as an object and the fluid through which it might pass; the awkward additives of drag, countered by inherent buoyancy as arises in the process of gravitational pull (F_G).[6]

The equations confronting velocity with "gas density..frontal area..drag coefficient"[7] where terminal velocity (V_t) equals the square root of 2xW (weight) over the Cd (drag coefficient) x ρ (gas density) x A (frontal area), and the function of time, are well enough studied and personally experienced over however so many millennia as to operate under the assumptions of various

"Beginner's Guides" fortified by the all-powerful *constants* of math, physics and aerodynamics.

Leaving, it would appear, little light between what is known and what is presumed to be common knowledge. This was the assumption also held by Burke, with respect to freedom. Although certainly not to the ideal of a Utopia, any utopia, as Sir Thomas More recognized. Or anyone else, for that matter, who has jumped from a point higher than ten stories above ground or water (though there are remarkable exceptions to that rule, including an accidental fall from the 47th story of a building).[8/9] Isaac Newton's First Law of Motion all but guarantees that, short of an *unbalanced force* acting upon it, inertia and motion will not cease with respect to any object(s) that have achieved equilibrium. Our condemnation by gravity can also be read as its own equilibrium that keeps us rooted, standing, or lying down. But moving to Newton's Second Law, 1 Newton = 1 kg • m/s^2 involves far more variables. Conditionals by which *something happens*; acceleration impacts an object, or, for our purposes, an idea. That speed has magnitude and direction and, according to Newton, is "inversely proportional to the mass of the object."[10] Regardless of the mass, its approach to terminal velocity (speed) is asymptotic. It never actually reaches to the point of infinity, or an absolute net force that is zero (equilibrial). Even as we picture a falling object: When it hits the ground there is still an upward force degrading its speed into a hyperbolic function, like a creeping catenary (idealized curve) temporarily inert at the far tensile strength afforded its particular mass or viscosity.

It was Archimedes of Syracuse who had first explored the displacement of volume by the inherent mass factor, or, V_t (for terminal velocity) = $[2(m - \rho V)g/\rho AC_d]$[11]. Archimedes' principle, or proposition 6, describes the world of "floating bodies".[12] By this fixed, historic representation of a most familiar legacy in everyday nature, he also conjures forth a philosophical correlate described by Robert Nozick in his discussion of the Von Neumann-Morgenstern situation.[13] There, conditions, preferences and probabilities all vie for the satisfaction of a rational, a credible, a likely choice. As if to suggest that the "structure of preferences" is within our grasp, vulnerable to the clutches of any *rational* organism.[14] Or, as Henry Miller jotted in his "Journey To An Antique Land," "It is not a line, really, but an intention."[15] "Good or evil," to reiterate Burke. A "free government." Here, then is the rational, philosophical and political underpinning of a mathematical certainty which is not qualifiable. Its physics, true values, asymptotic tangentials all suggest that gravity, unlike hunger and a piece of bread, do not actually exist in philosophical discourse.

If that is *true*, ecological philosophy may then take any detour to grasp even the basics of biophysical conditionals. This is the most essential facet of the syndrome by which terminal philosophy is vested in the inertia of thought itself, which at every inroad confronts the resistance of the atmosphere of the cerebral. While, yes, we can measure speed, whether of blood flow or electricity, or of a falling body above the earth's atmosphere, unaffected by most chemical densities, speed and velocity differ in the awareness of direction that characterizes the latter.[16] Because it is understood that not all governments, indeed, few if any by definition, are *free*, our primary agency for refuting and walking away from the generalized postulation requires imagination. The first Jewish Aesop, the wandering mystic Isaac ben Solomon Sahula, wrote his *Meshal ha-kadmonim* in the 13th century to refute more than a millennium of perceptions that the world was flat, in terms of other species.[17] A lion, for example, yearns to make a pilgrimage to Jerusalem.[18] Attributions, influences, motives, superstitions, correlations: all can be described in the languages we choose: of the fable, or of calculus and cosmology. That we are stuck in our singular linguistics, notwithstanding the more than 31,000 known human languages to have existed, over 6,000 in present day,[19] underscores a powerful component, call it failing, of both psycholinguistics and rationality. That would be the two central premises of the Sorites Paradox. A heap of sand, regardless of the precise number of grains, remains the same *heap*. Supervaluationism allows us to disregard vagueness, and to tame the relentless beast that is logical positivism. In other words, to assert an anti-empirical pathway towards life. The Dutch-American philosopher Bastiaan Cornejlis van Fraassen (b. 1941) has called this approach "constructive empiricism," a brilliant means to unleashing the imaginative embrace of science without its traditional proof-positive requirements or credentials.[20]

Bertrand Russell's *Paradox* lends additional precision to the imprecision. By that we locate his "unrestricted comprehension" linking classes, sets, sub-sets and sub-classes in an arena of the all inclusive axions, predicates, symbols, foundations and new foundations.[21] This is the *deductive explosion*[22] that is catapulted by a paraconsistent logical series of anti-maxims that can hold true or false, or some other value (the "paradox of entailment") that gives to the biological sciences any taxon, or storyline to work with. It would have been inherent to the Aesop Principle; to *modus tollens*, and to the affirmative premises in a Moses ben Maimon's (Maimonides, 1138-1204) *The Guide for the Perplexed* (*Moreh Nevukhim*- מורה נבוכים, c.1190). Explanations of life that have conditionals that are biologically neither logical nor illogical. They simply are. Arguments in and of and for themselves. Arguments that are implicative of Others. Conditionals that are notationally without human involvement or contrivance; conditioned by a first, second, third, fourth, etc. layer of both independent and interdependent rationales.[23]

This gets particularly interesting at the instant, as Michael Strevens writes, that "everything turns on explaining the stochastic independence of microdynamic probabilities."[24] In examining detail and large schema, Strevens ponders whether certain mechanisms within the realm of "the neural code" are "biologically realistic"?[25] Leonardo himself asked a similar set of questions when he considered the "similarities" between "nature-made and artist-created things" which, today, complicate modern ideas of style and aesthetics."[26] And that *condition* harkens to "the landscape of Genesis on the third day, still without people…"[27] But, writing about Hieronymus Bosch (c. 1450-1516), Cees Nooteboom notes, "Rarely has a man who has become invisible left behind so much that can be seen."[28] Bosch, in a sense, has hit the ground, expressed mathematically as the conclusion of a drag force on the nature of a free fall.[29] His identity, in its fullest brushstrokes, has achieved immortality.

Mathematics has always intruded into the formulation of ethics, and in the case of our species, it should. Why not with trillions of ants, midges, flies? Allometry, isometry, and other identification rules for body size and scaling ratios[30/31] have crystallized our formulations of nature's rules, as we think of them. Equations are thrown at every leg, muscle, metabolic rate and heartbeat of an organism that arrives at length upon its embryological beginning and conclusion. But this is simply the compulsion of science to project, estimate, interpolate and assign number categories of human perception of others. Or, in the case of a Rembrandt's 80 self-portraits, to describe our own evolving personage in the fading light and aging nuances of what it means to be human. In the case of such analyses as those by Adam Smith or Rev. Thomas Malthus, exponents applied to the human condition comport with our size, consumption and extraction rates, mounting famines and our likely exceeding of ecological carrying capacity, almost by rule. With over 15,000 known ant species or the more than 2,500 species of fleas, their size matters in as much as any biome is finite. This is a lesson that astonishes us – what if ants were the size of people? – but does little to persuade, in terms of even the most basic concept of sustainability.

All the combined oceans amount to some 71% of the planet, containing roughly 15% of known species, whereas 80% occupy the terrestrial earth, with another 5% in freshwater.[32] Some biologists argue that the "tipping point" for this enormously disproportionate geographical allocation occurred within the evolving architecture of earth during the Cretaceous period, some 125 million years ago.[33] It was as radical a moment in time, as the Cambrian Explosion of life forms 400 million years earlier in the seas. But it has always been easier for us to inquire about life on land than in water.[34] This is a dominant variable throughout natural history and little was done to alter its paradigmatic reign over science until the British HMS Challenger Expeditions (1872-1876) sought out new findings in oceanography, including species within ocean depths. Four thick reports from Challenger landed in the hands of the German zoologist Ernst Haeckel (1834-1919) whose own artistic gifts enabled him to draw and paint newly discovered creatures, like Radiolaria, for the general public. To hazard the reality of a world abounding in rarified and fragile beauty by which "ontogeny recapitulates phylogeny,"[35] a theory of little purchase in today's genomic laboratories for refining and manipulation of the nature of evolution; but an idea – we grow just as our ancestors, and those of all others, grew – that seemed suddenly obvious. In that sense, we must all be connected.

Frameworks of Biological Numbers

Molecular biology relies upon numbers in every narrative, from geometry to information systems and their AI graphic translations that have continually refined our understanding of DNA codes.[36] The Reynold's Number (named after the Irish fluid dynamics innovator, Osborne Reynolds, 1842-1912) determines the forces turning laminar flow into turbulence. It has exercised an aeronautical hold on the imagination in its attempts to relate inertia and viscous forces (the Re division), and eventually the very "boundary (horizon) layer concept" (think of every airfoil as it confronts drag).[37] The layer also differentiates artificial from biological intelligence. *BI* infuses every drag with lift, but only within a finite timeframe that is death. For mammalian *species*, on average, a million-year life expectancy. For invertebrates generally-speaking 11 million years. Only Dinoflagellates exceed that horizon, at an average extinction rate of 13 million years.[38] For individuals, and – as propagated by a number of eco-dynamic barriers and constraints, populations – the relativity of the event horizon provides for spectacular inferences. Four strains of Permian bacteria found in New Mexico appear to be capable of surviving for 250 million years.[39] Other "bacteria, fungi and viruses" half-mile down in the ocean suggest lively endurance at the individual level in the many millions of years, with 10,000 year old reproductive cycles.[40] Great Basin Bristlecone Pines can live for 5,000 years, but that is the full blush of youth compared with tens-of-millions of halcyon years old yeast, the 80,000 year old "Pando" aspen glen in the Fishlake National Forest of Utah, a 43,600 year old King's Holly in Tasmania's Southwest National Park, Ice Age flowers still surviving in Siberia, as well as Late Pleistocene Jurupa Oak in California's Jurupa Mountains, and Box Huckleberry in Pennsylvania.[41] The average bacterium lives about 12 hours; a housefly two weeks; a house mouse, one year; a human cell, 7-12 years; a Greenland shark, 272 years, the Quahog clam over 500 years, the Giant Barrel Sponge 2,300 years, and at least one species of Northern Atlantic Black Coral (*Leiopathes glaberrima*) over 4,300 years. Most celebrated of all is the so called "immortal jellyfish" – *Turritopsis dohrnii*.[42]

There are no averages, but *H. sapiens* certainly have no bragging rights when it comes to longevity, as can be deciphered from the above. The BI (Biological Intelligence) Index, as we'll term it, appears to have no incorporation of gray matter, neurobiology, language, fertility rate, socialization, artistic or ethical ideas as the basis for duration. And yet, these latter two variables, aesthetics and moral conviction, seem to predicate the only antidotes to our otherwise largely hostile existence as a species among so many others. The natural machinery of our physiology tires and expires for no known reason, beyond the mechanics themselves. Knowing this for millennia, one might have expected human evolution to have self-directed in ways more propitious to perpetuation. At best we have doubled life expectancy, and only during the last century of our presence here. And by mechanisms that have also allowed us to utterly run riot over the very notion of ecological carrying capacity. Hence, the logical conclusion: by adding 40-50 years of life on average to each individual, we have – and can compute – the numbers of populations of other species (and their billions of other individuals) who have gone prematurely extinct as a result of our age-related meddling. That is anything but a solution. As has been proposed, we don't have the right language, or other means, of asking the right question in order to hopefully segue to an answer.

That is the fundamental problem for philosophy, as it looks quite desperately for feedback in biology, mathematics, ethics and politics.

Sets and Classes of Bias

We have earlier spoken of bias, anthropic coordinates that all but condemn us to us. In terms of what we have come to believe is intelligence belies the very same. Between 1915 and the early 1960s tests for "intelligence" were dispatched to thousands of Australian aborigines. By the 1960s the "culture-free" test had been developed, and then critiqued as being all but impossible. Wrote D. W. McElwain and G. E. Kearney, "a person brings to the solution of any complex problem tactics which are determined in part at least by experiences peculiar to his social history."[43] Perhaps the most telling irony accomplished by the so-called culture-free scores was the fact that Queensland aboriginal children were shown to be more or less equal to white children the more contact they had with one another. "The difference," wrote R. L. Kirk in analyzing the liabilities of such tests, was that "the difference is large in situations where contact has been moderate, and becomes greatest where contact has been low" referring to contact between white children and aboriginal children.[44] Many decades later, such inherently useless analytics – the standard *intelligence* scales used separately on adults and children – continue to be employed.[45] But the worst of these residually predisposed exercises has to do with the assent to common standard deviations that have no way of accounting for actual Beingness, creativity, dreamtime, or any other quality of mind that is both human, but also connected with a non-human past that is irrefutably part of a biotic Weltanschauung.[46] Not surprisingly, one of the most venerable studies of vertebrate intelligence recognizes "the possibility that there is in fact no such thing as 'general intelligence' so that comparisons between species are meaningless."[47]

At its face, Euan M. Macphail's categories for exploring vertebrate mind, or at least mental capacity, are straight forward. He examines "learning tasks," and their comparisons; "differing degrees of relatedness," forebrain structural qualities in fish, amphibians, reptiles, avifauna, and mammals. He looks at "brain organization" and speculates upon "general adaptiveness," "learning" and some "instrumental conditioning" and "habituation". But from the outset, Macphail acknowledges that a formal universal definition of intelligence is not the point, since it is a word as vulnerable to bias as was the word "instinct" which Charles Darwin had warned about.[48] Additionally, and much to his credit, Macphail quickly acknowledges the numerous pitfalls to experimentally thinking about appropriateness of context in which differing species are likely, under normal circumstances, to express behavior that in any sense may be related to the propensity for what we think of as intelligence. He is quite aware of the "unnatural situations" into which test methodologies can easily err in the choice of circumstances to which other species, as well as humans, are placed.[49] The best summary that can be affixed is this: "many of them [vertebrates] in fact perform in apparently similar ways over a relatively wide range of behavioural tasks, so that there are at least grounds for supposing some common behavioural capacities."[50]

But even this assumption is vulnerable. Macphail readily posits that "causation in different species" may well undermine any general theories; and that "comparative research of this kind" "need not hold good" in the sense that it is potentially "unlikely to provide conclusive evidence for a behavioral theory…"[51] In introducing the present "human condition", "the evolution of present-day reality amid countless other possible realities," Edward O. Wilson simplifies the definition of "intentional meaning" by suggesting that, ultimately it comes down to the "use of intentional meaning"; of "behavior that fulfills intention".[52] The tautological nature of reciprocal evasions tease forth the very flaws to which human language making are prone. We simply cannot assert authoritatively anything that includes ourselves within a subset of biological clarifications with respect to behavior or intelligence. This is the heart of the Russell's Paradox, which he articulated in 1901.[53] In essence, Russell suggests that there is a class of beings that includes all beings but itself. Since that *itself* is also part of *some* class of itselves, can the two classes ever be truly separate without contradicting the nature of that class of all beings? If so, or if not, as American logician/philosopher W. V. O. Quine (1908-2000) wrote of the paradox, it "can be accommodated by nothing less than a repudiation of our conceptual heritage."[54]

What is that heritage? Is it strictly racist? The fabrication of sets and classes in a social context that includes or excludes? A class system, a set system that discriminates on the bases of those qualities that determine membership? Quine spoke of an "epistemology naturalized" that argued "for seeing epistemology and empirical science as containing and constraining one another."[55] As Chase Wrenn points out in looking at Quine's response to German philosopher Rudolf Carnap's (1891-1970) attempt to resolve naturalization processes in logic, "Theoretical statements cannot, in general, be translated into purely observational vocabulary." Observation requires groups of "individual theoretical statements".[56]

Logic and mathematics are easily tangled in the paradox of the sheer number translation of other numbers, groups and kinds of numbers e.g., one basic list includes: natural, prime, composite, whole, integers, rational and irrational, real, complex and imaginary; negative, countable, fractions, greater than 1, and zero adjoined.[57] In the biosciences, particularly with respect to phylogenetics and taxonomy, the same material assemblages invoke enormous disparities, both of logic, systematics, and the imagination. Evolutionary trees are entirely, by definition, speculative, whether based upon rRNA genes or genomes, geological time, types of trees, or the proliferative cladistical studies, e.g., the delineation of ancestral clades. The details spiral from observation to hypothesis at the point of shared and derived traits (apomorphy and synapomorphy). Other characteristics of the evolutionary point of view encompass loss and gain, coalescence and division, convergence, reversal, homoplasy (loss or gain of derived traits), parallel and reverse homoplasy, etc.[58]

But in no less a manner than the assessment of intelligence that is hopelessly steeped in transparent biases, the question of a bias problem throughout all a priori knowledge raises the point of analysis that derives from previous analysis. Whereas experience does not. This indicts all history as post-history. There can be no *real history* (except in the sense of wild surmise) because our trajectories are not fixed, either before the present, during or after the present. We can make the same argument about phylogenetics, sub-atomic physics, and, indeed, every natural quantum caught out in the whorls of both time, human perception and perception by Others. If there is emphatic interdependency amongst these variables, their multiplication by the number of individual biotic components makes it even more imponderable to the sitting intellect. This is neither anti-realism nor anti-science. But it is an important form of skeptical inquiry because it is not selective. Both experiential and so-called empirical evidence are suspect within the consideration of what is actually happening in the world. History provides no real re-assurance, and certainly no guide. If soldiers throughout all the battles of time had said "No" to their commanding officers; if all physicists had refused to work at the Manhattan Project, or walked off the jobs at every national laboratory in every country; if every dictator had been perceived for who he/she really was and dispatched in a timely fashion (as earlier theorized); if if if…

In geometry p→q or, if-then laws of detachment, of syllogism, of generalization are neither a priori nor a posteriori. The problem is best cached in the terms of immediacy. The pico(trillionth of a)second-by-second pragmatric, with which every organism contends, whether in pico, nano (billionth), or other increments of evolutionary and geological time, can never meet the test of real time.

Knowing that we assimilate by our perceptual faculties, and imagine by laws as yet to be divined, we gravitate to the obvious, as a *new gravity* flush with the Gestalt psychology that so obsessed both philosopher Ludwig Wittgenstein (1889-1951) and German psychologist Wolfgang Köhler (1887-1967).[59] Like so many before and after him, Plato himself grappled, and could not satisfy the dialectics informed by Being and Becoming.[60] It was German philosopher Nicolai Hartmann (1882-1950) who is perhaps best remembered for his development of a metaphysical phylogenetics[61] which in turn provided a semantics to the famed German entomologist, Will Hennig (1913-1976) whose four biological categories continue to influence our views of evolution. Hennig discounted universals in favor of "levels" of biological reality; a systematics that included the "semaphoront"[62], or object in time; a transitive and ephemeral terminal by which ongoing hierarchies can be related, placed, and signified, a challenge for modern cladistic systematics.[63] The semaphoront concept as applied by Hennig acknowledged that neither the "organism or the individual (not to speak of the species)" should be viewed "as the ultimate element of the biological system." Instead, he emphasized points along the way of the biohistory of those beings, even "during a certain, theoretically infinitely small, period of its life."[64]

The emergence of such viewpoints are crucial to grasping the sheer complexities of both the quantum biosemiosphere[65], but equally, the ability to formulate the right questions if we are to tease forth in timely manners the answers to outright inflictions perpetrated by the social human fabrics of 21st century society. The same societies now demonstrably ignoring the ecological fate of so many millennia gone haywire in empire and hubris building.

As Philosophy Turns Toward a Mirror

A myriad of apologias have been proposed in defense of philosophical discourse having never achieved a single solution. The actual literature on this seemingly fundamental gap in the riddle that is alleged intellect proves that logic and illogic are perfect asymptotes. That thought comes close at times to a sub-set of closure, but never to the set itself.[66] Critic Robert Almeder, examining the work of John Kekes, cites as one "difficulty," the fact that "Seldom, if ever, does philosophy bear any relevance to basic problems about how to live in our complex and dangerous world."[67] Chris Daly, a professor of philosophy at the University of Manchester, cautions there are laws in science that differ substantially from the absence of such certainly in philosophy and logic, citing, "the inverse square laws governing light and sound, the Coulomb laws of magnetic and electric interaction, and Ohm, Ampère and Faraday's laws of electricity"[68] are each fitting examples of, in a sense, the triumph of scientific *constants* over the endless logical quibbling and grasping at irrelevant straws that seem to have always absorbed philosophical dialogue.

This in spite of the common assent to those basic goals of philosophy, in its broadest outlines, have always sought – certainly since the times of Mahavira, Plato, Lao Tzu and Aristotle – to understand how human beings can live happily and more virtuously. But many contemporary thinkers, like physicist Lawrence Krauss in dialogue with philosopher Julian Baggini, have suggested that philosophy is "impotent"; whereas Baggini suggests "I cannot see how mere facts could ever settle the issue of what is morally right or wrong, for example."[69]

Philosophy students are taught to question everything, from the beginning. Science students, conversely, must memorize and at least partially understand everything. As a rule, it is only much later that a scientist can legitimately question any of those basics. This is an enormous distinction which Daly summarizes: "…there are two awkward facts about philosophy. First no philosophical problems have been solved; second, philosophers cannot agree about anything beyond that."[70]

In the opening line of Bertrand Russell's *The Problems of Philosophy*, he asks: "IS there any knowledge in the world which is so certain that no reasonable man could doubt it?"[71] The 61-year old "invisible Ukrainian," Igor Pedin who, with his dog Zhu-Zhu, walked 225kms to escape the unrelenting destruction of Mariupol. Their survival epic, like that of Holocaust survivors, evinces a kind of knowledge that, when fully absorbed, not only permanently impacts identification with the victims, with the entire setting of war, but mirrors the very nomadic nature of philosophy whose true task is to wander through such a minefield.[72] To ask the same questions again and again, perpetually from a different out-of-sorts; abetted by no pillar of sustaining logic, no buttress of actual clarity. The formidability of the unknown is not the agency of philosophy, but of humanity searching for any tools to make fire without blowing up the world. So far, no luck, as Russian media discusses in cavalier fashion how long it will take to render London or Paris a wasteland.

That this intractable asseveration applies equally to science is no surprise. But that philosophical inquiry should spend forty years, at least, in the desert, lost, makes the task of being found that much more of an historical phenomenon that has ever been our plight as a species. This is certainly where philosophy and biology can acknowledge their shared frustration.

Political and legislative policies, like the vicissitudes of every quotidian act of the mundane, are irrelevant under any time-defined aegis. Talk of human rights, solving world hunger, criminalizing hate, etc. are not on par with millions of sudden human and other animal food refugees in East Africa, where three anticipated rainy seasons failed to materialize by the Spring of

2022.[73] The age of cynicism, the epoch of fatalism, of the onslaught of World War III in anyone's mind who watches or reads the news, even in fleeting soundbites, strikes one by one, in increments of fatalistic taxons, ruined ideals – like Umberto Eco's "legendary lands"[74] or Ray Ching's "fabled lands"[75]; irruptive hope that swarms around a headline today, and is all but gone by tomorrow. Take the example of the Madras High Court in India's southern state of Tamil Nadu declaring in 2022 "Mother Nature" a living entity with personhood that must be protected, citing legal precedents from a 2017 case in the state of Uttarakhand, and from similar declarations in countries like New Zealand, Ecuador and Bangladesh.[76] After thousands of years of desecration, the getting of religion suddenly is not going to do it. In 2021, researchers mapped the planet for ecosystems with datasets targeting the integrity of faunal communities. Their estimates show that no more than "2.8%" of the terrestrial earth "could be considered functionally intact" based on such criteria as Key Biodiversity Area qualifications, mammal diversity and density, number of extirpated species, and general persistence of in situ biological community assets.[77]

Conservation estates (governed by environmental authorities) and outright wilderness areas in countries like those aforementioned, comprise varying degrees of compromise, as defined per country. New Zealand shows approximately 29% as legally protected to some degree.[78] As we have analyzed in over 15 years of field research in New Zealand, conservation means a concerted nation-wide effort at killing many non-native species, as well as a multitude of designated recreational hunting blocks within conservation areas. While there is always trouble in paradise, New Zealand conservationists like Craig Potton are leaving a magnificent legacy of aesthetic and biological hope through their unflinching activism, inspiration and artistic legacies. Of course, in doing so, such outstanding individuals also reveal only too clearly how much there is to lose; how fine an edge that of hope and tragedy share.[79]

The *wilderness ideal* has been constrained by reality, in the broadest definition of the term, to six regions of the planet: the boreal forests of Canada and Alaska, the Amazon, Botswana's Okavango Delta, the great central desert of Australia and most of Antarctica.[80] These devolvings of ideal to reality are predicated upon one's definition of what we're speaking of: 20,000 pristine hectares by New Zealand terms; 5,000 acres in the U.S. legal framework, "Category 1b" for the IUCN.[81/82] The Wilderness Act of 1964 (Pub.L. 88–577) written by Howard Zahniser described and protected 9.1 million acres in the U.S. at the time of its codification.[83] But from India to Ecuador to Bangladesh;

from Columbia and Suriname to Bhutan; from the U.S. even to Antarctica, the incremental compromises involving poaching, unsustainable tourism, regional and global pollution, loss of rights by indigenous people (some of whom inhabit those wildernesses), and other forms of aggression by dint of the sheer human population explosion meted out directly or indirectly by imperfect or non-existent policies and ecological monitoring mechanisms, undermine the good will, and remarkable research endeavors by hundreds-of-thousands of people. Today's depreciated conservation achievements resemble the efforts by medieval monks to find a suitable wilderness in which to build a monastery. Historian Clarence J. Glacken describes how St. Boniface encouraged St. Sturm, the "indefatigable, psalm-singing hermit,"to keep looking until he had found a "place predestined by God". Eventually St. Sturm believed he had found such a sacred vortex and the first thing he did involved "cutting down the trees to make a circular defense to protect his ass"; but he was certain that the spot "was a blessed one, foreordained by God for such holy use" as a monastery. Another monk, "God's servant Cedd (d.659)" searched for his monastic site according to Isaiah's prophecy recommending "the fruit of good works to spring up where formerly lived only wild beasts…"[84] Some of those creatures were much admired, others feared, as witnessed in the horae illustrations, the Book Of Hours genre.[85] Such are the fluctuating values of what constitutes both wilderness and nature. The chaos of semantics, vocabulary, meaning and intent. The lists of "Protected and Conserved Areas" represent an extreme cartographical confusion of ever-changing coefficients, numeric assignations of quantity and quality; of human-divined aesthetics and the persistent tyranny or fringe tolerance of legal codes.

What were once beasts are today rare mammals, birds, trees and insects, etc. A flower has not always been the same flower, as Lucia Impelluso so beautiful details throughout the Middle Ages and Renaissance with respect to the tulip, lily, hyacinth, cyclamen, rose and so forth.[86]

While Ecuador – the nation that was allegedly "first to grant nature constitutional rights"[87] – served as a precedent for India's recent High Court decision, the World Data Base on Protected Areas of the IUCN[88] has nowhere near the levels of sensitivity and accuracy to determine real time on-the-ground consequences of political change or economic marginalization, as has been the case with oil drilling in Yasuní National Park, and other Key Biodiversity protected areas of Ecuador.[89] Poverty, the fact there are still uncontacted tribes in the country's Amazon regions, political wavering within a very few years from the inception of the so-called Yasuní-ITT fossil fuel restraint order ("initiative") under the former President Rafael Correa,[90] and the enormous power even within Ecuador's court system of multinational oil companies, all conspire to undermine progress in wilderness ratification, let alone human redress.[91] These are just the most salient variables in a collapsed *philosophical system* that would hope to meld with the biological basics. It is one of the emblematic and troubling coefficients of ecological antinomies that pervade other paradox-driven compromises in nation after nation.

There are so many competing definitions for wilderness in the human political and legal arenas, that we can begin to grasp from their expansive arguments the troubled, murky psyche behind these endless flash points for deliberation.[92] Christopher Tunnard reminds us that "acclimatization" to every aspect of our relation with Nature has been compressed. What required "years of effort, heartbreak, and acrimony" in searching for "the source of the Nile" in the nineteenth century, could now be accomplished in "an instant of satellite photography." And the same goes for the introduction of genetically modified organisms, or "dry rice cultivation in Indonesia," thereby eliminating "the time-honored water-filled paddy" system of agriculture, and so forth.[93] Throughout nineteenth century England, the tension between rigorous natural history and the Tractarian Movement[94] of ecological "sacramental imagination" propagated by Anglican priest and poet John Keble (1792-1866) in his book *The Christian Year* (1827)[95] would come to torture Darwin in his endlessly treated dark night of the soul.[96] Such that Darwin evidently remarked to his friend Thomas Huxley, "If I had been a friend of myself, I should have hated me."[97] The dialectic between Biblical nature and scientific explanations also hint at the current divide between GIS, Google Earth, all those forms of advanced cartography[98] that have occupied the imagination with instantaneous access to the previously unknown/unknowable quadrants of the world, down to the inch, the chemical, the sub-surface, even wireless communication "spectrum cartography" described as "a deep network architecture" which has as much applicability to neurons as to any object or space on the planet.[99]

In her extraordinary book, *Atlas Of Remote Islands – Fifty Islands I have Never Set Foot On and Never Will,* Judith Schalansky excites a mesmerizing realm of the merging of discovery and something beyond that, which chimes with the humanity that is so arrested by the thought of greener pastures. She writes of German adventurer August Gissler (1857-1935) searching for gold year after year on the Cocos Island of Costa Rica, ultimately determining that "the promise of the map was worth more to him than the treasure that was impossible to find."[100] Greek Nobel Laureate, the poet Odysseus Elytis would describe how legendary Ithaca was not the goal of exploratory obsessions. It was the journey itself to Ithaca that always mattered. One of countless versions of Gertrude Stein reflecting on the fact in her *Everybody's Autobiography* (1937) that the Oakland, California home of her childhood had ceased to exist. A fact of life hallowed three years after Stein echoed "there is no there" by Thomas Wolfe in his 1940 novel, *You Can't Go Home Again*. No better environmental debacle echoes Wolfe's title than the ongoing disaster relating to the survival of the fewer than 700 individual Asiatic (Gir) lions essentially trapped in Gujarat State by a Prime Minister, and a nation one-third the size of the United States with a population well over 1.4 billion people and counting.[101] That number, however, is a dramatic increase from the nadir of 177 individuals in 1968. Much dedicated work to save this remarkable big cat has been accomplished by Indian conservationists in and abutting the Gir National Park and Wildlife Sanctuary in Gujarat.[102] But India's various Forest Service biological opinions have recognized that there is no wilderness left in India where the prides can be translocated, only Wildlife Sanctuaries, of which there are 564 in the country, averaging in size 83 square miles each. The largest of them all is Ranthambore National Park in Rajasthan, at 515 mi^2. An area where poaching and "people laying claim to the forest" has been ongoing.[103] Ultimately, writes G. Seetharaman, "Gujarat's refusal to move some of Gir's lions to [the State of] Madhya Pradesh despite the death of 24 lions has more to do with politics than the effectiveness of translocation."[104] But, in fact, lacking an abundant food base, the average lion pride (2-to-40 individuals) requires some 150 square miles to eke out its livelihood. And as Poulomi Banerjee writes, "one can only hope that the pride of Gir does not fall prey to forces beyond the control of its protectors."[105]

The problem with the numbers is ultimately key to the crisis of Critically Endangered species worldwide. In the case of the rarest bear in the world, the Gobi Brown Bear (*Ursus arctos gobiensis, mazaalai*) in Mongolia, as of 2017 there were fewer than 40 individuals left.[106] They have an enormous area (over half-million square miles including contiguous habitat in China) across which to maintain discrete genetic populations, but their inbreeding and subsequent genetic vulnerabilities, in addition to extraordinarily meager, almost entirely herbivorous food base, have left them marooned in a hot desert environment, that is getting hotter all the time; and to which their adaptation – for a large mammal, albeit the smallest of the brown bear sub-species – is simply not enough. Their world has let them down. It is not conclusive, but near enough so, in the global scope of endangered species contexts, to suggest that human intervention is failing. Hunting of brown bear was outlawed in Mongolia in 1959. But they simply do not appear to have the necessary ecological infrastructure necessary to save them from extinction. None have ever survived in captivity and there is no known Gobi Brown bear anywhere in the world outside of the wild. One can say that this is a problem for philosophy. But not one that can be solved by human intellect or feeling. And that is a crucial dilemma with which we cannot, will not ever come to terms. It stares in the mirror and sees an earth in crisis, but all it can do, as a discipline, is to ponder its plight. There is simply too much human induced drag on its velocity, mass, and ineluctable gravity that is propelling most other species, on a severely time-limited directional vector, toward a ground zero finale.

As far as the African lion, it is estimated there are fewer than 20,000 individuals left in the wild.[107] As for Africa's human population, it is projected to rise from a current 1.34 billion continent wide, to nearly 2.5 billion in 2050.[108] If, as was the case with the U.S. Congress and China for so many years, a right-wing American-dominated international affairs policy pattern opposing termination of pregnancies and all trans-continental immigration were to emerge, tied perhaps to food aid or other humanitarian assistance, one can be absolutely certain that pro-life (as perceived by radical GOP politics) would translate into the extinction of lions, among many other species.

Some have thought of the moral conundrums associated with these stark policy interconnections the basis for something like "Noah's Choice," as Charles C. Mann and Mark L. Plummer titled their book on "The Future of Endangered Species" in 1995.[109] In the Appendix to their work, they questioned the efficacy of the (U.S.) Endangered Species Act as of twenty years after its enactment. Not surprisingly, in looking at the number of species that could be said to have recovered, out of 721 species added to the "list" by the U.S. Fish and Wildlife Service, "sadly," they wrote, "the number is small."[110] Psychologically, philosophically, pragmatically this is very bad news for a world where human agency is already so stricken by a patchwork of ineffective laws, feckless policing, or worse. Like lawmakers, conservation biologists, or artists, "practitioners of any aesthetic activity may be thoroughly alienated from what they are doing," writes Jerome M. Segal, in a work that lays out a troubling and fascinating study of human presence and, as Terry P. Pinkard characterized its impetus, "the philosophy of action."[111] When we idly consider human thought and its consequences it is almost unimaginable to consider targets as targets of ideas, objects of philosophical meditation. Any of the more than 300 squirrel species can remember where they had cached, in some instances, over *9,000 separate nuts*.[112] It is acknowledged that a speaker of about "10,000 words" makes them fluent, or certainly a "native-speaker".[113] Some have speculated that Shakespeare had a passive vocabulary of around 65,000 words.[114] And, like a squirrel, he had to know where to place each word. Had the poor fellow, in addition, needed to run all over the neighborhood during all four seasons (it's principally the tree squirrel species that hide so many nuts and they don't quasi-hibernate in Winter), the great bard might have picked up quite a few more words, anecdotes, and outright tales. Who knows. The point is, every species that becomes rare, threatened, endangered and eventually ends up on the brink, like New Zealand's flightless parrot, the Kakapo, Ecuador's Critically Endangered Black-Headed Spider Monkey, India's Gir lions, Bhutan's Hispid Hare, Columbia's Santa Marta Bush-Tyrant, or the South China Tiger – down to zero individuals in the wild[115] – represents a mirror on human actions that have failed the world; undermined the very credibility of what most of us propose as one of the unique gifts of our humanity: an activist metaphysics of protection,[116] pragmatic idealism.

As with the last living speaker of a language, of which at least six individuals have been known,[117] such categories of loss manifest what has always occurred to bigger picture idealists as a wanton cruelty built into the very matrix of Nature. Where to champion one's energies? Whether to be active or reactive, in terms of the very practical-minded preoccupation with tenable outcomes? In conservation biology this has meant investing time, research, resources into those fixable problems. Or, at the very least, situations that lend themselves to some quantum of reasonable amelioration (e.g., a no kill animal shelter). Theoretical research has a long view that does not address the moment-by-moment hope v. hopelessness debate in philosophy. And it *is* a debate that has infiltrated every aspect of human thought, pervading all those urgencies where paroxysms of inertia are obviously useless. Hence, the realm of philosophy concerned with activism as a fundamental responsibility of all meditation, the next logical step upon the *ladder of being*; or biological notations of phylogeny that have been so core to natural history and philosophical speculation (however different those two activities may be defined).[118] This was Jean-Paul Sartre's possibly greatest point: that *because* humans *must* be free (even when so many are not), it is our sublime, often desperate duty to be activists.

Hope and Hopelessness

All norms are fast loosing traction in human social settings, everywhere. "Offense"[119] has masterminded action and reaction. Anger roils; compassion and tolerance are strained, like mercy, as the species-level circumstances loom larger than any previous generation thought possible, though there have been more than sufficient past centuries of documented terror, widespread grievance, and irremediable, justified nihilism, to have informed us in advance.

Maybe this is why – at the height of philosophical duty – some female octopuses have been evolutionarily programmed to self-destruct "after laying eggs" and protecting them for some time. Perhaps it is simply one more biochemical pathway, the alleged "precursor to cholesterol;"[120] or perhaps something far more savvy, much deeper in its advanced prescience.

Bias, injustice, polarization, contest, the fated discourse. Each of these builds an analytical narrative that panhandles for resolution,[121] for the psychological tools that can empower our grasp of, and resolve to rationally embrace "actuality."[122] Shelly Kagan questioned such tools in her work, *The Limits of Morality*[122] concluding that the ethical standards enshrined by any society, "can demand a significant overall sacrifice of one's interests,"[123] and they do. The conceptualization of policies and activist orientations that can work alone, or in tandem with others, has never posed impediments. This is the human tragedy: that we can imagine how to rescue victims, prevent disasters, assist others in need on so many levels, but fail to do so in the actual moment(s) when we are called upon. A hero's welcome is always a singularity, in mind; the ecology of aftermaths, its contour. Much has been written of classical hope, despair, the bestiality of the Gods in Homer, of the Swan-song in Euripides.[124] Elpis and Spes, hope in Greek and Latin. Versus apelpisia (despair) and desperation. A dialectic that has shaped every philosophical discussion since, let us say the origins of discussion. French philosopher Comte de Volney (1757-1820) naively calls upon the philosopher who secretly or not so, resides in every politician to "teach us, after so many religions of error and delusion, the religion of evidence and truth."[125] Of the 170 or so most famous quotations regarding "hope" that have been ordained in English literature[126] it is little surprising that Nietzsche should have covered the mantle with a solemnity exclusive to himself when he wrote in *Human, All Too Human* (1878) "... die Hoffnung: sie ist in Wahrheit das übelste der Übel, weil sie die Qual der Menschen verlängert. ("Hope in reality is the worst of all evils because it prolongs the torments of man.")[127] But it was also Nietzsche, in the same book, who spoke of "Man" as an "undetermined animal" which, as biographer Rüdiger Safranski writes, corresponds with Nietzsche's belief in a human containing a "profusion" of personages and their "voices"; and that we have the ability to discriminate between this internalized "medley" and make a determined "choice."[128] Morality for Nietzsche did not necessarily evolve from morality. There is the possibility of something new under the Sun. That is a vast distinction which, in the flames of his same torment is conjured forth in the name of *hope* that so many have seen fit to ridicule, if not despise outright. Why so? Perhaps, in one's most unsettled and cynical frame, because it is the very spirit of a twisted yearning that remains forever undermined by our very dualistic humanity.[129]

To best illustrate this psychotic break in the demonstrative urgings of a philosophical verdict on human morality and its chances in the world, we consider the depth intoned by the 24th Jain Tirthankara, or Jina: an Indian sage known to history as Mahavira (599 BC – 527 BC). An elder mentor to Gautama Buddha, Mahavira presents to interfaith ecosystem logic the prime example of renunciation, total non-violence, and a life during which he wandered from village to village conveying a singular message of peace to all beings, interdependent beings, he emphasized. His ecological acumen exceeded that of any pre- or Socratic Greek thinker. Indeed, we know of no other individual in the history of ethics who has espoused so perfect a mirror on ahimsa, non-violence in Sanskrit, and revivified it within a human life. As we have written elsewhere, "In negotiating their way through the maze of destructive behavior that is endemic to most human life, the Jains have managed to a remarkable degree to impede the accumulation of ill-thoughts, ill-deeds, even inadvertent imposition. This, they say, is the only way to achieve peace. At every juncture of human behavior, the Jains have sought to enshrine gentleness, finding a viable path toward love that can be embraced by an entire community. This ecology of the soul (*jiva*) consists of care taken in all actions and thoughts; forgive, to be universally friendly, compassionate, and affirmative; to exercise critical self-examination at all times, as well as restraint in all matters; to fast frequently and meditate on non-violence for forty-eight minutes at the beginning of every day (*samayika*); to follow a holy path that ultimately leads to total renunciation."[130]

Today's fewer than 100 earlier referenced Digambara monks, walk naked, as they have for thousands of years of documented history across India, carrying a gourd filled with boiled water (purified water); and a pinchi, peacock feathers that have naturally fallen to the ground, been collected and made into a little broom to (gently) sweep away the slightest insect that might get under food. They eat but one meal a day – strictly vegetarian – when they are not fasting. The meal is given to the monk by clerical disciples who vow that the food is pure (vegetarian) and for whom it is a great honor to bestow food into the hands of the monk who otherwise will never touch another living being; who will never walk on grass, touch a tree or a flower, or shake someone's hand. Out of the question. And, of course, they are celibate, but for reasons perhaps unexpected. They believe that the obvious fluids produced in such prodigious acts as sexuality, are a total killing field of spermatazoa, etc. Their diet is also rigorously restricted to only one-sensed plants, not two, or three, or four or five. A one sensed plant, for example, is butter lettuce, as was earlier remarked upon.[131]

"Parasparopagraho jivanam," said Mahavira in Sanskrit, later propounded in the famed *Tattvārtha Sūtra* (5.21) by famed Jain scholar, Umaswati, who lived sometime between the 1st and 5th centuries CE.[132] Current interdisciplinary eco-dynamic studies globally attest to this vision. But where the natural sciences agree that all biological beings are in one way or other dependent upon one another, the crucial element in Jainism is the subtle translation of Being into Soul. Even more globally congenial, forthright, and reassuring is the Jain insistence on activism, care for all others – all of them. Frankly, Jainism goes where no other vast spiritual tradition has emphatically accompanied, namely, by declaring, "a wise man should not act sinfully towards earth, nor cause others to act so, nor allow others to act so…"[133]

The Jains are by no means alone in challenging the sinister vision that so consumed Friedrich Nietzsche. Among other anthro-ecological models of a testable, tenable reality, we include such biocultural examples as the Fore peoples of Okapa District in the Eastern Highlands Province of Papua New Guinea (as described by anthropologist E. Richard Sorenson), the early Tahitian peoples (as investigated by Robert I. Levy), the Tasaday of Mindanao (studied in depth by John Nash), the Yurock Indians of California, the West Malaysian Semai who so intrigued the scholar Robert Knox Dentan, the Tanzanian Hadza, the Australian Murngin and Warlpiri peoples, the Dani of Irian Jaya, the Inner Badui of West Java, the Bishnoi of Rajasthan and Toda of Tamil Nadu, the Pantaneiros, Qollahuaya and Runas of Bolivia, the ancient Essenes of Qumran, the Gnostics of the Manichaean religion founded by Mani in AD 242, Paulicians of Armenia (followers of Paul of Samosata), and the Bulgarian Paterenes of the tenth century, followers of a charismatic priest they called Bogomil. In Italy the Patarenes would found the non-violent Cathar creed, also known as the Albigensians in France. Later Renaissance Christian monastic orders upheld similar views, most notably as depicted in the life of Saint Francis who propounded the celebrated perspectives endowing all plants and animals with a soul, and thus considered sacred and inviolate. Carthusians, Trappists, Camaldolesian hermits of Mount Corona, and Seventh Day Adventists each adhere to the same vegetarian philosophy, predicated upon the famed *Genesis* passage 1:29 that reads to its own intrinsic rhythm that seems a universal through-story too many have forgotten: "And God said, behold, I have given you every herb bearing seed, which is upon the face of all the earth, and every tree, in which is the fruit of a tree yielding seed; to you it shall be for meat."[134]

It is this precise activist interjection by Jain ethical endowment that we first glimpse what Mahavira knew to be the *Samavasarana*[135] or *Samosharana*, a gathering place (literally: a refuge for all) from which the Jain animal sanctuaries would arise, goshalas (animal refuges for bovines)[136] and panjarapols, other Jain sanctuaries found all over India, all over the world. Uncannily, according to multiple Jain oral and written traditions, Mahavira spoke to thousands of animals at the Samavasaranas he conducted. From Aesop to Saint Francis, this deep ethological conservation was nothing less than a harmonious conversation betwixt an interspecies politic, a means of resolving anything on anyone's mind. Among the Todas of the Nilgiris, this podium of resolutions is called a *noyim* and long normalized.[137] Thus, inherent to the political structure of the Jain refuge concept is the foregone belief (in humans and all others) that any real political progress can only occur through acceptance at, excitement by, the progress, ethological truth of the famed *parliaments*. One thinks of Geoffrey Chaucer's (1425-1475) middle English masterpiece, "Parlement of Foules" or "The Conference of the Birds," by that nomadic heart in one sublime Persian poem by Attar of Nishapur (c. 1145-c. 1220). These human designs in nature call upon all the species in the region to come together (lion and lamb); to sit, perch, lounge around and engage peacefully in a dialogue that is not merely the fantasy of children's highest literature – rebuked at every turn by gun violence shattering the lives of children in their very schools, from Ukraine to Texas[138] – but, indeed, a very real societally-grasped means towards an end.

In the stark reality of that end, a Samavasarana will not expedite our cavalier insistence on such engines of adamantine self-interest as "ammonia (for fertilizer), steel, cement and plastic".[139] Nor will Kierkegaard's vague reliance on some expectation that the future will move toward goodness (an agnostic quavering between hope and hopelessness)[140] easily be characterized as the pre-condition for some level of courageousness, as has been suggested by the Italian philosopher Giorgio Agamben.[141] In an interview with Juliette Cerf, Agamben declares, "Philosophy is not an academic discipline, but a way of measuring oneself up to this event that never stops taking place and which determines the humanity and inhumanity of mankind;" his biopolitical *Homo sacer*, sacred and accursed man in one – anyone other than a theologian may kill him.[142] The ambiguity may be ignored by those who have transcended the cynicism that marked the *learned hopelessness* in dogs and rats first publicized by Martin Seligman and Steven Maier over half-century ago.[143] A cure? Eudaimonia, says Seligman. A life lived in service of something greater than oneself.[144] Such logic ignores the frailty, the total mathematical probability distribution fracture lines of traditional hypothetical syllogisms and the *transitivity of the implicative*.[145] That would entail, for example, the nearly 11 million prisoners in the world, the highest rate being that of the paradise islands, the Seychelles, with 799 inmates per 100,000 inhabitants.[146] For so many of those caught out in the so-called "correctional" world, there is little hope. Much like what Elliot R. Wolfson has meditated upon in his discussion of "the messianic belief in a future that must be perpetually deferred" (in his essay examining the common threads of melancholy in a variety of great such thinkers including Kafka and Derrida).[147] Our consciousness is rooted to hope, declares one age after another of misery. We are vulnerable but we can make more than merely comfortable decisions. In German psychoanalyst and philosopher Erich Fromm's (1900-1980) work *The Revolution of Hope: Toward a Humanized Technology* (American Mental Health Foundation edition, 2010) our very vulnerability is a pillar of our strength; his eight described needs a combined alchemy of freedom providing for avenues of transcendence but also of identity beyond the fact, as he put it, humans are "a freak of nature"; and the ability to accomplish meaningful ends.[148] We can gauge through the lens of the remarkable Rumanian intellect, Emil Cioran, that failure is everything, so contrasted by Fromm. Failure, and the "ruins" of philosophy which pre-start our futilities in the midst of plenty, such that it is in keeping to admit that only after philosophy has ceased might we start to live.[149] That may be the courage Kierkegaard was thinking of.

It was at such a moment, when Herries Beattie reminded us that "As with the birds, so it is also with races – there is a sentimental satisfaction in alluding to those who are extinct…"[150]; that Albert Schweitzer, speaking of a "Fellowship of those who bear the Mark of Pain" will go out "in the colonies" and dispatch amelioration "among the miserable in far-off lands all that ought to be done in the name of civilization, human and humane…" Actions that are required in the extra-territoriality of truth, noting, as Schweitzer did, that "Europe is ruined and full of wretchedness". That the world knows truth not by time of day, or location. "Its hour is now – always, and indeed then most truly when it seems most unsuitable to actual circumstances," he went on to say.[151] Schweitzer's involvement with the poor, the sick, and all animal species he could help, does not comport exactly with any one philosophical tradition, which should come as no surprise to the purveyor of all those schools of thought that are simply institutionalized settings for debate, not true places of unbiased and unsupported engagement in everyday life.

The time, temperament and pressing urgency of the outside world does little to abet engagement of that proliferation of norms which is philosophy. As editors Jussi Suikkanen and Yiying Peng elaborate in their overview of topics under the aegis of "normative ethics," the categories invite endless consideration of topical entry points into "Consequentialism," "Utilitarianism," "Deontological Moral Theories," "Virtue Ethics," "Moral Value" and "Phenomena," every possible modality therein.[152] But a person actually grappling from a wheel chair with these issues is likely to come back to reality far more convincingly than any abstraction.[153] Similarly, a politically dispossessed individual, or an animal on an assembly line heading rapidly towards slaughter, will have none of it.[154]

Here is the great divide that has, for as long as documentation affords some insights, separated goodness and evil; kindness and hatred; tolerance and self-absorption; humility and super-ego. All of the antipodes. To live without contradiction is to have ignored paradox in oneself and in the world. Is that even possible to do? The contradictory-free existence is a disease that cannot exist, except in the vacuum that is destined to die alone, without notice, care, or value. A valueless death is acceptable on a planet that sees suffering without the least gesture or condolence. Indeed, the proverbial killing fields of human history, or of the Serengeti's is proof positive beyond any doubt that nature is, in part, a horror. Nothing our psychological, social or technological innovations may accomplish will change the biological basis of evolution which will remain repulsively opportunistic, not withdrawn into gentle thought, or certainly not entirely. We see and always underestimate its beauty, because we are subsumed within our aesthetic freedoms. So, we are confronted with this challenge of impossible ambiguity. If we are to assemble questions, lines of inquiry that have meaningful answers, responses worthy of the best of humanity, we must break bread together on the cusp of overwhelming hope, despair and destruction. We have no evidence this is possible, or not in any large confines of dialectical existence where we awake to antipathies every day.

Nonetheless, it is worth comparing the two roadmaps to see how a community, even a nation state might avow its allegiance to peace and prosperity in absence of all the sad, heinous and irrational ruins upon which dictatorships and brutality are fashioned. There may never be a correlation between an individual and its species; an individual and the biological connections that can be discerned. No Being who is tantamount to a village or population. We, each of us, is blinded by the numbers that surround us, retreating to the One in Mind, in reverie, in hopes for itself. Hopes for the world are the blind hands extended into air. The dreams that have always been dreamt. Thinking of tomorrow, addicted to present moments. Every cemetery mentors them. Builds up reminders of their value and peril. Residual disappointments cannot re-fabricate the intricacies of a successful evolutionary change because we have no way to believe in any of it. We can't see it happening, not in a moment. A bacterium or fly can, but we cannot. Only the customs of biology give us the predictability of seasons, more or less. Of every weather, however fickle and rapidly changing. Of life and death before we, or anyone else, knows what has happened. These embers roam like ghost species mounting their age-old argument in favor of the monstrous, necessary, all-consuming mortality that is the breezy, almost cavalier underpinning of all evolution. As Robert Frost sought to dissect when he wrote, "Griefs, not grievances, are the stuff of poetry."[155]

Hobbesian Brutality and Buddhist Legal Narratives

We arrive at length at the most remarkable and literarily acrid political philosopher in Western history, Thomas Hobbes (1588-1679), most famed for four of his books, most incisively, *Leviathan* (1651).[156] Alongside Hobbes, and in stark contrast, is that of Bhutan's Constitution and the legal writings of its principal author, Lyonpo Sonam Tobgye, that nation's former Supreme Court Chief Justice, and Chairman of the Constitution's drafting committee.[157]

It is important to note that we (the Authors) have sat for many hours on different occasions at Lyonpo Sonam Tobgye's home high above Thimphu discussing these issues and principles and have, in sum, come away recognizing without question that there are people, like Tobgye who defies with outspoken goodness and breathtaking intellect, the gravity and terminal repercussions of the endless circumlocutions that have absorbed humanity during its entire odyssey.

If we may take the idea of liberty to adduce, then Tobgye's pellucid, ethical convictions – as expressed, outlined and manifested in Bhutan's newly Democratically elected government, which took place between 2007 and 2011, when Bhutan's population was between 664,000+ and 693,000+ – represent a strangely elusive, opposite corollary to the frightening propositions masterfully amassed by Hobbes.

How does one reconcile two distinct futures, both imperfect, one far more so than the other, but both inherently seductive at different times, for different reasons, as the human condition unfolds? The variables of each of the two paradigms – Hobbesian and Buddhistic – in a glance seem equally prone to the vicissitudes of human nature, aspiration, greed and/or unstinting modesty and compassion. In Bhutan the national elections of 2007 seemed straightforward, after a century of paternalistic monarchy, four beloved and noble majesties and their Queens. Four parties, 47 constituencies, a bicameral Parliament with 25 members, 5 chosen by the King (His Majesty Jigme Singye Wangchuck, b. November 11, 1955) and 20 members elected, one per 20 of the dzongkhags (states) throughout the country. There were, at the time (2007), 312,817 eligible voters on the "final electoral roll".[158] Nearly 70% of those eligible voted, an astonishing turnout given the nation's logistical complexities topographically (it is the most mountainous region of any country). It is also amazing that the 4th King voluntarily and quite suddenly decided that the monarchial modality, which his family, the Wangchucks had overseen for 100 years, was no longer the appropriate legislative formula for the 21st century. He would step down, abdicate all of his official duties and live in a log cabin in the hills of Thimphu, thereby setting in motion the formative preconditions for what was at the time the newest democracy in the world. This was the same leader who, as a teenager, decided that Bhutan must forever leave at least 60% of its standing canopy of old forest intact.[159] That the reverence for nature that is largely inherent to his country's state religion of Vajrayana Buddhism be codified throughout the laws of the land. There would have been very few Bhutanese who were not more than a little saddened by these political turns, for the people love their Kings and Royal Family who have only shown wise benevolence. Democracy, for the Bhutanese, represented nothing less than a profound challenge, electrifying though it may be.

How extraordinarily different was Hobbes' England when he wrote *Leviathan*, with a population of approximately 5.6 million, 91.7% of them living in the English countryside.[160] The year the book was published, England's monarch, Charles II was defeated by Oliver Cromwell at the Battle of Worcester, the last bloody conflict of the country's Civil War, and fled to Europe. Two years earlier, Charles' father, Charles I, King of England, Scotland and Ireland had been executed. England would not have been the destination of choice for most tourists. The "de facto republic" of Cromwell was one of continued violence, absolutism and much chaos. The idea of a constitutional monarch meant essentially nothing. The ideals of a Democracy did not exist, not in any country (with the possible exception of Iceland, which was under Danish rule). And Hobbes considered such authoritarianism as was constantly arising in the course of normal affairs all across the world as the essential binding of subjects and their sovereign leaders as the basis for any safe escape from the otherwise deathly state of nature. A set of inexorable local circumstances across the geography of international relations which, despite such rational pleas as those of a Hugo Grotius (*On the Law of War and Peace*, 1625) and the 1648 conclusion of the Eighty Years' War involving Spain, Netherlands and Germany at the Peace of Westphalia, was, according to Hobbes, a logically doomed complex, the "summum malum" or ultimate fear of death, the basis for Hobbesian political theory.[161]

Hobbes thought little of humanity, suggesting that beasts no more than one year of age were far more capable and could "pursue that which is for their good, more prudently, than a child can do at ten."[162] While humans can theorize, analyze, add and subtract, citing Cicero, "there can be nothing so absurd, but may be found in the books of philosophers"; that only we among all the other species possess the "privilege of absurdity."[163] Hobbes' other fixation with philosophy concerned "natural philosophy" which, he believed was the result of "accidents of bodies natural". *Accidents*. Science, physics, politics...each discipline "consequences from the accidents" of various quantities, qualities and other aspects of "bodies".[164] As with these misadventures and contretemps, he also spoke of "a great deal of grief" which arose from "keeping company, where there is no power able to over-awe them."[165] Only our companions, Hobbes asserted, could lend us enough value in our lives to keep us from instantly killing one another ("in [a] quiet") mode.[166]

This quietism, or need for a dictator to give us succor, could not be stayed by any ethological resolution because, according to Hobbes, the idea of biophilia (he did not use such a word) was an incorrect assessment of the relations between species. Indeed, says he, "To make covenant with brute beasts, is impossible, because not understanding our speech, they understand not, nor accept of any translation of right; nor can translate any right to another; and without mutual acceptation, there is no covenant."[167] Moreover, nature does not grant us the "force of words" sufficient to either our causes or consequences, any more than it does to other species, he alleges. Leaving us all bound to one invalid guarantee after another. There is no giving or receiving that is not premature, and without "propriety". It is the nature of politics to surmise ways by which to ensure the maintenance of "valid covenants."[168] But let us imagine such a warped premise of propositions, that only the passionate drive towards self-preservation can ultimately inform any necessarily contingent "commonwealth" that survives by its concatenate power to "tie them [constituents] by fear of punishment to the performance of their covenants…" and that such "terror" as may be discerned among "the laws of nature" "cannot apply to humans" who only subscribe to nature when their strength to do so has not abandoned their personage. Where the custom of small families preying upon one another has somehow ceased to exist. And when those same laws of nature can be applied "safely" to the human condition, which they cannot.[169] And so only the "sovereign power, whether placed in one man, as in monarchy, or in one assembly of men, as in popular, and aristocratical commonwealths, is as great, as possibly men can be imagined to make it." With inevitable evil consequences, either way, to follow.[170]

Hobbes is quite certain that laws to amend these adverse consequences cannot be made up, least of all by philosophers. He says quite explicitly: "The interpretation of the laws of nature, in a commonwealth, dependeth not on the books of moral philosophy." That it is of "great error, to call the laws of nature unwritten law." Humankind, in other words, must persist outside the rubrics of that which can safeguard our petty little pains and aspirations.[171] Only the Leviathan, as described in the first and fortieth books of *Job*, says Hobbes, can claim a natural right to be "King of the Proud"; "king of all the children of pride."[172] Even as he chides our moral equivalencies within a monarchy, Hobbes also recaptures the fallacies of differing ancient systems, like those of the Roman Senate, and the very "People of Rome"[173] who, in their various thrusts toward power were always going to be subject to the very same delimiting rubrics as defined the entire stage laid out by Edward Gibbon, or an Arnold Toynbee or Jared Diamond. Hobbes would have made the reading of such histories illegal, as if they had been written expressly to defy the monarchy, the commonwealth; as if the authors had been bitten by "a mad dog".[174]

All such divagations were conceived so as to espouse what is needed to sustain the authoritarianism of a dictator. Hobbes in this manner quite anticipated, for example, the fanatical controls levied by a Putin upon Russian journalists and their efforts to keep alive any honest social media. He forthrightly acknowledged that humanity cannot live without such tyrannical monsters, and hence, the double-example of the Biblical Leviathan, and the consumption whole of a human being, its communities gobbled up by the one threat to them that can force their obedience, just as a Trump demanded a diseased loyalty during his own vile reign. Or, as Hobbes describes the syndrome, "And because the first instruction of children, dependeth on the care of their parents; it is necessary that they should be obedient to them…"[175]

For Hobbes, human life is nothing more than "bellum omnium contra omnes" –"war of all against all [everyone against everyone]"[176] – where, in its purest ecological outpouring, nature propounds a state that is "the life of man [as] solitary, poor, nasty, brutish, and short."[177] As prolifically as Hobbes has been cited, the contradictory belief that led Hobbes to insist on the judicial need for a sovereign has for centuries been criticized as overly pessimistic, Machiavellian.[178] But tens-of-thousands of people were murdered during Hobbes' time; violence was normalized, and he had good reason to assume that pre-emptive strikes at both individual and commonwealth levels were the only antidote to the safety which humans, like all organisms, crave. Even as it means ceding one's own miniscule power, and waning sense of dignity to the voracious systems swirling around autocracy.[179/180] In Ireland alone, it was estimated that the Ulster Uprising of 1641 might have resulted in some "154,000" Protestants who were "butchered".[181]

The monarchies were assumed to provide safety nets for citizenry and others. We know from history that this is not the case, certainly not uniformly. The concept of psychopomp, angels of death that guide souls in one direction or another, has its shamanic counterparts in the multicultural apprehensions regarding the final present, of the terminus that always connotes death. Hobbes had obsessed on its inevitability, like every other living being who is aware at infinite levels of the tension, the terminal velocity teasing our ideas outward, and back inward. Life replacement fields of energy are inextricably woven into the politics that dominate our present; have always done so. In every charged meeting of dissenting minds the questions of a finality emerge. Monarchs and death deities hold similar spells over the mob. Classical mythology politicizes and animates these supreme beings who control the machinations of everyday. With so entangled a biocultural web of emotions run riot, little wonder that few political institutions have ever managed to grapple with the fundaments of human fear and willingness to be subjugated, aside from a very healthy revolution now and then.[182]

Bhutan's Constitution, in fact, has been said to grant its citizens a far greater voice as to the future of their country and individual "destiny" than is the case throughout the rest of the world, most notably as concerned "the drafting of the European constitution."[183] According to the 4th King's daughter, HRH Princess Sonam Wangchuck who studied comparative constitutional law at Harvard while her father was enacting the historic changes in Bhutan, "My father always said that you can't leave the future of the country in the hands of one person." But, she added, "people need to be educated to a certain level before they can embrace democracy."[184] Given that American journalists were chiding their readerships for "living in the Golden Age of Stupidity"[185] how could any democracy enforce the prerequisites necessary for making wise choices?

Buddhist Bhutan is a premiere case study in pushing the logic of governance to its possible boundaries of virtue, certainly in the biocultural sphere which is the only one that truly matters. Article 5 of its Constitution takes up quite succinctly the five pillars of true environmental sustainability. They include recognition that each citizen is a "trustee of the Kingdom's natural resources and environment for the benefit of the present and future generations…" They are intended to help conserve the country's "rich biodiversity" and prevent "ecological degradation including noise, visual and physical pollution through the adoption and support or environment friendly practices and policies." That "Parliament may, by law, declare any part of the country to be a National Park, Wildlife Reserve, Nature Reserve, Protected Forest, Biosphere Reserve, Critical Watershed and such other categories meriting protection."[186] In addition to its maintenance of a minimum of 60% forest cover, Bhutan's Article 5 was described by Helvetas, an independent Swiss development organization, as an "innovative and unique constitutional approach [that] may serve as a model for other constitutions."[187] Its emphasis on "intergenerational equity" lends additional weight to themes and definitions that no other founding documents of democracy anywhere in the world have ever recognized. Input from the Bhutanese public on issues pertaining to Article 5 were welcomed by officials and frank explanations given for the protective web of environmental components. For example, the potential, unsustainable greed of corporations and public authorities well into the future was openly acknowledged during discussions in central Bhutan in December 2005.[188]

In writing about the freedoms inherent to Bhutan, the conatus of an individual to pursue her/his best options in life through natural inclination, Tobgye references Liberty (dod bdang in Dzongkha) by ancient Greeks; to the French Declaration of 1789; and to a constellation of thinkers, from Aristotle to Hobbes; Rousseau and Spencer, Marx, Nietzsche and Freud to Robert Thurman's mention of Buddhist principles of "enlightenment, education, individualism, altruism and egalitarianism [that] are realized through democracy."[189]

For Buddhism it was the *Mahasammatta* who founded all political principles.[190] There is the characteristic legendary qualities to this "Great

Chosen One" in Mongolia who "preserved peace and settled the conflicts among the people by way of Dhamma" [norm] which Buddha himself had laid down centuries before. Buddha had declared that such a leader or Dhammaraja must think of others, not her/himself. They must embody "ten royal virtues"[191]: including "generosity," "charity," "high morality," "selflessness for common good," "courage," "civility and kindness," "self-control," to be "without prejudice," to promote "non-violence," "patience," to be "resilient" and possess "empathy"; and finally, to promulgate the qualities of "harmony," "non-obstruction and to respect the will of the people."[192]

While there is a literary abundance of Buddhist, ecological meditation, the essence of it comes down to this: "Under Buddhist philosophy, the planet earth is the abode for all sentient beings. Conservation and protection are thus the basis of the survival for all sentient beings, the refuge for posterity…" The Buddha, according to Bhutan's famed 8th-9th century saint, Guru Rinpoche Padmasambhava, declared that one must never "destroy plants," "vegetables," "dig ground or have it dug," "drink water with living germs in it," or "deprive any living being (animal etc.) of life."[193] In the United States and other democracies outside Bhutan, rights are very differently assigned: natural, inalienable and fundamental, as it concerns citizens. Citizens who, in the Constitution, Declaration of Independence and the Constitution's Bill of Rights, were a special class of Caucasian males.[194] "…let Facts be submitted to a candid world," wrote Jefferson and his 55 fellow signatories to the Declaration of Independence, before writing that King George had "endeavoured to bring on the inhabitants of our frontiers, the merciless Indian Savages, whose known rule of warfare, is an undistinguished destruction of all ages, sexes and conditions" among other so-called "usurpations".[195]

We quote our past, both embarrassed and perplexed by the blind alleys of history and of those otherwise astute performers on the myriad fronts of the offensives towards justice that have drenched this, and virtually every other nation in blood. That includes Bhutan itself, whose founding leader, Zhabdrung Ngawang Namgyal, a refugee from the Tibetan side of the Himalayas, found himself embroiled in wars with Tibet's rulers and ruling class from 1627 to 1634. Indeed, as early as the 11th century, Tibetan and Mongolian conscripts occupied by force and claimed Bhutan for themselves. Altercations occurred between the Bhutanese and the outside world well into the late eighteenth and nineteenth centuries. Great Britain even declared war on Bhutan in November 1864. A peace was signed in Sinchula (Bhutan) roughly one year later. Bhutan lost some 20% of its territory to what today is India.[196]

Hobbes had not overreached. No country exists without the "country" mandating the relations between peoples. While we might take that as a given, it is no given in nature. Thales, Aristotle, Lao Tzu (Laozi), Mahavira, Buddha, Christ, Percy Shelley, Alfred Wallace and Charles Darwin, and a rapturous succession of countless political philosophers and biologists, metaphysicians, psychologists and geneticists have tried to work through the mechanisms that preceded evolution and today appear to guide her bespoke dominions, complex as they are, through the many layers of acute obstructionism and defilement represented by *H. sapiens*. The Bhutanese have sought to repeal those inexplicable woes with some of the most impressive environmental beliefs ever achieved by ethical and political willpower. But even all 14,824 square miles of little Bhutan have succumbed, in part, to internal and external variables: poaching, road building, the excesses of certain industries like cement manufacture, rural-to-urban migration and with it pollution in all forms, climate change, population growth, and the contradictory challenges of animal rights and animal liberation in a Buddhist country that falls within a biological hotspot, wedged uncomfortably between the two most populous nations – still growing fast – on earth.

Beyond TVP (Terminal Velocity/Philosophy)

Sir George Stokes, 1st Baronet (1819-1903),[197] who held the Lucasian Chair of Mathematics at the University of Cambridge for an astonishing 54 years (a position once held by Isaac Newton as well as Stephen Hawking), was enamored of almost everything to which numbers and common sense could be attached, from rainbows and optics, astigmatism in particular, to the brittleness of cast iron bridges, politics, and natural theology. But he is most remembered for his obsessive fascination with the details (many of which he derived) of fluid dynamics. *Stokes' Law* (as well as the Claude-Louis Navier-Stokes equations), refers to his precise measurements of a sphere falling through a viscous medium up to its terminal velocity.[198] One delightful aspect of this "law" concerns *one of those questions*, "Why don't clouds fall?"[199] The answer concerns a combination. Of the radius, of say a raindrop, and the atmosphere's viscosity; the velocity and mass density of the raindrop, and the measure of turbulence as defined by Reynolds number. Simply put, little raindrops, a mist, may settle but not fall.[200] But why is any of it relevant? Or does *relevance* matter?

Terminal velocity is particularly complicated in that fluids, liquids and solids all have varying definitions as a medium through which an object is flowing or falling or moving. There are "ideal fluids" that offer no resistance. But the mechanics of sheer force, dispersion of energy, change in deformation, all move in terms of forces both external and internal mounting increasingly counterintuitive forms of inertia that all but culminate with Newton's Second Law of motion, and his Third Law of Reaction. Force equals mass times acceleration.[201]

We have seen how even a little rainbow-like Bhutan has been forced into war by a major world power, and now finds the physical forces of the world eating away at both its raindrops and glaciers, threatening more than a billion people downstream in India and Bangladesh, not to mention the Bhutanese themselves. Glacial Lake Outburst Floods, and wildfires have already shown their accelerating ferocity across Bhutan.[202] The interdependencies inherent to Bhutan's and to Buddhism's most noble revelations have come back to haunt the innocent, both at the individual, hamlet, community and political population levels. It torments our species with outright devastation, violence, injustice and every imaginable horror that we ourselves have perpetrated. Yet, even as we learn from our mistakes, another force, rich in demographic milestones, topples over that knowledge in one stampede after another. While we have analgesics to temporarily curb some pains, there is no such opium poppy whose seedpods appear capable of halting our species' infinite debacles.

"Conundrums Written in Stone, Ryoan-ji, Kyoto," Photo © M. C. Tobias.

Endnotes

[1] https://www.etymonline.com/word/incarnate

[2] See *The World's Best Fairy Tales*, Edited by Belle Becker Sideman, Illustrations by Fritz Kredel, Two Volumes, The Reader's Digest Association, In., Pleasantville, New York, 1977.

[3] From Observations On A Late Publication, Intituled [sic], "The Present State Of The Nation," *The Works of the Right Honourable Edmund Burke*, Collected In Three Volumes, Vol. 1, J. Dodsley, London, UK, 1792, p. 259.

[4] See *Utopia*, by Sir Thomas More, A New Edition with Notes, by Rev. T. F. Dibdin, Two Volumes, William Bulner, London, UK, Vol. 2, p. 5, 1808.

[5] See "Math Insight," by Duane Q. Nykamp, https://mathinsight.org/definition/magnitude_vector

[6] "Terminal Velocity (gravity and drag)," Edited by Nancy Hall, Glenn Research Center, NASA Official, NASA, https://www.grc.nasa.gov/WWW/K-12/airplane/termv.html

[7] Terminology and equation, NASA, ibid.

[8] Weckbach, Sebastian; Flierl, Michael A; Blei, Michael; Burlew, Clay Cothren; Moore, Ernest E; Stahel, Philip F (October 25, 2011). "Survival following a vertical free fall from 300 feet: The crucial role of body position to impact surface". Scandinavian Journal of Trauma, Resuscitation and Emergency Medicine. 19: 63. doi:10.1186/1757-7241-19-63. PMC 3212924. PMID 22027092.

[9] Parke, Caleb (April 22, 2019). "'Thank God for the miracle:' Man who survived 47-story fall from NYC skyscraper recounts story". *Foxnews.com.*

[10] "Newton's Second Law," Physics Classroom, https://www.physicsclassroom.com/class/newtlaws/Lesson-3/Newton-s-Second-Law

[11] Helmenstine, Anne Marie, Ph.D. "The Difference Between Terminal Velocity and Free Fall." ThoughtCo, Feb. 16, 2021, thoughtco.com/terminal-velocity-free-fall-4132455, https://www.thoughtco.com/terminal-velocity-free-fall-4132455#:~:text=Terminal%20velocity%20is%20defined%20as,buoyancy%20and%20the%20drag%20force; See also, http://hyperphysics.phy-astr.gsu.edu/hbase/airfri2.html

[12] See *The Works of Archimedes*, Cambridge University Press, Cambridge, UK, 1897. p. 257.

[13] See *Theory of Games and Economic Behavior*, by John von Neumann and Oskar Morgenstern, Princeton University Press, Princeton, NJ, 1944.

[14] See *The Nature of Rationality*, by Robert Nozick, Princeton University Press, Princeton, NJ, 1993, p. 141.

[15] "Journey To An Antique Land," Ben Ben Press, Big Sur, CA, 1962, p.14.

[16] See "Speed and Velocity," *The Physics Hypertextbook*, ©1998–2022 Glenn Elert, Author, Illustrator, Webmaster, https://physics.info/velocity/; See also, "Nerve conduction velocity," MedlinePlus, https://medlineplus.gov/ency/article/003927.htm

[17] See "Meshal ha-kadmonim, The Fable of the Ancient," Albert S. Cook Library, Towson University, MD, https://libraries.towson.edu/featured-item/meshal-ha-kadmonim-fable-ancient

[18] 2nd edition published in Venice by Meir Parenzo, 1546, https://www.abebooks.com/servlet/BookDetailsPL?bi=30699881226&cm_sp=snippet-_-srp3-_-tile2&

searchurl=fe%3Don%26bi%3D0%26ds%3D50%26bx%3Doff%26sortby%3D1%26kn%3DBirds%26recentlyadded%3Dall

[19] See "No. 2723: Language Death," by Richard Armstrong, Engines of Our Ingenuity, © 1988-2011 by John H. Lienhard, https://www.uh.edu/engines/epi2723.htm#:~:text=It's%20hard%20to%20come%20up,languages%20spoken%20in%20the%20world.

[20] See B. C. van Fraassen, "Singular Terms, Truth-value Gaps, and Free Logic", *The Journal of Philosophy* 63(17), September 1966:481–495. See also, *Scientific Representation – Paradoxes of Perspective*, by Bas c. Van Fraasen, Oxford University Press, Oxford UK, 2010.

[21] See Crossley, J.bN.; Ash, C. J.; Brickhill, C. J.; Stillwell, J. C.; Williams, N. H., What is mathematical logic?. Oxford University Press, London-Oxford-New York, 1972.

[22] Carnielli, Walter; Coniglio, Marcelo Esteban (2016). Paraconsistent Logic: Consistency, Contradiction and Negation. Logic, Epistemology, and the Unity of Science. Vol. 40. *Springer International Publishing*. ix. doi:10.1007/978-3-319-33205-5.

[23] See José Ferreirós, *Labyrinth of Thought: A History of Set Theory and Its Role in Modern Mathematics* (2nd ed.). Springer, New York, NY, 2008 - § Zermelo's cumulative hierarchy pp. 374-378.

[24] See *Bigger than Chaos – Understanding Complexity through Probability*, by Michael Strevens, Harvard University Press, Cambridge, MA, 2003, p. 275.

[25] ibid., pp. 328-330.

[26]. See *Leonardo's Paradox – Word and Image in the Making of Renaissance Culture*, by Joost Keizer, Reaktion Books, London UK, 2019, p.99.

[27] See *A Dark Premonition – Journeys to Hieronymus Bosch*, by Cees Nooteboom, Translated from the Dutch by Laura Watkinson, Schirmer/Mosel, Munich, Germany, 2016, p. 39.

[28] ibid., p.21.

[29] See "Drag Force with low Reynold's number," by "philosophicalmath", November 18, 2017, https://philosophicalmath.wordpress.com/2017/11/18/drag-force-with-low-reynolds-number/; See also, https://philosophicalmath.wordpress.com/2017/10/21/terminal-velocity-derivation/

[30] See R. H. Peters, *The ecological implications of body size*. Cambridge University Press, Cambridge UK, 1983.

[31] See Burness, G. P.; Diamond, Jared; Flannery, Timothy (2001). "Dinosaurs, dragons, and dwarfs: The evolution of maximal body size". *Proc. Natl. Acad. Sci. U.S.A.* **98** (25): 14518 23. Bibcode:2001PNAS...9814518B. doi:10.1073/pnas.251548698. PMC 64714. PMID 11724953.

[32] See "Why Are There So Many More Species on Land When the Sea Is Bigger?" by Sarah Zhang, The Atlantic, July 12, 2017, https://www.theatlantic.com/science/archive/2017/07/why-are-there-so-many-more-species-on-land-than-in-the-sea/533247/

[33] ibid.

[34] ibid. Zhang points out that there is no question of a prevailing bias in this sense. She also makes clear that we would need an entirely different discussion for unicellular life forms; microbes whose abundance both in the oceans and on land are so differently numerous as to, if you will, break all the normal rules of bias and inquiry.

https://www.theatlantic.com/science/archive/2017/07/why-are-there-so-many-more-species-on-land-than-in-the-sea/533247/

[35] See Smithsonian Libraries, Section 11, Curator's Note, https://library.si.edu/field-collection/field-section/678; See also "Haeckel Radiolaria Collection and the H.M.S. Challenger Plankton Collection," by Hoshiaki Aita, et al., *Joint Haeckel and Ehrenberg Project: Reexamination of the Haeckel and Ehrenberg Microfossil Collections as a Historical and Scientific Legacy*, edited by Y. Tanimura and Y. Aita, pp. 35-45. National Museum of Nature and Science Monographs, No. 40, Tokyo 2009.

[36] See "Mathematics and the Genome: Introduction," by Joseph Malkevitch, American Mathematical Society, © 2022, http://www.ams.org/publicoutreach/feature-column/fcarc-genome1

[37] See Reynolds, Osborne (1883). "An experimental investigation of the circumstances which determine whether the motion of water shall be direct or sinuous, and of the law of resistance in parallel channels". Philosophical Transactions of the Royal Society. 174: 935–982. Bibcode:1883RSPT..174..935R. doi:10.1098/rstl.1883.0029. JSTOR 109431. See also, David B. Dusenbery, *Living at Micro Scale*. Harvard University Press, Cambridge, Massachusetts, 2009.
See "History of Reynolds Number," n.a., n.d., https://www.nuclear-power.com/nuclear-engineering/fluid-dynamics/reynolds-number/history-of-reynolds-number/#:~:text=The%20concept%20was%20introduced%20by,exhaustive%20experiments%20in%20the%201880s. https://www.nuclear-power.com/about/copyright-notice/38 See the 7-volume *Encyclopedia of Biodiversity*, 2nd edition, "Modern Examples of Extinctions," by Gábor L. Lövei, 2013, https://www.sciencedirect.com/topics/earth-and-planetary-sciences/life-span

[39] See "250-Million-Year-Old Bacteria Revived in Lab/Spores were found deep in rock salt formation," By David Perlman, SF Gate, October 19, 2000, https://www.sfgate.com/news/article/250-Million-Year-Old-Bacteria-Revived-in-Lab-2733033.php

[40] "Soil beneath ocean found to harbor long lived bacteria, fungi and viruses," by Bob Yirka, Phys.org, August 29, 2013, https://phys.org/news/2013-08-soil-beneath-ocean-harbor-bacteria.html 29, 2013, 41 See "Oldest Living Organisms in the World," Shasha Neil, https://www.oldest.org/nature/living-organisms/

[42] See "How Long Animals Live – The Life Spans Of 50 Animals," n.a., n.d., https://alansfactoryoutlet.com/wp-content/uploads/2021/02/how-long-animals-live-life-spans-50-animals-6b.png, using the following sources: nationalzoo.si.edu, darwinfoundation.org, https://www.nationalgeographic.com/news/2016/07/animals-oldest-sponges-whales-fish/, https://marinebio.org, https://tpwd.texas.gov/publications/nonpwdpubs/young_naturalist/animals/animal_life_spans/

[43] See *Aboriginal Man Adapting – The human biology of Australian Aborigines*, by R. L. Kirk, Clarendon Press, Oxford University, UK, 1981, p. 149.

[44] ibid. See also, *Aboriginal Cognition Retrospect and Prospect*, Psychology Series, No. 1, Ed. By G. E. Kearney and Donald W. McElwain, Australian Institute of Aboriginal Studies, Canberra, Australia, 1976.

[45] See "Alfred Binet and the History of IQ Testing," by Kendra Cherry, Fact checked by Emily Swaim, verywell mind, April 13, 2022, https://www.verywellmind.com/history-of-intelligence-testing-2795581

[46] See Rindermann H, Becker D, Coyle T. Survey of expert opinion on intelligence: Intelligence research, experts' background, controversial issues, and the media. *Intelligence*. 2020;78:101406. doi:10.1016/j.intell.2019.101406; See also, Reynolds C, Altmann R, Allen D. The problem of bias in psychological assessment. *Mastering Modern Psychol Test*. 2021;1621:573-613. doi:10.1007/978-3-030-59455-8_15; See also, Spielman R, Dumper K, Jenkins W, Lacombe A, Lovett M, Perlmutter M. 40 measures of intelligence. Psychology - H5P Edition.

[47] See *Brain and Intelligence in Vertebrates*, by Euan M Macphail, Clarendon Press, Oxford, UK, 1982, p. 340.

[48] ibid., Introductory chapter, and p. 3.

[49] ibid., p.8.

[50] ibid. p.17.

[51] ibid.

[52] *The Meaning Of Human Existence*, by Edward O. Wilson, Liveright Publishing Corporation, A Division of W. W. Norton & Company, New York, NY, 2014, p.13.

[53] See 1903. "Appendix B: The Doctrine of Types," in Bertrand Russell, *The Principles of Mathematics*, Cambridge University Press, Cambridge, UK, 1903, 523–528.

[54] See W. V. O. Quine, *The Ways of Paradox and Other Essays*, Random House, New York, NY, 1966, p. 11.

[55] "Naturalistic Epistemology," by Chase B. Wrenn, University of Alabama, *Internet Encyclopedia of Philosophy*, https://iep.utm.edu/nat-epis/#:~:text=Naturalistic%20epistemology%20is%20an%20approach,theories%20from%20the%20empirical%20sciences. See also, W. V. O. Quine, *Ontological Relativity and Other Essays*, Columbia University Press, New York, NY, 1969; Columbia University Press. See also, W. V. O. Quine, "Norms and Aims" in *The Pursuit of Truth*, Harvard University Press, Cambridge MA, 1990.

[56] Wrenn, ibid., 1.a.

[57] See "Number Sets," Math Skills Overview Guide, Davenport University Libraries, https://davenport.libguides.com/math-skills-overview

[58] See Roderick D.M. Page and Edward C. Holmes *Molecular Evolution: A Phylogenetic Approach*, John Wiley & Sons, New York, NY, 2009. See also, Mayr, Ernst (1978), "Origin and history of some terms in systematic and evolutionary biology", Systematic Zoology, 27 (1): 83–88, doi:10.2307/2412818, JSTOR 2412818. See also Mayr, Ernst (1982), The growth of biological thought: diversity, evolution and inheritance, Cambridge, Massachusetts: Harvard University Press, and Farris, James S. (1983), "The logical basis of phylogenetic analysis", in Platnick, Norman I.; Funk, Vicki A. (eds.), *Advances in Cladistics*, vol. 2, Columbia University Press, New York, pp. 7–36

[59] See "'Blind' to the obvious: Wittgenstein and Köhler on the obvious and the hidden," https://escholarship.org/content/qt4j0433bp/qt4j0433bp_noSplash_f066f934c8d0146f69e7c50e33eb2e3e.pdf?t=nhs2lw, https://escholarship.org; See also, Davis, W.H. The morally obvious. *J Value Inquiry* 19, 263–277 (1985). https://doi.org/

10.1007/BF00172002; See also, "From Semiotics To Philosophy: Daring To Ask The Obvious," by David Z. Saltz, *Performance Philosophy*, Vol 1 (2015): 95-105, doi: http://dx.doi.org/10.21476/PP.2015.1124, ISSN 2057-7176

[60] See "A Glimpse of the obvious," by I. H. Sutherland, Australasian Journal of Psychology and Philosophy, Volume 10, 1932, Issue 1, https://doi.org/10.1080/00048403208540956, https://www.tandfonline.com/doi/abs/10.1080/00048403208540956

[61] See Tremblay, Frederic (2013), "Nicolai Hartmann and the Metaphysical Foundation of Phylogenetic Systematics", *Biological Theory*, 7 (1): 56–68 (2013), https://doi.org/10.1007/s13752-012-0077-8, S2CID 84932063, https://philarchive.org/rec/TRENHA

[62] ibid.

[63] See "Hennig's semaphoront concept and the use of ontogenetic stages in phylogenetic reconstruction," by Prashant P. Sharma, Ronald M. Clouse and Ward C. Wheeler, Cladistics, The Will Hennig Society, Wiley Online Library, March 11, 2016, https://doi.org/10.1111/cla.12156, https://onlinelibrary.wiley.com/doi/10.1111/cla.12156

[64] ibid, from Hennig, W., 1966, p.6. *Phylogenetic Systematics.* University of Illinois Press, Urbana, IL, PubMedWeb of Science®Google Scholar

[65] See *The Quantum Biosemiosphere*, by M. C. Tobias and J. G. Morrison, NOVA Science Publishers, New York, NY 2021.

[66] See "Whether Philosophical Questions Can Be Answered," by Justin Weinberg, April 23, 2018, DailyNous, https://dailynous.com/2018/04/23/whether-philosophical-questions-can-answered/

[67] See also Robert Almeder's review of John Kekes' book, The Nature of Philosophical Problems: Their Causes and Implications, Oxford University Press, Oxford UK, 2014, in *Philosophical Reviews*, Notre Dame, https://ndpr.nd.edu/reviews/the-nature-of-philosophical-problems-their-causes-and-implications/

[68] See, "Philosophy's lack of progress," by Chris Daly, edited by Nigel Warburton, *Aeon*, 11 June 2021, https://aeon.co/essays/why-doesnt-philosophy-progress-from-debate-to-consensus

[69] "Philosophy v science: which can answer the big questions of life?" by Julian Baggini and Lawrence Krauss, September 8, 2012, *The Guardian*, https://www.theguardian.com/science/2012/sep/09/science-philosophy-debate-julian-baggini-lawrence-krauss

[70] Chris Daly, II—Persistent Philosophical Disagreement, *Proceedings of the Aristotelian Society*, Volume 117, Issue 1, April 2017, Pages 23–40, https://doi.org/10.1093/arisoc/aow020, https://academic.oup.com/aristotelian/article/117/1/23/3572468

[71] Opening sentence in "Apperance And Reality," www2.lawrence.edu/fast/ryckmant/The%20Problems%20of%20Philosophy,%20Bertrand%20Russell.htm

[72] "The invisible Ukrainian who walked 2215km to safety from Mariupol," by Daniel Boffey, May 13, 2022, The Guardian, https://www.theguardian.com/world/2022/may/13/the-invisible-ukrainian-who-walked-225km-to-safety-from-mariupol

[73] See "East Africa faces worst hunger crisis in decades," by Thelma Mwadzaya and Mohamed Odowa DW, Retrieved May 15, 2022, https://www.dw.com/en/east-africa-faces-worst-hunger-crisis-in-decades/a-61320250#:~:text=Millions%20at%20risk%

20of%20severe%20hunger&text=The%20United%20Nations%20estimates%20that, driest%20conditions%20recorded%20since%201981.

[74] *The Book of Legendary Lands*, Umberto Eco, Translated by Alastair McEwen, Rizzoli ex libris, New York, NY 2013. See also, *The Dictionary of Imaginary Places*, by Alberto Manguel and Gianni Guadalupi, Illustrated by Graham Greenfield, Maps and Charts by James Cook, Macmillan Publishing Co., Inc., New York, NY, 1980.

[75] *Fabled Lands – Fables, Nonsense & Other True Stories*, by Ray Ching, Poorly Rabbit Press, Auckland, NZ, 2021.

[76] See "Indian Court Rules That Nature Has Legal Status on Par With Humans – and That Humans Are Required To Protect It" by Katie Surma, Inside Climate News, May 4, 2022, https://insideclimatenews.org/news/04052022/india-rights-of-nature/; See also, "Madras HC grants living being status to 'Mother Nature': What does it mean and what are its legal precedents?" by FP Explainers, May 4, 2022, https://www.firstpost.com/india/madras-hc-grants-living-being-status-to-mother-nature-what-does-it-mean-and-what-are-its-legal-precedents-10632831.html; See also, https://www.hindustantimes.com/india-news/mother-nature-is-a-living-being-with-rights-and-duties-madras-high-court-101651311461556.html

[77] See "Where Might We Find Ecologically Intact Communities?" by Andrew J. Plumptre, et al., Front. For. Glob. Change, 15 April 2021 | https://doi.org/10.3389/ffgc.2021.626635, https://www.frontiersin.org/articles/10.3389/ffgc.2021.626635/full; See also, "Taking the pulse of Earth's tropical forests using networks of highly distributed plots," by Cecilia Blundo et al., School of Geosciences, School of Biological Sciences, Deanery of Biomedical Sciences, Global Health Academy, College of Science and Engineering, The University of Edinburgh, Scotland, 25 May 2021, 10.1016/j.biocon.2020.108849, https://www.sciencedirect.com/science/article/pii/S0006320720309071, https://www.research.ed.ac.uk/en/publications/taking-the-pulse-of-earths-tropical-forests-using-networks-of-hig-2

[78] See "What are Wilderness Areas?" FMC, Federated Mountain Clubs, Wilderness Areas of New Zealand, https://fmc.org.nz/wilderness-areas/; See also, *New Zealand's Wilderness Heritage*, Text by Les Molloy, Photography by Craig Potton, Craig Potton Publishing, Nelson NZ, 2007.

[79] See *God's Country: The New Zealand Factor*, by M. C. Tobias and J. G. Morrison, A Dancing Star Foundation Books, Zorba Press, LA and Ithaca, NY, 2011, https://dancingstarfoundation.app.box.com/s/st72okcdfn; See also, "New Zealand's Biodiversity Crisis Prompts Extreme Measures," given that "Approximately 4,000 of the country's native species are classified as 'at risk' or 'threatened' – the highest proportion of threatened native species in the world." By Pete McKenzie, Photographs by Jim Huylebroek, *The New York Times*, June 5, 2022. See also the very spectacular and optimistic book, *New Zealand's Wilderness Heritage*, by Les Molloy & Craig Potton, Craig Potton Publishing, Nelson New Zealand, 2007.

[80] See "Five maps that reveal the world's remaining wilderness," by Steve Carver and Lex Comber, *The Conversation*, January 29, 2019, https://theconversation.com/five-maps-that-reveal-the-worlds-remaining-wilderness-110061

[81] See "Wilderness areas," 16 USC § 1131(a), https://www.law.cornell.edu/definitions/uscode.php?width=840&height=800&iframe=true&def_id=16-USC-

1581012044-1053370792&term_occur=4&term_src=title:16:chapter:23:section: 1131; See also the Final Process Paper of August 21, 2008, entitled, "Guidance on How to Conduct the 'Potential Wilderness Area Inventory' for the Revision to the Revised George Washington Forest Plan," a "Framework" for evaluation under the Wilderness Act of 1964 that elaborates upon the "Inventory Criteria," and the "Identifying [of] Areas That Generally Appear To Have Been Affected Primarily By The Forces Of Nature, With The Imprint Of Man's Work Substantially Unnoticeable," https://www.fs.usda.gov/Internet/FSE_DOCUMENTS/stelprdb515 7866.pdf

[82] See IUCN, "Wilderness Protected Areas: Management guidelines for IUCN Category 1b protected areas," Prepared by the IUCN WCPA Wilderness Specialist Group, Sarah A. Casson, Vance G. Martin, Alan Watson, Angie Stringer and Cyril F. Komos, *Best Practice Protected Area Guidelines Series No. 25*, https://portals.iucn.org/library/sites/library/files/documents/pag-025.pdf, https://portals.iucn.org/library/node/46541\

[83] "Complete Text of the Wilderness Act". See also, Wilderness area, List of U.S. National Forests, List of U.S. National Parks

[84] From *Traces on the Rhodian Shore – Nature And Culture In Western Thought From Ancient Times To The End Of The Eighteenth Century*, by Clarence J. Glacken, University of California Press, Berkeley and Los Angeles, 1967, pp. 306-307.

[85] See https://www.getty.edu/art/exhibitions/bestiary/; See also, *The Grand Medieval Bestiary (Dragonet Edition): Animals in Illuminated Manuscripts*, by Christian Heck and Rémy Cordonnier, Abbeville Press, 2018.

[86] *Nature and Its Symbols*, by Lucia Impelluso, Translated by Stephen Sartarelli, The J. Paul Getty Museum, Los Angeles, CA, 2004, pp. 82-129,

[87] See "Ecuador First to Grant Nature Constitutional Rights," by Karen Charman, Capitalism Nature Socialism, Volume 19, 2008, Issue 4, Taylor & Francis Online, 28, November 2008, https://doi.org/10.1080/10455750802575828, https://www.tandfonline.com/doi/abs/10.1080/10455750802575828?journalCode=rcns20#:~:text=On%20September%2028%2C%202008%2C%20the,the%20world%20to%20do%20so.

[88] "World Database on Protected Areas," https://www.iucn.org/theme/protected-areas/our-work/world-database-protected-areas; See See "A Polygon and Point-Based Approach to Matching Geospatial Features," by Juan J. Ruiz-Lendínez, Manuel A. Ureña-Cámara and Francisco J. Ariza-López, December 5, 2017, *International Journal of Geo-Information*, https://pdfs.semanticscholar.org/67f9/2b05d2c02b1f6eab9813d2fbebdbb8899478.pdf, Accessed February 21, 2020; https://www.protectedplanet.net/c/world-database-on-protected-areas; https://www.protectedplanet.net. https://www.cbd.int/sp/targets/; https://sustainabledevelopment.un.org/?menu=1300; http://www.ipbes.net; See https://www.protectedplanet.net/c/united-nations-list-of-protected-areas/united-nations-list-of-protected-areas-2018; and https://www.protectedplanet.net/c/protected-planet-reports/report-2018, Accessed March 3, 2020; See *2018 United Nations List of Protected Areas – Supplement on protected area management effectiveness*, United Nations Environment Programme (Eric Solheim, Executive Director) and UNEP-WCMC

(Director Neville Ash), UNEP-World Conservation Monitoring Centre, Cambridge, UK 2018, in Collaboration with the CBD (Executive Secretary, Cristiana Pasca Palmer), the IUCN (Director General, Inger Andersen), the WCPA (World Commission On Protected Areas, Chaired by Kathy MacKinnon) and UN environment, Editors: Marine Deguignet, Heather C. Bingham, Neil D. Burgess and Naomi Kingston, https://wdpa.s3.amazonaws.com/UN_List_2018/2018%20List%20of%20Protected%20Areas_EN.pdf.
See https://www.un.org/depts/los/convention_agreements/texts/unclos/unclos_e.pdf. See https://pame.protectedplanet.net; ibid., https://wdpa.s3.amazonaws.com/UN_List_2018/2018%20List%20of%20Protected%20Areas_EN.pdf, p.8.

[89] See https://www.youtube.com/watch?v=AJP_jlw3brw; See also, "Heart of Ecuador's Yasuni, home to uncontacted tribes, opens for oil drilling," by Kimberley Brown, 5 July 2019, Mongabay Series: Global Forests, https://news.mongabay.com/2019/07/heart-of-ecuadors-yasuni-home-to-uncontacted-tribes-opens-for-oil-drilling/

[90] See "Policy Debate: Ecuador's Yasuní-ITT Initiative: What Can We Learn from its Failure?" by Pamela L. Martin and Imme Scholz, Policy Debates, International Development Policy, Geneva Graduate Institute, 5.2/2014, https://doi.org/10.4000/poldev.1705, OpenEdition Journals, https://journals.openedition.org/poldev/1705; See also, "Ecuador's Imperiled Paradise – One of the World's Most Important, If Least-Known Battles: A Conversation with Dr. Ivonne Baki," by Michael Charles Tobias, *Forbes*, Sep. 27, 2011, https://www.forbes.com/sites/michaeltobias/2011/09/27/ecuadors-imperilled-paradise-one-of-the-worlds-most-important-if-least-known-battles-a-conversation-with-dr-ivonne-baki/?sh=6c8473da5330; See also, "Ecuador's Vice President Lenín Moreno, 2012 Nobel Peace Prize Nominee, Reflects on Human Welfare and the Rights of Nature," by Michael Charles Tobias, Forbes, Oct. 5, 2012, https://www.forbes.com/sites/michaeltobias/2012/10/05/ecuadors-vice-president-lenin-moreno-2012-nobel-peace-prize-nominee-reflects-on-human-welfare-and-the-rights-of-nature/?sh=51a59fa6b85d

[91] See, for example, "Lawyer Who Battled Chevron Over Amazon Oil Spills Found Guilty of Contempt," by Gabriela Barzallo, nacla, August 31, 2021, https://nacla.org/news/2021/08/25/ecuador-chevron-donziger#:~:text=In%202011%2C%20an%20Ecuadorian%20judge,never%20complied%20with%20the%20ruling. See also, "Ecuador Lawsuit – The Facts About Chevron and Texaco in Ecuador," by Chevron, https://www.chevron.com/ecuador

[92] See Watson, James E.M.; Shanahan, Danielle F.; Di Marco, Moreno; Allan, James; Laurance, William F.; Sanderson, Eric W.; Mackey, Brendan; Venter, Oscar (November 2016). *"Catastrophic Declines in Wilderness Areas Undermine Global Environment Targets"*. Current Biology. **26** (21): 2929–2934. doi:10.1016/j.cub.2016.08.049. PMID 27618267. See also, "The Wilderness Act," https://wilderness.net/learn-about-wilderness/key-laws/wilderness-act/default.php; Allan, James R.; Kormos, Cyril; Jaeger, Tilman; Venter, Oscar; Bertzky, Bastian; Shi, Yichuan; Mackey, Brendan; van Merm, Remco; Osipova, Elena; Watson, James E.M. (February 2018). "Gaps and opportunities for the World Heritage Convention to contribute to global wilderness conservation". *Conservation Biology*. 32 (1): 116–126.

doi:10.1111/cobi.12976. PMID 28664996. S2CID 28944427. William. Cronon, *Uncommon ground : rethinking the human place in nature*. W.W. Norton & Co., New York, NY, 1996, OCLC 36306399. See also, Max Oelschlaeger, *The Idea of Wilderness. From Prehistory to the Age of Ecology*. New Haven & London, Yale University Press, New Haven, CT, 1991.

[93] See *A World with a View – An Inquiry into the Nature of Scenic Values*, by Christopher Tunnard, Yale University Press, New Haven, CT, 1978, pp. 12-13.

[94] See "The Tractarian Movement," by Herbert Schlossberg, The Victorian Web, n.d., https://victorianweb.org/religion/herb7.html

[95] See "The Sacramental Imagination," by G. B. Tennyson, in *Nature And The Victorian Imagination*, Edited by U. C. Knoepflmacher and G. B. Tennyson, University of California Press, Berkeley, Los Angeles and London, 1977, pp. 170-190.

[96] See "The Evolution of Darwin's Religious Faith," by Ted Davis, November 3, 2016, BioLogos, https://biologos.org/articles/the-evolution-of-darwins-religious-faith; See also, *Darwin's Origin of Species – A Biography*, by Janet Browne, Doublas & McIntyre, Vancouver/Toronto, Canada, 2006, Chapter 4, "Controversy," pp.84-117.

[97] ibid., cited by Janet Browne, p. 117.

[98] See "ArcGIS API for Python," "Advanced Cartography (Part 1)," https://developers.arcgis.com/python/guide/advanced-cartography-part1/; See also, "The future of maps: Cartography in the 21st century," by Marianna Cerini, CNN, June 27, 2018, https://www.cnn.com/style/article/cartography-in-the-21st-century/index.html

[99] "Data-Driven Spectrum Cartography via Deep Completion Autoencoders," by Yves Teganya and Daniel Romero, Technical Report, December 2, 2019, https://arxiv.org/pdf/1911.12810.pdf

[100] *Atlas of Remote Islands – Fifty Islands I have Never Set Foot On and Never Will,* Judith Schalansky, Translated from the German by Christine Lo, Penguin Books, New York, NY 2010, p. 21.

[101] See Sudipta Mitra, *Gir Forest and the saga of the Asiatic lion*. Indus Publishing, New Delhi, India, 2005, pp. 226–227. See also, "Asiatic lions in Gujarat's Gir forest dying of Canine Distemper Virus: ICMR". Press Trust of India. New Delhi: *The Hindustan Times*. 2018-10-05. Retrieved 2018-10-05. See also, Dionne Bunsha, 20 May 2007, "A kingdom too small". *Frontline*. 22 (10). Archived from the original on 12 February 2012.

[102] See the excellent overview of the crisis of the Gir Lion in Poulomi Banerjee's essay, "Pride is in numbers: We saved Gir's Asiatic lions, but is it enough?" *Hindustan Times*, June 8, 2015, https://www.hindustantimes.com/india/pride-is-in-numbers-we-saved-gir-s-asiatic-lions-but-is-it-enough/story-I14dNL1v2drhC5uwkenbMN.html

[103] See "Murder in the Sanctuary," n.a., June 7, 2015, https://www.downtoearth.org.in/indepth/murder-in-the-sanctuary-30995

[104] See "What's stopping the Asiatic lions of Gir from getting a new home?" by G. Seetharaman, *The Economic Times*, October 20, 2018, HTTPS://ECONOMICTIMES.INDIATIMES.COM/NEWS/POLITICS-AND-NATION/WHATS-STOPPING-THE-ASIATIC-LIONS-OF-GIR-FROM-GETTING-A-NEW-HOME/ARTICLESHOW/66296056.CMS?FROM=MDR

[105] op. cit., Poulomi Banerjee, *Hindustan Times*.

[106] See Tumendemberel, Odbayar; Tebbenkamp, Joel M.; Zedrosser, Andreas; Proctor, Michael F.; Blomberg, Erik J.; Morin, Dana J.; Rosell, Frank; Reynolds, Harry V.; Adams, Jennifer R.; Waits, Lisette P. (August 2021). "Long-term monitoring using DNA sampling reveals the dire demographic status of the critically endangered Gobi bear". *Ecosphere*. 12 (8). doi:10.1002/ecs2.3696. ISSN 2150-8925. See also, Chadwick, Douglas (April 2014). "Can World's Rarest Bear Be Saved?". *National Geographic*. Joe Riis (photography).

[107] See "Population Dwindling – Only about 20,000 wild lions remain in Africa, occupying less than 5% of their former range," panthera.org, https://panthera.org/cat/lion#:~:text=Only%20about%2020%2C000%20wild%20lions,5%25%20of%20their%20former%20range.

[108] See "Forecast of the total population of Africa from 2020 to 2050," statista, https://www.statista.com/statistics/1224205/forecast-of-the-total-population-of-africa/

[109] *Noah's Choice: The Future Of Endangered Species*, by Charles C. Mann and Mark L. Plummer, Alfred A. Knopf, New York, NY 1995.

[110] ibid., p. 240.

[111] See *Agency And Alienation – A Theory Of Human Presence*, by Jerome M. Segal, Rowman & Littlefield Publishers, Inc., Savage, Maryland, 1991, p. 112.

[112] See "How surprisingly brainy and amazingly agile squirrels thrive in the wild," by Erin Blakemore, November 10, 2018, *The Washington Post*, https://www.washingtonpost.com/national/health-science/how-surprisingly-brainy-and-amazingly-agile-squirrels-thrive-in-the-wild/2018/11/09/44368de4-e1fb-11e8-b759-3d88a5ce9e19_story.html

[113] See "Lexical facts," by R.L.G., *The Economist*, May 29th 2013, https://www.economist.com/johnson/2013/05/29/lexical-facts

[114] "How Many Words Does the Average Person Know?" by Nickee De Leon Huld, wordcounter, © 2016-2022, https://wordcounter.io/blog/how-many-words-does-the-average-person-know/#:~:text=According%20to%20lexicographer%20and%20dictionary,vocabulary%20is%20around%2040%2C000%20words.%E2%80%9D

[115] See Tilson, R.; Defu, H.; Muntifering, J.; Nyhus, P. J. (2004). "Dramatic decline of wild South China tigers *Panthera tigris amoyensis*: field survey of priority tiger reserves" (PDF). *Oryx*. 38 (1): 40–47. doi:10.1017/S0030605304000079. See also, "China's Three-Fold Environmental Degradation," by Fengshi Wu and Richard L. Edmonds, early draft for the Chapter "Environmental Degradation," in *Critical Issues in Contemporary China*, 2nd edition, edited by Czeslaw Tubilewicz, Routledge, London, UK, 2017. https://www.academia.edu/29884644/Chinas_Three_Fold_Environmental_Degradation?email_work_card=view-paper

[116] See the *Metaphysics of Protection*, by M. C. Tobias and J. G. Morrison, Waterside Productions, Cardiff by the Sea, CA, 2014, https://www.textbooks.com/Metaphysics-of-Protection-14-Edition/9781939116987/Michael-Charles-Tobias-and-Jane-Gray-Morrison.php?kpid=9781939116987U

[117] "6 Last Living Speakers of Dying Languages," by Nadia Jones, Omniglot, n.d., https://omniglot.com/language/articles/lastspeakers.htm#:~:text=Doris%20Jean%20

Lamar%20McLemore&text=Language%3A%20Wichita-,Ms.,language's%20only%20remaining%20fluent%20speaker.

[118] See "Workshop on the Philosophy of Activism," Sep. 7-22, 2020, Australian Catholic University, https://philevents.org/event/show/82566; See also, https://www.philosophyofactivism.com/

[119] See "Activism and offense: a philosophical analysis," by Stef McGraw, University of Northern Iowa Honors Program Theses, 2014, https://scholarworks.uni.edu/cgi/viewcontent.cgi?article=1130&context=hpt

[120] "Scientists Figure Out Why Female Octopuses Self-Destruct After Laying Eggs," by Margaret Osborne, *Smithsonian Magazine*, May 16, 2022, https://www.smithsonianmag.com/smart-news/scientists-figure-out-why-female-octopuses-self-destruct-after-laying-eggs-180980088/

[121] See *The Political Turn in Analytic Philosophy*, Edited by David Bordonaba-Plou, Víctor Fernández-Castro, and José R.Torices, De Gruyter, Berlin, Germany, 2022, https://doi.org/10.1515/9783110612318-toc

[122] See, for example, "Activism, Philosophy and Actuality in Deleuze and Foucault," by Paul Patton, Deleuze Studies, December 2010, vo. 4, No. supplement: pp.84-103, *Edinburgh University Press Journals*, https://www.euppublishing.com/doi/abs/10.3366/dls.2010.0207

[123] See *The Limits of Morality*, by Shelly Kagan, Oxford Scholarship Online, November 2003, First published in 1991 by the Oxford Ethics Series, doi: 10.1093/0198239165.001.0001, https://oxford.universitypressscholarship.com/view/10.1093/0198239165.001.0001/acprof-9780198239161-miscMatter-1

[124] See Richard Paul Jodrell, *Illustrations of Euripides*, Three Volumes, Printed by J. Nichols, London, UK, 1781-1789. See also, *Hope in Ancient Literature, History, and Art*, Edited by George Kazantzidis and Dimos Spatharas, Volume 63 in the series, *Trends in Classics* – Supplementary Volumes, including the chapter, "Hope and Hopelessness in Euripides," by Nick Fisher, and "'A Historian Utterly Without Hope': Literary Artistry and Narratives of Decline in Tacitus' Historiae I," by Sophia Papaioannou, https://doi.org/10.1515/9783110598254, DeGruyter, Berlin, Germany 2018, https://www.degruyter.com/document/doi/10.1515/9783110598254/html; See also Harris, John P. "The Swan's Red-Dipped Foot: Euripides, 'ION' 161—9." *The Classical Quarterly*, vol. 62, no. 2, 2012, pp. 510–22, http://www.jstor.org/stable/23470119. Accessed 17 May 2022.

[125] *The Ruins: or A Survey of the Revolutions Of Empires*, by M. Volny, J. Johnson, London UK, 1792, p. 326.

[126] See *Familiar Quotations*, by John Bartlett, 14th edition, Revised And Enlarged, Emily Morison Beck, Editor, Little, Brown and Company, Boston, MA, 1968, pp. 1399-1400.

[127] Source: https://quotepark.com/quotes/1080246-friedrich-nietzsche-in-reality-hope-is-the-worst-of-all-evils-becaus/

[128] *Nietzsche – A Philosophical Biography*, by Rüdiger Safranski. Translated by Shelley Frisch, W. W. Norton & Co., New York, 2002, p. 184.

[129] See "Hoping for Hopeless Hope," by Frank Seeburger, *Trauma And Philosophy*, February 14, 2022, https://www.traumaandphilosophy.com/blog-1/2022/2/14/hoping-for-hopeless-hope?format=amp

[130] See *World War III: Population and the Biosphere at the End of the Millennium*, by M. C. Tobias, 1st edition, Bear & Co., Santa Fe, NM, 1994, p.437.

[131] See *Life Force: The World of Jainism*, by M. C. Tobias, Asian Humanities Press, Freemont, CA 1991. See also the film version, "Ahimsa-NonViolence," one hour documentary Written and Directed by Michael Charles Tobias, KRMA/PBS, Denver, CO 1987. In addition, see the novel, *A Naked Man*, by Michael Charles Tobias, Jain Press, Freemont, CA, 1994.

[132] *Tattvartha Sutra, That Which Is*, Translated with an introduction by Nathmal Tatia, With a Foreword by L. M. Singhvi and an introduction to the Jaina faith by Padmanabh S. Jaini, The Institute of Jainology, Harper Collins Publishers, San Francisco, CA 1994.

[133] See *The Akaranga Sutra*, Book 1, Lecture 1, Lesson 3, in Jaina Sutras, Translated by Hermann Jacobi, Motilal Banarsidass, New Delhi, India, 1980 (first published by Oxford University Press, Oxford, UK, 1884), pp.4-5.

[134] See *The Heretic's Feast – A History of Vegetarianism*, Fourth Estate, London, UK, 1993. See also *Nonviolence to Animals, Earth and Self in Asian Traditions*, by Christopher Key Chapple, State University of New York Press, Albany, NY, 1993, pp. 113-114; See also, Ashley Montagu, edited, *Learning Non-Aggression – The Experience of Non-Literate Societies*, Oxford University Press, Oxford UK, 1978. And finally, see Chapter 4, "Ahimsa," pp.96-118, in *A Vision of Nature – Traces of the Original World*, by Michael Tobias, Kent State University Press, Kent, Ohio, 1995. In addition, see also, "Complete Guide," healthline, https://www.healthline.com/nutrition/seventh-day-adventist-diet#:~:text=The%20Seventh%2Dday%20Adventist%20diet,deems %20to%20be%20%E2%80%9Cunclean.%E2%80%9D, and, "Why Seventh-day Adventists are so often vegan or vegetarian," by Tamas Lestar, The Conversation, May 24, 2022. https://theconversation.com/why-seventh-day-adventists-are-so-often-vegan-or-vegetarian-177298

[135] op. cit., *Life Force*.

[136] See "A Safe Home for Cows," Govinda Goshala Cow Haven, https://www.safehomeforcows.org/; See also, "300 cattle head for goshala everyday," *The Times of India*, Wayback Machine, http://articles.timesofindia.indiatimes.com/2001-08-17/bangalore/27235240_1_goshala-cattle-fodder

[137] See *The Toda Landscape – Explorations In Cultural Ecology*, by Tarun Chhabra, Harvard University Press, Orient BlackSwan, 2015.

[138] See, for example, "Beto O'Rourke confronts Texas Gov. Greg Abbott at Uvalde press conference; 'This is on you,'" *The Texas Tribune*, by Patrick Svitek, May 25, 2022, https://www.texastribune.org/2022/05/25/beto-orourke-greg-abbott-uvalde-shooting/

[139] See "A scientist's inconvenient truths about decarbonizing the economy," by Charles Lane, *The Washington Post*, Opinion, a review of Vaclav Smil's book, *How the World Really Works* (Penguin, New York, 2022), https://www.washingtonpost.com/opinions/2022/05/25/inconvenient-truths-about-decarbonizing-economy/

[140] See "Kierkegaard On the Metaphysics of Hope," by Roe Fremstedal, *The Heythyrop Journal*, LIII (2012), pp. 51-60, https://www.sfu.ca/~poitras/hj_kierkegaard-hope_12.pdf

[141] See "Thought is the courage of hopelessness: an interview with philosopher Giorgio Agamben," by Juliette Cerf, Verso, https://www.versobooks.com/blogs/1612-thought-is-the-courage-of-hopelessness-an-interview-with-philosopher-giorgio-agamben

[142] ibid. See also, "Homo Sacer y violencia divina en el caso judío: Lo insacrificable sometido a castigo," by Ely Orrego Torres, *Revista Pléyade* 2 (2008): 22-32, https://www.academia.edu/517231/Homo_Sacer_y_violencia_divina_en_el_caso_judio_Lo_insacrificable_sometido_a_castigo

[143] See "Learned Helpless: Seligman's Theory of Depression (+ Cure)," by Courtney Ackerman, March 24, 2018, PositivePsychology.com, https://positivepsychology.com/learned-helplessness-seligman-theory-depression-cure/#seligman-learned-helplessness; See also, "The History and Development of the Hoplessness Depression Theory," by W. Harrison Combs, Student Publications, Spring 2021, The Cupola Scholarship at Gettysburg College, https://cupola.gettysburg.edu/cgi/viewcontent.cgi?article=2004&context=student_scholarship

[144] See https://www.youtube.com/watch?v=9FBxfd7DL3E

[145] See "Discussion: Hypothetico-Deductivism is Hopeless, by Clark Glymour, *Philosophy of Science*, Volume 47 Issue 2, April 1, 2022, https://www.cambridge.org/core/journals/philosophy-of-science/article/abs/discussion-hypotheticodeductivism-is-hopeless/E7882F0BF7676CE76F6614136537D9DF; See also, Robert May, *Logical form: its structure and derivation*. MIT Press, Cambridge, Mass, 1993.

[146] See "World Prison Population List/11th Edition," https://nicic.gov/world-prison-population-listeleventh-edition#:~:text=1).,100%2C000%20of%20its%20total%20population. See also, "Hope and Hopelessness in an Age of Mass Incarceration," by Professor Lori Gruen, a philosophy course at Duke University, https://carceralstudies.duke.edu/2021/10/22/hope-and-hopelessness-in-an-age-of-mass-incarceration/

[147] See "Melancholic Redemption and the Hopelessness of Hope," by Elliot R. Wolfson, *The Journal of Jewish Thought and Philosophy*, 31 Mar 2022, Brill Publishers, https://brill.com/view/journals/jjtp/30/1/article-p130_8.xml

[148] See "An Antidote to Helplessness and Disorientation: The Great Humanistic Philosopher and Psychologist Erich Fromm on Our Human Fragility as the Key to Our Survival and Our Sanity," by Maria Popova, *the marginalian*, https://www.themarginalian.org/2020/03/22/erich-fromm-revolution-of-hope/

[149] See "The Philosopher of Failure: Emil Cioran's Heights of Despair," by Costica Bradatan, Los Angeles Review of Books, November 28, 2016, https://lareviewofbooks.org/article/philosopher-failure-emil-ciorans-heights-despair/; See also, "Hopeless Philosophy," by Marcel Rus, January 20, 2019, quoting from Cioran's *précis de décomposition*, Éditions Gallimard, Paris, France, 1949, https://echinox25.wordpress.com/2019/01/21/hopeless-philosophy/

[150] *Moriori – The Morioris of the South Island*, by Herries Beattie, Facsimile Edition With Preface and Index, Cadsonbury Publications, Christchurch, New Zealand 1993, p. 5.

[151] See *On The Edge Of The Primeval Forest – The Experiences and Observations of a Doctor in Equatorial Africa,* by Albert Schweitzer, Adam And Charles Black, London, UK, 1954, p. 125.

[152] See "Normative Ethics," Edited by Jussi Suikkhanen, Ass.Ed., Yiying Peng, Search PhilPapers, https://philpapers.org/browse/normative-ethics

[153] See "Hope and hopelessness: theory and reality," by Thaïs Helène Downman, 2008 Aug;101(8):428-30. doi: 10.1258/jrsm.2008.080193, PMID: 18687867, PMCID: PMC2500241, https://www.ncbi.nlm.nih.gov/pmc/articles/PMC2500241/; See also, Ahmed Al-Awamer, Physician-assisted suicide is not a failure of palliative care]. Al-Awamer A. Can Fam Physician. 2015 Dec;61(12):1045-7, https://pubmed.ncbi.nlm.nih.gov/26668278/

[154] See "7 Factory Farming Practices Straight out of a Horror Film," Mercy For Animals, https://mercyforanimals.org/blog/7-factory-farming-practices-straight-out/; See also, "We Will Look Back on This Age of Cruelty to Animals in Horror," by Ezra Klein, *The New York Times*, December 16, 2021, https://www.nytimes.com/2021/12/16/opinion/factory-farming-animals.html; See also *Man's Search for Meaning*, by Viktor Frankl (*Ein Psychologe erlebt das Konzentrationslager*), published by Verlag für Jugend und Volk and Beacon Press, 1946/1947. See also, Noble, Holcomb B. (September 4, 1997). "Dr. Viktor E. Frankl of Vienna, Psychiatrist of the Search for Meaning, Dies at 92". *The New York Times*. p. B-7.

[155] See Anthony Hecht, *On the Laws of the Poetic Art,* The A.W.Mellon Lectures In The Fine Arts, The National Gallery of Art, Washington D.C., Bollingen Series XXXV: 41, Princeton University Press, Princeton, NJ, 1993, p. 172. See also, "The Poetry of Grief: Beyond Scientific Portrayal," by Margaret Stroebe, *Journal of Death and Dying*, August 8, 2018, PubMed, SAGE Perspectives, https://doi.org/10.1177/0030222818792706, https://journals.sagepub.com/doi/full/10.1177/0030222818792706

[156] See also Hobbes' *De Cive* (1647), *De Corpore* (1655) and *Behemoth* (1681). For *Leviathan* we are utilizing the London Folio Society edition of 2012, Edited by J. C. A. Gaskin © 1996, Introduced by Alan Ryan, Illustrated by Mike Wilks, London, UK, 2012. This edition, in turn, follows "with minor emendations" the 1996 Oxford University Press World's Classic edition, also edited by J. C. A. Gaskin.

[157] See *The Constitution of Bhutan – Principles and Philosophies*, by Lyonpo Sonam Tobgye, July 18th, 2008, Thimphu, Bhutan, ISBN: 978-99936-658-7-8; See also, *The Constitution of The Kingdom of Bhutan, Draft of Tsa Thrim Chhenmo as on 1st February 2007*, Thimphu, Bhutan; See also, *The Judiciary of The Kingdom of Bhutan*, Royal Court of Justice, Thimphu, Bhutan, ISBN: 99936-658-4-3; and *Buddhist Jurisprudence And Pre-Constitutional Principles*, by Sonam Tobgye and Jeffrey Avina, Kuensel Corporation Limited, Thimphu, Bhutan, 2021.

[158] See "312,817 voters on final electoral roll," 1 December 2007, Kuensel Online, https://web.archive.org/web/20120722070043/http://www.kuenselonline.com/modules.php?name=News&file=article&sid=9480

[159] *National Forest Policy of 1974*: See *Bionomics in the Dragon Kingdom – Ecology, Economics and Ethics in Bhutan*, by Ugyen Tshewang, Jane Gray Morrison and Michael Charles Tobias, Springer Sciences, New York, NY 2018, p. 150.

[160] "Demographics," Britannica, https://www.britannica.com/topic/history-of-Europe/Demographics

[161] ibid., Alan Ryan Introduction, p. xiii

[162] *Leviathan*, 1., lll, 9., p. 23.

[163] ibid., 1, v, 7., p. 35.

[164] ibid., pp. 61 a,b (charts)

[165] ibid., 1, x111, 5., p. 91.

[166] ibid. "So that in the nature of man, we find three principal causes of quarrel. First competition; secondly, diffidence; thirdly, glory."

[167] ibid., 1, xiv, 22., p. 100.

[168] ibid., 1, xv, 3., p.105.

[169] ibid., Chapter XVII, 1., p. 123.

[170] ibid., 2, xx, p. 151.

[171] ibid., 2, xxvi, 23., p. 199.

[172] ibid., 2, xxviii, 27., p. 230.

[173] ibid., p. 233.

[174] ibid., 2, xxix, 14., p. 235.

[175] ibid., 2, xxx, 11., p. 245.

[176] See Kavka, Gregory S. "Hobbes's War of All Against All." *Ethics*, vol. 93, no. 2, 1983, pp. 291–310. *JSTOR*, http://www.jstor.org/stable/2380421. Accessed 28 May 2022.

[177] ibid., 1, x111, 9., p. 92. See also "Is life in the state of nature solitary, poor, nasty, brutish, and short?" by Theoria Beograd, ResearchGate, 56(3):41-78, by Igor Zivanovic, doi:10.2298/THEO1303041Z, https://www.researchgate.net/publication/274269001_Is_life_in_the_state_of_nature_solitary_poor_nasty_brutish_and_short

[178] See, for example, Williamson, Colwyn. "A Contradiction in Hobbes' Analysis of Sovereignty." *The Canadian Journal of Economics and Political Science/Revue Canadienne d'Economique et de Science Politique*, vol. 32, no. 2, 1966, pp. 202–19. *JSTOR*, https://doi.org/10.2307/139797. Accessed 29 May 2022. See also, "A Contradiction in Hobbes' Analysis of Sovereignty," Published online by Cambridge University Press: 07 November 2014, Colwyn Williamson, https://www.cambridge.org/core/journals/canadian-journal-of-economics-and-political-science-revue-canadienne-de-economiques-et-science-politique/article/abs/contradiction-in-hobbes-analysis-of-sovereignty/ADF496C613F22F712D20282AB761FECD; See also, Illinois Political Science Review, Spring Volume 12 2008, Edited by Teri J. Bengtson and David M. Dolence, https://www.eiu.edu/ipsa/docs/IPSR_Spring_2008.pdf; See also, "Thomas Hobbes's substantially constrained absolutism: the fundamental law of the commonwealth as a substantial constraint on the sovereign's power," Facundo Rodriguez, in *Jurisprudence – An International Journal of Legal and Political Thought*, Volume 12, 2021, Issue 4, Taylor & Francis Online, Pages 447-465 | Published online: 21 Apr 2021, Download citation, https://doi.org/10.1080/20403313.2021.1912901, https://www.tandfonline.com/doi/full/10.1080/20403313.2021.1912901

[179] See also "Hobbes's Moral and Political Philosophy," April 30, 2018, by Sharon A. Lloyd and Susanne Sreedhar, © 2018, *Stanford Encyclopedia of Philosophy*,

https://plato.stanford.edu/entries/hobbes-moral/#:~:text=Hobbes%20argues%20that%20the%20state,to%20escape%20this%20miserable%20condition.

180 See also, P. Zagorin, P., *Hobbes and the Law of Nature*, Princeton University Press, Princeton. NJ, 2009. See also S. A. Lloyd, *Morality in the Philosophy of Thomas Hobbes: Cases in the Law of Nature*, Cambridge University Press, Cambridge, UK 2009.

181 See Ohlmeyer, Jane H.. "English Civil Wars". *Encyclopedia Britannica*, 30 Nov. 2021, https://www.britannica.com/event/English-Civil-Wars. Accessed 28 May 2022, https://www.britannica.com/event/English-Civil-Wars

182 See *Le Chamanisme Et Les Techniques Archaîques De L'Extase*, by Mircea Eliade, Librarie Payot, Paris, France, 1951 (*Shamanism: Archaic Techniques of Ecstasy*, Pantheon Books, New York, NY, 1964; See also, Rosemary Radford Ruether, *Goddesses and the Divine Feminine: A Western Religious History*. University of California Press, Berkeley, CA 2006. See also, "Death, Angel of," by Kaufmann Kohler and Ludwig Blau, Jewish Encyclopedia, https://jewishencyclopedia.com/articles/5018-death-angel-of, and After Life and Funeral Customs, Zoroastrian Heritage, by K. E. Eduljee, http://heritageinstitute.com/zoroastrianism/death/index.htm, and "UK says EU trade talks face 'moment of finality' on weekend," Independent via AP news wire, December 20, 2020, https://www.independent.co.uk/news/world/americas/us-politics/uk-says-eu-trade-talks-face-moment-of-finality-on-weekend-uk-eu-trade-deal-foreign-minister-ap-b1769178.html

183 See "Democratization from above: The case of Bhutan," by Klaus Hofmann, Democracy International, Revised by Ronald Pabst and Stefan Wolf, V i.1 – 4/1/2006, WaybackMachine, http://www.democracy-international.org/fileadmin/di/pdf/papers/di-bhutan.pdf, https://web.archive.org/web/20110610012322/http://www.democracy-international.org/fileadmin/di/pdf/papers/di-bhutan.pdf

184 See "Elevation," by Emily Newburger, July 1, 2007, *Harvard Law Today*, https://today.law.harvard.edu/feature/elevation/

185 See, for example, "You Are Living in the Golden Age of Stupidity," by Lance Morrow, *The Wall Street Journal*, April 29, 2021, https://www.wsj.com/articles/idiocy-stupidity-afghanistan-covid-vaccine-maga-trump-civility-privacy-common-sense-11630271666

186 See "Article 5 – Environment," *The Constitution of the Kingdom of Bhutan*, Draft of Tsa Thrim Chhenmo as on 1st February 2007, pp.8-9. See also Tshewang, Tobias and Morrison, *Bionomics*, p. 136.

187 See *The Constitution of Bhutan – Principles and Philosophies*, by Lyonpo Sonam Tobgye, July 18th, 2008, Thimphu, Bhutan, p. 123, ISBN: 978-99936-658-7-8

188 ibid., p. 124.

189 ibid., p. 145, citing an interview in Kuensel, Thimphu, Bhutan, November 21, 2006.

190 See Walther Heissig, *The Religions of Mongolia*, University of California Press, Berkeley and Los Angeles, 1980, p. 69. See also, "Mahasammata," https://www.palikanon.com/english/pali_names/maha/mahasammata.htm

191 op. cit., Tobgye and Avina, 2021, pp.9-10.

192 ibid., p. 10.

[193] ibid., pp. 161-162. Buddha's credo cited from D.N.Bhagvat, *Early Buddhist Jurisprudence, Theravada Vinaya Laws*, Cosmos Publications for Genesis Publishing Private Ltd., New Delhi, India, 2013.

[194] See "Natural Law and the American Constitution," by Charles S. Desmond, Fordham Law Review, Volume XXII, December, 1953, Number 3, https://ir.lawnet.fordham.edu/cgi/viewcontent.cgi?article=1424&context=flr; See also, Robert S. Barker, "Natural Law And The United States Constitution," *The Review of Metaphysics*, vol. 66, no. 1, 2012, pp. 105–30. *JSTOR*, http://www.jstor.org/stable/41635554. Accessed 29 May 2022.

[195] See "Declaration of Independence: A Transcription," of the Congressional text of July 4, 1776, America's Founding Documents, https://www.archives.gov/founding-docs/declaration-transcript

[196] See *The Dragon Country: The General History of Bhutan*, by Nirmala Das, Orient Longman, Hyderabad, India, 1974. See also, *Bhotan And The Story Of The Dooar War*, by Surgeon Rennie, John Murray, London, UK, 1866; and *Views of Medieval Bhutan – The Diary and Drawings of Samuel Davis, 1783*, by Michael Aris, Serindia Publications, London, and Smithsonian Institution Press, Washington, D.C., 1982.

[197] See "George Gabriel Stokes 1819-1903: An Irish Mathematical Physicist," https://web.archive.org/web/20060208033233/http://www.cmde.dcu.ie/Stokes/GGStokes.html

[198] See Stokes, G. G. (1851). *"On the effect of internal friction of fluids on the motion of pendulums"*. Transactions of the Cambridge Philosophical Society. 9, part ii: 8–106. Bibcode:1851TCaPS...9....8S. The formula for terminal velocity (V) appears on p. [52], equation (127).

[199] Hadley, Peter. "Why don't clouds fall?". Institute of Solid State Physics, TU Graz. http://lamp.tu-graz.ac.at/~hadley/whydontcloudsfall.html

[200] See "Numerical model for the fall speed of raindrops in a rainfall simulator," by J. van Boxel, UvA-Dare (Digiral Academic Repository), University of Amsterdam, 1998, *I.C.E. Special Report*, 1998/1, 77-85, https://pure.uva.nl/ws/files/2778495/171269_VanBoxel_1998_GENT_ModelFallSpeedRaindrops.pdf

[201] See Sir Isaac Newton's *Philosophiae Naturalis Principia Mathematica* (1687). See Philosophiae naturalis principia mathematica. Auctore Isaaco Newtono, equite aurato. Editioultima, Isaac Newton, Published by sumptibus Societatis, Amstaelodami, 1714. And, Selections from Newton's *Principia*, Green Lion Press, Santa Fe, NM, 2004.

[202] See *Bhutan: Conservation and Environmental Protection in the Himalayas*, by Ugyen Tshewang, Michael Charles Tobias, and Jane Gray Morrison, Springer Nature, New York, NY, 2021; See also, *Bionomics in the Dragon Kingdom: Ecology, Economics and Ethics in Bhutan*, by Ugyen Tshewang, Michael Charles Tobias, and Jane Gray Morrison, Springer Nature, New York, NY, 2018.

Chapter 8

Credendum

Compound Expressive Potentials

The *quantum biosemiosphere* represents what the Authors have elsewhere described as the "compound expressive potential" ("CEP") of any incipient, passive or active relationship amongst individuals, taxons, and every other configurative exchange of Beingness, regardless of the taxonomic designations, constraints and liberations posed by every concerned discipline. That includes molecular biology, ecosystem dynamics, and conservation biology; but also, sub-atomic physics and quantum mechanics. The orientation of quanta is herewith explored briefly as a paradigm shift in better understanding the signaling and receiving of biological information that is likely to prove crucial, at most scales, for near-term human survival.

CEP[1] pertains both to surfaces, as in every mathematical dimension (e.g., the rhombitrihexagonal), as well as to the evolution of structure in all aspects of genetics.[2] But CEP abridges one fundamental notion inherent to scientific modeling, namely, the ability to test or replicate any proof. This conditional has been reiterated for centuries.[3] As Ethan Siegel has written, "it wouldn't be possible to measure every state of every particle under every condition all the time."[4] We might aspire to do so in order, for example, to finalize the number of digits for an irrational number like pi.[5] As of August 2021, that number was 62.8 trillion.[6] Or to try and fathom the actual relevance to survival of measuring brain mass encephalization quotients in worms, humans and whales.[7] But given the presumed absence of a spinal cord within the invertebrate world, there are significant allometric, and central nervous system gaps in any theory that might presume to work out a relevant correlation in the effort to define, or even condone the importance of so called *intelligence* across the entire spectrum of life-forms.[8]

If CEP is immune to measurement or proof, we ask, what is its use? For that matter, why recognize as scientifically relevant the characters, say, of Lassie, Bambi, or the Prophet Isaiah (11:6) promulgating the vision such that "the wolf will live with the lamb, the leopard will lie down with the goat, the calf and the lion and the yearling together; and a little child will lead them."[9]

The computational power of this yields feelings rather than algorithms. We enjoy the riddle of paradise teased in so many artistic endeavors throughout time.[10] CEP is a riddle within a paradigm that can be translated differently, not indifferently, as a politic, an economics, a modality of Being that is nothing more than companionship. And leave it synesthesially at that.[11] As we have written, "No social system has ever resolved the differences posed by all its individuals."[12]

With this breakdown of certainty in the sciences, as conferred by so much inexplicability defining both the core and margins of interspecies relations, we are focusing our research on content meaningfulness, not meaning. The distinctions are enormous. Defining "effective scalar ethics" is crucial to the biosemiotics impulse: What do we (as individuals and as a species) hope to engender socially, locally, globally? At a time when genocide is being conducted in Ukraine, and the human ecological inflictions throughout the world have cumulatively, geologically defined the epoch of the Anthropocene[13] with a resulting 6th mass biological extinction, our models for approaching biodiversity, and the philosophical/ethical thrusts which derive from, and most certainly challenge such models – must fundamentally change. We simply cannot solve problems alone (as one species). This presents a monumental challenge to the survival of life on earth. If we cannot work together as a species, what other taxonomic grouping *would* promote collaboration? And to what end?

Logistica Biosemiotica

Modern biosemiotics logistics, powered principally by Estonian philosopher Yuri Lotman (1922-1993), Baltic German philosopher Jakob Johann von Uexküll (1864-1944) and Hungarian American semiotician Thomas Sebeok (1920-2001) have provided psycholinguistic foundations for registering the *other minds problem*[14] within the realm of holosemiotics[15]. For over a decade we have known that the symbiotic metagenome comprising some "1000 major bacteria groups in our gut microbiome"[16] is "about 150 times larger than that of the human eukaryotic genome."[17] But this is, as it turns out, rather irrelevant. The number of genes in an organism may have "nothing to do with the organism's complexity."[18] Such multidimensionality within every individual that is a population that is, itself, an individual, presents to mind a tautological heurism that is ontologically anthropic in its oddly out-advantaged biases.[19] Add to that fickle system of inbred prejudice the notion of what is biologically of necessity, with what has for several thousand years been deemed scientific. Philosophy is loath to grant such bias, but has never found a way to elegantly quash the problem. They are at their best when they disagree, these two disciplines. The resulting confusion is often thought of as some global complex of consciousness, with a verdict that declares: that's just the way it is.

This strikes at the heart of the biology of quantum entanglement in the human mind[20]; the condition going back to the origins of life that require all holobionts to work together.[21] Is it possible that primordial methods of life sustaining teamwork will not work in the 21st century? That is hardly a rational supposition, or tenable perspective, but only to the point of it not requiring human thought to require it. The important message here is that coral reefs, neotropical rainforests, prairies, mangroves, and the entire panoply of relational consortia of pollinators would be extraordinarily content to ignore *H. sapiens*; not to mention the phylogenetic circumstances over time that have made for the emergence of the vertebrate subphylum nearly 600 million years ago.[22]

By around 350,000 years ago, our kind began to whisper. By now, the embarrassment of our species is all but impossible to ignore. For some of the more precocious microbes, particularly viruses, we obviously represent a bonanza with whom to engage in fine sport.

Of course, our principal difficulty has been our collective consciousness, with its most pernicious ecological hand- and footprints. Our second challenge concerns any reason left to communicate what has already gone far past the probability for any redemption or re-engineering of what we have done as a species to the earth. We know this from sufficient bulwarks of data that are unambiguous in their extinction-level event dissections. We thought that, perhaps, good storytelling and the human repertoire of sociolinguistics might fathom some miracle cure for the vast majority of those within the human community who refuse to be tethered to kindness. But multilingualism has not done more than enrich the familiar chatter,[23] or drawn attention to Foreign Accent Syndrome within a variety of native and extra-spatial language acquisition or loss situations.[24]

A veritable renaissance of research into "extralinguistic cognition"[25] has demonstrated fascinating features of hominin language capacity at levels, recently discerned, of neuroarchitecture in various parts of the brain, responsible to various degrees for "attentional orienting," "word-level resolution," as well as the ability to "capture signal changes" and grasp "demonstratives."[26] We will continue to identify the endless minutiae of our kind, but thousands of years of this incessant philosophical bent has not ethically rebalanced a statistically ascertainable number of individuals within the greater community. We can generalize upon such standards of behavior, as if there might be actual courtesies in an ideal biological world, from the brute force that is the continued penchant, and escalating tools, for consequential human violence. Conceptually, we have not altered the course of bloodshed. We might escape temporarily, as individuals, "the cloud imposed by symbols,"[27] as C.D. Scott referred to it, or convince ourselves (again and again) that we are apex linguists with corresponding behavioral wisdom, given the "multiple-network view" that has been advanced in attempting to understand all that which is happening "beyond the information…that enter primary sensory cortices."[28]

Small language communities, like that of the Brazilian Kaixana, with all of one known remaining speaker, or Ongota in southern Ethiopia, with eight known adherents,[29] offer pressing opportunities to determine whether there are any words, designations, representations, or other salutary qualities and nuances of the engaged and biosemiospherically entangled human-language dynamic that could change our problem as a species. New York's Central Park, as earlier referenced, provides another kind of horizon to be tested, bioextraterritoriality within the accessible synanthroposphere. Divining something –"language-contact phenomena"[30] – or other conceptually derived nuances tied to linguistics, the rest of us had missed.

But, more soberly, the imagined contagion of softening permutations – anodynes – come down to the same vested hopes in communities that might gather their last-ditch efforts to go beyond conventional modalities of merely the early stages of restoration ecology.[31] These endo-, exo-, and homophoric ranges of individual or collective expressions derive from the accumulated antecedents that are human history. They give loft to what we would call "idiosympatric" compulsions between speakers and listeners; between readers, viewers and all other relational minds within the experience of a human community. Linguistic anaphorae and deictic centrality refer to this dependence on context, as has been notably studied amongst Inuktitut Eskimo groups.[32] In essence, the basic discovery for new contexts of understanding that do not repeat the miseries of our history and the perpetual assault on all Others that we perpetuate to this very moment.

As with all ecological crisis studies, so too, psycholinguistics – in apprehending the variety of anaphora as such contextualization impacts our world views in a repetition as concretized as language itself – gives us to recognize an all but fatal pattern locked away in our species' behavior, or the empiric perfect aspect. It is a habituality that locks in the generic antecedents of experience. And while they differ from hamlet, to community to city, they represent an ineluctable repetition, as one finds, for example, in data processing variables, such as the ANSI Common Lisp LOOP facility, with its test features, defaults, and myriad strange codes for understanding the mechanics of language in information technologies.[33] Philosophers of language have emphasized a continuous narrowing/expansion that is the paradox of subjectivity in the metalanguage universe of human iterations and biocultural dispersion throughout history.[34/35] Philosopher David Kaplan (b.1933) has greatly expanded the theory of contexts and the logic of indexicality, exploring referentials in a way that offers propositional validity to the very core of so-called "truth-value" and "possible-worlds semantics".[36]

Philosophy Has Always Pondered The Imponderable: What Is Possible?

These aforecited difficulties of research challenge metrics of all kind and scale to succeed in making relevant the comparisons between differing life forms for the purpose not of human utility, dismissal, or ethic. In essence, our assertiveness constitutes a biospheric "paradox" we have not yet come close to qualifying.[37] Even the quantitative modeling of extinctions falls far short of our being able to even *approach* alleged understanding of how extinction risks exert the full range of behavioral alterations on ecosystem dynamics.[38] We know there is an ecological ineluctability i.e., a biological system of feedback, that promises of reciprocity.[39] That is as far as any philosophical disposition has ever reached. But, beyond that, wrote David Hume, "Tis an establish'd maxim in metaphysics, That whatever the mind clearly conceives includes the idea of possible existence, or in other words, that nothing we imagine is absolutely impossible. We can form the idea of a golden mountain, and from thence conclude that such a mountain may actually exist."[40]

"Ecosystem Dynamics, Yosemite Falls, California," Photo © M. C. Tobias.

Endnotes

[1] *The Quantum Biosemiosphere*, by Michael Charles Tobias and Jane Gray Morrison, Foreword by Con Slobodchikoff, Prologue by Alexander N. Chumakov, Nova Sciences Publishers, New York, NY, 2022, p.10.

[2] See "The Mathematics of Phylogenomics," by Lior Pachter and Bernd Sturmfels, February 1, 2008, https://arxiv.org/pdf/math/0409132.pdf

[3] "Scientific Proof Is A Myth," by Ethan Siegel, Senior Contributor, *Forbes*, November 22, 2017, https://www.forbes.com/sites/startswithabang/2017/11/22/scientific-proof-is-a-myth/?sh=5d2413cf2fb1

[4] ibid., Siegel.

[5] "Euler's formula: e^(i pi) = -1," by Alex Lopez-Ortiz, February 20, 1998, https://cs.uwaterloo.ca/~alopez-o/math-faq/mathtext/node13.html

[6] "Why bother calculating pi to 62.8 trillion digits? It's both useless and fascinating," by Julia Collins, *The Conversation*, August 17, 2021. Her essay follows scientists at the University of Applied Sciences Graubünden, Switzerland. https://theconversation.com/why-bother-calculating-pi-to-62-8-trillion-digits-its-both-useless-and-fascinating-166271#:~:text=We%20believe%20in%20the%20free%20flow%20of%20information&text=Swiss%20researchers%20at%20the%20University,a%20staggering%2062.8%20trillion%20figures.

[7] See, for example, Haier, R.J.; Jung, R.E.; Yeo, R.C.; Head, K.; Alkired, M.T. (2004). "Structural brain variation and general intelligence". *NeuroImage*. **23** (1): 425–433. doi:10.1016/j.neuroimage.2004.04.025. PMID 15325390. S2CID 29426973.

[8] See "Bligh's Bounty," by Stephen Jay Gould, *Natural History*, September 1985, Vol. 94; p.2, https://web.archive.org/web/20010709234346/http://yoyo.cc.monash.edu.au/~tzvi/GOULD.html: the essay, of course, establishes the breaking of traditional rules with respect to the echidna, often thought of as the mysterious, groundbreaking mammal in the world. See https://animals.howstuffworks.com/mammals/echidna.htm#:~:text=While%20the%20echidna%20(pronounced%20ih,a%20class%20of%20its%20own.

[9] See "Bible Hub," "Isaiah 11:6," https://biblehub.com/isaiah/11-6.htm

[10] See *Jan Brueghel The Elder - The Entry of the Animals into Noah's Ark*, by Arianne Faber Kolb, The J. Paul Getty Museum, Getty Museum Studies On Art, Los Angeles, CA, 2005, p. 34. Faber provides a concise overview of the empirical thrusts of the Renaissance when it came – in the hands of a Leonardo, a Dürer or a Breughel the Elder – of the "direct observation" of animals into the painter's brush.

[11] op. cit., Tobias/Morrison, p.11.

[12] ibid., Tobias/Morrison, p. 139.

[13] See *Anthrozoology: Embracing Co-Existence in the Anthropocene*, by Michael Charles Tobias and Jane Gray Morrison, Springer Nature Publishers, New York, NY, 2017.

[14] See Ludwig Wittgenstein, 1992, *Last Writings on the Philosophy of Psychology, Volume two: The Inner and The Outer, 1949–1951*, G. H. von Wright and Heikki Nyman (eds.) and C.G. Luckhardt & Maximillian A.E. Aue (trans.), Oxford: Blackwells. See also, Tsouna, Voula, 1998a, "Remarks About Other Minds in Greek Philosophy", *Phronesis*, 43(3): 245–263. doi: 10.1163/15685289832111972

[15] See "Towards a Holo-semiotic Framework for the Evolution of Language," in Meanings & Co. The Interdisciplinarity of Communication, Semiotics and Multimodality, 2019, by Jeremiah Cassar Scalia, Acadmeia, https://mcgill.academia.edu/JeremiahCassarScalia

[16] "A Symbiotic View of Life: We Have Never Been Individuals," by Scott F. Gilbert, Jan Sapp and Alfred I. Tauber, Handling Editor James D. Thomson, and Associate Editor Stephen C. Stearns, *The Quarterly Review of Biology*, Volume 87, Number 4, The University of Chicago Press Journals, https://www.journals.uchicago.edu/doi/full/10.1086/668166

[17] op. cit., Tobias/Morrison, *The Quantum Biosemiosphere*, p. 24.

[18] See "Eukaryotic Genome Complexity," by Leslie A. Pray, © 2008 Nature Education, 1(1): 96. https://www.nature.com/scitable/topicpage/eukaryotic-genome-complexity-437/

[19] Tegmark, M. (1998). "Is 'the theory of everything' merely the ultimate ensemble theory?". *Annals of Physics*. 270 (1): 1–51. arXiv:gr-qc/9704009. Bibcode: 1998AnPhy.270....1T. doi:10.1006/aphy.1998.5855. S2CID 41548734. See also, Dicke, R. H. (1957). "Gravitation without a Principle of Equivalence". *Reviews of Modern Physics*. 29 (3): 363–376. Bibcode:1957RvMP...29..363D. doi:10.1103/RevModPhys.29.363; and, "Anthropic Explanations in Cosmology," by Jesús Mosterín, http://philsci-archive.pitt.edu/1658/1/Anthropic_Explanations_in_Cosmology_pdf, PhilSci Archive, 2004, http://philsci-archive.pitt.edu/1658/

[20] op. cit., Tobias/Morrison, *The Quantum Biosmemiosphere*, p. 150.

[21] See *Earth's Earliest Biosphere – Its Origin And Evolution*, Edited by J. William Schopf, Princeton University Press, Princeton, NJ, 1983; See also, *Genetic takeover and the mineral origins of life*, by A. G. Cairns-Smith, Cambridge University Press, Cambridge, UK, 1982; and *The Forest: A Year's Watch in Nature*, by David George Haskell, Viking Press, New York, NY, 2012.

[22] Ota, Kinya G.; Fujimoto, Satoko; Oisi, Yasuhiro; Kuratani, Shigeru (25 January 2017). "Identification of vertebra-like elements and their possible differentiation from sclerotomes in the hagfish". *Nature Communications*. 2: 373. Bibcode:2011Nat Co...2E.373O. doi:10.1038/ncomms1355. ISSN 2041-1723. PMC 3157150. PMID 21712821.

[23] For an examination of current perspectives in sociolinguistics, see *Communicating Beyond Language – Everyday Encounters with Diversity*, by Betsy Rymes, Routledge (Taylor & Francis), Abingdon-on-Thames, UK, 2014.

[24] See "Language beyond Words: The Neuroscience of Accent," by Ignacio Moreno-Torres, Peter Mariën, Guadalupe Dávila and Marcelo L. Berthier, *Front. Hum. Neurosci.*, 20 December 2016 | https://doi.org/10.3389/fnhum.2016.00639, https://www.frontiersin.org/articles/10.3389/fnhum.2016.00639/full

[25] See, for example, "Language beyond the language system: Dorsal visuospatial pathways support processing of demonstratives and spatial language during naturalistic fast fMRI," by Roberta Rocca, Kenny R. Coventry, Kristian Tylén, Marlene Staib, Torben E. Lund, Mikkel Wallentin, https://doi.org/10.1016/j.neuroimage.2019.116128 Get rights and content, https://doi.org/10.1016/j.neuroimage.2019.116128. https://www.sciencedirect.com/science/article/pii/S1053811919307190, Elsevier, NeuroImage, Volume 216, 1 August 2020, 116128

[26] ibid. See also, P. Hagoort, The core and beyond in the language-ready brain. *Neurosci. Biobehav. Rev.* 81 (Pt B), 194–204 (2017). http://dx.doi.org/doi:10.1016/j.neubiorev.2017.01.048; and, L. Menenti, S. M. E. Gierhan, K. Segaert, P. Hagoort, Shared language: Overlap and segregation of the neuronal infrastructure for speaking and listening revealed by functional MRI. *Psychol. Sci.* 22, 1173–1182 (2011). https://doi.org/10.1177/0956797611418347

[27] Scott, C.D.. (2011). Understanding beyond language: Perceiving meaning in reality. Koers - Bulletin for Christian Scholarship. 76. 10.4102/koers.v76i4.415, https://www.researchgate.net/publication/269969177_Understanding_beyond_language_Perceiving_meaning_in_reality; See also, P. A. M. Seuren, *Language in Cognition: Language From Within*, Oxford University Press, Oxford UK, Vol. 1., 2009.

[28] See "The neurobiology of language beyond single-word processing," by Peter Hagoort, *Science*, 4 Oct 2019. Vol 366, Issue 6461, pp. 55-58, doi: 10.1126/science.aax0289, https://www.science.org/doi/10.1126/science.aax0289

[29] See "Rare and Dying Languages of the World," by Lisa Morrow, *Far & Wide*, May 29, 2019, https://www.farandwide.com/s/rare-dying-languages-world-810f0b59a27940e1

[30] See *Language Contact and Change in Mesoamerica and Beyond*, edited by Karen Dakin, Claudia Parodi, and Natalie Operstein, Studies in Language Companion Series, 185, 2017, https://doi.org/10.1075/slcs.185. See also, Ochs, Elinor. "Indexicality and Socialization". In J. Stigler, R. Shweder & G. Herdt (eds.) *Cultural Psychology: Essays on Comparative Human Development*, Cambridge University Press, Cambridge, UK, 1990.

[31] See, for example, Naro, E.M., Lichtenfeld, L.L. (2021). Transcending the Boundaries of Conservation and Community Development to Achieve Long-Term Sustainability for People and Planet. In: Underkoffler, S.C., Adams, H.R. (eds) *Wildlife Biodiversity Conservation.* Springer, Cham. https://doi.org/10.1007/978-3-030-64682-0_2, https://link.springer.com/chapter/10.1007/978-3-030-64682-0_2#citeas

[32] "Semantics of the Inuktitut (Eskimo) Spatial Deictics," by J. Peter Denny, *International Journal of American Linguistics*, Volume 48, Number 4, University of Chicago Press Journals, October 1982, https://doi.org/10.1086/465747, https://www.journals.uchicago.edu/doi/abs/10.1086/465747?journalCode=ijal; See also, De Swart, H. "(In)definites and genericity." In *Quantifiers, Deduction and Context.* Edited by M. Kanazawa and others. Stanford: CSLI: 171–199, and Helge Lødrup. "Norwegian Anaphors without Visible Binders." *Journal of Germanic Linguistics* 19 (2007): 1–22. Available at http://journals.cambridge.org.

[33] See "What would be an example of an anaphoric conditional in Lisp?" edited by "ThinkingStiff," January 18, 2012, https://stackoverflow.com/questions/3920193/what-would-be-an-example-of-an-anaphoric-conditional-in-lisp/3922204#3922204

[34] See Austin, J.L.. *How to Do Things With Words*, Harvard University Press, Cambridge, Massachusetts: 1962, p. 5.

[35] See Peirce, C.S., "Division of Signs" in *Collected Papers*, 1932 [1897]. OCLC 783138

[36] See "An architect, pianist, philosopher and mathematician are the recipients of this year's Rolf Schock Prizes, 24 March 2022, *Kungl. Vetenskaps-Akademien*, https://www.kva.se/en/pressrum/pressmeddelanden/arkitekt-pianist-filosof-och-matematiker-far-are

[37] See *On The Nature Of Ecological Paradox*, by Michael Charles Tobias and Jane Gray Morrison, Foreword by Bob Gillespie, Prologue by G. Wayne Clough, Springer Nature Publishers, 2nd edition, New York, NY, 2022.

[38] See *The Hypothetical Species – Variables of Human Evolution*, by Michael Charles Tobias and Jane Gray Morrison, Foreword by Melanie L. DeVore, Springer Nature, New York, NY, 2019, p. 229.

[39] See *Ecological Reciprocity – A Treatise on Kindness*, by Michael Charles Tobias and Jane Gray Morrison, Greek Translation by Niki Stavrou, NOVA Science Publishers, New York, NY, 2021.

[40] From David Hume's *Treatise on Human Rights*: *Being an Attempt to Introduce the Experimental Method of Reasoning into Moral Subjects*, London, UK 1739-40, texts online, T 1.2.2.8, SBN 32, https://davidhume.org/texts/t/1/2/2#:~:text='Tis%20an%20establish'd%20maxim,a%20mountain%20may%20actually%20exist, taken from *World War III – Population And The Biosphere At The End Of The Millennium*, by Michael Tobias, 1st edition, Bear & Co., Santa Fe, NM, 1994, p. 474. See also, "Enormous stingray sets world record for largest freshwater fish," by Stefan Lovgren,

National Geographic, June 20, 2022. (The magnificent, utterly gentle Mekong River giant was weighed -661 pounds-, admired by human members on shore of the Megafishes Project, then sent back out into the murky, unexplored Cambodian waters from whence it had been temporarily captured).

Index of Names

D

E

F

G

O

P

Q

R

S

X

Y

Z

Index of Terms

B

C

F

G

H

I

N

O

P

Q

R

S

T

About the Authors

Michael Charles Tobias, long-time president of the Dancing Star Foundation (dancingstarfoundation.org), earned his PhD in the history of consciousness from the University of California-Santa Cruz, specializing in global ecological ethics and biological systems, as well as the interdisciplinary humanities. His wide-ranging work embraces the global ecological sciences, art, comparative literature, the history of ideas, philosophy, and natural history. Dr. Tobias is the author of over 60 books – fiction and non-fiction – and has written, directed, and/or produced over 50 films (mostly documentaries, docudramas, and TV series). Tobias' works have been read, translated, and broadcast throughout the world, and he has, in addition, conducted ecological field research in nearly 100 countries. Most recently, his books, *The Earth In Fragments: A Memoir, Ecological Reciprocity: A Treatise on Kindness,* and *The Quantum Biosemiosphere* were published by NOVA Science Publishers (2021).

Jane Gray Morrison is an ecologist whose work has taken her to over 40 countries. As a filmmaker, Ms. Morrison has produced numerous films for such networks as Discovery, PBS (where she co-directed "A Day in the Life of Ireland" for Irish Television and WNET/New York), "Hotspots" (www.hotspots-thefilm.com), and Turner Broadcasting, for which she served as senior producer for "Voice of the Planet," a 10-hour dramatic series based upon the history of life on Earth. As a Goodwill Ambassador to Ecuador's Yasuni National Park, she produced the short film "Yasuni – A Meditation on Life," which premiered at the United Nations Rio+20 Summit in 2012. Her books include *Sanctuary: Global Oases of Innocence* (www.sanctuary-thebook.com), *Donkey: The Mystique of Equus Asinus*, *God's Country: The New Zealand Factor*, and *No Vacancy* (co-edited). She has co-written seven books published by Springer Nature. Since 1999, Jane Morrison has served as the executive vice president of Dancing Star Foundation, a nonprofit organization that focuses on animal rights, the interdisciplinary humanities, and social and ecological justice movements as they concern humankind's relationship to the natural world.